CRITICAL
HELLO! BUDGET HOTEL GUIDES

"You couldn't ask for a better traveling companion in Europe than Margo Classé. She scours the continent for the best hotel deals and shares her information in her series of Hello! Budget Hotel Guides."
—*AAA Westways, Southern California's Lifestyle Magazine*

"From Amalfi to Verona, this book (one in a series) focuses on the kind of practical information that plan-it-yourselfers need to make informed lodging decisions."
—*Chicago Tribune*

"I'll tell you up front that I am a great fan of Margo Classé's hotel guides. I used her "Hello Italy" to find a nifty, inexpensive place in Positano with a stunning ocean view."
—*Detroit News and Free Press*

"These are practical guides to low-cost hotels in Spain, Italy and France, and a guide to reasonable lodgings in England, Scotland and Ireland."
—*Orlando Sentinel*

"Some out there cares about you. That is, those of you who prefer to plan your own budget travels in the United Kingdom. Ireland, Italy, France and Spain."
—*St. Petersburg Times*

"Few travel writers would dedicate this time and effort that Margo Classé has done in preparing these excellent detailed hotel guides."
—*International Travel News*

"Margo is the guru when it comes to good well-priced hotels."
—*www.journeywoman.com*

"Even the most ambitious books rarely devote as much space to listing accommodations. For sheer number of entries…the books can't be beat."

—*The Wichita Eagle*

"It's a great guide and one that we highly recommend."

—*Paul Lasley and Elizabeth Harryman,*
The Touring Company

"This book is a dream. Not only does it list over 200 accommodations, all of them are well documented including addresses, phone numbers, credit cards, etc. …This book is definitely a winner."

—*Shoestring Travel*

"Make no mistake; Margo Classe is the independent travel's friend. Her books are clearly a labor of love, and her readers have benefited from the depth of her passion. No one else pro-vides such a range of coverage for budget hotels nor details the amenities of each establishment with an informed, personal touch."

—*Wichita Eagle*

"[For] cost-conscious travelers who are too old for hostels and dormitories, but don't care if the curtains match the bedspread."

—*The Times-Picayune*

"You'll find…cheap quarters in Margo Classe's *Hello France!*"

—*Washington Post*

"What this book does is allow you the freedom of not making reservations until you get to Italy…"

—*Pasadena Weekly*

"I found a very acceptable hotel [in Paris]…comfortable, in a great location, was clean and offered breakfast and friendly service."

—*Joanne Gerber, French Government Tourist Office*

WHAT READERS ARE SAYING
ABOUT *HELLO!* BUDGET HOTEL GUIDES

"Thank you for the insight that you had in writing this book to help meet the needs of the American Traveler to Italy. Thank you again for the obvious attention to detail."

—Jim Cancilleri, New Jersey

"It has been two years since our wonderful trip to Italy, made more wonderful by the terrific hotel (Desiree) you recommended in Sorrento. We are planning a trip to Portugal in July of this year and I was so disappointed to learn that you have not done a book on that country. I feel lost regarding how to go about picking hotels."
Lost without Hello Portugal!

—Ken Mijeski

"I used your book for Italy and it was great."

—Leslie Runyon

"I have "Hello Italy", which I found very useful for my last couple of trips."

—Lesli Sjostrom, California

"We just completed a wonderful trip to Italy. Thanks to your "Hello Italy" we stayed in many comfortable, affordable hotels. We went on to Sicily and really missed your help. Our experience in Italy was completely wonderful. Thanks so much for your contribution to that success. Should we travel to Spain or France we will certainly use your guides in planning our trip."

—Diana Blank and Arthur Simon, California

"I received your book and went to work immediately....wow! Your book is like finding a GOLD MINE."
Ciao,

—Mary

"Your books have become my travel bible for hotel bookings. The choices in your books are wonderful. My 2nd trip from now will hopefully be Milan and Barcelona. You will be my bible for Barcelona and I will consult your Italy book for Milan."
Thanks again, I love your books,

—Mitch

"MClassé knows her hotels…I used her book for our entire trip through France and found her descriptions 100% accurate in every respect…I selected the Muguet from her " printed words of wisdom"…Merci Margo — now when do you publish a book for other European countries??? Portugal & Spain perhaps???? I meant what I said about your recommendations…they were OUTSTANDING…"

—Sally

"I am overwhelmed by all that great information. All that stuff is so up to date and insightful. I will read it carefully and make good use of it. You have a beautiful writing style for travel books; it reads like warm caring advice from a good friend."
Your fan,

—James (Dr. Lee), California

"Your style of writing is the most helpful I've seen because the reader knows that you have either checked out the hotel and rooms by staying there or at least inspecting them. This is the best reassurance to people who don't travel that often, or to those traveling to a new city."
Thanks again,

—Diana and Bill Price, California

"Who could have thought that traveling through Europe was so affordable. Hello Spain! did an excellent job of compiling affordable, clean, and centrally located hostels with plenty of character. This book is a lifesaver for any type of traveler."

—Sal and Sylvia Sances, California

"I received your book Hello Spain! this weekend and it's great. Thank you for all those tips and advice I haven't found in other Spain travel books; it's like talking to a close friend who's been there. There are so many details in planning a trip that having this book comforts me because now I know I won't miss a lot of them. Planning a trip on my own (first time!) is very exciting but also very stressful. At least now, with your book, I have additional information on those little things that nobody warns you about before leaving."
Sincerely,

—*Karen Ferrer, Puerto Rico*

"I was very pleased to see that most of the hotels I've reserved or am considering are listed in your book. It's so helpful to get a firsthand report from someone with similar requirements that includes a detailed description and the helpful information on location and directions that you provide. Another thing I appreciate is that some of the hotels you list aren't covered in most other guidebooks. I'd like to thank you for all of your help."
—*April Amaral, New Jersey*

"I love your books. You stay in my kind of hotels and these places, for the most part are not listed on the Internet or known by travel agents. You provide a valuable resource, especially to solo travelers, and I am delighted to recommend your books."
Continued success,

—*Sharon*

"After such a great experience with Hello France!, I have now gotten Hello, Spain! for our first trip to Spain. My husband and I travel with two children, ages 5 and 9. If we couldn't find inexpensive lodging, we would never be able to afford traveling like we have"
—*Denise Montana, Arizona*

"I've read many, many books on tourism and hotels for specific areas, and quite honestly none of them is bad. They're all helpful in different ways, but yours absolutely stands apart from the rest. You not only give the basics of each hotel, but the details such as which rooms to request or which rooms are among the least desirable is invaluable. The preceding chapters before the hotel recommendations contains a lot of information that often only well-seasoned travelers can know, other guide books don't tell, and those new to traveling *need* to know! The list of resources and websites is so inexhaustible that if I looked up every one of them, I'd miss my trip to Paris. Thank you very much for an absolute treasure trove of information that will make my trip to Paris even more enjoyable! I am also quite impressed that you visited each hotel individually (which, to me, is the only real way to write about them) and take such pride and care of your work. You certainly seem like an endless bundle of energy who makes the most out of life while being extraordinarily helpful to everyone along the way. You are one classy dame, Madame Classé!"
All my best,

—Jennifer Metcalf, Iowa

"I just purchased your Hello Spain! book today & know I will find it infinitely useful as I plan my first trip to Spain this August."

—Lynn Williams, California

"My family and I just got back from two weeks in Spain. We used your book for hotel reservations in Cordoba (Hotel Gonzalez), Granada (Hotel Sacromonte), and Sevilla (Hotel Maestranza.) We were very happy with all three hotels; all are clean, safe, comfortable, well-located and very good value. Everything that is written about your books is true. I will never take a trip without them again, if I'm going anywhere that you have written about! Thank you very much."

—Deborah Maltby, Missouri

"You're providing a much-needed (and long overdue) service for travelers to Europe. I think it would be great if you could eventually expand your listings to include Benelux, Germany, Austria and Switzerland. At any rate, keep up the good work."

—Arlice Davenport, Kansas

"Keep up the good work. I think the books are fabulous."

—John Flinn, California

"Thank you for putting out such great books that make traveling much easier!"
Kind Regards,

—Amiee

"I used your Hello France! with great success. Thanks."

—Paul Tubb

"First, I picked your book — Hello France! A Hotel Guide to Paris — off the shelf in a bookstore in Aug. It was ONLY BY USING YOUR BOOK, especially the Hotels of France web site you mentioned, and especially using the email addresses you provided, that I finally found us a room at the Hotel La Serre. So first of all, THANK you for introducing us to using email for reservations, and for introducing us to the 7th Arondissement.

P.S. We also read all your other tips closely and took your advice in several key areas. THANK YOU for your tips on the CARTE ORANGE — it was a godsend! And for your tips about transportation between CDG and Paris — we used the Carte Orange coming and the airport shuttle van leaving."

—Astrid Dodds, Massachusetts

"I have all your other three books and they've been a godsend throughout my travels. I've even bought a couple as gifts. Thanks again."

—Cherryl

"I bought and used your Hello France book for my trip to France last March. Yours is the best book I've ever used for hotel . . . thank you for writing and researching it. I'll be looking for your books the next time I start planning a trip." Thanks again.

—Sandy Behrens

"I am familiar with your publications and I am an admirer of your work. Thanks Again!" Sincerely

—BillySki

"A big compliment on Hello Britain & Ireland! What a delight to discover you have also included groceries, laundries, internet cafes and (my absolute favorite place to stop) bookstores! Wow!! My sincere thanks. Again, thank you very much."

—Peggy Vaughn

"I am a big fan of your guide books."

—Amita Gopinath, Maryland

"Thanks for writing your books. We found them useful a few times in Italy and Spain. Let us know whenever you have any new books coming out."

— Anne Colon

"We spent this past June in Italy and used your book for almost all of our accomodation choices. We were extremely happy with all of them. Thanks for all your hard work!"

—Eric Brahm & Yvonne Wiebelhaus

"I have recommended your book to a lot of people. Most of the travel books (other than Rick Steves) do not have the excellent type of information that you do and his are not nearly as extensive. You have been very helpful! Thank you again."

—Maryellen Federico, Arizona

"Thanks to you and your book, I was able to book everything here and have faxes and e-mails with the needed info. Thank you for these wonderful publications. Since our daughter has been in France so many times and we plan to visit her again next summer, guess that I will need the hotel book for France also! Please let me know your site address again. (www.Hello Europe.com) Thanks for everything!"

—*Michel Puckett, Ohio*

"I am happy to report that I am a purchaser of your great book regarding Italy. I have "dog-earred it to death in preparation for our trip next month. Again, thank you for your great book."

—*Mitch Harada, Washington*

"I just wanted to say that the hotel recommendations from *Hello Italy!* worked out great. We stayed at the Pausania in Venice. Thanks for writing a great guide book."

—*Mike Frey, California*

"Thank you for your great guide *(Hello Italy) An Insiders Guide Italian Hotels!* We have just returned from 18 days in Italy where we had reservations in three hotels you recommended (Hotel Canal in Venice, Hotel Caschi in Florence and Hotel Primavera in Rome). I was so curious about the accuracy of your book that I visited two additional hotels you recommended (Hotel Lidomare and Hotel Amalfi) while staying in Amalfi. The rooms and terms were just as you had described , the locations were great, and the staff very friendly and helpful."

—*Mara and Charles Walter, Maryland*

"I usually follow Frommer, Fodor, and Rick Steves, but I have a new leader, Margo Classé. It offers pricing, location, discounts available, directions, tips on reservations, packing, etc. Try it, you'll like it."

—*Mary Anna Bramberg, California*

"The book was worth the money! It did what it purported to do, namely get us into hotels for under $80 consistently. Most were around the $40-$50 range."

—David Dingee, Florida

"As a woman traveling alone, I was concerned about security as well as economy. I found your comments about the neighborhoods 'right on the money.' I never was disappointed in any of the hotels where I stayed."

—Mary Redmond

"I am an avid European traveler and have found your books extremely helpful…they fill a serious need for the independent traveler."

—Arlice W. Davenport, Kansas

"I have access to a copy of your excellent book *Hello Spain!* Thank you."

—Raymond Moreno

"This is a great little book about mid-priced hotels in Spain. The author has obviously visited all of them in person. This is a book for the independent traveler and belongs in their luggage. It won't take up a lot of space either."

—Martin Fritze

"I recently returned from a trip to Italy. I like being able to go with the flow. Classé read my mind in answering questions I wanted to ask."

—Teresa A. Jones, California

"We were able to secure a room at the Centrale [in Siena, Italy] with the help of your guide. Great recommendation. Thank you so much for your information in your book."

—Mark De Wit and Carrie L. Brody

"We recently used your book as a hotel guide in France. The Hotel Nicolo in Paris was delightful! We would certainly recommend your book to anyone traveling in France!"

—*John & Bebe Vink*

"I made a reservation with the Plaza hotel in Barcelona by e-mail and had confirmation in under one hour for a quiet affordable room! Your overall strategies are as good as the detailed information for each hotel. Great job Margo!"

—*Jeannette Belliveau*

"Just back from paris. Found your recommendations right on target. Will always use your guides in the future."

—*Mimi Greenberg*

"I simply must write and tell you how glad I was to find your book. We are happy to be saving money as most everything has been under $100 per night."

—*Maryellen and Gil Federico*

"About your book — it is a very excellent book. You are doing a very good job and I hope you become very successful, because there is definitely a need for what you are doing. Keep up the good work!!!!"

—*Michelle Patterson*

"I have recommended your book. Your book was worth the two hotels we stayed in!"

—*Ken Mijeski*

"I love what you have done. That is, pair travelers with smaller, more intimate hotels with a personal touch. You have helped us and so many others find the wonderful, small, intimate hotels that really make the trip rather than a large impersonal "American" hotel just like the ones here in the States."

—*Michel Puckett, Ohio*

"I have had great fun marking places in your book. Your descriptions are wonderfully thorough. I am so glad someone is finally doing what you are doing."

—Hebe Smythe, Mississippi

"I love your book because you embrace one of my big requirements....clean!! And the other huge thing you added into some descriptions that helped me with the yeah/nay decision… 'popular with students' which can often mean…late night kinds of folk..also was glad to see the designation 'quiet' or 'noisy' P.S. Thanks for all your hard work. I certainly can trust your recommendations in the future, which says a lot because there's so many 'guide books' out these days ya never know!"

—Andrea Egan

"I received the book yesterday and really enjoy reading it. So helpful."

—Pizza Hair

"My companion and I just returned from our 2 week trip and we used your book to choose our hotels. I wanted to thank you and to tell you about our good experiences. I wanted you to know that we thought your book was WONDERFUL and would recommend it."

— Amy Soelzer

"Got your book yesterday and haven't put it down – it's great."

—Larry Handley

"Got your book today. Man, are you efficient, and it's great. Loved seeing all the rave reviews."

—Maggie Tom (The Other Margaret), Vermont.

"Thanks for your help. I just purchased your book and I find it to be very helpful!"

—Barbara Maniscalco, California

"I am writing you to thank you for your excellent book on Spain. My husband and I travelled from Halifax, N.S., Canada, to Spain on November 2 and stayed a month. We used your book to travel the southern part of Spain and do not know what we would have done without your help. We had wonderful places to stay and great people to meet. My husband is 63 and I am 56 and it was the first trip we took without relying on travel agents."
—*Ruth R.Harvey*

"I found your book early in my travel planning and found it very helpful."
—*Gail*

"Your guidebooks make Europe so accessible. Your book was recommended on the Frommer site, as you know. I was going to go on an Alitalia tour because I thought I couldn't plan a trip to Italy without prior experience. Ha, your book makes me a genius!! Now I can stay in Italy twice as long for the price of a tour. I have told several of my friends about your book and will tell both Borders and Barnes & Noble (where I found your book) to stock up and recommend your books to travelers."
—*Mary*

"I have used your books for Italy, Spain and France and love them. Thanks for your help."
—*Kathy Kawulok, Colorado*

"Thank you Margo! I used your book for Italy on my first trip there and found it extremely useful. Have also recommended you to others. I think one of the things your books offer that most others don't, are your detailed directions for walking to the hotels from the train station, and your identification of lots of good rooms and bad."
—*Carol Gordon*

"Returned from a wonderful trip to Rome, Florence and Venice this week. Wanted to let you know that we just loved the Primavera Hotel in Rome. It was charming and the location was perfect. The staff was very friendly and helpful as well. We stayed at the Hotel Bellettini in Florence which was a good value for its central location. Thanks so much for your wonderful recommendations - I recommend your books to all my friends travelling to Europe."

—*Colleen Kochman*

"I just got back from a trip to Italy. I used your book for all of my hotel accomodations except for Bellagio and you are wonderful. Your descriptions of the hotels were accurate. Your directions to the hotels were accurate. We stayed at the Antica Locanda Mercanti in Milan, the Hotel Pasquale in Monterossa, the Hotel Duomo in Siena, the Hotel Bellitini in Florence, the Hotel Marin in Venice and the Hotel London in Milan for the last night. All of the hotels were immaculate and the staff was very helpful and friendly. I am very glad I used your book and thank you very much. You definitely have more of an idea of what a woman is looking for than does Rick Steve. I also use his book, however, I find that I am happier with your suggestions for hotels and restaurants. Please go to Germany and write a book for that area. We are going there in two years. I'm very glad there is someone like you to help the rest of us. Happy travels."

—*Sharon Cruz, Florida*

"What a great book!! I have used it almost exclusively to plan my first trip to Italy. I have 6 guide books and I am always referring to yours for the best information!! Planning this trip has been almost effortless due to your travel experience and foresight. Brava!!"

—*Mary Scudder*

"Thank you very much. Your book is making our trip to France easier to plan."

—*David Swingle*

"I found your book to be helpful and informative about the small hotels in Italy. I can only hope you continue to travel to expand upon the number of books you have. Personally, one for Israel would be my dream come true!! Margo, I think your book was excellent and I will recommend it to all of my friends. Keep up the travels!!!"

—*Jason Samansky*

"I love your books. The choices in your books are wonderful. When I picked up the Spain edition and saw my hotel Aguilar on San Jeronimo I knew you were legit! A friend's brother living in Madrid found it and it was $40 a night with bathroom - unbelievable! I then used your book for a Paris hotel- Grand Hotel des Balcons - $100 for 3 people and spotless! Your books are now my bible for booking hotels in these countries. I like the number of choices near the train station in Rome on Via Amadeo where I stayed last year when I found only 1 listing for that street in another book, so thank-you for more choices for my next trip (when I use Rome as a base for day-trips I prefer to stay near the train stations) Thank-you for your help and I have to say your books are great - now that I travel more I realize paying more than $100 is almost always completely unnecessary and I agree with your choices!"

—*Mitch Chaitin*

"I am a travel agent working for Thomas Cook Travel in Canada. We traveled throughout Italy with your guidebook as our friend. I just wanted to let you know how helpful your books are. We found your restaurant recommendations especially helpful, particularly in Rome. Keep up the good work."

—*Jill Clark, Canada*

"Your book [*Hello France!*] *A Hotel Guide to Paris* is the best. I am so grateful to you for writing it. I have every book written on where to stay in Paris and yours is by far the best. Thank you. I grew up in Paris and have been back to visit many times so I know it well but I still need a book like yours each time I go. Thank you very, very much."

—*Susan Russell*

"I learned about your books online listening to several others who swear by your books and not the so called big boys. It seems to me that the so called big boys just rehash the same listings and haven't actually stepped foot inside the hotels, but you have! I read lots of opinion message boards, and sometimes I read that the hotels and restaurants recommended by the big boys are inaccurate. I wonder if the big boys actually go to the places they recommend or just reword the same lists. I have read on the internet that you have actually gone to these hotels and then write reviews that shoot straight from the hip, which I sincerely appreciate. I will spend my travel budget on what you say, not them."

—*Cyndi*

"I have found your recommendations invaluable in both Paris and Nice! But when I'm in London, I find I have to pay the proverbial arm and a leg for clean, comfortable and well-located hotels…is there something I'm missing? With thanks for your time."

—*Jule Williams*

"I used your Italy guide extensively on my trip the summer before last (Thankyou!) I am planning a greek island trip for next summer and was disapointed that you have not published a hotel guide for that area yet."

—*Carol Marino*

"My wife and I enjoyed your book. I particularly like the way you get right to the point. We both like the extras you suggested we take along with us like apple cutter etc. Thank you for your help."

—*Miles and Candyce Hackley*

"Your advice on places to stay enabled my husband and I to spend 21 days in France instead of 14…amazing how those dollars saved can stretch to buy more time."

—*Sally*

"Just a short note to thank you for all the helpful information that your provided in your *Hello France!* guide. We are not first time travelers but we found your book to be most enjoyable and extremely informative. We also had Rick Steves' book and used yours as a 1st rate guide for our evening stays. Your recommendations were so complete & at times filled with fun....Oscar the hotel mascot at the hotel Ponteil in Antibes for one. In Arles we stayed at the Cloitre and Agnes was a delight and most helpful. Thanks again for all the tips & just to let you know I just purchased another book for our friends who are planning a trip to France the first of the next year."

PS We were in France for almost a month and only stayed in your recommended hotels !!!!!!!!!!!!!!

—*Diana & Brian Reeves*

"I love this book. I had bought your 1st one 4 years ago. It was actually the thing that pushed me over the edge to go to Paris in the first place…finding a cheap accessible place to stay. In fact, I stayed in 4 different places over 8 nights, just to experience different worlds. I would never have done it without all your hard work! I loaned the book to someone a year ago, and never saw it again. Then I found your revised edition."

—*Ed Grady, Michigan*

HELLO ITALY!

Best Budget Hotels *in* *Italy*

28 Italian Cities

- ▶ *Centrally Located Hotels*
- ▶ *Best Rooms* ▶ *Hotel Web Sites*
- ▶ *Restaurants* ▶ *Travel Tips & More*

Margo Classé

Wilson Publishing
Los Angeles, California

HELLO ITALY!
BEST BUDGET HOTELS
in Italy
By Margo Classé

Published by: **Wilson Publishing**
5554 Spokane St., Los Angeles, CA 90016 U.S.
Tel: (323) 939-0821 Fax: (323) 939-7736
http://www.HelloEurope.com/
E-mail: margo@helloeurope.com
Order toll-free: (888) 663-9269
3rd Edition

Cover designed by Pamela Terry, Opus1design.com

Cover photographs by Tyrell Wilson

Map illustration by Opus1design.com

Text designed by Opus1design.com

Edited by Brenda Koplin

Printed by United Graphics, Inc.
Manufactured in the United States of America
ISBN: 0-9653944-8-4
Library of Congress Catalog Card Number: 2002102417

Normally, I use this page to thank my husband, Tyrell Wilson, whose love, passion and support allow me to continue pursuing my dream and making it a reality.

However, this particular book would not have been published without the assistance and support of American Airlines & Rail Europe. I want to acknowledge and thank them both for believing in me and supporting me so that I can continue to write and publish these guides on the best budget hotels in Europe and that you, the reader, will be able to benefit from the information.

Acknowledgments

Without the support and friendship of the following people, completing this book would have been a more difficult task.

Geovanni Brewer, my buddy who always rescues me from myself, shares my love of traveling and constantly gives me the freedom to release my stress.

My close friends Lillian Martin, Marvinia Anderson, Sheryl Carey, Christy Hervey, Judy Robilotti, Jeff Fischgrund, Linnie Washington and Pamela Terry. Pamela, I continue to owe you a special gratitude. Esther Wilson, my adopted mom, for all her contributions.

As a one-woman business competing in the big-league publishing world, I never would have come this far without the continuing help of the following people in the media:

Millie Ball, travel editor, *New Orleans Times-Picayune*

Barbara Shea, travel writer, *Newsday*

Arlice Davenport, travel editor, *Kansas Wichita Eagle*

Pucci Meyer, travel editor, *New York Post*

Ava Plakins, executive editor, *Moneysworth*

Evelyn Hannon, editor, *Journeywoman.com*

Shirley Davis, travel editor, *Quad-City Times*

Elaine Glusac, contributing editor, *American Way*

Jerry Morris, travel editor, *Boston Globe*

Gerry Volgenau, travel editor, *Detroit News/Detroit Free Press*

Don Groff, travel writer, *Philadelphia Inquirer*

Editorial Staff, *International Travel News*

Paul Lasley and Elizabeth Harryman, Touring Company

Don Schaffer, Drive Time, KSL

Jerry Reno, Drive Time, WHO

Jane DeGrow and Marsha Miller, WGIM "Travel Queen"

Valarie D'Elia, WOR 710 "Travel Show"

Jackie Wolfer, "Travel Smart"

John Clayton, "John Clayton's Travel with a Difference"

Location of Cities

TABLE OF CONTENTS

TABLE OF CONTENTS

TO READERS OF MY BOOKS:

I traveled by myself to 28 of the most popular cities in Italy, which took ten consecutive weeks (no days off), to visit each of these hotels in person. This is no easy task. I am literally a one-woman company. I worked extremely hard to bring you an extensive resource guide on clean, safe, inexpensive, centrally located and charming hotels (with private bathrooms) in these wonderful 28 cities so that you would be able to have a more affordable, enjoyable vacation. The book is filled with lots of tips and information gathered from actual experience. Please take the time to read it so that you may benefit from it.

My husband, Tyrell, and I pay for all our expenses including the cost of publishing our own books. No hotel or restaurant pays us to be in our books. Any discounts I get are passed on to my readers. I have included my contact information in the front of the book and I encourage you to use it. However, if any details in this book are not totally correct or you experienced something beyond my control, please forgive me and have a good time.

INTRODUCTION

Many of us lead very structured lives. Most of our days include strict timelines, so when it is time for a vacation, I would think you would want a more relaxed schedule. You can accomplish this by planning your own vacation. Take charge of your trip, arrange your own day tours and have some fun at your own pace. Select your hotel by reading this book and making your own reservations. I have made it quite easy by doing all the research for you. I have put together a list of hotels that offer rooms for rates between $69-$149 a night for double occupancy. I have included detailed information on affordable rooms for people traveling alone, with a companion or as families. This means you can spend your money on the important things such as sightseeing, food, shopping and more food! With the expert help of the Italian Tourist Boards in Los Angeles, California; New York City, New York; & Vern Kenney (a long-time very experienced independent traveler), we selected 28 of the most popular cities in Italy. (I wish I could have done more, but I am only one person.) I then visited each hotel in every city listed in this book. These selected cities are fabulous sights in themselves, but they also make great bases to explore the various regions of Italy. All that is left for you is to decide what city you want to visit, what sights you want to see and how long you want to be in each city. I have included the phone, fax numbers and most Web sites of the local tourist offices for each city in this book. You can write, fax or e-mail them and request detailed information on day tours, maps and events that might not be available from the tourist offices in the U.S. & Canada. (See Appendix II.)

My criteria for selecting hotels are that they must be *very clean*, safe, inexpensive, centrally located and, above all, have a private toilet and shower in the room. Of course, I also try to include charming and quaint as criteria. All the hotels listed in this book are family-run unless otherwise indicated, and have at least one room with a toilet. For me, the sole purpose of a hotel room is to provide a *safe* and comfortable place to sleep after an enjoyable day. *Many of the hotel owners agreed in writing to give a discount when you show them this book (no copies or rip-out pages will be accepted) before (not after) you check into the hotel. (Please see "Tips on Hotel Accommoda-*

INTRODUCTION

tions" for more specific details on this subject.) I made a notation in each hotel listing where a discount is offered. Depending on the time of year, it ranges from about 5% to 10% or more per room. However, all discounts go out the window when you arrive during any major festivals that take place in the cities. (For a calendar of events, see Appendix V.) I have organized this book by listing the 28 Italian cities alphabetically. All our traveling through Europe is done by train or bus, so I use the train station squares as my starting point in most of the listings for directions to the hotels. Hotels are listed alphabetically within each city, with street (mailing) address, phone, fax number and/or e-mail address along with a detailed description of the hotel including the best rooms for people traveling alone, with a companion or as families. The Appendixes list information on packing tips, tourist offices in the U.S. & Canada, using telephones in Italy, Italian phrases for checking in and a schedule of holidays and special events when hotels are crowded, so you can plan ahead.

This book *will* allow you the freedom of making or not making reservations until you get to Italy, arm you with plenty of choices and information on inexpensive hotels and some great restaurants. To avoid any misunderstandings, always confirm the rate and what it includes at the time you check into the hotel.

RESTAURANTS
My criteria for selecting restaurants are that they must have great food using local ingredients, be moderately priced, have a friendly atmosphere and be family-owned. **Tip:** Forget about finding smoke-free restaurants in Italy. They don't exist. The only trick is to get to the restaurant as soon as it opens. If you can't decide which pasta or dessert dishes to order, many times the restaurant will allow you to order two (2) half servings as one order for an additional charge.

LAUNDRIES
The use of self-service or service *lavanderias* throughout our travels helps us tremendously because we pack light. I have tried to include locations of the various laundries for most cities listed in this book. The cities that don't have the information do not have public laundries.

SUPERMARKETS

Take advantage of these well-priced markets that usually take major credit cards (some have a minimum purchase). I have tried to include locations of various supermarkets for most cities listed in this book. Buy your wine, cheese, fruit, candy and stock up on bottled water (that sells for three times as much on the street). If you are lucky enough to have a minibar (frigobar) or small fridge in your room you can keep these items cold and have them later for midnight snacks. Sometimes I buy a pastry or two and keep the leftovers in the minibar for the following evening.

THE MOST IMPORTANT TIP OF ALL: If I could give you one piece of advice to follow, it would be this: Be extremely patient and polite with everyone you talk to. If you treat each person you meet with respect and exhibit the attitude that you know you are a guest in their country, hopefully you will never have any difficulties. I do not speak Italian, but I do know how to say "Thank you," "Good morning" and "Please" with a smile. (See Appendix IV.)

Some things you learn from pictures.
Some things you learn from books.
Some things you learn from your brother.

Granted, not all of it is repeatable. But it's something you share.
And when you put it together, you realize that brothers and sisters have
more in common than height marks in a doorway. So with low fares available
on AA.com, isn't it time to visit those you share so much with?

AmericanAirlines®

Great low fares now available on A̐A.com®

BEFORE YOU LEAVE HOME

Please read your travel guide for all the basic information on what to do before you leave home. The following is intended to be used as additional advice only.

Anticipate hotels' busy times: Familiarize yourself with the schedule of local holidays, traditional events, fashion shows and religious celebrations in the cities you are planning to visit so that you know which times of the year hotels are likely to be especially busy. This will help you decide whether you need to make advance reservations. If a public holiday falls on a Tuesday or Thursday, many businesses also close on the nearest Monday or Friday for a long weekend. For each city in this book, I have included the phone, fax numbers and most Web sites of the city's local tourist office. Take advantage of this and write, fax or e-mail them prior to your leaving home. Request that they send you information on the city, a detailed list of local events for the month you plan to visit the city, hotels, and most important, a map of the city. Their information is usually more detailed than what you will get from the tourist offices of Italy within your country.

ATM/Credit Cards: Confirm with your bank that your ATM/credit cards can be used in Europe and that they will be recognized by the Cirrus or Plus systems. For a list of ATMs while in Italy call MasterCard Cirrus Network toll-free at 900971231 or Visa Plus System toll-free at 900974445 or try Web sites: http://www.mastercard.com/atm or http://www.visa.com/pd/atm/ Carry several cards from two or more different banks. Apparently demagnetization seems to be a common problem and ATMs have been known to eat the cards. Usually there are no letters on the key pads of European ATMs. (The ATM at the Rome airport had letters and numbers on the keypad.) Make sure the PIN (Personal Identification Number) code is numeric and not alphanumeric and is only four digits. If it is more than four digits, change it before you go. Without a 4-digit numeric PIN code, you will be unable to withdraw cash with your credit card abroad. ATMs will eat the card if you punch the wrong code into the ATM 3 times. You may also want to arrange with your bank to have your daily withdrawal limits raised in the account attached to the ATM card before departing from home, since you incur a fee each time you do a transaction. Call your credit card company to let them know you will be in Italy using the card. I had been unable to use my card when the credit card company put a hold on it because they thought it was stolen. I found out when I called them from Europe. Get the lost/stolen phone numbers from your bank for all your ATM & credit cards. Most banks have collect call numbers that you can use since 800 numbers do not work from Europe. Speaking of lost/stolen cards, make sure your bank offers the same protection on your ATM/Visa or ATM/MasterCard as regular credit cards because those cards are attached to your checking/savings account. If those cards get lost/stolen, all the money in your checking account can be wiped out. Carry cash, traveler's checks and credit cards as a back-up because there could be computer glitches, or as I mentioned, your card could be eaten by the ATM. If by chance your card does get eaten, report it immediately to your bank. I have heard stories where people did not report it to their bank, thinking the useless card and the unwritten PIN were safe, but found out the funds in their checking account were wiped out because of an inside job at the bank.

Books recommended: The following books will contribute to planning your trip: **1.)** *Italy Fever: 14 Ways to Satisfy Your Love Affair with Italy,* Darlene Marwitz, ISBN: 0-9664998-2-4. $24.00. It is a wonderful & entertaining book to read about Italy before you leave home. **2.)** *The Collected Traveler, Central Italy*, Barrie Kerper, ISBN: 0-609-80443-X. $16.00. An inspired anthology and travel resource guide book. **3.)** *The Travel Detective: How to Get the Best Service & the Best Deals from Airlines*, Peter Greenberg, ISBN: 0-375756663. $15.95. It is a great guide to getting you the best fares on airlines.

The following are convenient and handy for traveling and you should have them with you. **1.)** One good guide book. Make sure the guide book tells you what to see in each city, hours of operation for museums and sites, and transportation information for doing day trips to nearby towns. **2.)** *Hello Italy!* (this book) Many of the hotels will give you a discount if you show them this book. **3.)** *Eating & Drinking in Italy,* Andy Herbach & Michael Dillon, ISBN: 1-892975-59-9 $9.95. This user-friendly guide is my first, best and only choice of menu readers because it alphabetizes the food and drinks and is compact. Andy & Michael can be reached at e-mail: EatnDrink@aol.com

4.) *Lonely Planet Italian Phrasebook,* ISBN: 0-86442-475-6 or *Italian: A Rough Guide Phrasebook,* ISBN: 1-85828-147-4 (make sure whatever book you purchase has a two-way dictionary). **5.)** *Thomas Cook European Timetable,* ISSN: 0952-620X, for train schedules (rip out the pages on Italy and you are ready to go).

Cellular phone: This is one of the best and most comforting thing I have ever done for myself on a trip. I move around a lot from town to town, hotel to hotel, and having the portable phone made it possible for my husband to keep up with my travels and eased his worries about my traveling all alone in a foreign country. My family and friends didn't have to struggle with broken Italian to reach me. It also made it quite convenient for me to keep in touch with home as well as make advance hotel reservations along the way. What was really great was being able to use it while I was on a seven-hour train ride. I didn't have a chance to make hotel reservations before leaving the last city, so I called while I was on the train. There are several companies in operation but I recommend Cellhire, USA, because of their low rates and excellent reputation. Cellhire, USA: (888) 476-7368 or Web site: http://www.CellHire.com/

Hotel reservations: Please see hotel reservations in "Tips on Hotel Accommodations" for very important tips.

Language tapes: As I mentioned earlier in the introduction, I do not speak Italian but I do try to learn several basic phrases to make my traveling a little more fun. About a month before I leave, I keep an Italian language tape for travelers in my car and play it over and over while I rehearse the phrases.

Luggage: The amount of luggage you carry can make or break your trip. European hotels do not offer a lot of closet space. Also, there are no porters in these charming small hotels. My husband and I are in our late forties and we still travel a month or more at a time with only two bags each. Therefore, we do not require a lot of closet space. We use the Eagle Creek's *Cargo Switchback® Plus* convertible suitcase & *Cargo SB Traveler*. These are bags that work together as a system. The *Switchback®* is a 2-in-1 modular system. The first is a 14x21x8 (14x23x8) w/wheels) suitcase that comes with an extension handle that allows it to roll on wheels; or it can be carried as a backpack or by hand-handle. This luxury of choices is very convenient when cobblestone streets sometimes makes it almost impossible to navigate the wheels. I can't say enough about these bags. I pulled, wheeled, banged and dragged them (sometimes through pouring rain) up and down stairs in train stations, cobbled streets and country roads in 28 cities throughout Italy. I stuffed them with my notes, brochures and information collected after visiting more than 500 hotels, which tested the strength of the zippers and handles. The *Switchback®* has a day pack (12x16x5) that attaches (zips) to it. The second is the *Cargo SB* bag (21x13x8) that slips over the handle of the Switchback but can also be carried as a backpack or on the shoulder. The best feature about these bags is that they both meet the now revised specifications for carry-ons allowed on airlines. I also love their *Sidekick* (waist & shoulder bag). I wear it around my waist when I board the plane so it is not counted as an extra bag. Then I use it as a shoulder bag when I arrive at my destination. It is roomy enough to hold my paperback book, cellular phone, umbrella, camera, flashlight, water bottle, etc. Web site: http://www.eaglecreek.com/ Self-service laundries throughout our travels help us tremendously because we pack light. I have tried to include locations of the various laundries for most cities listed in this book.

Maps: Obtain a map of each city you are planning to visit. If you have enough time, contact those cities and request that they mail you a map. (See individual chapters for contact information on the different tourist offices.) Having the map ahead of time will help you to familiarize yourself with the layout of the city as well as the location of the hotels. I cannot stress enough how important this information is because it also helps you to determine whether you can walk or should take the bus, train or taxi to the hotel. If you forget to pick up a map before you leave home, you can always purchase one at the convenience stores located at the train stations. It amazes me when I hear tourists who don't speak Italian asking for directions. The time you spend getting lost will cost you more than an investment in a good map. Most travel guides suggest picking up a free map from the local tourist information centers located within the city. This is a great idea. However, given the hours of the tourist offices and the time of day that you may arrive in the city, this suggestion will not always be possible to follow. Besides, how will you find the tourist office? Numerous bookstores carry an abundance of information regarding traveling. (Check my Web site: http://www.HelloEurope.com/ for a complete list of travel stores.) Whatever map you decide to purchase, make sure it has an index to help you find the street you are looking for. If you can't find the first name of the street, then try the second name. Tip: For Rome, Florence & Venice, I loved using the compact, useful and informative *Popoutmaps*, size 5"x 4", $6.95US, Toll-free (800) 617-6768, Web site: http://www.popoutmaps.com/ E-mail: info@popoutmaps.com. They have a street index and are convenient to carry around.

Packing: As a result of my years of traveling, I have compiled a packing list of seldom thought-of but very necessary items. (See Appendix I.) These items will make your trip more enjoyable and hassle-free. Most of these items are available at your local favorite travel store. Check my Web site: http://www.HelloEurope.com/ for a complete list of travel stores or you can contact Magellan's travel catalog at (800) 962-4943 or Web site http://www.magellans.com/

Precautions for safe travel: As an experienced traveler, I take certain precautions that I assumed everyone takes or knows about. I was wrong. I met people on my many journeys to Europe who shared their negative experiences with me on how they were pickpocketed. What surprised me was how simple it was for the thief. I don't consider any city in Italy, including Rome or Naples, to be as dangerous as New York City (where I was born and raised) or Los Angeles (where I currently live). But you must be aware of the huge number of pickpocketing incidents that take place within Italy. They use so many different scams to distract you: making believe there is a bird dropping on your jacket; putting a newspaper or cardboard up to your face; mother with the infant baby; simply bumping into you; watching you in a gift store to see where you put your wallet; person on a Moped grabbing your bag and your arm with it; or just running up to you and grabbing your purse off your arm, etc. Pickpockets dress for the job in clothes ranging from the typical gypsy look to the elegant look of a well-dressed Italian tourist. Leave your valuables locked in your room or with the hotel management. Nowadays most hotels including 1-stars have safety boxes inside the room. (See tips on rooms for my opinion on safety boxes.) If you are uncomfortable with that, then invest in a deluxe undercover wallet that is worn underneath your clothes. They come in different shapes and styles to be worn around your waist, shoulders, legs or neck. Buy whatever is comfortable for you but get one. Once I leave my hotel room there is never any reason for me to go into or open my deluxe undercover wallet because I also use *Eagle Creek's Departure* pouch (wallet/purse) that loops onto my belt to carry the estimated money I plan to use for the day, one credit card, a pen and a small memo pad. Remember professional pickpockets are always watching where you reach for or put your money. If I underestimated the money I needed for the day, I replenish my funds from inside a stall in a ladies' bathroom and nowhere else. These items are carried by your local favorite travel store. Check my Web site: http://www.HelloEurope.com/ for a list of travel stores or you can contact Magellan's travel catalog at (800) 962-4943 or Web site http://www.magellans.com/ I do not use fanny packs but if you want to use one, do not put anything of value in it. Use a separate wallet for your money and put all the unimportant items you will need for the day in the fanny pack, and put a small combination lock on the zipper. Do not assume because you have a fanny pack that it is safe from the pickpockets. *Make photocopies of all your important documents: airline ticket, passport, traveler's checks, credit card numbers and phone numbers of the credit card companies in case they are lost or stolen.* Make sure someone at home has the duplicate set of everything you photocopied. Remember pickpockets also work airports.

Train travel in Italy: I travel to all the cities in Italy by train or bus. I always purchase an Italy Flexi Rail Card from Rail Europe before I leave the country. There are so many variations of passes that are sold by Rail Europe. The following is a brief summary of the different passes available for Italy. 1.) Eurailpass-a multicountry pass sold either as a consecutive days usage pass or flexipass, which is a certain amount of days in a time frame (1st class only). 2.) Eurailpass Saver is the same as the Eurailpass but is cheaper if two or more people are traveling together on the same schedule (1st class only). 3.) Europass-a specified number of days for specific number of countries (1st class only). 4.) Europass Saver-same as Europass but is cheaper if two people are traveling together on the same schedule

(1st class only). 5.) Europass Drive-a combination rail/drive pass (1st class only). 6.) Italy Flexi Rail Card-a specified number of days in a month (1st or 2nd class). 7.) Italy Flexi Rail Card Saver, same as the Italy Flexi Rail Card but cheaper if two or more people are traveling together. 8.) Italy Rail 'n Drive-a combination pass for train and car (1st or 2nd class). 9.) France 'n Italy Pass for travel in Italy and France. This pass is available in first and second class and also has a cheaper Saverpass version. Most of the passes mentioned above are available for people under 26 at discounted prices and would include the use of 2nd class travel. Railpasses must be purchased before you leave home. Call Rail Europe at 1-888-382-7245 or check out their Web site: http://www.raileurope.com. The Web site also has useful trip planning information, showing fares and schedules for specific rail journeys. You can also buy point-to-point rail tickets from Rail Europe. Please note that whether you have a rail pass or not, reservations are mandatory on the Eurostar Italia (ES*), EuroCity (EC), InterCity (IC), the Pendolino and EuroNight (EN) night trains.

To make our train travel more efficient throughout the country, we use the *Thomas Cook European Timetable*, which is sold in most travel bookstores like the Complete Traveler, Kansas, at toll-free Tel: (888) 862-0888, Web site: http://www.completetrav.com/; Distant Lands Travel, California at toll-free Tel: (800) 310-3220, Web site: http://www.distantlands.com/ California Map & Travel Center, California at Tel: (310) 396-6277, Web site: http://www.mapper.com/ or you can order it directly from the Forsyth Travel Library, Tel: (800) 367-7984 in the U.S. or Canada. (Check my Web site http://www.HelloEurope.com/ for a more complete list of travel stores.) The *Thomas Cook European Timetable* is the best timetable available in the north continent and is published on the first day of each month. It is worth its weight in gold because it can save you hours of standing on information lines at various train stations. Otherwise, you can visit Rail Europe's Web site: http://www.raileurope.com/ or call them toll-free at (888) 382-7245 for the USA and (800) 361-7245 for Canada or fax them at (800) 432-1329. I use these numbers to get an idea of the cost, distance and time it takes to travel to each city's train station. Rail Europe also has an information-by-fax-on-demand system. The prices and information you get from contacting Rail Europe will help you to decide what type of rail pass you will

BY RAIL

need, if any. One to two days before I depart a city in Italy, I usually go to the train station to make my advance reservations for the next leg of my trip. This cuts down on the stress of finding out that the departure times or seats you want are sold out, which has happened to me more than once when I waited to the last minute to make my reservation. However, once I get to Italy, I try to buy the Italian FS "InTreno" which is the official train timetable that the train conductors use for information. The FS "InTreno" timetable comes in quite handy for the Italian Riviera and Cinque Terre which is not covered by the Thomas Cook Timetable. The FS "InTreno" is available at newsstands inside most of the train stations. State Railways in Italy (FS) Information: Tel: 848888088. Web site: http://www.fs-on-line.com/ Hrs.: 7am-9pm.

Train tips:
1. Always purchase your ticket as soon as you know your departure time. Don't wait until the morning of departure, especially if you plan to catch Eurostar Italia (ES*), EuroCity (EC), InterCity (IC), the Pendolino and EuroNight (EN) night trains. It doesn't matter whether it is 1st or 2nd class, always make reservations as soon as you are sure of your departure times, as these trains fill up quickly. This rule also applies to railpass holders. Be sure to bring your cable locks (see packing tips) because Eurostars have separate compartments for luggage. Many times you are too busy looking out the window to watch your luggage.

2. If a train ride is more than three hours and I am traveling with luggage, I always buy 1st class tickets if I am not using my 1st class rail pass. It is less crowded and allows me to spread out comfortably. The only time I use 2nd class on trips longer than three hours is if the train is Eurostar Italia (ES*), EuroCity (EC) or InterCity (IC). 2nd class is extremely comfortable on these trains.

3. When you look at the departure board at the train stations, it is not always easy to identify which train is yours. Here are some tips to assist in assuring you catch the right train: a. Using your timetable as a reference, look on the board for the number of the train. b. The city you are going to may not be listed on the board. Look for the train's final destination. c. Look at the departure time of your train. The trains

are listed chronologically. d. There are also large detailed displays on walls throughout the trains stations that include the departure times, train numbers, track number (sometimes changes) and a list of most of the cities the train is stopping at before its final destination.

4. When waiting on the platform to board your train, look for the display boards that may have diagrams of the layout of the train. These diagrams are quite useful. They will show you the direction the train is going and approximately where the 1st & 2nd class cars will stop at the train station. In the case of a Eurostar Italia (ES*), it will show you what part of the platform your assigned car will stop. Check your Eurostar Italia (ES*) ticket for the number of your car & pre-assigned seat number.

5. When boarding a train without reserving a seat, make sure you sit in a nonreserve seat. Just look at the back of the seat near the window or on the glass door (depending on the type of train you are boarding) for little tags with reserve seat numbers on it. I can't tell you how many times I've heard our fellow Americans get upset because they were not told that they were in the wrong seats until they were comfortably on their way.

6. When using individual train tickets (including supplement tickets), make sure you stamp your ticket before you board the train, using any one of the convenient orange machines. Always check the ticket to make sure it got stamped. You'll get a hefty fine if you board the train without a stamped ticket.

7. When the train conductor comes by to stamp your ticket, always confirm with them that you are in the right car. Some trains split up their cars at certain train stops and will travel in different directions. There is nothing more frustrating than having to grab your luggage because you found out at the last minute that you were in the wrong car. (I speak from experience.)

8. Don't forget to pack water, fruit peeler, towelettes, inflatable head pillow, book, toilet seat covers and snacks for long trips.

9. The great advantage of having a rail pass (& this book which gives you lots of choices on affordable hotels) is you can change your destination while you are on the train. I have done this several times. Example: I was on my way to Santa Marguerita and decided to stop in Camogli at the last minute. I got off in Camogli then caught a train to Santa Marguerita the next day.

10. If you are doing day trips, purchase your round-trip tickets ahead of time even if you are not sure of your departure time.

11. When purchasing train tickets always indicate whether you want aisle (*passaggio*), window (*finestra*), smoking (*fumare*), nonsmoking (*non fumare*), 1st class (*prima classe*) or 2nd class (*secondo classe*). After you purchase your train ticket & before you leave the window, always double-check on the time and departure date printed on the ticket. Several times the attendants made mistakes on either the day I wanted or the departure time of the train. Tip: Most train stations take credit cards.

12. Most of the train stations do not have elevators. Before you drag your suitcases up and down the steep stairs, check to see if there are platforms that cross over the tracks. Ask the train personnel for permission to use this platform. I can't tell how many times I didn't see these platforms until it was too late. I would drag my bags up and down the stairs, feeling totally exhausted only to see the locals using the platforms to cross over the tracks.

13. There are certain advantages to having an Italian rail pass or Eurostar ticket. They both entitle you free entré into the Eurostar clubs which are similar to the clubs at the airports. They are located in most of the major train stations in Italy such as Bologna, Florence, Milano, Naples and Rome, etc. You can make or change your train reservations at no extra charge at these clubs without having to wait on the long ticket lines.

TIPS ON AIR TRAVEL

The following information from American Airlines AA should help you navigate the new rules & regulations regarding air travel and security.

1. BEFORE YOU GO

http://www.aa.com (award-winning site)
Net SAAver & Special Offers (basically Internet discounts)
Online AAdvantage® award-booking feature
Proactive flight-status notification by voice or text-message (notifies you via your cell phone or pager of flight arrival & departure times, gate info, baggage info, etc.)

2. AT THE AIRPORT

Carry-on Baggage Allowance: New FAA security measures now limit customers on all AA flights to one carry-on bag plus one per-sonal item. The one carry-on bag must fit in an overhead compart-ment or under the seat. It should not exceed 45 linear inches (length + width + height) or weigh more than 40 lbs/18 kgs.

Newly Recommended Airport Arrival Times: Customers travel-ing internationally should be at the airport two hours prior to depar-ture. Customers should extend their arrival times during holidays and other high-demand periods.

Security Procedures: Have a photo ID out and available at all times for inspection. Have a ticket confirmation available if traveling on an electronic ticket. Ensure that luggage bears traveler's name and con-tact information inside and out. Pack sharp objects such as razors and sewing scissors in checked baggage rather than in carry-ons. Take laptops out of carrying cases prior to putting them through se-curity screening devices at checkpoints. Be prepared for hand searches of carry-ons. Be ready to remove footwear for additional screening.

3. ON THE PLANE

More Room - Row after row only on American Airlines: We've been busy removing rows of seats from every aircraft to give our Coach customers more legroom to relax and enjoy their flight in com-fort. Only American Airlines offers more room throughout Coach.

4. ITALY NUMBERS/CONTACTS

AA Travel Center: Via G.B. Pirelli 20, 5th Fl., Milan. Tel: 02-6968-2464. **AA Reservations:** Milan Tel: 02-6968-2464; Rome Tel: 06-6605-3169.

FIRST TIME ABROAD?

After spending almost three months traveling throughout Italy, I heard lots of stories from the locals about American tourists who experienced Europe for the first time. Some of them are quite funny and, of course, some are not. However, I could relate to all the stories at one time or another. We are usually used to large hotel rooms even in the most basic of hotels. We take certain standards for granted and are surprised when we don't find them. This is the reason I promised many of the hotel owners and managers that I would include the following statements about budget hotels in Italy, which might help reduce the culture shock and any possible misunderstandings.

Facts (most of the time) about budget hotels & their rooms

There are no ice machines. 90% of the time, there are no elevators. 90% of the time, there is no air-conditioning. There are no porters. There are very few handicapped-equipped rooms. There are no face cloths in European hotels. There usually is no 24-hour telephone reception. This means your family will not be able to call you after 11pm in Italy. Hotels do charge for every local phone call. There is usually no such thing as a king-size bed. You are lucky if they have a queen-size bed. If you are over 5' 11", your feet will hang over the end of the double bed. (My husband is 6' 4".) The size of the hotel rooms are the size of a master bathroom in the U.S. The bathroom is about the size of a linen closet in the U.S. The clothes closet is about the size of a kitchen cabinet. You may have to live out of your suitcase. Check-out time is usually 10am. Check-in time is usually after 2pm. If breakfast is included in the rate, the rate is nonnegotiable whether you eat breakfast or not. Always ask about their parking facilities in advance.

TIPS ON HOTEL ACCOMMODATIONS

Air-conditioning: I know how important this feature is to many people. I specifically asked each hotel if they had air-conditioning in the hotel rooms and not just the hotel lobby. Each hotel that I list in this book as having air-conditioned rooms assured me that it is in the rooms. If you are reserving a hotel because the hotel has air-conditioned rooms, always ask what time the air-conditioning is turned on and off each day. Please keep in mind, the hotel may charge extra to use the air-conditioning and it may not be adjustable from your room.

Balconies (*balcone*): I have included whether hotels have rooms with balconies because this is such a special feature. However, a balcony facing the street can be quite noisy at night even if the windows are double-paned. Don't forget to pack your earplugs. Also, please keep in mind that the sizes of the balconies vary from one foot to the size of a full terrace. A balcony is great to have when your traveling buddy needs to grab a smoke.

Bathroom facilities: One of the biggest complaints I hear about is the small bathroom size. Some bathrooms are so small, you can shower, brush your teeth and use the toilet all at the same time. I realize this is an adjustment but we should not compare European bathrooms in most 1-, 2- and 3-star hotels to American-size standard bathrooms. We forget that some of the buildings that house these hotels are centuries old. Even when the hotel renovates the rooms, there isn't much left over for a full-size bathroom. The only thing that matters to my husband and me regarding a bathroom is that it is clean, private and has a shower, toilet and sink in it. Speaking of bathrooms, sometimes there is a difference in price between rooms with a bathtub and rooms with a shower. A room with a shower is cheaper than one with a bathtub. A room with a bathtub = *vasca da bagno*; without bathtub = *senza vasca da bagno*; with shower = *con doccia*; without shower = *senza doccia*. Do not assume anything when it comes to a bathroom in an Italian hotel room. Some rooms have a toilet and sink, or a sink only with no shower or toilet, or a shower but no toilet. I think you get my drift. Make absolutely sure of what you are getting. Use the convenient Italian phrases I have included in Appendix IV to confirm the facilities. European hotels do not have facecloths. I always pack mine. *Showers:* I haven't figured out why some showers don't have shower curtains on them. This inconvenience sometimes makes it impossible for two people to use the bathroom at the same time.

Beds: A double bed (*letto matrimoniale*) is usually cheaper than twin beds (*due letti singoli*). Be specific when requesting a room for two. Indicate whether you want *letto matrimoniale* or *due letti*. It is important that you ask to see the room and check firmness of the bed to make sure it is satisfactory. **French (small) double beds:** I have noted whenever possible in the individual hotel listings which rooms have small double beds. A small double bed is larger than a twin bed but smaller than a standard double bed. I jokingly describe it as a nice-size bed for one person or two slim people in love. **Zip & lock queen-size bed** or **zip & lock king-size bed** is when the hotel zips two twin-size beds together to make one queen-size or king-size bed.

Breakfast (*colazione*): Most hotels in Italy serve a continental breakfast at an extra charge unless otherwise specified in the hotel listing. The price ranges from 3€ (euro) to 12€ (euro) per person (pp) per day. Always check before turning it down. Sometimes you might luck out and get a buffet (assorted breads, yogurt, cheese, eggs, ham, chocolate milk, juice, jam plus the basics), but normally it consists of *caffe latte* (coffee with hot milk) and a choice of bread (not always croissants), toast or baguettes and awful canned juice. The bread is not always fresh and the coffee might be reheated from the day before. Politely make yourself perfectly clear when you are checking into the hotel whether or not you plan to have breakfast in the hotel. The only time you have no choice is when they post signs on the wall stating that breakfast is included in the room rate and that the hotel room rate is the same whether you eat breakfast or not. Breakfast is usually served from 7:30am to 10am. Some budget hotels do not have an area where they can serve breakfast, so be prepared for them to serve breakfast in your room. Confirm the serving time with them and what the meal consists of and where they serve it. Tyrell and I prefer to enjoy our breakfast at the local café, with the conversation of Italian people on their way to work as the background, at half the price the hotel will charge. *Note:* Half-board rates means room plus breakfast and one other meal. Full-board rates means room plus breakfast, lunch and dinner.

TIPS ON HOTEL ACCOMMODATIONS

Buildings: Don't get discouraged by an unimpressive entrance or lobby as you enter a building to your hotel. You can walk through the most magnificent lobby and your room can be small and drab or you can walk through a shabby entrance of a building, take the elevator up to the hotel and when the doors open and you are escorted to your room, you will be pleasantly surprised at how charming & nicely furnished your room will be.

Car parking: If there is parking available at the hotels, assume there will be an additional daily charge for the convenience (about 14€ (euro) a day).

Checking in: Never pay for a room in advance for more nights than you will need. You may not always get your money back. Never check into a room without seeing it first, and remember to check the firmness of the bed. If they refuse to show you the room, politely leave. If a hotel is holding your deposit for a room but you know in advance that you will be arriving after 1700 hrs. (5pm), contact the hotel immediately. The hotel is within their rights to give away your room after that time, regardless of the fact that they have your money. **If you made advance reservations, please remember to pack and bring your hotel confirmation with the person's name on it along with you.**

Checking out: 10-11am is the normal checkout time in Italy. Do not assume you have the right to leave your luggage in the hotel's care while you finish your day. Not all hotels have this service, and keep in mind they are not responsible for lost or stolen property. I have offered to pay them to hold my luggage. They usually don't accept the offer. When departing the hotel, always make sure you get a receipt marked "paid in full." If you plan to leave very early in the morning, **I recommend paying the hotel bill the night before**. This relieves the stress of trying to catch that early-morning train or bus and allows time to clear up any discrepancies or misunderstandings regarding the final bill.

Children: The general rule most of the time is that hotels will charge for children if they require an additional bed in the room. Always confirm before you make a reservation to see if you can have your children in the room at no charge or at least 50% off the extra-person price.

TIPS ON HOTEL ACCOMMODATIONS

Closet space: Please see **Luggage** in chapter "Before You Leave Home."

Credit cards: Hotels and restaurants prefer cash over credit cards. Because I personally visited each hotel, I have indicated wherever possible whether the hotels take credit cards or cash. Do not let them intimidate you into paying cash, which some may try to do (unless, of course, they are willing to give you a cash discount). I listened to one hotel manager ask a tourist, "Don't you have any cash?" when there was a sign on his wall next to the desk stating "Credit cards accepted." The young lady said "No" and whipped out her credit card.

Discounts on hotel rooms: Please do not choose a hotel room based on this feature. This is a very confusing area for me and I haven't figured out a perfect solution. Many of the hotel owners agreed in writing to give a discount if you show them this book when you check into the hotel. The question regarding discounts is part of a questionnaire they fill out when I visit each hotel. The questionnaire is written in Italian so there is no misunderstanding. I made a notation in each hotel listing where it applies. Depending on the time of year, it ranges from about 5% to 10% or more per room. I included a name wherever possible. If I did not give an amount, it is because they did not state how much they would give. It could be given in the form of **one** free breakfast. On occasion, some of the hotels after they agree in writing to give my readers a discount will suddenly forget about it. I guess they do not like giving them. Please do not be surprised if they give you a distasteful look when you ask for one. Do not let them intimidate you. (Sometimes this is easier said than done.) If you arrive at the hotel and are having problems getting your discount, you can always try asking the hotel manager to contact me via fax (323) 939-7736 and request to have the written form I received from the hotel authorizing the discount. This may not always work and I may not be around but it's worth a try. Also disregard all discounts when it comes to national holidays or festival celebrations.

Eating in hotel rooms: Management frowns upon eating in the rooms. If you plan on this type of activity (which I am guilty of), don't leave gingerbread crumbs in the room as evidence. Please be neat and use paper towels as coasters and napkins.

TIPS ON HOTEL ACCOMMODATIONS

Elevators: I know a hotel elevator is an important feature to some people. Using the elevators in most 1-, 2- and 3-stars hotels can be an experience in itself. Elevators come in different sizes in these small family-owned hotels. Most of them have elevators that are just big enough for one person. The elevators can be so small that sometimes my husband goes up with the bags and I'll either wait for the elevator to come back or take the stairs. This is another reason why I advise people to pack light because porters are nonexistent in these hotels.

E-mailing & faxing hotels: Please see Appendix III for the specifics & tips on making hotel reservations via e-mail & fax. Also, see hotel reservations in this section.

English: Where I indicate in the listings that limited English is spoken at a hotel, this means they speak enough English to confirm what type of room and bathroom facilities you want. Use the Italian phrases in Appendix IV to help you with hotel reservations.

Exchange rate: I quoted the hotel room rates in euro (€). I rounded off the exchange rate at $1 U.S. per each €.

Family rooms: I have noted in the individual hotel listings which hotels have rooms for families. My definition of a family is 4 people. It can be 4 adults; 2 adults with 2 children; or 3 adults and 1 child. I identify the rooms that can accommodate more than 4 adults by using the terms quint (5 adults) or sextet (6 people).

Floors: Usually Americans call the ground floor the first floor, but the Italians call it *piano terreno* (ground floor). In Italy the first floor (*piano primo*) is our second floor. I have followed the Italian convention in this book. In the addresses for the hotel listings where it states "2nd flr.," it means 2 floors above the ground floor. The ground floor is noted by "T" or "O" on the elevator panel.

Frigobar: It is a compact mini-refrigerator. Similar to a minibar in a hotel but without food or drinks inside it.

Hotel ratings: I think the rating system is misleading. It has nothing to do with the charm or the quality of the hospitality. The hotel's star rating is based on things like the location of the hotel in the building, percentage of rooms with full baths, the size of the bathrooms, reception area or breakfast room, whether the hotel has TVs, elevator, bar or restaurant. The only difference between a 1-star hotel and a 2-star hotel could be that the 2-star has an elevator, a restaurant or a bar. The difference between a 3-star and a 4-star may be that the 3-star doesn't have separate bathrooms for men and women in their restaurant. The number of rooms that an establishment has can also determine whether it is a 2-star or 3-star hotel. The higher the star the more the hotel has to pay in taxes. The ratings are allocated once only, unless the hotel requests a reassessment. None of this information should matter to you as much as your specific room. Some hotels have no rating because the hoteliers have never asked the government to rate them. Do not place any importance on the rating system; I stayed in 2-star hotels that were better equipped than 3-star hotels.

Hotel reservations: To make reservations ahead of time from home, do it during the Italian business day when the owner/manager is available to give you a confirmation or a discount. You may have to fax them three or four times before you get a confirmation or a response back. If you don't hear back it doesn't always mean they don't have a room. I can't express the level of frustration I experience when I try faxing requests for friends of mine. The hotel's reasons for not responding vary: reservation is too far in advance for them to take seriously, they are too busy to respond or they just don't feel like responding. On the other hand, it could be because you didn't put your country of origin and/or the proper telephone fax number for them to respond back to. I was told by numerous hotels that Americans are the only group of people who do not do this on their request for reservations.There is no magic formula for dealing with these small family-owned hotels. You must be persistent and constantly follow up. Make it a point to confirm about three to ten days before your arrival date. Make sure you get a written confirmation of the agreed-upon arrangements. Examples: bath or shower, toilet, balcony, number of people (if children, what is the cutoff age), which floor, front or back of hotel, extra charge for air-conditioning, room number, with or without breakfast and total cost per night (including the service charge and tax). You may still have to insist upon these same arrangements when you arrive at the hotel, but it is a lot easier when you have a copy of the written confirmation with you. I cannot emphasize this enough. **If you made advance reservations, please remember to pack and bring your hotel confirmation with the person's name on it along with you. Also, always ask what is the hotel's cancellation policy. If you have to make any changes in your reservations be sure to fax the hotel with the changes. Do not rely upon a verbal confirmation of your change. Try to get a confirmation from the hotel indicating the new changes. I cannot stress this enough.** A sample of a hotel fax form has been provided for you at the back of this book. (You can adjust the size of the form by going to my Web site: http://www.HelloEurope.com/) Obviously, it is a lot easier to confirm reservations via fax and with a credit card, but many of the smaller, inexpensive family-run hotels do not accept credit cards. They usually require you to mail one night's deposit (usually a foreign-currency draft). Contact your bank or call Thomas Cook Foreign Exchange at (800) 287-7362 or International Currency Exchange at (888) 842-0880 East Coast or (888) 278-6628 West Coast to purchase an international draft. Mailing a deposit may present a problem if you decide to cancel your reservation because getting the deposit back may not always be a pleasant task. The U.S. Postal Service doesn't includes Italy in its "Global Priority" overseas mail program. If you choose to make reservations in writing before you leave home, try to include an International Reply Coupon (found at post offices), which saves the hotel return postage and will almost guarantee a response. A reader (Sydney Swiger) sent the hotel a traveler's check as a deposit via Federal Express. She stated that this gave her a certain amount of security to know that not only did the hotel receive the deposit but also who signed for the package. Sending your deposit Federal Express makes a statement that you are quite serious. You might be able to accomplish this at a cheaper rate using the Express mail from U.S. Postal Service which also goes to Italy. Never pay for a room in advance for more nights than you need. You may not always get your money back. Please check the section on bathroom facilities in the Italian phrases in Appendix IV for specific types of rooms and facilities. *Tip:* If there are no English-speaking staff members at the hotel, refer to Appendix IV or to your Italian travel phrase book, and fax or repeat the phrases regarding accommodations. Also, familiarize yourself with military time and calendar days. *Example*: Arrival time 4pm is 1600hour and June 7-15, 2003 is 7/6/

03 to 15/6/03. (To find out how to call, fax or e-mail from the United States to Italy, see Appendix III.)

Hotel room payment: There are still some hotels left in Italy that do not accept credit cards. Payment is on a "cash only" basis. These hotels usually offer greater value than the others. This means they are often booked far in advance. If you plan to stay at these hotels without making reservations, get there early in the morning!! If you plan to leave very early in the morning, **I recommend paying the hotel bill the night before**. This relieves the stress of trying to catch that early-morning train or bus and allows time to clear up any discrepancies or misunderstandings regarding the final bill.

Hotel room rates: If the rooms are described and the rates are quoted for a triple (3 adults) or a family (4 adults), this doesn't mean that two people cannot have the room. The rates for two people for the same room that can accommodate three or more people may be a little higher than a room that can only accommodate two people. All rates for the rooms have to be displayed in a prominent place. Look for the rate chart either by the entrance or near the reception desk and in your room. The rates displayed usually include tax and service. The city tax (per room, per night) is normally included in the quoted price for the room. Always confirm before registering that the total price quoted for the room includes the city tax. The staff doesn't always offer their cheapest room at first so you usually have to ask for it. Regardless of the reason, the hotel cannot legally charge you more than the maximum rate shown in the display that is either on the back of your hotel door or at the front desk. If they do, you can tell them that you will send a letter of complaint about the extra charge either to the address that is stamped on the display or local municipal office. You can find out the correct address from the tourist office. The Italian government is very strict and will issue steep fines to hotels that gouge tourists. *Note:* Half-board rates means room plus breakfast and one other meal. Full-board rates means room plus breakfast, lunch and dinner. Single = 1 person; double = 2 people; triple = 3 people; quad/family = 4 people; quint = 5 people; sextet = 6 people; pp = per person.

TIPS ON HOTEL ACCOMMODATIONS

Hotel safes: I still don't trust them. I have heard too many stories about people having negative experiences with safes whether they stayed at a 5-star or a 3-star hotel. As a matter of fact, I think I feel more secure in a smaller 2-star hotel because the management recognizes the residents, the staff is usually smaller, visible, and has been with the hotel longer than the staff of the larger hotels.

Streetside vs. rooms in the back: Rooms that face the street may offer you more light and interesting views but this is usually accompanied by lots of noise, which may force you to keep your windows closed at night. Not a great idea if it is a hot night and the hotel doesn't have air-conditioning. Rooms that face the back are likely to be darker but quieter.

Telephone and faxing hotels: Please see Appendix III for how to call and fax hotels in Italy.

Useful Web sites & information:

Around the World Travel: (800) 590-7778 or
http://www.atwtraveler.com/
eTravel Tips: http://www.etravel.org/
Europe Travel: http://www.eurotrip.com/
Shoestring Traveler: http://www.stratpub.com/
Traveling Smart E-mail: cuber@dragonflyerpress.com/
Travel Abroad: http://www.transabroad.com/
http://www.beaumonde.net/
Information on discount airfares, accommodations, hostels & rental
cars, bus, train information, embassies, visas, health and road safety,
backpacking, currency conversion, Internet: cybercafes, laptop hook-
ups, meeting travelers, study & live abroad.

Air travel
American Airlines: (800) 433-7300 or http://www.aa.com/

Airports in Europe
http://www.airwise.com/airports/euroboard.html/

Cars
Auto Club of Italy: http://www.aci.it/
Auto Europe: (800) 223-5555 or http://www.autoeurope.com/
Avis Rent-a-Car: (800) 331-1084 or http://www.avis.com/
Europe by Car: (800) 223-1516 or http://www.europebycar.com/
Europcar: (800) 800-6000 or http://www.europcar.com/
Hertz: (800) 654-3001 or http://www.hertz.com/
Kemwel: (800) 678-0678 or http://www.kemwel.com/
Kilometers between places: http://www.iti.fr/

Cellular phone
Cell Hire: (888) 476-7368 or http://www.CellHire.com/

Credit cards & money
American Express: (800) 843-2273 or http://www.aexp.com/
Cirrus Network: (800) 424-7787. Call for a list of locations.
Currency Converter: http://www.oanda.com/
International Currency Exchange: (888) 842-0880 East Coast, (888)
278-6628 West Coast, or http://www.foreignmoney.com/

USEFUL WEB SITES & INFORMATION

MasterCard: (800) 999-0454 or http://www.mastercard.com/atm/
Plus System: (800) 843-7587. Call for a list of locations.
Thomas Cook Foreign Exchange: (800) 287-7362 or
http://www.thomascook.com/
Universal Currency Converter: http://www.xe.com/ucc/
Visa: (800) 336-8472 or http://www.visa.com/
World Cash: (800) 434-2800 or fax (800) 434-2822.
Worldwide Currency Converter: http://www.olsen.ch/
currency_converter.html/

Culture
http://www.culturekiosque.com/

Customized Tours in Italy
http://www.takemymotherplease.com/

Customs, embassies, tourist office & warnings
Italy Tourist Board: http://www.italiantourism.com/
Embassy of Italy: http://www.emb.org/
U.S. State Dept. warnings:
http://www.travel.state.gov/travel_warnings.html/
Travel laws & protection:
http://www.nolo.com/ChunkCTIM/ctim.index.html#1/

Cyber cafes
http://www.netcafeguide.com/
http://www.cybercaptive.com/

Ferries
Ferries Italy to Greece: http://www.greekislands.gr/sff/

Hotels in Italy
http://www.vacanzeonline.it/
http://www.saritel.interbusiness.it/TPHOTEL/
http://www.italyhotels.it/
http://www.venere.it/home/italy.html/
http://www.hoteldirect.com/
http://www.room-service.co.uk/ITALY-BROCH/italy.html/
http://www.lodgingintuscany.com/

USEFUL WEB SITES & INFORMATION

http://www.bookeurohotels.co.uk/

Italian sculpture
http://www.thais.it/SCULTURA/

Italy
Italy Tourist Board: http://www.italiantourism.com/
Italy Tourist Webguide: http://www.itwg.com/
Italy Tourist Web Guide: http://www.masternet.it/
Italy Travel info: http://www.travel.it/
Italy site: http://www.initaly.com/
Italy Fever: http://www.italyfever.com/
Museums: http://www.museionlineit/
World Travel: http://www.wtgonline.com/navigate/world.asp/
Planet Italy: http://www.planetitaly.com/
Untours in Italy: http://www.untours.com/italian.htm/
Italy tour: http://www.italiatour.com/
http://www.city.net/countries/italy/
http://www.travel-italy.com/
http://www.piuitalia2000.it/
http://www.traveleurope.net/
http://www.italiansites.com/

Language
Travel Language Home Page: http://www.travlang.com/
Web Italian Lessons: http://www.june29.com//Italian/

Maps
California Map & Travel Center http://www.mapper.com/
Complete Traveler http://www.completetrav.com/
Distant Lands http://www.distantlands.com/
MapLink: (805) 692-6777 or http://www.maplink.com/
Maps of Italy/Our Heritage: http://www.initaly.com/ads/

Newsletters & magazines
Independent Traveling: http://www.footloosetravel.com/
International Travel News: http://www.intltravelnews.com/
Italy Fever: http://www.italyfever.com/
Journey Woman: http://www.journeywoman.com/

USEFUL WEB SITES & INFORMATION

Shoestring Travel: http://stratpub.com/
TheTravelzine: http://www.thetravelzine.com/
Travel Abroad: http://www.transabroad.com/
Travel Books Reviews:
http://members.aol.com/travbkrev/recentreviews2.html/

Trains
Rail Europe: (888) 382-7245 or http://www.raileurope.com/
Italy Rail Information: http://www.fs-on-line.com/ Tel: 848-888088.
Italy Rail Information: http://www.amicotreno.com/
Eurostar: http://www.eurostar.com/
http://www.trenitalia.com/

Travel clothes & necessities
Magellan's Travel Supplies: (800) 962-4943 or
http://www.magellans.com/
(Don't forget to check my packing list at the back of this book.)
Packing Tips: http://www.oratory.com/travel/index.html/
TravelSmith: (800) 950-1600 or http://www.travelsmith.com/
Universal Packing List: http://www.henricson.se/mats/upl/

Travel insurers & medicine
International SOS Assistance: (800) 523-8662 or
http://www.intsos.com/
Travel Insurers: Access America (800) 284-8300
                   Carefree Travel (800) 323-3149
                   Travelex (800) 228-9792
Travel Medicine: (800) 872-8633 or http://www.travmed.com/

Weather
http://www.weather.com/
http://travel.epicurious.com/travel/
http://www.usatoday.com/weather/

Wilson Publishing (my Web site)
(888) 663-9269 or http://www.HelloEurope.com/

World Clock
http://www.timeanddate.com/worldclock/

USEFUL WEB SITES & INFORMATION

ITALY CITIES & REGIONAL WEB SITES

Amalfi
http://www.starnet.it/onda_verde/
Amalfi coast: http://www.starnet.it/italy/amalfi/
http://www.ondaverde.it/

Bellagio
http://www.fromitaly.net/bellagio/

Bologna
http://www.bolognaonline.it/
http://www.provincia.bologna.it/

Capri
Hotels: http://www.capriweb.com/Capri/hotels/
http://www.caprionline.com/
http://www.capri-island.com/
http://www.capriweb.com/Capri/hotels/zona5.html/

Cinque Terre
http://www.cinqueterrenet.com/
http://www.aptcinqueterre.sp.it/
http://www.riomaggiore.net/
http://www.monterossonet.com/
http://home.sunrise.ch/avong/cinque_terre/
Ferry shuttle: http://www.navigazionegolfodeipoeti.it/
Vernazza: http://www.fast.mi.it/eia/vernazza/
Lerici: http://www.village.it/lerici/
http://italianvillas.com/liguria/cinque.htm/

Cortina D'Ampezzo
http://www.sunrise.it/dolomiti/
http://www.cortinanet.it/casatua/indexames/

Florence
Taste of Florence: http://www.divinacucina.com/
http://www.weekendafirenze.com/

USEFUL WEB SITES & INFORMATION

Hotels in Florence: http://www.firenzealbergo.it/
Florence & Tuscany: http://www.fionline.it/
http://www.arca.net/
http://www.tiac.net/users/pendini/index.html/
http://www.vps.it/propart/
http://www.whatsuptuscany.com/
http://www.firenze.net/events/
http://www.comune.firenze.it/english/homenglish.htm/

Lake Como
http://www.lakecomo.com/ E-mail: lakecomo@tin.it
http://www.traveleurope.net/comolake.htm/
http://www.traveleurope.it/bellagio.htm/
http://www.lagodicomo.com/
http://www.highonadventure.com/Hoa98apr/Lakecomo/

Lake Garda
http://www.lagodigarda.it/lakegarda/
http://www.telmec.it/Uk/Arena_frame.htm/
Hotel Rock: http://www.hotelrock.com/ Zambiasi Renato

Lucca
http://www.lucca.turismo.toscana.it/

Milano
Walking art tours: http://www.provincia.milano.it/
Hotels in Milan: http://www.mebs.it/hotels/
http://www.rcs.it/inmilano/english/
http://www.hellomilano.it/
http://www.milanoin.it/
http://lascala.milano.it/
http://www.vivimilano.it/
Reservations for Last Supper 02-89421146

Orvieto
http://www.eng.uci.edu/~alberto/orvieto/
http://www.orvietounderground.it/
http://www.orvienet.it/

USEFUL WEB SITES & INFORMATION

http://www.argoweb.it/orvieto/orvieto.uk.html/
http://www.argoweb.it/orvietano/

Naples
http://www.itb.it/metroNA/english/home.htm/
http://www.comune.napoli.it/
http://www.aziendaturismonapoli.com/

Padua
Brenta Canal: http://antoniana.it/mainuk.html/

Parma
http://www.parmaitaly.com/

Perugia
http://www.perugiaonline.com/
Map: http://hppg04.pg.infn.it/images/hotelmap.gif/

Pisa
http://www.csinfo.it/PISA/

Pompeii
http://www.marketplace.it/pompeionline/

Positano
http://www.starnet.it/positano/welcome.html/
http://www.positanonline.it/

Ravello
http://www.starnet.it/italy/ravello/ingrawel.htm/

Riva del Garda
http://www.gardaqui.it/
http://www.gardatrentino.de/

Rome
http://www.informaroma.it/ or http://www.comune.roma.it/
Walking architectural Itineraries: http://www.scalareale.org/

USEFUL WEB SITES & INFORMATION

Rome, walks, numbers, maps, events: http://www.romeguide.it/
Getting in/out of Rome: http://www.enjoyrome.it/
Public Holidays: http://www.inforoma.it/romepage.htm/
Forum: http://library.thinkquest.org/11402/
History: http://www.ukans.edu/history/index/europe/
Vatican: http://www.vatican.va/
City Guide: http://www.romanhomes.com/rome-guide.htm/
Guided Tours: http://www.romeguide.it/FILES/visite/guided.htm/
Hotels near Termini: http://rome.hotelguide.net/hl1te.htm/
Public transportation: http://www.atac.roma.it/trasroma/biglietti/
coveruk.htm/

San Gimignano
http://www.sangimignano.com/
http://www.firenze.net/events/itineraries/sangim.htm/

Sicily
http://www.osolemio.it/sicily/turismo/default.nclk/

Siena
http://www.turismoverde.com/
http://www.sienaweb.it/territorio/

Sirmione
http://www.comune.sirmione.bs.it/
http://www.sirmionehotel.com/
http://www.comune.sirmione.bs.it/index-en.html/

Sorrento
http://www.sorrentotourism.it/

Taormina
http://taol.taormina-ol.it/sunshine/
http://www.taormina-ol.it/host/aastao/aastao.html/

Umbria
http://www.argoweb.it/umbria/umbria.uk.html/
http://www.umbria.org/

USEFUL WEB SITES & INFORMATION

http://www.rai.it/
http://www.regione.umbria.it/
http://www.umbria-turismo.it/

Venice

Welcome to Venice: http://www.port.venice.it/
Venice info: http://web.vemod.it/aptve/inghome.asp/
Marco Polo airport: http://www.veniceairport.it/vce/eng/home.asp/
Venice boats: http://www.venetia.it/boats/
Hotels in Venice: http://www.venicehotel.com/
Walks: http://pathfinder.com/travel/TL/801/venice1.html/
Venice hotels: http://www.veniceinfo.it/
Texan in Venice: http://www.iuav.unive.it/~juli/
Guide to Venice: http://ucgi.venere.it/venezia/guida/
Grand Canal: http://www.gondolavenezia.it/
http://www.stb.dircon.co.uk/
http://www.venetia.it/
http://www.webcom.com/~italys/
http://www.tradenet.it/veniceworld/
http://www.provincia.it.venezia.it/
http://www.provincia.venezia.it/aptve/
http://www.comune.venezia.it/
http://www.portve.interbusiness.it/wetvenice/wetvenice.html/
http://www.govenice.com/ or http://www.governice.com/

Verona

http://www.verona-apt.net/

Vicenza

http://www.ascom.vi.it/aptvicenza/

AMALFI
Amalfi Coast, zip code 84011
Country code 39, city code 089

Amalfi's Tourist Information Center (AAST)
Corso Repubbliche Marinare 19- 27. **Tel/Fax:** 089-871107. Hrs.:
Mon.-Fri. 8:30am-1:30pm & 3pm-5:15pm; Sat. 8:30am-1pm. Longer
hours in summer. With your back to the water, walk along the waterfront to your right, located just before the post office. **Web site:** http:/
/www.azienturismamalfi.com/
E-mail: aziendasoggiornoeturismoamalfi@katamail.com

HOTELS
AMALFI: Via Pastai 3. **Tel:** 089-872440 **Fax:** 089-872250. **Web site:**
http://www.starnet.it/hamalfi. **E-mail:** hamalfi@starnet.it (40 rms., all
w/toilet & bath or shower.) 98€ single; 126€ double; 173€ triple;
231€ quad. Breakfast (7:30-10:am) is included in the rates & can be
served on the veranda in warm weather. Visa, MC, AX, DC. English
spoken (Carmela & Paola, sisters), phones, cable TV w/CNN, wonderful charming renovated hotel w/identically nicely furnished bright
airy pretty rms., shiny tiled flrs., #405 (small bathroom w/shower &
view of mountainside) & 406 (small view of mountainside) both w/2
twin beds or zip & lock queen-size beds are for a double; #411 (1 step
up to bathroom w/bathtub) & 412 (1 step up to bathroom w/shower)
both w/2 twin beds or zip & lock queen-size beds & face garden are
for a double; #104 (nice-size rm. w/2 twin beds or zip & lock queen-
size bed, bathroom w/bathtub & small balcony that faces the street) is
for a double; #407 (large rm. w/3 twin beds or 1 zip & lock queen-
size bed & twin bed, bathroom w/bathtub & faces garden) is for a
triple; #306 (3 twin beds or 1 zip & lock queen-size bed & twin bed,
bathroom w/shower & balcony w/no view) is for a triple; #410 (3
steps down to large rm. w/2 twin beds or zip & lock queen-size bed &
bathroom w/shower) is for a double but can fit an extra twin bed for a
triple; #307 (4 twin beds or 1 zip & lock queen-size bed & 2 twin
beds, bathroom w/shower & balcony w/no view) is for a family; 10
rms. w/balconies but none of the rms. (except #405 & 406) have views,
rooftop terrace w/magnificent view overlooking the town, wonderful
citrus garden, bar, 5th flr. restaurant with veranda, quiet location, el-

evator, 5 flrs., garage parking (16€ per day). Half-board rates required Aug.-Sept. 5. Owned/managed by the wonderful & charming Salvatore & Carmela Lucibello. Walk up the main street, past the Duomo, continue uphill, turn left at the meat market (look for hotel sign) up a flight of steps to the hotel. (Closed Jan.-March.)

FONTANA: Piazza Duomo.**Tel:** 089-871530. (16 rms., 13 w/toilet & bath or shower.) 87€ double; 121€ triple; 146€ quad. Call for quint rates. The rooms without bathrooms are cheaper. Cash only. Breakfast (8-10:30am) is included in the rates. English spoken (Aldo), phones, cable TV, grand old plain hotel w/old-fashioned furnished plain airy bright nice-size rms., #3 (large rm. near the reception area w/2 twin beds or zip & lock queen-size bed, bathroom w/bathtub & wonderful view of waterfront) is for a double; #8 (2nd flr. rm w/2 twin beds or zip & lock queen-size bed & sea view) & 12 (2 twin beds or zip & lock queen-size bed, bathroom w/o shower curtain & small balcony w/view of Piazza) are for a double; #5 (huge 2nd flr. rm. w/2 twin beds or zip & lock king-size bed, high ceiling & small balcony w/wonderful view of waterfront) &11 (huge rm. w/double bed, bathroom w/o shower curtain, high ceiling & wonderful view of Piazza & Duomo) are for a double but can fit extra twin beds for a triple; #19 (3rd flr. rm. w/2 twin beds or zip & lock queen-size bed, bathroom w/o shower curtain & window w/no view) &1 (not-so-bright nice-size rm. near reception area w/double bed, bathroom w/o shower curtain & small window w/no view) are for a double; #18 (huge 3rd flr. rm. w/3 twin beds or 1 zip & lock queen-size bed & twin bed, private bathroom outside the room & wonderful view of Piazza & Duomo) is for a triple; #14 (3 twin beds or 1 zip & lock queen-size bed & twin bed & small balcony w/wonderful view of Piazza & Duomo) & 6 (sea view) are for a triple; #2 (huge rm. near the reception area w/double bed, 2 twin beds, high ceiling, bathroom w/o shower curtain & small balcony w/wonderful view of waterfront) is for a family but can fit an extra twin bed for a quint; #7 (single rm. w/sea view),10 (double rm.) & 9 (double rm.) all have no bathrooms; wonderful noisy location near the waterfront, the rooms that face the water are quieter than the rooms that face the Piazza, antique marble staircase, no elevator, 3 flrs. Owned/managed by the charming Aldo & his sisters for more than 30 years. (Closed Oct.-Easter.)

LIDOMARE: Largo Duchi Piccolomini 9. **Tel:** 089-871332. **Fax:** 089-871394. **Web site:** http://www.lidomare.it/ **E-mail:** lidomare@amalficoast.it (15 rms., all w/toilet & bath or shower.) 50€ single; 100€ double; 126€ triple; 141€ quad. Breakfast (8-10:30am) is included in the rates. Air-conditioned (6€ extra per day.). Visa, MC, AX, DC. English spoken (Maria & Santolo), phones, cable TV w/BBC, wonderful charming 13th-century hotel w/beautiful antiquish to modern furnished large pretty rms., shiny tiled flrs., #45 (twin bed & no view) is the only single; #31 (bathroom w/Jacuzzi ™ bathtub @6€ extra per day), 43 (large rm. & bathroom w/bathtub), 44 & 56 (all w/2 twin beds or zip & lock queen-size beds & balconies w/sea views) are for a double; #53 (honeymoon rm. w/2 twin beds or zip & lock queen-size bed, 18th-century headboard, bathroom w/bathtub w/hand-held shower & balcony w/no view) is for a double; #41 (Jacuzzi shower @6€ extra per day) & 42 (both huge rms. w/2 twin beds or zip & lock queen-size beds, high ceilings & balconies w/sea views) are for a double but can fit an extra twin bed for a triple; #55 (2 twin beds or zip & lock queen-size bed, futon convertible chair/bed & small balcony w/no view) is for a double or triple; #56 (large rm. w/2 twin beds or zip & lock queen-size bed & balcony w/no view) is for a double but can fit an extra twin bed for a triple; #34 (huge rm. w/queen-size bed & 2 twin beds) & 35 (both w/ balconies w/sea views) are for a family; hairdriers, minibars, warm atmosphere, bar, no elevator, 2 flrs. Owned/managed by Santolo & Maria Camera (sister & brother) & their family since they were children. *5% rm. discount when you show them this book.* Located in Piazza Piccolomini through the passageway across from the Duomo. Take a left up the stairway into the Piazza.

RESIDENCE AMALFI: Via Repubbliche Marinare 9. **Tel:** 089-872229 or 871183. **Fax:** 089-873070. (27 rms., all w/toilet & bath or shower.) 98€ single; 137€ double; 173€ triple; 205€ quad. Breakfast (7:30-10am) is included in the rates & served in a huge breakfast room or in warm weather on the terrace w/fabulous view. Visa, MC, AX, DC. English spoken (Enzo), charming simple hotel w/old-fashioned furnished rms., phone, cable TV w/CNN, shiny tiled flrs., #8 (huge rm. w/2 twin beds or zip & lock queen-size bed, bathroom w/ bathtub, high ceiling & small balcony w/side sea view) is for a double;

#5 (queen-size bed & balcony w/sea view) is for a double; #28 & 29 (3rd flr. rms. w/balconies & sea views) are for a double; #4, 19, 20 & 22 (all have sea views); #7 (corner rm. w/queen-size bed, bathroom w/bathtub & balcony) & 6 (queen-size bed & balcony that faces the street) are for a double; #9 (3 twin beds or zip & lock queen-size bed & 1 twin bed, high ceiling & balcony w/side view of Piazza), 24 (balcony w/view of sea & Piazza) & 22 (balcony w/sea view) are for a double or a triple; #10 (huge rm. w/3 twin beds or zip & lock queen-size bed & 1 twin bed, bathroom w/bathtub, decorative antique high ceiling & view of Piazza) is for a triple but can fit an extra twin bed for a family; #25 (no view) is for a family; all rms. have balconies & old-fashioned bathrooms; the higher the better the view, terrace w/ magnificent panoramic view, dramatic 14th-century ironstone staircase, elevator, 3 flrs., parking (16€ per day). Owned/managed by Gargano Galtano & his family since he was a baby. Located on the waterfront in front of the dock. (Closed Nov.-Feb.)

RESTAURANT
AL TEATRO: Via E. Marini 19. Tel: 089-872473. Fax: 089-873359. Visa, MC, AX, DC. (Minimum charge 27€). Hrs.: Thurs.-Tues. 11:30am-1:30pm & 7:30pm-11pm. Closed Wed. & Jan. 6-mid-Feb. Fabulous delicious food. Highly recommended by Santolo, Hotel Lidomare. Walk up the main road.

ASSISI
Northern Umbria, zip code 06081
Country code 39, city code 075

Assisi's Tourist Information Center
Piazza Comune 12. **Tel:** 075-812534 or 812450. **Fax:** 075-813727.
Hrs.: Mon.-Fri. 8am-2pm & 3:30pm-6:30pm; Sat. 9am-1pm &
3:30pm-6:30pm; Sun. 9am-1pm.
Web site: http://www.umbria2000.it/ **E-mail:** info@iat.assisi.pg.it

TRANSPORTATION TIPS
Assisi's main train station is inconveniently located in Santa Maria
degli Angeli, a challenging 5km downhill below the town, outside
the center. It is too far and too steep to walk from the train station to
the center. Purchase your bus ticket (1€ pp) at the newsstand before
you exit the train station. Look to your left when you exit the train
station to catch (every 30-min.) the shuttle bus (20-min. ride) to Piazza Matteotti (the center of Assisi). Taxi: 15€ . From Piazza
Matteotti, you can walk downhill to most of the hotels listed below.

Assisi hotels listed alphabetically
ALEXANDER
BELVEDERE
FORTEZZA (LA)
IDEALE
IL PALAZZO
PALLOTTA
PRIORI
SOLE
UMBRA

HOTELS (in the center where the bells ring loudly)
ALEXANDER: Piazza Chiesa Nuova 6: **Tel/Fax:** 075-816190. **Web
site:** http://www.assisihotels.it/ **E-mail:** hpriori@tiscalinet.it (8 rms.,
all w/toilet & shower.) 66€ single; 95€ double; 108€ triple; 136€
quad. Call for quint & superior rates. Breakfast (7:30-10am) at 7€
pp is served across the street at Hotel Priori or can be served in the
room (6€ extra pp). Visa, MC. English spoken (Marco & Milena),

phones, cable TV w/CNN, wonderful charming hotel w/nicely old-fashioned & identically dark wood furnished rms., carpeted flrs., #2 (large rm. w/2 twin beds or zip & lock king-size bed) is for a single or double; #7 (nice-size ground-flr. rm. near the reception area w/2 twin beds or zip & lock queen-size bed, high wood-beamed ceiling & faces the back overlooking an active pizza shop) is for a single or double & is the worst room; #3 (wonderful huge rm. w/2 twin beds or zip & lock king-size bed, convertible chair/bed & small bathroom) & 1 (wonderful huge rm. w/3 twin beds or 1 zip & lock king-size bed & twin bed, wood-beamed ceiling & faces the back) are for a double or triple; #8 (4 twin beds or 1 zip & lock king-size bed & 2 twin beds, wood-beamed ceiling & faces the side street) is for a family; #4 (wonderful huge nonsmoking rm. w/5 twin beds or zip & lock king-size bed, zip & lock double bed & twin bed & faces the cathedral) is for a family or quint; #5 (huge nonsmoking superior rm. w/2 twin beds or zip & lock king-size bed, wood-beamed ceiling & wonderful views of countryside & rooftops) & 6 (nonsmoking superior rm.) are for a double; #9 (minimum stay 2 wks.); fabulous terrace w/magnificent panoramic view, no elevator, 2 flrs., parking (12€ per day). I stayed at this hotel and loved it. Owned/managed by Simone Fittuccia who also owns/manages Hotel Priori. *15% rm. discount when you show him this book.*

BELVEDERE: Via Borgo Aretino 13. **Tel:** 075-812460. **Fax:** 075-816812. **E-mail:** assisihotelbelvedere@hotmail.com (16 rms., all w/ toilet & shower.) 71€ single; 110€ double 142€ triple. Breakfast (7:30-9:30am) at 7€ pp. Visa, MC, AX. English spoken (Enrico & Maria), phones, TV, wonderful charming hotel w/nice old-fashioned & individually furnished rms., #2 (smallest rm. w/2 twin beds or zip & lock king-size bed, small bathroom w/shower, curved high ceiling & balcony w/fabulous view of countryside), 3 (2 twin beds or zip & lock king-size bed & balcony w/fabulous view of countryside), 4 (2 twin beds or zip & lock king-size bed, bathroom w/shower, high ceiling, & fabulous view of countryside), 5 (nice-size 2nd flr. rm. w/ queen-size bed, small bathroom w/shower & view of countryside), 6 (2 twin beds or zip & lock king-size bed & view of countryside), 7 (queen-size bed, high ceiling, bathroom w/circular shower & fabulous view of countryside) & 16 (large 3rd flr. rm. w/queen-size bed

& large bathroom) are for a double; #19 (large rm.), 18 & 20 (all 3rd flr. rms. that face the garden) are for a double; #8 (large rm. w/queen-size bed, large bathroom w/shower & 2 sinks & fabulous view of countryside), 10 (large rm. w/king-size bed, large bathroom w/shower & balcony that faces the back w/no view) & 9 (faces back w/no view) are for a double but can fit an extra twin bed for a triple; hairdriers (some rms.), newly renovated bathrooms w/large shower stalls & towel heaters, rooms that face the back have larger bathrooms, 3rd flr. terrace w/fabulous view of countryside, delightful ambience, bar, great restaurant (see below), elevator, 3 flrs. Owned/managed by wonderful & accommodating Olympia, Maria, Enrico & Francesco Maddalena (mother, daughter & sons). *10% rm. discount when you show them this book.* (Closed Jan. 8-March 10.)

FORTEZZA (LA): Vicolo Fortezza 19b. **Tel:** 075-812993. **Fax:** 075-8198035. **Web site:** http://www.lafortezzahotel.com/ **E-mail:** lafortezza@lafortezzahotel.com (7 rms., all w/toilet & shower.) 63€ double; 87€ triple; 102€ quad. Breakfast (8-9am) at 7€ pp. Visa, MC, AX. DC. English spoken (Luca & Lorenzo), phones, TV (some rms.), charming renovated 14th-century hotel w/simply old-fashioned furnished rms. that all face the street, parquet flrs., #44 (king-size bed & small balcony), 46 (nice-size rm. w/king-size bed, bathroom w/o shower curtain & rooftops view) & 3 other rooms similar to #46 but may have 2 twin beds are for a double; #48 (king-size bed, twin bed & bathroom w/shower) is for a triple; #43 (huge ground-flr. rm. near reception w/3 twin beds or 1 zip & lock king-size bed & twin bed, futon convertible chair/bed & large bathroom w/bathtub) is for a triple or family; all the rooms except #48 have bathrooms w/show-ers; you have to walk outside to the restaurant to have breakfast, no elevator, 1 flr. Owned/managed by Luca & Lorenzo Chiocchetti (brothers) & their family for more than 40 years. They offer half-board rates. (Closed Feb.)

IL PALAZZO: Via San Francesco 8. **Tel:** 075-816841. **Fax:** 075-812370. **Web site:** http://www.hotelilpalazzo.it/
E-mail: info@hotelilpalazzo.it (10 rms., all w/toilet & bath or shower.) 63€ single; 116€ double; 142€ triple. Breakfast (8-10am) at 7€ pp served in a beautiful breakfast room w/authentic frescoed ceiling &

view of countryside. Visa, MC, AX. English spoken (Giselda, Simone & Ariana), phone, TV, wonderful charming 16th-century hotel w/ old-fashioned & individually furnished pretty rms., #101 (1st flr. rm.) is for a single; #102 (large 1st flr. rm. w/canopy queen-size bed, wood-beamed ceiling, bathroom w/shower & faces the street), 103 (step down into 1st flr. rm. w/2 twin beds or zip & lock king-size bed w/ antique headboard, wood-beamed ceiling, bathroom w/shower & faces the street) & 105 (1st flr. rm. w/queen-size bed w/antique headboard, wood-beamed ceiling, bathroom w/bathtub & interior balcony that faces the back) are for a double; #104 (step down into large 1st flr. rm. w/queen-size bed, twin bed, wood-beamed ceiling, bathroom w/bathtub & faces the street) is for a triple but can fit an extra twin bed for a family; you have to walk outside of the bldg. & one flight upstairs to get to the rooms on the 2nd flr.: #203 (wonderful large, bright, airy 2nd flr. rm. w/canopy king-size bed & antique wrought-iron headboard, small bathroom & patio door w/fabulous views of countryside & rooftops), 205 (large 2nd flr. rm. w/queen-size bed, frigobar & fabulous views of countryside & rooftops), 201 (step down into wonderful huge 2nd flr. rm. w/2 twin beds or zip & lock king-size bed w/antique wooden headboard, 2 steps up to large bathroom w/shower & small window that faces the interior w/no view) & 202 (2nd flr. rm. w/queen-size bed & antique brass headboard, antique mirror, bathroom w/shower & small view of countryside) are for a double; #204 (step down into large 2nd flr. rm. w/2 twin beds or zip & lock king-size bed & antique wrought-iron headboard, frigobar, bathroom w/shower & patio door w/fabulous view of countryside & rooftops) is for a double but can fit an extra twin bed for a triple; terrace w/no views, warm ambience, restaurant, fabulous location 1/2 block from the Basilica, charming authentic sitting area, original stone staircase, no elevator, 3 flrs. Owned/managed by Arianna Bartocci Fontana. *5% rm. discount when you show her this book.* Bus stop: Basilica. Walk up Via San Francesco. (Closed Nov.-Feb.)

PALLOTTA: Via San Rufino 6. **Tel/Fax:** 075-812307. **Web site:** http://www.pallottaassisi.it/ **E-mail:** pallotta@pallottaassisi.it (7 rms., all w/toilet & shower.) 37€ single; 58€ double; 73€ triple. No breakfast served. Visa, MC, AX, MC. English spoken (Elisabetta), phone, TV, charming renovated 15th-century hotel w/simply old-fashioned furnished nice-size rms., parquet flrs., #7 (smallest rm. w/2 twin beds & cubicle bathroom) is for a single or discounted for a double; #14 (large rm.) 13 (faces street), 12 (2 small arched windows), 18 (small window near ceiling) & 15 (all w/2 twin beds or zip & lock king-size bed) are for a double; #16 (3 twin beds or 1 zip & lock king-size bed & twin bed & faces the street) is for a triple; all have small bathrooms w/o shower curtains, there is narrow circular staircase that leads to a small sitting room w/fabulous panoramic view, nearby restaurant serves delicious food (see below), no elevator, 1 flr. Owned/managed by a wonderful & accommodating family. Walter & Margherita (father & mother), Elisabetta Simonelli (daughter), Stefania (daughter), Stefano (son) & Sabrina (Stefano's wife).

PRIORI: Corso Mazzini 15. **Tel:** 075-812237. **Fax:** 075-816804. **Web site:** http://www.assisihotels.it/ **E-mail:** hpriori@tiscalinet.it (34 rms., all w/toilet & bath or shower.) 83€ single; 124€ double; 162€ (superior) double; 162€ triple; 215€ (superior) triple; 200€ quad. Add 50% more to rates during the weeks of Easter & New Years. Breakfast (7:30-10am) is included in the rates & can be served in the room (6€ extra pp). Air-conditioned. Visa, MC, AX, DC. English spoken (Ignazio, Nadia, Samir & Simone), phones, cable TV w/CNN, wonderful charming elegant hotel w/beautifully & identically furnished nice-size rms., beautifully carpeted flrs., #107 (nonsmoking rm. w/twin bed, bathroom w/bathtub, minibar & faces the back w/no view) is for a single; #106 (large rm. w/2 twin beds or zip & lock queen-size bed, high decorative curved ceiling, large bathroom w/bathtub, minibar & faces the back w/no view) & 101 (queen-size bed, bathroom w/shower, minibar & face the side street) are for a double; #201 (large superior rm. w/2 twin beds, bathroom w/bathtub, minibar, high decorative curved ceiling & faces the street) & 201 (large superior rm. w/queen-size bed, bathroom w/bathtub, minibar, high decorative curved ceiling & faces the street) are for a double; #207 (large rm. w/3 twin beds, large bathroom w/unusual shaped bathtub) is for a triple; #102 (loft rm. w/queen-size bed on top flr., 1 twin bed & bathroom on the bottom flr.), 103 (loft rm. w/2 twin beds on top flr., 1 twin bed & bathroom on the bottom flr.) & 104 (loft rm. w/king-size bed & frescoed wall on top flr., sitting area & bathroom w/bathtub on the bottom flr. & faces the street w/no view) are for a double or triple; #211 & 407 both have balconies; bathrooms w/ hairdriers & towel heaters, minibars (15 rms.), nonsmoking rms. available, bar, restaurant that serves delicious well-priced food in a sterile windowless atmosphere, elevator, 4 flrs., parking (11€ per day). They offer half- and full-board rates. Owned by Simone Fittuccia, managed by wonderful & accommodating Ignario Campoccia. Same family owns/manages Hotel Alexander. *15% rm. discount when you show them this book.*

SOLE: Corso Mazzini 35. **Tel:** 075-812373 or 812922. **Fax:** 075-813706. **E-mail:** sole@techonet.it (40 rms., all w/toilet & bath or shower.) 48€ single; 74€ double; 100€ triple; 127€ quad. Breakfast (8-9:30am) at 6€ pp can be served in the room (2€ extra pp). Air-conditioned (10 rms. at 10€ extra per day). Visa, MC, AX, DC. English spoken (Michelle), phones, TV (some rms.), charming renovated 13th-century 2-bldg. hotel w/simply & identically furnished nice-size rms. Main bldg. (20 rms.): #32 (wonderful large 3rd flr. attic rm. w/2 twin beds or zip & lock queen-size bed, bathroom w/ bathtub, sitting room & balcony w/wonderful views of countryside & rooftops) is for a double; #14 (large 1st flr. rm. w/2 twin beds or zip & lock king-size bed, futon convertible chair/bed, no TV, bathroom w/o shower curtain & 2 steps up to balcony that faces the street w/rooftops view) & 12 (nice-size 1st flr. rm. w/2 twin beds or zip & lock king-size bed, futon convertible chair/bed, no TV, bathroom w/o shower curtain & terrace that faces the street w/rooftops view) are for a double or triple; #6 (nice-size 1st flr. rm. w/2 twin beds or zip & lock king-size bed, no TV, bathroom w/shower & faces the street) & 26 (rm. w/2 twin beds or zip & lock king-size bed & bathroom w/ shower) are for a double; #28 (large 3rd flr. rm. w/3 twin beds or 1 zip & lock king-size bed & twin bed & bathroom w/bathtub w/hand-held shower) is for a triple. Annex (20 rms.): #72 (fabulous large 4th flr. attic rm. w/French double bed, small bathroom w/shower & small low window w/view) & 60 (attic rm. w/French double bed, bathroom w/shower & red wrought-iron furniture) are the only rooms in the annex for a single; #76 (fabulous large 4th flr. attic rm. w/queen-size bed, twin bed, bathroom w/bathtub w/hand-held shower & terrace w/ fabulous view of countryside & rooftops), 54 (nice-size 1st flr. rm. w/ 2 twin beds or zip & lock king-size bed, convertible chair/bed & bathroom w/bathtub w/hand-held shower) & 50 (large 1st flr. rm. w/2 twin beds or zip & lock king-size bed, convertible chair/bed, yellow wrought-iron furniture & large bathroom w/bathtub w/hand-held shower) are for a double or triple; #56 (large 1st flr. rm. w/3 twin beds or 1 zip & lock king-size bed & twin bed, convertible chair/bed & bathroom w/shower), 52 (nice-size 1st flr. rm. w/3 twin beds or 1 zip & lock king-size bed & twin bed, convertible chair/bed, yellow wrought-iron furniture & bathroom w/bathtub w/hand-held shower), 64 (large rm. w/2 twin beds or zip & lock king-size bed, convertible chair/bed, small bathroom w/shower & faces the street), 68 (king-size bed, twin bed, convertible chair/bed & small bathroom w/shower), 62 (queen-size bed, twin bed, convertible chair/bed, large bathroom w/bathtub & faces the back w/no view) & 58 (attic rm. w/2 twin beds or zip & lock queen-size bed, arched ceiling, red wrought-iron furniture, small bathroom w/shower & small window w/partial view) are for a triple or family; the hotel is renovating a room in the annex that will have handicapped access, terrace w/wonderful view (annex), if you stay in the annex, you have to walk outside to the main bldg. to have breakfast, restaurant, no elevator (main bldg.), 3 flrs., elevator (annex), 4 flrs. Owned/managed by the wonderful & accommodating Antonio, Ilvana & Michele Modestini (father, mother & daughter) for more than 40 years. They offer half- and full-board rates.

UMBRA: Vicolo Archi 6. **Tel:** 075-812240. **Fax:** 075-813653. **Web site:** http://www.hotelumbra.it/ **E-mail:** humbra@mail.caribusiness.it (25 rms., all w/toilet & bath or shower.) 83€ single; 120€ double; 140€ triple; 165€ quad. Breakfast (8-10am) is included in the rates. Air-conditioned. Visa, MC, AX, DC. English spoken, phone, cable TV w/CNN, charming hotel w/simply old-fashioned & individually furnished nice-size rms., #33 & 37 (both w/French double beds & views of valley) are for a single; #30 (French double bed) & 47 (twin bed) are for a single; #22 (French double bed & no view) is for a single & the last to be rented; #36 (huge rm. w/2 twin beds or zip & lock queen-size bed, sitting area, large bathroom w/bathtub & views of valley & rooftops), 34 (large corner rm. w/2 twin beds or zip & lock king-size bed, sofa, bathroom w/bathtub & small terrace w/view of valley), 46 (2 twin beds or zip & lock king-size bed & small terrace view of valley), 21 (small terrace) & 20 (small terrace) are for a double; #50 (small terrace) & 51 (both attic jr. suites w/views of garden) are for a double; hairdriers, minibars, wonderful terrace w/ view of valley, lots of public areas to relax, bar, restaurant. Owned/ managed Alberto Laudenzi. They offer half-board rates. (Closed Jan. 10-March 15.)

HOTEL (Piazza Matteotti)
IDEALE: Piazza Matteotti 1. **Tel:** 075-813570. **Fax:** 075-813020. **Web site:** http://www.hotelideale.it **E-mail:** hotelideale@libero.it (12 rms., all w/toilet & shower.) 55€ single; 70€ (rm. #25) single; 90€ double; 118€ triple. Buffet breakfast (7:30-10:30am) is included in the rates. Visa, MC, AX. English spoken (Ilaria), phones, cable TV w/CNN & BBC, charming modern hotel w/simple modern & identically furnished nice-size rms., #2 (French double bed & small bathroom) & 23 (twin bed) are for a single; #25 (small rm. w/2 twin beds or zip & lock king-size bed, minibar & balcony w/views of countryside & rooftops) is for a single or double; #31 (nice-size rm. w/fabulous view), 26 (corner rm w/fabulous view), 21 (large rm. w/cubicle bathroom), 30 & 29 (all have 2 twin beds or zip & lock king-size bed, minibars & balconies w/views of countryside & rooftops) are for a double; #27 (nice-size rm. w/2 twin beds or zip & lock king-size bed, minibar & small window) is for a double; #24 (double rm. w/2 twin beds or zip & lock king-size bed, minibar & balcony w/ views of countryside & rooftops) & 23 (twin bed for a single) which have connecting doors can be rented separately or together as one triple rm.; #22 (ground-flr. rm near reception w/3 twin beds or 1 zip & lock king-size bed & twin bed, minibar, wood-beamed ceiling, 2 steps up to an unusual bathroom & faces back w/no view) is for a double or triple; small bathrooms w/showers & hairdriers, terrace w/ wonderful panoramic view, wonderful peaceful location near bus stop & 10-min. walk from center, no elevator, 2 flrs., free parking. Owned/ managed by Bernardo, Marisa, Ilaria & Lara Pampaninia (husband, wife & daughters) for more than 20 years. The same family also owns Hotel Ascesi which is managed by Lara but I did not see it. Hotel Ascesi: Via Frate Elia 5. Tel/Fax: 075-812420. Located near the Basilica.

RESTAURANTS

BELVEDERE: Via Borgo Aretino 13. Tel: 075-812460. Fax: 075-816812. E-mail: assisihotelbelvedere@hotmail.com Visa, MC, AX, DC. Wonderful simple restaurant that serves delicious homemade food. Closed Thurs. & Jan. 8-March 10. Owned/managed by Olympia/chef, Maria, Francesco/chef & Enrico Maddalena (mother, daughter & sons).

CANTINE DI ODDO: Via San Francesco 8. Tel: 0758-13692. Fax: 0758-12370. Visa, MC, AX, DC. Closed Thurs. Wonderful quaint restaurant that serves delicious homemade food. Owned/managed by Bartocci Fontana (husband) & Orietta Lupi (wife/chef) & their family since 1950. *Show Orietta this book and get a complimentary Vin Santo.* Highly recommended by Hotel Il Palazzo.

PALLOTTA: Vicolo Volta Pinta. Tel: 075-812649. Web site: http://www.pallottaassisi.it/ E-mail: pallotta@pallottaassisi.it Visa, MC, AX, MC. Reservations required. Wonderful energetic restaurant that serves delicious homemade food. The hotel's symbol is the cat because a cat is known for continuing to return home for good food, warmth & hospitality. Owned/managed by a wonderful & accommodating family. Walter & Margherita (father & mother), Elisabetta Simonelli (daughter), Stefania (daughter), Stefano (son) & Sabrina (Stefano's wife).

BELLAGIO
Lake Como, zip code 22021
Country code 39, city code 031

Bellagio's Tourist Information Center
Piazza Mazzini. **Tel/Fax:** 031-950204. Hrs.: Tues.-Sat. 9am-12noon
& 3pm-6pm. Closed Sun. & Mon. Longer hours in summer. Located
at the boat landing. **Web site:** http://www.bellagiolakecomo.com/ **E-mail:** prombell@tin.it

TRANSPORTATION TIP
Before purchasing individual boat tickets to see the different towns,
look into the all-day ticket (7€ pp). They are great, you can hop on &
off the boats to the different towns. Visa, MC. **Web site:** http://
www.navigazionelaghi.it/ **E-mail:** navicomo@navigazionelaghi.it

HOTELS
GIARDINETTO: Via Roncati 12. **Tel:** 031-950168. (14 rms., 12 w/
toilet & shower.) 64€ double; 88€ triple. Call for quad rates. The
rooms without bathrooms are cheaper. Breakfast (8-10:30am) at 7€
pp. Cash only. English spoken (Eugenio & Laura), warm charming
simple 2-in-1 hotel w/plainly & identically pinewood furnished airy
bright rms. which vary in size. Main bldg. (4 newly renovated rms.):
#5 (small 2nd flr. rm. w/2 twin beds, bathroom w/shower & small
window w/rooftops view) & 6 (small 2nd flr. rm. w/queen-size bed,
bathroom w/shower & small window w/rooftops view) are for a double;
#7 (corner rm. w/king-size bed, twin bed, huge bathroom w/shower
& 3 windows w/rooftops view) is for a triple; annex (10 rms. facing
the garden): #20 (2nd flr. rm. w/2 twin beds or zip & lock queen-size
bed, large bathroom w/bathtub w/hand-held shower & balcony w/
mountain view) & 18 (2nd flr. rm. w/2 twin beds or zip & lock queen-
size bed, 2 steps down into bathroom w/shower & balcony w/moun-
tain view) are for a double; #12, 14 & 15 (all nice-size rms. w/queen-
size beds, bathrooms w/showers & balconies w/partial lake views)
are for a double; #9 (nice-size ground-flr. rm. w/2 twin beds or zip &
lock king-size bed, bathroom w/shower & no view) is for a double;
#10 & 11 (nice-size ground-flr. rms. w/queen-size beds, twin beds,
bathrooms w/showers & face the garden) are for a triple; #16 & 19
both have no bathrooms; reception area w/working fireplace, huge

vine-covered garden/terrace, bar, wonderful quiet location, original stone staircase, no elevator, 2 flrs. Owned/managed by wonderful & charming Eugenio & Laura Ticozzi. From the tourist office (waterfront), walk up the stairs on Salita Plinio, continue to walk up the steep stairs to the entrance of the hotel. (Closed Nov. 7-Feb.)

ROMA: Salita Grandi 6. **Tel:** 031-950424. **Fax:** 031-951966. (25 rms., 16 w/toilet & bath or shower.) 53€ single; 72€ double; 98€ triple; 114€ quad. Call for quint rates. The rooms without bathrooms are cheaper. Breakfast (8-10am) is included in the rates & can be served on the terrace in warm weather. Visa, MC, AX, DC. English spoken (Claudio & Carla), no phones, no TV, charming simple hotel w/plainly furnished nice-size airy bright rms., original wooden flrs., #33 (small rm. w/2 twin beds or zip & lock queen-size bed, compact bathroom w/ shower & small window w/wonderful lake view) is perfect for a single; #49 & 40 (both w/twin beds, compact bathrooms w/showers & face the back w/no views) are for a single; #42 & 34 (both large rms. w/2 twin beds or zip & lock queen-size bed, compact bathrooms w/showers & small balconies w/wonderful lake views) are for a double; #41 (nice-size rm. w/2 twin beds or zip & lock queen-size bed, compact bathroom w/shower & small balcony w/wonderful lake view) is for a double; #44 (large corner rm. w/2 twin beds or zip & lock queen-size bed, bathroom w/bathtub w/hand-held shower & window w/wonderful lake view) is for a double but can fit an extra twin bed for a triple; #48 (nice-size rm. w/2 twin beds or zip & lock queen-size bed, compact bathroom w/shower & faces the back w/no view) & 27 (corner rm. w/2 twin beds or zip & lock queen-size bed, bathroom w/shower & faces the back w/no view) are for a double; #35 (huge rm. w/4 twin beds or 1 zip & lock queen-size bed & 2 twin beds, large bathroom w/ bathtub w/hand-held shower & small balcony w/wonderful lake view) is for a family but can fit an extra twin bed for a quint; #43 (twin bed, no bathroom & balcony w/wonderful lake view) is for a single; #44 (see above) & 42 (see above) have connecting doors & make a great family room; the 4 rms. on the 5th fl. (all w/no bathrooms but have lake views) share 3 communal toilets & 2 showers; #54 (nice-size 5th flr. rm. w/2 twin beds or zip & lock queen-size bed, no bathroom & balcony w/wonderful lake view) is for a double; old-fashioned bathrooms, bar, restaurant w/terrace, elevator only goes to 4th flr., 5 flrs. Owned/managed by Carlo, Carla & Claudio Cinzia (father, mother &

son) for more than 30 years. Rony (Claudio's brother) does the cooking. Carla is wonderful, charming & very attentive. I would stay here just to experience her hospitality. From the tourist office (waterfront), walk up the stairs on Salita Grandi to hotel. (Closed Nov.-Easter.)

Hotel in Pescallo
PERGOLA (LA): Piazza Porto 4. **Tel:** 031-950263. **Fax:** 031-950253. **Web site:** http://www.lapergolabellagio.it/ **E-mail:** lapergola@tin.it (11 rms., all w/toilet & shower.) 56€ (rm. #3) single; 87€ (rm. #3) double; 102€ (rms. #7 & 8) double; 112€ (large rms.) double; 133€ triple. Call for quad rates. Buffet breakfast (8-10am) is included in the rates & is served on the terrace in warm weather. Visa, MC, AX. English spoken (Maria Maddalena), phones, cable TV w/CNN, wonderful charming old waterfront hotel w/beautifully old-fashioned & individually furnished nice-size to huge bright airy rms., #3 (small quaint 1st flr. rm. w/double bed, bathroom w/shower & balcony w/magnificent lake & mountain views) is for a single or discounted for a double; #2 (quaint nice-size 1st flr. rm. w/2 twin beds or zip & lock queen-size bed, bathroom w/shower & balcony w/magnificent lake & mountain views) is for a double; #5 (fabulous huge corner 1st flr. rm. w/queen-size bed, wood-beamed ceiling, huge bathroom w/showers & shares huge terrace w/rm. #4 that has a magnificent lake view) is for a double but can fit an extra twin bed for a triple; #11 (fabulous huge corner 2nd flr. rm. w/queen-size bed, twin bed, bathroom w/bathtub & balcony that faces the parking lot w/ partial lake view) is for a double or triple; #4 (fabulous huge 1st flr. rm. w/king-size bed, convertible sofa, stone nonworking fireplace, bathroom w/shower & shares huge terrace w/rm. #5 that has a magnificent lake view) & 10 (fabulous large corner 2nd flr. rm. w/2 twin beds or zip & lock queen-size bed, convertible sofa, bathroom w/ shower & windows w/2 patio doors that face the parking lot w/partial lake view) are for a double, triple or family; #8 (nice-size 2nd flr. rm. w/king-size bed, bathroom w/shower & window w/magnificent lake & mountain views) & 9 (nice-size 2nd flr. rm. w/double bed, bathroom w/shower & window w/magnificent lake & mountain views) are for a double; #12 (nice-size 2nd flr. rm. w/2 twin beds or zip & lock queen-size bed, large modern bathroom w/shower & faces the garden) is for a double; #1 (1st flr. rm. w/balcony) & 7 (2nd flr. rm.). I didn't see these 2 rooms but both have lake views; huge 16th-

century beautiful painting greets you as you walk to your rooms, ceiling fans, many of the original architectural features remain, lots of character, warm ambience, bar, waterfront restaurant (see below), wonderful peaceful location in a tiny village on the eastern side of Bellagio, no elevator, 2 flrs. Owned/managed by wonderful, charming Maria Maddalena Mazzoni who was born in the hotel. I suggest you taxi to hotel. If you want to walk (20 min.) from the waterfront (ferry stop), walk to your right, look for Salita Genazzini at the far edge of town, take the 1st set of steep stairs on your right to the main road, cross the main road, look for the sign "Village of Pescallo," continue to walk up the 2nd set of steep stairs, then down the steps, turn right onto Salita Cappucini, follow the road around, which becomes Via Sfondrati, then Via Pescallo. (Closed Dec.-Feb.)

HOTEL TO AVOID
I have received many complaints regarding the lack of hospitality at Hotel Suisse.

LAUNDROMAT (Lavanderia)
Il Pinguino: Via Centrale 7. Hrs.: Mon.-Sat. 9am-1pm & Tues.-Sat. 3pm-7:30pm. Closed Sun. & Mon. afternoon. Dry cleaning, drop-off & pick-up service only.

SUPERMARKET
Minimart: Via Centrale 7. Hrs.: Mon.-Sun. 7:30am-1pm & Mon.-Sat. 3pm-7:30pm. Closed Sun. afternoon.

RESTAURANTS
GROTTA (LA): Salita Cernaia 14. **Tel**: 031-951152. Visa, MC. (20€ min.) Hrs.: Daily 12noon-2:30pm & 7pm-12midnight. Closed Nov. 12-Dec. 26. Visa. MC. (20€ min.) Delicious food. Owned/managed by Giorgio Benzi & Adriana Rizzi. Highly recommended by Eugenio, Hotel Giardinetto.

PERGOLA (LA): Piazza Porto 4. **Tel**: 031-950263. **Fax:** 031-950253. **Web site:** http://www.lapergolabellagio.it/ **E-mail:** lapergola@tin.it Visa, MC, AX. Hrs.: 12:30pm-2pm & 7:30pm-9pm. Closed Tues. Specialty: Fresh seafood & fish. I did not eat here but have heard wonderful things about the food.

BOLOGNA
Emilia Romagna, zip code 40121
Country code 39, city code 051

Bologna Tourist Information Centers
1.) Piazza Medaglie d'Oro. Train station. Hrs.: Mon.-Sat. 9am-7pm, closed Sun. & holidays except trade fair days. **2.)** Piazza Maggiore 1. Hrs.: Mon.-Sat. 9am-7pm; Sun. & holidays 9am-2pm. **Web site:** http://www.comune.bologna.it/bolognaturismo/
E-mail: touristoffice@comune.bologna.it **Call Center: Tel:** 051-246541. **Fax:** 051-6393171.

HOTELS
DUE TORRE: Via Usberti 4. **Tel:** 051-269826. **Tel/Fax:** 051-239944. **Web site:** http://www.hotelduetorri.net/
E-mail: info@hotelduetorri.net (14 rms., all w/toilet & bath or shower.) 123€ single; 163€ (Trade fair days) single; 170€ double; 212€ (Trade fair days) double; 207€ triple; 255€ (Trade fair days) triple. Call for quad rates. Buffet continental breakfast (7-11am) is included in the rates. Air-conditioned. Visa, MC, AX, DC. English spoken (Luigi, who is wonderful), phones, TV, fabulous wonderful charming hotel w/beautifully & individually furnished pretty rms., shiny tiled flrs., #205 (small 2nd flr. rm. w/French double bed) is for a single; #103 (nice-size 1st flr. rm. w/double bed) is for a single or discounted for a double; #204 (nice-size 2nd flr. bright rm. w/2 twin beds or zip & lock queen-size bed & faces the street) & 203 (nice-size 2nd flr. rm. w/2 twin beds or zip & lock queen-size bed & faces the interior) are for a double; #303 (2 steps down into small 3rd flr. bright rm. w/queen-size bed, small bathroom w/shower & faces the street) & 301 (small 3rd flr. rm. w/2 twin beds or zip & lock queen-size bed, standard-size bathroom w/shower) are for a double; #105 (nice-size 1st flr. rm. w/3 twin beds or 1 zip & lock king-size bed & twin bed & standard-size bathroom w/shower) & 106 (nice-size 1st flr. rm. w/king-size bed & twin bed, standard-size bathroom w/shower & interior terrace) are for a triple; #202 (large 2nd flr. rm. w/3 twin beds or 1 zip & lock king-size bed & twin bed, roll-out bed & bathroom w/bathtub) is for a triple or family; new modern bathrooms, minibars, ceiling fans, many of the original features remain, beautiful frescoed paintings, warm ambience, small rooftop terrace w/view of

church tower, wonderful quiet location, bar, no elevator, 3 flrs., special street parking (5€ per day), garage parking (20€ per day). Owned by Cristina Malaguti & managed by Mario Dallanave. Taxi to hotel.

ROSSINI: Via Bibiena 11. **Tel:** 051-237716. **Fax:** 051-268035. (22 rms., 18 w/toilet & shower.) 76€ single; 112€ double. The rooms without bathrooms are cheaper. Air-conditioned (6 rms.) Breakfast (8-10am) at 6€ pp. Visa, MC, AX, DC. English spoken (Paola & Guido), phones, TV (18 rms.), charming renovated monastery simple hotel w/plainly to nicely pinewood furnished nice-size rms. that have no views, #44 (newly renovated large 3rd flr. air-conditioned rm. w/ twin bed & handicapped-access bathroom & sloped ceiling w/small window) is for a single; #42 (newly renovated large 3rd flr. air-conditioned attic rm. w/queen-size bed & sloped ceiling w/small window) is for a double; #43 (newly renovated large 3rd flr. air-conditioned attic rm. w/queen-size bed, futon convertible chair/bed & sloped ceiling w/small window) & 41 (newly renovated large 3rd flr. air-conditioned rm. w/double bed & twin bed & sloped ceiling w/ small window) are for a double or triple; #45 (newly renovated large 3rd flr. air-conditioned rm. w/queen-size bed, handicapped-access bathroom & sloped ceiling w/small window) is for a double; #40 (1 step down to newly renovated large 3rd flr. air-conditioned rm. w/3 twin beds or 1 zip & lock queen-size bed & twin bed & 2 tiny windows that face the street) is for a triple; #27 (2 twin beds or zip & lock queen-size bed, futon convertible chair/bed, cot & huge bathroom w/bathtub w/hand-held shower) is for a double, triple or family; bar, elevator, 3 flrs. Owned by Guido & managed by Guido & Paola (employee), who are both wonderful and charming. Taxi to hotel or catch bus #C to Piazza Verdi, turn right onto Via Bibiena. (Closed 10 days in July or Aug.)

SAN VITALE: Via San Vitale 94. **Tel:** 051-225966. **Fax:** 051-239396 (17 rms., all w/toilet & shower.) 63€ single; 89€ double; 114€ triple; 136€ quad. Call for quint & sextet rates. No breakfast is served. Cash only. English spoken (Daniela Po' & Valerio), phones, TV, wonderful charming simple hotel w/simply & identically furnished nice-size rms. that face the garden w/no views, shiny tiled flrs., #103 (large ground-flr. rm. w/twin bed) is the only room for a single; #104 (ground-flr. rm. w/2 twin beds or zip & lock queen-size bed) & 115

(1st flr. rm. w/2 twin beds or zip & lock queen-size bed) are for a double; #105, 106 (interior patio) & 107 (all large ground-flr. rms. w/3 twin beds or 1 zip & lock queen-size bed & twin bed) are for a triple; #119 (2nd flr. rm. w/3 twin beds or 1 zip & lock queen-size bed & twin bed & small window w/rooftops view) is for a triple; #116 (huge 1st flr. rm. w/3 twin beds or 1 zip & lock queen-size bed & twin bed, convertible sofa & faces the garden) is for a triple or family; #109 (huge rm. w/4 twin beds or 1 zip & lock queen-size bed & 2 twin beds) is for a family but can fit extra twin beds for a quint or sextet & is the only room that faces the street; all w/standard-size bathrooms, ceiling fans, garden/terrace, quiet location, no elevator, 2 flrs. Owned/managed by Daniela Po' & Valerio. Located at the eastern edge of the city, about a 10-min. walk to the center of town. Cross street: Via Sant' Apollonia. Taxi to hotel or catch bus #32 to Piazza di Porta San Vitale or bus #25 to Via Broccaindosso/Strada Maggiore near Via San Vitale.

LAST OPTION HOTEL
Hotel Centrale was not able to show me any of the rooms. However, I included it because I had stayed here on one of my trips and found the rooms acceptable. The reason I have it as a last option is that I don't know if the rooms are still up to the standard they were when I last visited the hotel in 1999.

CENTRALE: Via Zecca 2, 3rd fl. **Tel:** 051-225114. **Fax:** 051-235162. **E-mail:** werterg@tin.it (25 rms., 20 w/toilet & shower.) 72€ single; 98€ double; 131€ triple. The rooms without bathrooms are cheaper. Breakfast (8-10am) at 8€ pp can be served in the room. Air-conditioned. Visa, MC, AX. English spoken (Gionair), phones, TV, modern sterile hotel w/no ambience, #20 is for a single; wonderful noisy location, bar, elevator, 2 flrs. Owned/managed by Werther Guizzardi. Taxi to hotel or catch bus #25 to Via Ugo Bassi, turn left onto Via Zecca.

LAUNDROMATS (Lavanderia)
Lavarapido Wash & Dry: Via Petroni 38b. Hrs.: Daily 9am-9pm. Cross street: Piazza Verdi; **Onda Blu:** Via Saragozza 34a/b. Hrs.: Daily 8am-10pm.

BOOKSTORES

Feltrinelli: Piazza Ravegnana1. Tel: 051-261392. Fax: 051-264492. Hrs.: Mon.-Sat. 9am-8pm & Sun. 10am-1:30pm & 3pm-7:30pm; Feltrinelli International: Via Zamboni 7b. Tel: 051-268070. Fax: 051-228745. Hrs.: Mon.-Sat. 9am-7:30pm. Closed Sun. E-mail: bologna.international@feltrinlib.it Feltrinelli: Piazza Galvani 1h. Tel: 051-239990. Fax: 051-237389; Web site: http://www.feltrinelli.it/ Touring Club Italiano: Strada Maggiore 29. Tel: 051-2961476. Great for maps. Web site: http://www.touringclub.it/

RESTAURANT

DANIO: Via San Felice 50a. **Tel:** 051-555202. Hrs.: Daily 12noon-3pm & 7pm-11pm. Visa, MC, AX. Nonsmoking room available. Casual restaurant with family atmosphere that serves delicious home-made food with lots of love to locals. It is one of the few restaurants I know of that doesn't have a 2-people minimum on ordering *risotto*. I usually travel alone and am not always able to order it. Owned/managed by Franco & Pina (husband & wife), a wonderful warm couple. Franco moved from Italy to Boston, U.S., and back to Italy again. Franco works the room while Pina makes her fresh pasta in the kitchen. Franco raises ostriches on his land close to Naples on his time off. In April, he prepares dishes using the ostrich eggs. *Show owner/waiter Franco or son/waiter Fabian this book and they will give you a complimentary limoncello.* From Piazza Maggiore, walk up Via Ugo Bassi, which becomes Via San Felice.

CAMOGLI (House of Wives)
Italian Riviera, zip code 16032
Country code 39, city code 0185

Camogli's Tourist Information Center
Via XX Settembre 33r. **Tel/Fax**: 0185-771066. Hrs.: Mon.-Sat. 9am-12pm & 4pm-6pm; Sun. 9am-1pm. Longer hours in summer. Located across the street to the right of the train station. **Web site:** http:www.camogli.it/

TRANSPORTATION TIP
Ticket window at the train station hrs.: Mon.-Sat. 6am-12:30pm & Sun. 1pm-7:30pm. If they are closed, you can purchase both train & bus tickets at the tourist office. It is about 1€ pp by train (5-min. ride) or by bus (1/2-hr. ride) to Santa Margherita.

HOTELS
CAMOGLIESE (LA): Via Garibaldi 55. **Tel**: 0185-771402. **Fax:** 0185-774024. **E-mail:** camogliese@libero.it (21 rms., all w/toilet & shower.) 65€ (rms. #1, 10, 12, 15, 19 & 21) single; 82€ (rms. #1, 10, 12, 15, 19 & 21) double; 89€ double; 121€ triple. Call for quad rates. Buffet breakfast is included in the rates & can be served in the room (6€ extra pp). Visa, MC, AX, DC. English spoken (Mario), phones, cable TV w/CNN, fabulous wonderful charming w/contemporary & identically furnished nice-size modern rms., shiny tiled flrs., #1, 10, 12, 15, 19 & 21 (all w/small double beds, small bathrooms & no views) are for a single or discounted for a double; #3 (large corner rm. near reception w/double bed & wonderful sea view) & 18 (large rm. w/2 twin beds or zip & lock queen-size bed & small balcony w/side sea view) are for a double; #5 & 14 (both large rms. w/2 twin beds or zip & lock queen-size bed & balconies w/side sea views) are for a double; #4 (large rm. near reception w/2 twin beds or zip & lock queen-size bed, convertible chair/bed & balcony w/wonderful sea view) is for a double or triple; #23 (large rm. w/2 twin beds or zip & lock queen-size bed & balcony w/side sea view) & 13 (large corner rm. w/2 twin beds or zip & lock queen-size bed & view of mountain w/partial sea view) are for a double but can fit an extra twin bed for a triple; #22 (nice-size corner rm. w/2 twin beds or zip & lock

queen-size bed, small bathroom & no view) is for a double but can fit an extra twin bed for a triple; #16B (large corner rm. w/double bed, twin bed & 2 windows w/wonderful sea views) is for a triple; #6 (corner rm.) & 20 (large rm. w/2 twin beds or zip & lock queen-size bed & no view) are for a double; most w/standard-size bathrooms, wonderful quiet location, no elevator, 2 flrs. Owned/managed by wonderful & charming Mario & Stefania (husband & wife). *5% rm. discount when you show them this book.* I love everything about this hotel. With your back to the train station, look across the street to your right for the hotel's blue sign at the top of the stairs, walk down the steep stairs to the hotel. (Closed Nov. 15-30 & Jan. 15-Jan. 30)

CASMONA: Salita Pineto 13. **Tel**: 0185-770015. **Fax:** 0185-775030. **Web site:** http:www.casmona.com/ (26 rms., 24 w/toilet & bath or shower.) 33€ (annex rm. w/o view) single; 46€ (main bldg.: rm. #5 w/church view) single; 52€ (main bldg.: small rm. #6 w/o toilet & sea view) single; 52€ (bldg. #2: med. rm. w/sea view) single; 59€ (main bldg.: large rm. w/sea view) single; 67€ (main bldg.: large rm. w/terrace & sea view) single; 52€ (annex rm. w/o view) double; 62€ (main bldg.: rm. #5 w/church view) double; 72€ (main bldg.: small rm. #6 w/otoilet & sea view) double; 72€ (bldg. #2: med. rm. w/sea view) double; 75€ (main bldg.: large rm. w/sea view) double; 81€ (main bldg.: large rm. w/terrace & sea view) double; 91€ (bldg. #2: med. rm. w/sea view) triple; 95€ (main bldg.: large rm. w/sea view) triple; 101€ (main bldg.: large rm. w/terrace & sea view) triple. Call for quad rates. Visa, MC, AX, DC. Buffet breakfast (8-10:30am) is included in the rates & can be served on the terrace in warm weather. Air-conditioned (main bldg.). No English spoken, phones, TV, charming 3-in-1 renovated 19th-century villa hotel w/simply & identically furnished rms., 3-star main bldg. #1 has 15 rms. that all face the sea; 3-star bldg. #2 has 5 rms. that all face the sea; 2-star annex has 7 rms. w/no views & is closed from Nov.-March. They have 2 rooms w/o private bathrooms in the main bldg. that have connecting doors which can be rented separately as a double or together as one family rm. If you stay in bldg. #2 or the annex, you have to walk outside to the main bldg. #1 to have breakfast, wonderful quiet location, no elevator, free parking. Owned/managed by Carlo Brambilla. With your back to the train station, turn left and walk (5 min.) towards hotel.

TAXI
0185-771143.

SUPERMARKET
Doro Centry: Via XX Settembre 35. Hrs. Mon.-Sat. 8am-12:30pm & 2:30pm-5:30pm. Closed Sun.

RESTAURANT
IL PORTICO: Via Garibaldi 197A. Tel: 0185-770254. Hrs.: Mon.-Fri. 7:30pm-12midnight. Sat. & Sun. 12noon-12midnight. Cash only. Specialty: Pasta. Fabulous new (2000) restaurant location near the sea that offers an unbelievable selection of delicious homemade pastas at good prices. You can have a great time tasting a variety of pastas w/different types of sauces. Owned/managed by Francesca.

CAPRI
Country code 39, city code 081
zip code 80073

CAPRI
Tourist Information Centers
1.) Marina Grande. **Tel:** 081-8370634. **Fax:** 081-8370918. Hrs.: Nov.-May Mon.-Sat. 9am-1pm & 3:30-6:45pm. June-Sept.: Open daily w/longer hrs. As you exit the ferry, it is on the walkway before you hit the main dock. **2.)** Piazza Umberto I. **Tel:** 081-8370686. Hrs.: Nov.-May Mon.-Sat. 9am-1pm & 3:30-6:45pm. June-Sept.: Open daily w/longer hrs. Located in center of Capri under the big clock. **Web site:** http://www.capritourism.com/
E-mail: touristoffice@capri.it

ANACAPRI (above Capri)
Tourist Information Center
Via Giuseppe Orlandi 59/Piazza Vittoria. **Tel:** 081-8371524. Hrs.: Mon.-Sat. 9am-1pm & 3:30-6:45pm. Open daily & longer hrs. in summer. Located off Piazza Vittoria (the center of Anacapri). When you exit the boat in Marina Grande port, look to your right to catch a bus to get to Anacapri.

TRANSPORTATION TIPS
All ferries and hydrofoils dock at the Marina Grande which is located at the base of Capri. You can reach the center of Capri several ways from the port. Walk the very, very steep Via Marina Grande (30 min.) uphill and follow the signs to Piazza Umberto I (the heart of Capri town); or catch the funicular (1.5€ pp + luggage charge) which connects Marina Grande port with Piazza Umberto (every 15 min.); or catch a taxi. There are buses (1.5€ pp) just to the right of the tourist office at Marina Grande that will also take you to Piazza Umberto or directly to Piazza Vittori, the center of Anacapri. From Capri town, an Anacapri bus will also take you to Piazza Vittori, the center of Anacapri. If you have a lot of luggage, I suggest you taxi to the hotels. If you decide to walk or catch a bus to your hotel, there are uniformed men at the shuttle service next to the taxi stand at Marina Grande (9€ per bag) or Piazza Umberto (5€ per bag) to handle your luggage.

Boats

Navigazione Libera Golfo: Tel: 081-8370819 Capri; Tel: 081-5527209 Naples. Cost of fast boat ticket from Capri to Naples: 11€ pp. Cash only. Length of trip: 35 min. Departure time to Naples: Approx. every hour until 6pm; Capri to Positano: 25 min. ferry ride, 14€ one-way ticket; Capri to Sorrento: 20 min. ferry ride, 9€ one-way ticket. Cash only.

Capri hotels listed alphabetically
BELSITO
BELVEDERE E TRE
GUARRACINO
PRORA
QUATTRO STAGIONI
STELLA MARIS
TOSCA

Anacapri hotels listed alphabetically
BELLAVISTA
BIANCAMARIA
IL GIRASOLE
LORELEY
SAN MICHELE

CAPRI HOTELS

BELSITO: Via Matermania 9/11. **Tel:** 081-8370969 or 8378750. **Fax:** 081-8376622. **Web site:** http://www.hotelbelsito.com/ **E-mail:** info@hotelbelsito.com or eduardo@hotelbelsito.com (13 rms., all w/toilet & shower.) 116€ double; 163€ triple; 178€ quad. Breakfast (8-10am) is included in the rates & can be served in the room (3€ extra pp). Visa, MC, AX. English spoken (Lilliana, Eduardo & Mario), phones, no TV, wonderful charming 18th-century renovated villa w/simply furnished nice-size bright airy rms., #27 (corner rm.) & 26 (both w/2 twin beds or zip & lock double bed, balconies & magnificent views) are for a double; #23 (2 twin beds or zip & lock double bed), 22 & 24 (all w/balconies & magnificent views) are for a double or a triple; #28 (not-so-bright rm. w/double bed & balcony that faces the garden) is for a double; #19 (ground-flr. rm. w/2 twin beds or zip & lock double bed & wonderful view although you do get pedestrians walking past your window) is for a double; #25 (large rm. w/2 twin beds or zip & lock double bed, bunk beds, balcony & magnificent views) is for a family; #20 (ground-flr. rm. w/2 twin beds or zip & lock double bed, bunk beds & wonderful view although you do get pedestrians walking past your window) is for a family; #29 (large not-so-bright old-fashioned furnished rm. w/2 twin beds or zip & lock double bed, bathroom w/bathtub w/hand-held shower & balcony that faces the garden) is for a double but can fit 2 more twin beds for a family, hairdriers, frigobars, bar, wonderful restaurant w/spectacular panoramic view (see restaurants below), roof-top terrace, lots of greenery, no elevator, 1 fl. Owned/managed by Lilliana & Eduardo Catuogno (mother & son). *10% rm. discount when you show them this book.* They offer half-board rates which may be required in July & Aug. With your back towards the tourist office in Piazza Umberto, walk to your left near the tobacco shop, turn onto Via Botteghe, continue as it becomes Via Fuorlovado, then Via Croce, turn right onto Via Matermania. It is 20-min. steep walk uphill to the hotel. (Closed Nov. 6-mid-Dec.)

BELVEDERE E TRE: Via Marina Grande 264.
Tel/Fax: 081-8370345. **Fax:** 081-8378822.
Web site: http://www.belvedere-tre-re.com/ **E-mail:** info@belvedere-tre-re.com (16 rms., all w/toilet & shower.) 100€ single; 116€ (ground flr. rm.) double; 126€ (balcony) double; 137€ (terrace) double; 173€ (balcony) triple; 190€ (terrace) triple; 215€ (terrace) quad. Breakfast (8-10am) at 6€ pp can be served in the room & on the terrace in warm weather. Visa, MC, AX, DC. English spoken (Francesco), phones, TV, wonderful charming 19th-century renovated hotel w/simply to nicely furnished nice-size rms., shiny tiled flrs., #210 (large corner rm.), 208 & 209 (all w/2 twin beds or zip & lock queen-size bed & terraces) are for a double; #310, 311 (both share the sundeck terrace) & 309 (separate terrace) are all simply furnished rms. w/2 twin beds or zip & lock queen-size bed for a double; #314 (corner rm.) & 308 (both simply furnished rms. w/2 twin beds or zip & lock queen-size bed & balconies) are for a double; #107, 108, 109 & 110 (all ground flr. rms. w/2 twin beds or zip & lock queen-size bed) are for a double (you will get pedestrians & hear the traffic

passing by your window); #207 (terrace), 312 (simply furnished large rm. w/tiny balcony) & 308 (small balcony) all w/3 twin beds or 1 zip & lock queen-size bed & twin bed & are for a triple; #203 (2 twin beds or zip & lock queen-size bed, bunk beds & huge terrace) is for a family; hairdriers, this hotel faces the main road but the all rms. have sea views, the higher the floor the better the view and the more quiet, small terrace on the 3rd floor to relax in the sun, bar, no elevator, 3 flrs., free parking. Owned/managed by very accommodating & warm Constanzo, Francesco & Salvatore Ruocco (brothers). *10% rm. discount when you show them this book.* I stayed at this hotel and loved it. I love this location because it is very convenient to the Marina Grande (ferry dock) and the bus depot where you catch buses to Capri & Anacapri. As you exit the ferry, turn right past the taxi stand & bus stop, walk up the curved road, turn right onto Via Marina Grande. (Closed Jan.-March.)

GUARRACINO: Via Mulo 13. **Tel/Fax:** 081-8377140. (13 rms., all w/toilet & shower.) 74€ single; 84€ (view) single; 103€ double; 113€ (view) double; 121€ triple; 131€ (view) triple. No breakfast. Cash only. English spoken (Luigi & Lilliana), no phones, no TV, charming plain hotel w/simply furnished rms., shiny tiled flrs., #6 is for a single; #14 & 15 (2 twin beds or zip & lock double bed & balconies w/mountain views) are for a double; #5 & 27 (both w/ mountain views) are for a double; #21, 22 & 23 (all lower-level rms. w/2 twin beds or zip & lock double bed & share a ground-flr. terrace w/mountain views) are for a double; #16 (3 twin beds or zip & lock double bed, twin bed & balcony w/mountain view) is for a triple; #18, 19 & 20 (all small rms. that face the back w/no views) are for a double; wonderful quiet location, no elevator. Hotel is located outside the center of Capri on the way to Anacapri. Catch bus from the port to Anacapri. Ask bus driver for stop Due Golfi. Take the stairs near the main road down to the hotel. (Closed 15 days in Nov.)

PRORA: Via Castello 6. **Tel/Fax: 081-8370281**. (10 rms., all w/toilet & shower.) 74€ single; 137€ double; 147€ (balcony/terrace) double; 179€ triple; 200€ (rm. #2) triple; 205€ quad; 231€ (rm. #2) quad. Large continental buffet breakfast (8-10am includes homemade cakes) is included in the rates & served in a small breakfast room.

Air-conditioned (11€ extra per day). Visa, MC, AX, DC. English spoken (Adela), phones, TV, wonderful charming hotel w/nicely furnished pretty rms., shiny tiled flrs., #12 (twin bed, no a/c, no TV & small balcony w/view) is for a single; #15 (small corner rm. w/2 twin beds or zip & lock double bed & no view) is for a single or double; #20 (large wonderful rm. w/terrace & wonderful view) is for a double; #11 (large corner rm. w/2 twin beds or zip & lock double bed, balcony w/3 windows & wonderful view) is for a double; #19 & 18 (both w/2 twin beds or zip & lock double bed & wonderful views) are for a double; #1 (ground flr. w/2 twin beds or zip & lock double bed & wonderful view) is for a double; #14 (large rm. w/2 twin beds or zip & lock double bed & small balcony w/wonderful view) is for a double but can fit an extra bed for a triple; #16 (large corner rm. w/2 twin beds or zip & lock double bed, futon convertible chair/bed, frigobar & balcony w/wonderful view) is for a triple; #2 (private ground flr. duplex rm. located outside of the hotel w/double bed on the top flr. & view, walk down the narrow circular stairs to twin beds or zip & lock double bed on the lower flr.) is for a family, all rms. have views of the Gulf of Naples except rm. #15, climb steep narrow stairs up to the rooftop terrace where the hotel's laundry is hanging and get a magnificent panoramic view, bar, wonderful quiet location, no elevator, 2 flrs. Owned/managed by the warm & accommodating Caterina Rizzo, Adela Caso & Mariana (all sisters). Walk up the stairs from the main bus stop in Capri, turn immediate right, continue straight as the street changes names to hotel. (Closed Jan. 10-March 19.)

QUATTRO STAGIONI: Via Marina Piccola 1A. **Tel/Fax :** 081-8370041. **Web site:** http://www.hotel4stagionicapri.com/ **E-mail:** quattro.stagioni@libero.it (12 rms., all w/toilet & bath or shower.) 53€ (rm. #8) single; 74€ single; 103€ (no view) double; 147€ double; 136€ (no view) triple; 179€ triple. Breakfast (8-10:30am) is included in the rates & served on the terrace in warm weather. Air-conditioned. Visa, MC, AX. English spoken, phones, no TV, wonderful charming plain hotel w/simply furnished nice-size bright pretty rms., #8 (twin bed & small terrace w/garden view) is for a single; #1 & 2 (both w/2 twin beds or zip & lock queen-size bed & share terrace w/sea views w/room #3) are for a double; #3 (large rm. w/2 twin beds or zip & lock queen-size bed & shares terrace w/sea view) is for a double but can fit an extra twin bed for a triple; #9 (bathroom w/ bathtub), 10 (bathroom w/bathtub), 11(bathroom w/shower) & 12 (bathroom w/shower) are w/2 twin beds, terraces w/garden views & are for a double; #13, 14, 15 & 16 (all not-so-bright lower-level rms. w/2 twin beds or zip & lock queen-size bed, large bathrooms w/ bathtubs & no views) are for a double but can fit an extra twin bed for a triple; restaurant (summer), garden, terrace w/fabulous view, wonderful quiet location, no elevator, 2 flrs., free parking. Owned/ managed by Cecchini Alessandro. *10% rm. discount when you show him this book.* Hotel is located outside the center of Capri on the way to Anacapri. Catch bus from the port to Anacapri. Ask bus driver for stop Due Golfi. Walk to your left down Via Marina Piccola to hotel. (Closed Nov.-March.)

STELLA MARIS: Via Roma 27. **Tel:** 081-8370452. **Fax:** 081-8378662. (10 rms., all w/toilet & shower.) 48€ single; 84€ double; 126€ triple; 147€ quad. Air-conditioned (rms. #11 & 12 at 11€ extra per day). Breakfast (8-10am) at 11€ pp is served in the room. Visa, MC, DC. English spoken (Rosaria), phones, cable TV, charming plain hotel w/simply furnished nice-size bright rms., #10 (compact rm. w/no view) is for a single; #21 (twin beds or zip & lock double bed & faces the sea) is for a double; #18 & 19 (both small adorable 2nd flr. rms. w/2 twin beds or double beds & face the sea) are for a double; #20 (2nd flr. rm. w/double bed) is for a double; #15 (small balcony & faces the square) & 14 (both are large rms. w/2 twin beds or double beds & private bathrooms outside the rooms) are for a double; #12 (double bed & small balcony) & 11 are for a double; #16 (large rm. w/double bed, roll-out bunk beds, 2 shower stalls & view of sea) is for a family; most rms. have sea views w/a view of the bus depot; frigobars, climb up to the small rooftop terrace where the hotel's laundry is hanging and get a wonderful view, noisy location close to the square, no elevator, 2 flrs. Owned/managed by Rosaria.

TOSCA: Via Dalmazio Birago 5. **Tel/Fax:** 081-8370989. **Web site:** http://www.caprionline.com/latosca/ **E-mail:** h.tosca@capri.it (11 rms., all w/toilet & shower.) 71€ single; 126€ double; 171€ triple; 218€ quad. Rooms w/no views are cheaper. Breakfast (8-10:30am) at 7€ pp can be served in the room or on the terrace in warm weather.

Air-conditioned (11€ extra per day). Visa, MC. English spoken (Ettore, Michele & Alessandro), phones, no TV, wonderful charming renovated villa w/nicely furnished large bright airy rms., shiny tiled flrs., #51 (small rm. w/twin bed & small balcony w/view of countryside & side view of ocean) is for a single; #48 (nice-size rm. w/large terrace) is for a double; #54 (cozy rm), 56 (view of countryside), 57 & 53 (all w/2 twin beds or zip & lock queen-size bed) are for a double; #55 (large rm. w/2 twin beds or zip & lock queen-size bed & view of countryside), 47 (large rm. w/2 twin beds or zip & lock queen-size bed & balcony w/wonderful view) & 52 are for double but can fit an extra bed for a triple; #50 (large rm. w/2 twin beds or zip & lock queen-size bed, convertible sofa, minibar & huge terrace w/view of countryside & side view of ocean) & 46 (nice-size rm. w/ 3 twin beds & wonderful view) are for a triple or a family; ask about the room w/kitchenette located under the hotel that can accommodate a family; electric shutters on the windows, jasmine garden/courtyard, bar, wonderful quiet location, no elevator, 1 fl. Owned/managed by the charming Ettore Castelli & Michele Tine (American wife). *5% rm. discount when you show them this book.* Ettore spends a lot of time in Connecticut, U.S. Walk up the stairs from the main bus stop in Capri, turn immediate right, walk past Hotel Prora, when you get to the fork, bear left down the road onto Via Birago, stay straight on the road to hotel. 20 min. walk. (Closed Nov.-March 15.)

ANACAPRI HOTELS
BELLAVISTA: Via Giuseppe Orlandi 10. **Tel:** 081-8371463. **Fax:** 081-8370957. (15 rms., 14 w/toilet & bath or shower.) 74€ (rm. #7) single; 90€ single; 126€ (rm. #9) double; 168€ double; 199€ (rm. #18 & 19) double; 204€ triple. Call for quad rates. The room without a bathroom is cheaper. Breakfast (7:30-9:30am) is included in the rates & served in a beautiful room w/terrace. Visa, MC, AX, DC. English spoken (Sergio), phones, cable TV w/CNN & BBC, one of the oldest hotels on the island w/nicely furnished large rms., beautiful tiled flrs., #7 (twin bed, no view & private bathroom outside the room one level down) near the breakfast room is for a single; #10 (lower-level rm. w/twin bed & shares a huge terrace w/3 other rms. that face the garden) is for a single; #9 (lower-level small rm. w/2 twin beds, small bathroom w/shower & terrace that faces the garden)

is for a single or a double; #4 (unusual shaped rm. w/2 twin beds or zip & lock queen-size bed, window w/view of sea & shares a balcony w/garden view) near the breakfast room is for a double; #15 (large rm. w/2 twin beds or zip & lock queen-size bed, bathroom w/ bathtub & terrace that faces the garden) is for a double; #11 & 12 (both are nice-size lower-level rms. w/2 twin beds or zip & lock queen-size bed, huge bathrooms w/bathtubs & share a huge terrace w/2 other rms. that face the garden) are for a double; #5 & 6 (both ground-flr. huge rms. w/2 twin beds or zip & lock queen-size bed, bathrooms w/bathtubs & large windows w/views of sea & garden) are for a double but can fit an extra twin bed for a triple; #8 (lower-level large rm. w/ 2 twin beds or zip & lock queen-size bed & shares a huge terrace w/ 3 other rms. that face the garden) is for a double but can fit an extra twin bed for a triple; #19 & 18 (both large duplexes w/upper levels that have 2 twin beds or zip & lock queen-size bed, bathrooms w/ bathtubs & wonderful views and lower levels w/twin bed & balconies w/wonderful views) are for a double or triple; #14 (huge lower-level rm. w/2 twin beds or zip & lock queen-size bed, convertible sofa & shares huge terrace w/3 other rms.) is for a double, triple or family; electric shutters on the windows, hairdriers, pool, tennis court, garden, bar, restaurant w/wonderful sea view, wonderful quiet location, free parking, no elevator, 2 flrs. Owned by Sergio Gargiulo & managed by Salvatore Ruocco. They offer half- and full-board rates. Located close to Piazza Vittoria. (Closed Nov.-March.)

BIANCAMARIA: Via Giuseppe Orlandi 54. **Tel:** 081-8371000. **Fax:** 081-8372060. **Web site:** http://www.caprionline.com/ (25 rms., 21 w/toilet & shower.) 109€ single; 145€ double; 184€ triple; 209€ (rm. #11/12 & 13/14) quad; 220€ quad. Breakfast (8-10am) is included in the rates & can be served in the room (5€ extra pp). Air-conditioned. Visa, MC, AX, DC. English spoken (Rosa & Biancamaria), phones, cable TV w/CNN, wonderful charming hotel w/nicely furnished airy bright pretty rms., shiny tiled flrs., #26, 27, 28, 36, 37 & 38 (all w/2 twin beds or zip & lock queen-size bed & magnificent views of the sea) are for a double; #24, 35 (both w/2 windows & magnificent views of the sea) & 30 (terrace & mountain view) are all large corner rms. w/2 twin beds or zip & lock queen-size bed for a double but can fit a convertible chair/bed for a triple; #32 (large terrace & bathroom w/bathtub), 33 (large terrace), 31(terrace), 39 (tiny balcony w/partial view of sea & mountain) & 29 (all w/2 twin beds or zip & lock queen-size bed & mountain views) are for a double; #11/12 & 13/14 (both w/2 rms. w/4 twin beds, private bathrooms outside the room & large terraces w/no views) are for a family but should have private bathrooms by this book's publication date; electric shutters on the windows, garden, wonderful quiet location, elevator, 2 flrs. Located close to Piazza Vittoria. (Closed Nov.-March.)

IL GIRASOLE: Via Linciano 47. **Tel:** 081-8372351. **Fax:** 081-8373880. **Web site:** http://www.ilgirasole.com/ **E-mail:** ilgirasole@capri.it (24 rms., all w/toilet & shower.) 84€ (rm. #4) single; 132€ single; 137€ (rm. #5C) double; 141€ (rm. #3) double; 168€ (standard rm.) double; 184€ (rm. #3) double; 195€ (superior rm.) double; 226€ (superior rm.) triple; 210€ (rm. #B) quad; 257€ quad. Call for quint & sextet rates. Buffet breakfast (8-10am includes hot beverages, cheese, ham, salami, butter, assorted breads, cakes, fruit, juices, & jams) at 8€ pp can be served in the room (5€ extra pp) or in the garden in warm weather. Air-conditioned (16 rms.) at 19€ extra per day. Visa, MC, AX. English spoken (Angela), phones, cable TV w/CNN (21 rms.), wonderful charming hotel w/nicely to beautifully furnished pretty rms., shiny tiled flrs., #4 (not-so-bright rm. w/twin bed, no a/c & no view) is for a single; #12 & 13 (both standard rattan furnished rms. w/2 twin beds or zip & lock double bed & wonderful views) are for a double; #5 & 6 (all are standard rms. w/2 twin beds or double beds & share terrace w/views) are for a double; #18 (2 twin beds or zip & lock double bed, small bathroom & small view) is for a double; #15 (large bathroom) & 16 (both are large standard rms. w/2 twin beds or zip & lock double bed & face the side w/no views) are for a double; #20 (standard rm. w/2 twin beds or zip & lock double bed & no view) is for a double; #5C (not-so-bright rm. w/2 twin beds or zip & lock double bed, no a/c & no view) is for a double; #8 (superior rm. w/double bed, twin bed & wonderful view) & 9 (superior rm. w/double bed, convertible sofa suitable for 2 children & wonderful view) both share a terrace & are for a double or triple; #7 (superior rm. w/3 twin beds or 1 zip & lock double bed & twin bed & wonderful view) is for a triple; #14 (superior large rm. w/double bed, convertible sofa suitable for 2 children

& wonderful view) & 19 (standard rm. w/3 twin beds or 1 zip & lock double bed & twin bed & convertible sofa) is for a triple or family; #3 (not-so-bright standard rm. w/double bed & twin bed & no view) is for a triple; #B (lower-level 2 bedroom w/2 twin beds or zip & lock double bed in each rm., living rm. w/convertible sofa & convertible chair/bed, 2 bathrooms w/showers & no view) is for a family, quint or sextet; hairdriers, minibars (21 rms.), Internet access available at 6€ per 1/2 hr., garden, laundry services, pool w/solarium, fabulous peaceful location where you can totally relax, no elevator, 1 fl. Owned/ managed by Arnaldo, Silvana & Angela Orlando (father, mother & daughter). If you call ahead from the Marina Grande port, they'll pick you up (6€ pp & 3€ per luggage) and take you to the hotel door. You can catch a taxi but it can only take you as far as the footpath & you'll have to walk the rest of the way with your luggage. You can catch a bus from the Marina Grande to Anacapri, get off at the last bus stop (terminal), then walk the footpath where you'll see the hotel sign with a red arrow on your left, cross the road & up the 3 steps, walk down the pathway, you'll come to a fork, walk straight down Via Linciano to hotel. (Closed Feb.)

LORELEY: Via Giuseppe Orlandi 16. **Tel:** 081-8371440. **Fax:** 081-8371399. **Web site:** http://www.loreley.it/ **E-mail:** loreley@caprinet.it (14 rms., all w/toilet & bath or shower.) 79€ single; 110€ (rms. #2, 3, 4, 5 & 6) double; 116€ double; 121€ (rms. #11, 12, 15 & 16) double; 115€ (rms. #2, 3 & 4) triple; 146€ (rm. #11) triple; 168€ quad; 178€ (rms. 5 & 6) quad. Breakfast (8-10:30am) is included in the rates & can be served in the room or on the terrace in warm weather. Visa, MC, AX. English spoken (Michele Luisa), phones, cable TV w/CNN, charming hotel w/simply to nicely furnished bright airy large pretty rms., #18 (balcony but no view) is for a single; #16 (large bathroom w/bathtub) & 12 (small bathroom w/shower) both large rms. w/2 twin beds or zip & lock queen-size bed, large balcony w/wonderful view of sea & rooftops are for a double; #15 (nice-size rm. w/2 twin beds or zip & lock queen-size bed, small bathroom w/ shower & view) is for a double; #6 (small rm. w/2 twin beds or zip & lock queen-size bed) & 5 which share a terrace w/no view & have connecting doors can be rented separately or together as one family rm.; #11 (3 twin beds or 1 zip & lock double bed & twin bed, small bathroom w/shower & balcony w/no view) is for a triple; #3 (balcony w/no view), 2 (corner rm. & 2 large windows) & 4 (all large ground-flr. rms. w/2 twin beds or zip & lock queen-size bed) are for a double but can fit an extra twin bed for a triple; terrace w/magnificent panoramic view, 1 rm. has handicapped access, wonderful quiet location, no elevator, 2 flrs., free parking. Owned/managed by Michele Carotenuto. *5% rm. discount when you show him this book.* Located close to Piazza Vittoria. (Closed Nov.-March.)

SAN MICHELE: Via Giuseppe Orlandi 5. **Tel:** 081-8371427 or 8371442. **Fax:** 081-8371420. **Web site:** http://www.sanmichele-capri.com/ **E-mail:** smichele@capri.it (60 rms., 59 w/toilet & bath or shower.) 101€ single; 158€ (mountain view) double; 170€ (sea view) double; 170€ (sea view) double; 191€ (rm. #202) double. Call for triple, quad & suite rates. The room without a bathroom is cheaper. Add 6% to all rates during August & Easter. Breakfast (7-10am) is included in the rates & can be served in the room (2€ extra pp) or on the terrace in warm weather. Air-conditioned (1st & 2nd flr. rms. at 10€ extra per day). Visa, MC, AX, DC. English spoken (Norma & Attilia), phones, cable TV w/CNN, wonderful charming beautiful hotel w/nicely furnished bright airy large rms., #218 (corner rm. w/ twin bed & sea view) is for a single; #204 (corner rm.), 200, 201, 203, 211, 212, 214, 216, 219, 220, 221 & 222 (all 2nd flr. rms. w/2 twin beds or zip & lock queen-size bed & small balconies w/sea views) are for a double; #101, 102, 103, 104, 105, 112, 114, 116, 118 & 119 (all 1st flr. rms. w/2 twin beds or zip & lock queen-size bed & terraces w/sea views) are for a double; #111 (bathroom w/bathtub), 106, 107, 108, 109 & 110 (all 1st flr. rms. w/2 twin beds or zip & lock queen-size bed & terraces that face the mountain) are for a double; #205, 206, 207, 208, 209, 212, 214 & 215 (all 2nd flr. rms. w/2 twin beds or zip & lock queen-size bed & small balconies that face the mountain) are for a double; #2, 3, 4,10, 11,12 14, 15 16 & 18 (all ground-flr. rms. w/2 twin beds or zip & lock queen-size bed & terraces w/no views) are for a double; #202 (huge corner rm. w/small balcony & 3 windows w/magnificent sea views) is for a double, triple or family; hairdriers, minibars (15 rms.), garden, bar, solarium, huge terrace & restaurant w/magnificent panoramic views, semi-Olympic size pool, wonderful enchanting location overlooking the Gulf of

Naples, elevator, 2 flrs., free parking. Owned by Norma Scoppa & managed by Massimo Coppola. *5% rm. discount when you show them this book.* They offer half- and full-board rates. Located close to Piazza Vittoria. (Closed Nov.-March.)

INTERNET CAFES
CapriOnline: Via Longano, 37, Capri. Web site: http://www.capri.online.com/ Capri Internet Point: Piazza Vittoria 13, Anacapri. Web site: http://www.capri.-Internetpoint.com/

LAUNDROMATS (Lavanderia)
Capri: Via Castello 1 & Via Madonna Grazie 11; Anacapri: Via Caprile 50.

TAXI
Capri Tel: 081-8370543; Anacapri Tel: 081-8371175. Rates 15€ (1-4 people & extra charge for luggage) from Marina Grande port to Capri and 19€ (1-4 people & extra charge for luggage) from Marina Grande port to Anacapri.

GROCERY SHOPS
Via Matermania 10B. Hrs.: Mon.-Sat. 9am-1:30pm & 3:15pm-8:45pm. Closed Sun; Via Matermania 21. Hrs.: Daily 9am-9pm; Via Marina Grande 238. Hrs.: Daily 7:30am-9pm. Located near Hotel Belevedere.

RESTAURANTS
ARCATE (LE): Viale Tommaso de Tommaso 24, Anacapri. **Tel:** 081-8373588. Hrs.: Tues.-Sun. 12noon-3pm & 7:30pm-12midnight. Closed Mon. & Feb. Visa, MC, AX, DC. Owned/managed by Miguel & Luigi (brothers). Fabulous pizzas, great homemade pastas & desserts. Recommended by Angela, Hotel Il Girasole. *Show Miguel or Luigi this book and get a complimentary limoncello.*

BELSITO: Via Matermania 11, Capri. Tel: 081-8370969 or 8378750. Fax: 081-8376622. Web site: http://www.hotelbelsito.com/ E-mail: ristorantebelsito@libero.it or eduardo@hotelbelsito.com Hrs.: 12noon-3:30pm & 7pm-11:30pm. Visa, MC, AX. Owned/managed by Lilliana & Eduardo Catuogno (mother & son). Two restaurants in one w/spectacular panoramic views from terrace. I was very impressed with charming Eduardo, who speaks great English and is extremely knowledgeable about wines and the preparation of foods and desserts. Eduardo's grandfather (also named Eduardo) opened this charming restaurant in 1950 which serves the best pizzas from a wood-burning oven, homemade pastas, breads & cakes (delicious chocolate skinless almonds & white limoncello) and wines made from the family's winery. In July & Aug., they have a fish tank where you can select your fish for grilling. Try to get here to enjoy the sunset while you sip an aperitif, then watch the fishermen catch the calamari in the evening. Eduardo's grandfather owns/manages La Savardina on Via Lo Capo 8. It is surrounded by lemon & orange trees in a beautiful garden. *Show Lilliana or Eduardo this book and get a complimentary after-dinner drink at their restaurants. If you stay at their hotel, you get a 10% rm. discount.*

BUCA DI BACCO: Via Longano 35, Capri. Tel: 081-8370723. Hrs.: Thurs.-Tues. 12noon-3pm & 7pm-11pm. Closed Wed. & Nov. Visa, MC, AX, DC. Highly recommended by Ettore, Hotel Tosca. *Show the waiter Paulo this book and get a free limoncello.*

IL TINELLO: Via L'Abata 1. Tel: 081-8376712, Capri. Hrs.: Daily 8pm-11:30pm. Cash only. Small cozy restaurant that serves great food. Owned/managed by Peppino who speaks enough English to translate the menu for you. Highly recommended by Ettore, Hotel Tosca.

SAN COSTANZO: Via Marucella 28, Capri. Tel: 081-8377947. Hrs.: Daily April-Oct. 7:30pm-11:30pm. Cash only. Fabulous delightful well-hidden family-owned outdoor/indoor restaurant w/a view; serves delicious homemade food & scrumptious cakes. Owned/managed by the Savastano family. Alfredo (son) & Raffaella (father) are the chefs and Josephina (daughter) serves you. Walk up Via Marina Grande, past the Hotel Belvedere, continue uphill until you get to Via Strada Fenicia, turn right, continue on Via Strada Fenicia until you get to a fork near a brick wall (look for restaurant's sign), turn left, walk uphill to restaurant. Bring a flashlight for the evening stroll back to your hotel. Highly recommended by Francesco, Hotel Belvedere.

CINQUE TERRE (5 Lands)
Country code 39, city code 0187
zip code 19016

Cinque Terre Tourist Information Center
Via Fegina 38, Monterosso Al Mare. **Tel:** 0187-817506. **Fax:** 0187-817825. Hrs.: April-Oct. Mon.-Sat. 10am-12:30pm & 3-5:30pm. Sun. 10am-12:30pm. Located directly under the train station. **Web site:** http://www.cinqueterre.it/ **E-mail:** informazioni@cinqueterre.it

TRANSPORTATION TIPS
Depending on the length of your stay in Cinque Terre, you may want to inquire about the different types of Cinque Terre cards that are available before buying the individual tickets to each town. There are 1-day (7€ pp), 3-day (12€ pp) or 7-day (17€ pp) tickets. During the ticket's time period, you get boundless number of trips on 2nd class trains between Levanto-LaSpezia, unlimited usage of transport services (buses & trains) in each of the Cinque Terre towns and the entrance fee (required since 08/01) to walk from Vernazza to Riomaggiore. The 24-hr. period starts from the time you validate your ticket. They are great, you can hop on & off the buses or trains without ever waiting on line to purchase an individual ticket or validate it only to miss the train. When you purchase the Cinque Terre card, you also get a train timetable & a map of the hike through the five towns. **Parco Nazionale Cinque Terre**. **Tel:** 0187-760000. **E-mail:** parconazionale5terre@libero.it You can purchase these cards in the train stations of Monterosso Al Mare, Vernazza & Riomaggiore.

Cinque Terre hotels listed alphabetically
BAIA (Monterosso Al Mare)
CA' D'ANDREAN (Manarola)
DA BARANIN ROOMS(Manarola)
LOCANDA IL MAESTRALE ROOMS(Monterosso Al Mare)
MARINA PICCOLA (Manarola)
MIKE & FRANCA CASTIGLIONE ROOMS(Vernazza)
PASQUALE (Monterosso Al Mare)
TORRETTA ROOMS (Manarola)
VILLA DA CECIO (Corniglia)
VILLA STENO (Monterosso Al Mare)

MONTEROSSO AL MARE HOTELS

BAIA: Via Fegina 88. **Tel:** 0187-817512. **Fax:** 0187-818322. (29 rms., all w/toilet & bath or shower.) 111€ single; 141€ double; 200€ triple; 231€ quad. Breakfast (8-10:30am) is included in the rates & can be served on the terrace in warm weather. Visa, MC, AX. English spoken (Katruscia), phones, cable TV w/CNN & BBC, charming waterfront hotel w/nicely & identically furnished nice-size modern pretty rms., #14 (small 1st flr. rm. w/double bed, compact bathroom & balcony w/fabulous sea view), 18 & 19 are for a single; #33, 34 & 35 (all 3rd flr. rms. w/2 twin beds or zip & lock queen-size bed & balconies w/fabulous sea views) are for a double; #32 & 36 (both large 3rd flr. rms. w/2 twin beds or zip & lock queen-size bed, futon convertible chair/bed & balconies w/fabulous sea views) are for a double or triple; #23 & 25 (both 2nd flr. rms. w/2 twin beds or zip & lock queen-size bed & balconies w/fabulous sea views) are for a double; #12 & 16 (both w/balconies w/fabulous sea views) are for a double; #24 (2nd flr. rm. w/2 twin beds or zip & lock queen-size bed & fabulous sea view) is for a double; #38 (2 twin beds or zip & lock queen-size bed, small bathroom & no view) is for a double; #9 (huge rm. w/4 twin beds or 1 zip & lock queen-size bed & 2 twin beds, compact bathroom & small balcony w/no view) is for a family; most w/standard-size bathrooms, minibars (20 rms.), the higher the floor the better the view, bar, fabulous noisy location near the beach, elevator, 3 flrs. Owned/managed by Lori & Katruscia (mother & daughter). With your back to the train station, turn right and walk to hotel. (Closed Nov.-Feb.)

LOCANDA IL MAESTRALE: Via Roma 37, 1st fl. **Tel:** 0187-817013. **Fax:** 0187-817084. **Mobile:** 3384530531. **Web site:** http://www.monterossonet.com/ **E-mail:** maestrale@monterossonet.com (6 rms., all w/toilet & bath or shower.) 86€ single; 149€ double; 207€ (suite) double. Call for triple & quad rates. Breakfast (8:15-11am) is included in the rates & can be served on the terrace in warm weather. Air-conditioned. Visa, MC. English spoken (Giovanni), phones, cable TV w/CNN, fabulous wonderful charming new (2001) renovated 6th-century palace hotel w/beautifully & identically furnished pretty rms. that are named after the region & the five villages in Cinque Terre. Cinque Terre (1st flr. rm. w/twin bed, standard-size bathroom w/large shower stall & no view) is for a single; Riomaggiore (1st flr. rm. w/2 twin beds or zip & lock king-size bed, small bathroom & view of street); Corniglia (1st flr. rm. near the breakfast room w/2 twin beds or zip & lock king-size bed, standard-size bathroom w/large shower stall & no view) & Manarola (2nd flr. rm. w/2 twin beds or zip & lock king-size bed, small bathroom & no view) are for a double; Monterosso (1st flr. suite near the breakfast room w/wooden stairs up to loft bedroom w/king-size bed, original frescoed high ceiling, lower-level w/ large sitting area & standard-size bathroom w/large shower stall & view of street) & Vernazza (1st flr. suite near the breakfast room w/ wooden stairs up to loft bedroom w/king-size bed, original frescoed high ceiling, lower-level w/small sitting area & small bathroom w/ large shower stall & view of street) are for a double; hairdriers, minibars, many of the original features remain, huge terrace w/no view, warm ambience, wonderful quiet location, marble staircase, no elevator, 2 flrs. Owned/managed by Stefania & Giovanni. With your back to the train station, turn left onto Via Fegina, continue walking through the tunnel, walk past Hotel Pasquale, turn left onto Via Roma.

PASQUALE: Via Fegina 4. **Tel:** 0187-817477 or 817550. **Fax:** 0187-817056. **Web site:** http://www.pasini.com/ **E-mail:** pasquale@pasini.com (15 rms., all w/toilet & shower.) 85€ single; 130€ double; 155€ triple; 180€ quad. (Rates are cheaper if you pay cash.) Breakfast (8-10am) is included in the rates. Air-conditioned. Visa, MC, AX. English spoken (Felicita, Marco & Gloria), phones, cable TV w/CNN, wonderful charming carved-out-of-a mountain hotel w/nicely & identically bright airy modern nice-size rms. that all face the front & have sea views, #1 & 2 (both 1st flr. rms. w/3 twin beds & small bathrooms) are for a triple; #3 (large rm. w/4 twin beds or 1 zip & lock queen-size bed & 2 twin beds) is the only room for a family; it is 1/2 flight up to each floor but the higher the floor the better the view, hairdriers, bar, wonderful noisy location, lots of stairs, marble staircase, no elevator, 4 1/2 flrs. Owned/managed by Angelo & Marco Pasini (father & son) whose family also owns Hotel Villa Steno. With your back to the train station, turn left onto Via Fegina, continue walking through the tunnel to hotel.

VILLA STENO: Via Roma 109. **Tel:** 0187-817028 or 818336. **Fax:** 0187-817056. **Web site:** http://www.pasini.com/ **E-mail:** steno@pasini.com (16 rms., all w/toilet & bath or shower.)

85€ single; 120€ (rms. #10 & 16) double; 130€ double; 155€ (rm. #1) double; 155€ triple; 180€ quad. Breakfast (8-10am) is included in the rates & served on the terrace in warm weather. Air-conditioned. Visa, MC, AX. English spoken (Matteo & Carla), phones, cable TV w/CNN, wonderful charming hotel w/contemporary & identically pinewood furnished bright airy modern rms., the rooms are on the lower-level floors of the hotel, #1 (lower lower-level nice-size rm. w/ twin bed, small bathroom & terrace w/wonderful view), 9 (ground-flr. nice-size rm. w/twin bed & balcony w/wonderful view) & 7 (nice-size rm. w/twin bed & balcony w/wonderful view) are for a single; #16 (small ground-flr. rm. w/2 twin beds or zip & lock queen-size bed, small bathroom & interior patio w/no view) & 10 are discounted for a double; #11, 12 & 13 (all large ground-flr. rms. w/2 twin beds or zip & lock queen-size bed, small bathrooms & balconies w/wonderful views of the sea & hillside) are for a double; #6 (huge lower-level rm. w/3 twin beds or 1 zip & lock king-size bed & twin bed & small patio w/wonderful view) is for a triple; #5 (huge lower-level rm. w/4 twin beds or 1 zip & lock queen-size bed & 2 twin beds, large bathroom w/bathtub w/hand-held shower & L-shaped terrace w/wonderful views of the sea & hillside) is the only room for a family; hairdriers, private gardens, bar, no elevator, 3 flrs., lots of steep stairs surround the hotel, free parking but call ahead to reserve a space. Owned/managed by Angelo, Matteo & Carla Pasini (father, son & daughter-in-law). Matteo is warm, charming, attentive & much nicer than his brother Marco who owns/manages the Hotel Pasquale. Taxi to hotel. (Closed Nov.-March.)

VERNAZZA (AFFITTA CAMERE)
MIKE & FRANCA CASTIGLIONE ROOMS: Via Carattino 16, 19018. **Tel:** 0187-812374. (2 rms., both w/toilet & shower.) 80€ (small rm.) double & 85€ (large rm.) double. Cash only. No breakfast is served. English spoken (Mike & Franca), no phones, no TV, 2 small basic rooms w/sea views. Franca, who lived in New York for 20 years along with her husband, Mike (who was born in New York), is wonderful, informative & quite helpful. Always confirm your reservation 2 days before your arrival date or she will give the room away. If Franca doesn't have a room available, she tries hard to find you another room within the village. Franca will meet you upon arrival at the train station.

MANAROLA HOTELS & AFFITTA CAMERE

CA' D'ANDREAN: Via Discovolo 101. **Tel:** 0187-920040. **Fax:** 0187-920452. **Web site:** http://www.cadandrean.it/ **E-mail:** cadandrean@libero.it (10 rms., all w/toilet & bath or shower.) 60€ single; 83€ double; 113€ triple. Breakfast (8-11am) at 6€ pp & can be served in the room or in the garden in warm weather. Cash only. English spoken (Simone), phones, no TV, wonderful charming hotel w/nicely & identically furnished bright rms., most w/no views, shiny tiled flrs., #1 (1st flr. rm. w/French double bed, small bathroom & terrace w/view of the trail) is for a single or discounted for 2 slim people in love; #9 & 10 (nice-size 3rd flr. rms. w/2 twin beds or zip & lock queen-size bed & huge terraces w/wonderful views of mountains) are for a double; #7 (huge rm. w/2 twin beds or zip & lock king-size bed & terrace w/rooftops view) is for a double but can fit an extra twin bed for a triple; #5 (large rm. w/2 twin beds or zip & lock king-size bed, huge bathroom & faces the back w/no view) & 8 (nice-size rm. w/2 twin beds or zip & lock queen-size bed & faces the back w/no view) are for a double; #4 (large rm. w/2 twin beds or zip & lock king-size bed & futon convertible chair/bed) & 6 (large rm. w/2 twin beds or zip & lock king-size bed, futon convertible chair/bed & faces the back w/no view) are for a double or triple; #2 has a terrace; most w/standard-size bathrooms w/hairdriers, beautiful garden w/lemon trees, bar, wonderful quiet location, lots of stairs, no elevator, 3 flrs. Owned/managed by Morio & Simone Rollandi (father & son). Simone's great-grandfather built the house which is why it is called Andrean's house. From the train station, walk through the tunnel, turn right after you exit tunnel, walk up the very steep hill. 10-min. walk. (Closed Nov.-mid-Dec.)

DA BARANIN ROOMS: Via Rollandi 29. **Tel/Fax:** 0187-920595. **Web site:** http://www.baranin.com/ **E-mail:** info@baranin.com (6 rms., 3 apts., all w/toilet & shower.) 86€ (no view) double; 91€ (view) double; 129€ (view) triple. Call for quad & apt. rates. Breakfast (8-10am) is included in the rates & can be served on the terrace in warm weather. Cash only. They only take credit cards to reserve the room. English spoken (Sara, Andrea & Silvia), no phones, cable TV w/CNN, charming 2-in-1 B&B w/contemporary & identically pinewood furnished modern rms., shiny tiled flrs., #1 (very small rm. w/2 twin beds or zip & lock king-size bed), 2 (queen-size bed, compact bathroom, small window & front door opens out to view of countryside) & 3 are for a double; apt. #1 (steep circular staircase that goes to upper-level w/convertible sofa, kitchenette w/dining area, terrace w/view of countryside & lower-level w/queen-size bed, small bathroom & 2 windows w/views of countryside) is for a double, triple or family; annex (2 rms.): small 1st flr. rm. w/queen-size bed & small terrace w/fabulous views of mountain & sea) is for a double; #6 (huge ground-flr. rm. w/king-size bed, twin bed, & small terrace w/fabulous views of mountain & sea) is for a triple but can fit an extra twin bed for a family; you have to walk outside to have breakfast in a small room, terrace w/panoramic view, lots of steep stairs, no elevator. Owned/managed by Sara & Andrea Barani (wife & husband) & Silvia (Sara's sister) since 1998. From the train station, walk through the tunnel, turn right after you exit tunnel, walk up the very steep, steep hill past the church, continue to your right up the steep flight of stairs to hotel. (Closed Jan.-Feb. 20.)

MARINA PICCOLA: Via Discovolo 120, 19010. **Tel:** 0187-920103. **Fax:** 0187-920966. **Web site:** http://www.hotelmarinapiccola.com/ **E-mail:** marijes@tin.it (10 rms., all w/toilet & shower.) 78€ single; 103€ double; 137€ triple; 182€ quad. Breakfast (8-10am) is included in the rates. Visa, MC, AX, DC. Limited English spoken (Jan), phones, cable TV w/CNN, wonderful charming 2-in-1 hotel w/nicely & identically furnished bright nice-size rms., shiny tiled flrs. Main bldg. (6 rms.): #5 (small rm. w/2 twin beds or zip & lock queen-size bed) is for a double; #3 (nice-size rm. w/2 twin beds or zip & lock queen-size bed, convertible chair/bed & partial sea view) is for a double or triple; #7 (corner rm. w/2 twin beds or zip & lock king-size bed, convertible sofa, 6 steps up to small bathroom & terrace w/wonderful sea view) is for a double, triple or family; annex (4 rms.): #9 (nice-size rm. w/2 twin beds or zip & lock queen-size bed & wonderful sea view) is for a double; #8 (small rm.) & 10 (both w/wonderful sea views) are for a double; 3 rms. w/terraces, minibars, bar, wonderful waterfront restaurant w/veranda & terrace around the corner, you have to walk outside to the restaurant to have breakfast whether you stay in the main bldg. or annex, lots of stairs, no elevator, 4 flrs. They offer half- and full-board rates. From the train station, walk through the tunnel to the left, follow the main road, you'll see the hotel's blue & white sign on the right. (Closed Nov.)

TORRETTA (LA) ROOMS: Via Vico Volto 20. **Tel/Fax:** 0187-920327. **Web site:** http://www.cinqueterre.net/torretta/ **E-mail:** torretta@cdh.it (7 rms., 3 apts., 4 w/toilet & shower.) 64€ single; 114€ double. Call for triple, quad & apt. rates. The rooms without bathrooms are cheaper. Breakfast is included in the rates. Visa, MC. English spoken (Gabriele), no phones, cable TV w/CNN, charming 2-in-1 B&B w/contemporary & identically furnished modern rms., shiny tiled flrs., main bldg.: #3 (2 twin beds or zip & lock queen-size bed, private bathroom outside the room & wonderful view of mountain w/partial sea view) is for a double; #1 (small rm. w/2 twin beds or zip & lock queen-size bed, no bathroom & small balcony w/mountain view & partial sea view) & 2 (2 steps down to rm. w/2 twin beds or zip & lock queen-size bed, no bathroom & balcony w/mountain view & partial sea view) share a large private bathroom w/triangular-shaped bathtub w/hand-held shower outside the room, have a separate common door and can be rented separately as a double or together as one family rm.; rooftop terrace w/magnificent panoramic view, wonderful location near the church & its bells, lots of steep stairs, no elevator. Owned/managed by architect Gabriele Baldini. From the train station, walk through the tunnel, turn right after you exit tunnel, walk up the very steep, steep hill to the church. Look to your right for the B&B. (Closed Nov. 15-Jan.)

CORNIGLIA HOTEL
VILLA DA CECIO: Via Serra 58. **Tel:** 0187-812043. **Fax:** 0187-812138. (12 rms., all w/toilet & shower.) 63€ double; 87€ triple. No breakfast served. Cash only. English spoken, no phones, no TV, charming simple hotel w/simply & identically furnished bright nice-size airy rms., original flrs., #5 (king-size bed & views of mountain & sea), 3 (corner rm. w/2 twin beds or zip & lock king-size bed, futon convertible chair/bed, small bathroom & 2 windows w/views of mountains) & 6 (corner rm. w/queen-size bed & small windows w/sea views) are for a double; #7 (king-size bed, futon convertible chair/bed & small windows w/views of mountains & sea) is for a double or triple; #8 (king-size bed & faces the street) & 1 (ground-flr. rm. w/queen-size bed, small bathroom & no view) are for a double; restaurant & terrace w/magnificent panoramic views, bar, wonderful quiet location, no elevator, 2 flrs. Owned/managed by Elia & Carmelo Castagnelto (mother & son). *15% rm. discount when you show them*

this book. They offer half-board rates. From the train station, walk up the stairs to the bus stop which drops you off in the center. Hotel is a steep uphill walk (10 min.) from the center. (Closed Wed. & Nov.)

LAUNDROMATS (Lavanderia)
Lavanderia: Via Giuseppe Mazzini 3/5, Monterosso Al Mare. Claudio's Mobile: 3335454115. Hrs.: Daily 9am-1pm & 3pm-8pm; Lavasciuga I Camiletti: Via Roma 49, Vernazza. Hrs.: Fri.-Wed. 8am-10pm. Closed Thurs. Owned/managed by the Blue Marlin bar next door which is where you get the coins for the machines.

SUPERMARKETS
Despar: Via Roma 61, Monterosso Al Mare. Hrs.: Mon.-Sat. 8am-1pm & 5pm-8pm. Closed Sun; Piazza Matteotti 9, Monterosso Al Mare. Hrs.: Mon.-Sat. 8am-1pm & 5pm-8pm. Closed Wed. afternoon & Sun.

INTERNET CAFES
Via Vittorio Emanuele 55, Monterosso Al Mare. Tel/Fax: 0187-817288. Web site: http://www.monterossonet.com/ E-mail: info@monterossonet.com. Hrs.: Daily 10am-1pm & 3pm-7:30pm. Longer hrs. in summer; Blue Marlin Bar: Via Roma 43, Vernazza. Tel: 0187-821149. E-mail: bmarlin@tin.it Hrs.: Fri.-Wed. 7am-11:30pm. Closed Thurs.

RESTAURANT
TRATTORIA BILLY: Via Rollandi 122. Manarola. Tel: 087-920628. Hrs.: Fri.-Wed. 12noon-3pm & 7pm-11pm. Closed Thurs. (winter), 25 days in Nov. & 8 days in Dec. Cash only. Reservations required in-season. Specialty: Fresh seafood & fish. Owned/managed by George (waiter) & chef Paolo (brothers). Lots of steep stairs. From the train station, walk through the tunnel, turn right after you exit tunnel, walk up the very steep, steep hill to the church, look for trattoria's sign, continue walking up the stairs to trattoria. Highly recommended by Simone, Hotel Ca' D' Andrean.

CORTINA D'AMPEZZO
Dolomites/Veneto, zip code 32043
Country code 39, city code 0436

TOURIST OFFICES
1). Piazzatta San Francesco 8. **Tel:** 0436-3231. **Fax:** 0436-3235. Hrs.: Mon.-Fri. 9am-12:30pm & 4pm-7pm. **Web site:** http://www.apt-dolomiti-cortina.it/ **E-mail:** infocortina@apt-dolomiti-cortina.it **2).** Piazza Roma 1. **Tel.** 0436-2711. **Fax:** 0436-2944. This office is usually open when the above office is closed.

TRANSPORTATION TIPS
Catch a train to Calalzo di Cadore-Pieve, which is the nearest train station to Cortina D'Ampezzo. **Web site:** http://www.trenitalia.com/ It is about a 2 1/2 hr.-3 3/4 hr. (2nd class only) train ride to Calalzo di Cadore-Pieve (depending on what time & which train you catch) from Venice. When you arrive at the train station in Calalzo di Cadore, purchase your bus ticket to Cortina inside the train station at the same window that sells train tickets. Take the bus (1 hr. ride) from Calalzo di Cadore-Pieve to Cortina D'Ampezzo. The bus drops you off at the bus station in Cortina D'Ampezzo which overlooks the center of town. During high season, many of the hotels offer direct bus service from Venice to Cortina D'Ampezzo. Check with your hotel for rates and specifics.

NOTE: Most of the hotels in Cortina D'Ampezzo have a minimum 7-day stay and offer only weekly rates in high season. The rates are drastically reduced in low season. In you stay in town, you will hear the loud church bells ring from 7am-11pm.

HOTEL IN THE CENTER OF TOWN
MONTANA: Corso Italia 94. **Tel:** 0436-862126. **Fax:** 0436-868211. **Web site:** http://www.cortina-hotel.com/ **E-mail:** montana@cortina-hotel.com (30 rms., 26 w/toilet & bath or shower.) 67€ single; 122€ double; 126€ (rm. #119) double; 151€ triple; 198€ quad. Call for quint rates. The rooms with private bathrooms outside the rooms are cheaper. Buffet breakfast (8-10am, includes ham, cheese, yogurt, juices, assorted hot chocolates, 40 kinds of teas & assorted coffees)

is included in the rates & can be served in the room (2€ extra pp). Visa, MC, AX, DC. English spoken (Adriano & Roberta), phones, cable TV w/CNN, wonderful charming modern chalet hotel w/nicely pinewood & identically furnished nice-size to large rms., nice wooden flrs., #131 (nice-size rm. w/twin bed, standard-size bathroom w/ shower & balcony w/wonderful view), 117 (nice-size rm. w/twin bed, bathroom & balcony w/wonderful view), 124 (nice-size rm. w/twin bed, small bathroom w/shower & window w/wonderful view), 128 (bright nice-size rm. w/twin bed, bathroom w/bathtub & balcony w/ partial view), 130 (nice-size rm. w/twin bed, bathroom w/bathtub & small window), 111 (huge 1st flr. rm. w/twin bed, large bathroom w/ bathtub & access to terrace that is shared w/the other guests) & 6 other rooms are all for a single; #119 (wonderful large honeymoon rm. w/2 twin beds or zip & lock king-size bed, sofa, high wood-beamed ceiling, arched wall, bathroom w/Jacuzzi bathtub w/different color mood lighting for ambience & 4 windows w/wonderful view) is for a double; #140 (one flight up to a fabulous huge 4th flr. attic rm. w/2 twin beds or zip & lock queen-size bed, large bathroom w/bathtub, sitting area, wood-beamed ceiling & terrace w/magnificent panoramic view) is for a double but can fit extra twin beds for a triple or family; #127 (wonderful huge rm. w/2 French double beds or zip & lock super king-size bed, large bathroom w/bathtub & huge terrace w/magnificent panoramic view that is shared w/rms. #125 & 126) is for a double or triple; #133 (2 twin beds or zip & lock king-size bed, wood-beamed ceiling, standard-size bathroom w/bathtub & terrace w/wonderful view) is for a double; #139 (one flight up to a small 4th flr. attic w/queen-size bed & balcony w/magnificent panoramic view), 112 (huge 1st flr. rm. w/2 French double beds or zip & lock super king-size bed, wood-paneled walls, bathroom & huge terrace that is shared w/the other guests), 138 (one flight up to a large 4th flr. attic w/queen-size bed, sloped wood-beamed ceiling, large bathroom w/bathtub & small window w/partial view), 114 (1st flr. rm. w/2 twin beds or zip & lock queen-size bed, standard-size bathroom w/bathtub & balcony w/partial view), 122 (large rm. w/2 twin beds or zip & lock queen-size bed & standard-size bathroom w/bathtub) & 104 (1st flr. rm. w/2 twin beds or zip & lock king-size bed, standard-size bathroom w/bathtub & balcony w/no view) are for a double; #105 (1st flr. rm. w/2 twin beds or zip & lock king-size bed

& private bathroom outside the room) is for a double; #126 (large rm. w/2 twin beds or zip & lock queen-size bed, no bathroom & huge terrace w/magnificent panoramic view that is shared w/rms. #125 & 127) is for a double but can fit an extra twin bed for a triple; #126 & 127 (see above for both) have connecting doors & terraces but can be rented separately as a double or together as one family or quint rm.; #119 (see above) & 118 (2 twin beds positioned head-to-toe & no bathroom) have connecting doors but can be rented separately as a double or together as one family rm.; #133 (see above) & 132 (2 twin beds positioned head-to-toe & no bathroom) have connecting doors & terraces but can be rented separately as a double or together as one family rm.; the 4 rooms (#118, 126, 132 & 136) w/o bathrooms share 2 communal bathrooms; safety boxes, 15 rms. w/balconies, the higher the floor the better the view, warm ambience, elevator only goes to 3rd flr., 4 flrs., free parking. Owned/managed by wonderful, charming & attentive Adriano Lorenzi. All the paintings exhibited in the hotel are for sale; this is how Adriano helps support various artists. To walk from the bus station, cross the street, walk down the stairs, continue straight to the post office, turn left, turn right and walk to hotel. 10-min. walk. (Closed June & Nov. 10-Dec. 10.)

HOTELS (10-min. walk from the center)
BELLARIA: Corso Italia, 266. **Tel:** 0436-2505. **Fax:** 0436-5755. **Web site:** http://www.hbellaria.it/ **E-mail:** hbellaria.cortina@dolomiti.org (22 rms., all w/toilet & bath or shower.) 79€ single; 158€ double; 184€ triple. Call for quad rates. Breakfast (8am) is included in the rates & can be served in the room (3€ extra pp). Visa, MC. English spoken (Lorenzoe & Manuela), phones, TV, charming modern chalet hotel w/nicely pinewood & identically furnished nice-size rms., nice wooden or carpeted flrs., #302 (large 3rd flr. attic rm. w/2 twin beds or zip & lock king-size bed, bathroom w/bathtub & view), 108 (large 1st flr. rm. w/2 twin beds or zip & lock king-size bed, high wood-paneled ceiling & bathroom w/bathtub) & 101 (nice-size rm. w/2 twin beds or zip & lock king-size bed, huge bathroom w/bathtub & faces the parking lot) are for a double but can fit an extra twin bed for a triple; #102 (nice-size rm. w/2 twin beds or zip & lock king-size bed, bathroom w/ shower & balcony w/partial view) is for a double; there is a handicapped access bathroom on the 2nd flr. in between rms. #201 & 202;

most of the bathrooms have bathtubs, only 4 have showers, hairdriers, bar, restaurant, elevator, 3 flrs., free parking. Owned/managed by Lorenzoe Manuela Majoni. They offer half- and full-board rates. I suggest you taxi to hotel unless you are traveling light. To walk from the bus station, cross the street, walk down the stairs, continue straight to the post office, turn right, turn left, turn right onto Corso Italia.

IMPERO: Via C. Battisti 66. **Tel:** 0436-4246. **Fax:** 0436-4248. **Web site:** http://www.dolomiti.org/hotelimpero/ **E-mail:** hotelimpero@dolomiti.org (31 rms., all w/toilet & bath or shower.) 95€ single; 147€ double; 200€ triple; 242€ quad. Call for quint rates. Buffet breakfast (7:30-10am, ham, cheese & cereals) is included in the rates & can be served in the room (2€ extra pp). American breakfast available at extra cost. Visa, MC. English spoken (Pietro), phones, cable TV w/CNN, wonderful charming modern chalet hotel w/nicely pinewood & identically furnished nice-size to large rms., nice wooden or carpeted flrs., #44 (bright airy nice-size 3rd flr. rm. w/twin bed, frigobar, bathroom w/shower & balcony that faces the front w/wonderful view), 41 (large 3rd flr. rm. w/twin bed, bathroom w/bathtub & faces the back) & 4 other similar rooms are for a single; #47 (bright airy large 3rd flr. rm. w/2 twin beds or zip & lock king-size bed, sitting area, frigobar, huge bathroom w/bathtub & balcony that faces the front w/wonderful view) & 46 (bright airy large 3rd flr. rm. w/2 twin beds or zip & lock queen-size bed, large bathroom w/bathtub & balcony that faces the front w/wonderful view) are for a double; #48 (large 3rd flr. rm. w/3 twin beds or 1 zip & lock king-size bed & twin bed, large bathroom w/bathtub & no view), 58 & 33 are all for a triple; #32 (large 2nd flr. rm. w/2 twin beds or zip & lock queen-size bed, roll-out bunk beds, frigobar, standard-size bathroom w/shower & partial view) is the only 1 room for a family; #26 & 27 have connecting doors but can be rented separately as a double or together as one family or quint rm.; #36 & 37 have connecting doors but can be rented separately as a double or together as one family or quint rm.; #56 & 57 have connecting doors but can be rented separately as a double or together as one family or quint rm.; 17 rms. w/balconies, 6 rms. w/terraces, try to get a room facing the front & the higher the floor the better the view, hairdriers, frigobars (50%), whirlpool & sauna (6€ pp per hour), warm ambience, charming old-fashioned breakfast room, working fireplace, bar, wonderful location, elevator, 5 flrs., free street parking, garage parking (15€ per day). Owned/managed by Giovanni & charming Pietro Ghedina (father & son). Pietro requests that you be very specific about what you want when you book a room at his hotel. Indicate whether you want balcony, view, tranquility, frigobar, bathroom w/bathtub or shower & type of beds. I suggest you taxi to hotel unless you are traveling light. To walk from the bus station, cross the street, walk down the stairs, continue straight to the post office, turn left, turn right, walk past Hotel Montana down to the tourist office on Piazzatta San Francesco, turn right and walk straight to hotel. (Closed May.)

HOTEL (I didn't see because I ran out of time.)
CORONA: Via Val Sotto 12. **Tel:** 0436-3251. **Fax:** 0436-867339. **Mobile:** 336-669947. **Web site:** http://www.hotelcoronacortina.it **E-mail:** info@hotelcoronacortina.it (10 rms., all w/toilet & bath or shower.) 65€ single; 120€ double; 160€ triple; 205€ quad. Breakfast (8-10am) is included in the rates. English spoken (Stefano). Visa, MC, AX. *5% rm. discount when you show owner/manager Stefano Rimoldi this book.* (Closed April-May & Mid-Sept. to Dec.)

TAXI
Contac: Via Marconi 5. Tel: 0436-860888. Giorgio Alberti's Mobile: 3356371419 or 337495399. Web site: http://www.contac.it E-mail: info@contac.it

SUPERMARKETS
La Cooperativa: Corso Italia 40. Visa, MC. Hrs.: Mon.-Sat. 8:30am-12:30pm & Tues. -Sat. 3:30pm-7:30pm. Closed Mon. afternoon & Sun.; Kanguro: Via Franchetti. Hrs.: Tues.-Sat. 8:30am-12:30pm & Mon.-Sat. 3:30pm-7:30pm. Closed Mon. morning & Sun. Visa, MC. Cross streets: Corso Italia & Via Roma. Located opposite Hotel Villa Neva (not reviewed in this book.)

RESTAURANTS
BIRRERIA VIENNA: Via Roma 66/68. Tel: 0436-8666944. Hrs.: Thurs.-Tues. Kitchen 12noon-2:30pm & 7:30pm-10:30pm. Closed Wed. Visa, MC. Delicious fresh pizza. Highly recommended by Adriano, Hotel Montana.

RA STUA: Via Grohmann 2. Tel: 0436-868341. Hrs.: 12noon-3pm & 7pm-10pm. Visa, MC. Highly recommended by Adriano, Hotel Montana.

DESSERT
BAR SPORT: Corso Italia 132. Tel: 0436-868444. Hrs.: 8am-12midnight. Visa, MC. Assorted delicious fresh pastries & cakes.

CORTONA
Eastern Tuscany, zip code 52044
Country code 39, city code 0575

TOURIST OFFICE
Via Nazionale 42. **Tel:** 0575-630352/630353. **Fax:** 0575-630656. **E-mail:** info@cortonantiquaria.com Hrs.: Oct.-April Mon.-Fri. 9am-1pm & 3pm-6pm; Sat. 9am-1pm. Open longer hrs. & Sun. in summer.

TRANSPORTATION TIPS
Trains from Florence stop at the Camucia-Cortona train station, a challenging 5km downhill below the town, outside the center. Trains from Rome stop at Terontola-Cortona train station, 11km from Cortona. It is too far and/or too steep to walk from either of the train stations to the center. Shuttle buses connect both train stations to Piazzale Garibaldi (the center of Cortona). When you arrive at the Camucia-Cortona train station, walk up the street, look to your right for the travel agency. Hrs.: Mon.-Sat. 9am-1pm & Mon.-Fri. 4pm-7:30pm. Closed Sat. morning & Sun. This is where you can purchase your bus ticket (1€ pp). If the travel agency is closed, you can also purchase a bus ticket at the newsstand located farther up on the corner or at the bar across the street. The bus stop is in front of the bank near the newsstand. The shuttle buses depart (15-min. ride) about every 30-min. to Piazzale Garibaldi.

It is better to purchase your train ticket at the tourist office before you leave Cortona because the ticket window at the train station may not be open. Ticket window Hrs.: Mon.-Fri.- 6:40am-1pm. Closed Sat. & Sun.

HOTELS
SAN LUCA: Piazzale Garibaldi 2. **Tel:** 0575-630460. **Fax:** 0575-630105. **Web site:** http://www.sanlucacortona.com/ **E-mail:** info@sanlucacortona.com (57 rms., all w/toilet & shower.) 76€ single; 113€ double; 156€ triple; 178€ quad. Breakfast (7:30-10:30am) is included in the rates & can be served on the terrace in warm weather. Air-conditioned. Visa, MC, AX, DC. English spoken (Patricia), phones, TV, wonderful charming modern hotel w/beautifully & iden-

tically furnished nice-size pretty rms., nicely carpeted flrs., the rooms are on the lower level 4th, 5th & 6th floors of the hotel, #58, 59, 60, 61, 62, 63 & 64 (all nice-size 4th flr. rms. w/2 twin beds or zip & lock queen-size bed & balconies that face the front w/wonderful views of the countryside) are for a double; #68 (large rm. w/2 twin beds or zip & lock queen-size bed, futon convertible chair/bed & wonderful view of the countryside) is for a double; #71 (4 twin beds or 1 zip & lock queen-size bed & 2 twin beds & partial view of countryside) & 5 other rooms are for a family; many rooms that face the front have balconies w/wonderful views of the countryside, high ceilings, all w/ standard-size bathrooms w/hairdriers, minibars, safety boxes, Internet access available at 6€ per 1/2 hr., huge communal room & rooftop terrace w/magnificent panoramic view, restaurant, 2 elevators, 4 flrs., free parking. They offer half- and full-board rates. The shuttle bus drops you off right in front of the hotel.

SAN MICHELE: Via Guelfa 15. **Tel:** 0575-604348. **Fax:** 0575-630147. **Web site:** http://www.cortona.net/sanmichele/ **E-mail:** sanmichele@ats.it (40 rms., all w/toilet & shower.) 147€ double; 165€ (jr. suites) double; 173€ triple; 189€ quad. Buffet breakfast (7:30-10am) is included in the rates & can be served in the room (4€ extra pp). Air-conditioned. Visa, MC, AX, DC. English spoken (Margarita & Francesca), phones, cable TV w/BBC, fabulous wonderful charming renovated 15th-century palace hotel w/nicely & identically furnished pretty rms., original flr., #239 (large rm. w/2 twin beds or zip & lock king-size bed, large bathroom & balcony w/fabulous views of countryside & rooftops), 237 (large rm. w/2 twin beds or zip & lock king-size bed, high wood-beamed ceiling & faces the back w/rooftops view) & 243 (attic rm. w/2 twin beds or zip & lock king-size bed, arched wood-beamed ceiling & small window w/view of countryside) are for a double; #236 (loft rm. w/convertible sofa on lower level, 2 twin beds or zip & lock king-size bed & bathroom on upper level), 245 (2 attic rms. w/2 twin beds or zip & lock king-size bed, sitting area w/convertible sofa, sloped high wood-beamed ceiling & small window w/view of countryside) & 226 (2 twin beds or zip & lock king-size bed, convertible sofa, high ceiling & 1 step up to bathroom) are for a double or triple; #221 (huge rm. w/2 twin beds or zip & lock king-size bed & high ceiling) & 225 (2 twin beds or zip & lock king-size bed & high wood-beamed ceiling) are for a double; #242 (2 rms. w/3 twin beds or 1 zip & lock queen-size bed & twin bed, low wood-beamed ceiling & small window w/view) is for a triple; #227 (loft rm. w/queen-size bed on lower level, 2 twin beds or zip & lock king-size bed on upper level, high wood-beamed ceiling) & 5 other similar rms. are for a family; #241 (jr. suite w/2 twin beds or zip & lock queen-size bed, sitting area w/convertible chair/bed, wood-beamed ceiling, bathroom w/bathtub w/hand-held shower & small window w/view) is for a double or triple; #250 (walk up 2 flights of private stairs to unusual honeymoon loft tower suite that you walk up more stairs to get to upper level w/queen-size bed, small bathroom & 3 windows w/magnificent panoramic view) is for a double; most w/ standard-size modern bathrooms, beautiful breakfast room w/antique ceiling, doors & marble nonworking fireplace, minibars, bar, elevator, 4 flrs., parking (11€ per day). Owned/managed by Paolo Alunno. *5% rm. discount when you show him this book.* They offer half- and full-board rates. 5-min. walk from Piazzale Garibaldi.

VILLA MARSILI: Via G. Severini 48. **Tel:** 0575-630460. **Fax:** 0575-630105. **Web site:** http://www.villamarsili.com/ **E-mail:** info@villamarsili.com (23 rms., 3 suites, all w/toilet & bath or shower.) 137€ single; 177€ (classic rms.) double; 229€ (deluxe rms.) double; 322€ (suite) double. Call for triple & quad rates. Breakfast (7:30-10:30am) is included in the rates. Air-conditioned. Visa, MC, AX, DC. English spoken (Donato), phones, cable TV w/CNN & BBC, fabulous wonderful charming new (2001) renovated 15th-century palace hotel w/beautifully & individually furnished large pretty rms., shiny tiled flrs., #12, 22, 24 & 34 (all w/twin bed, bathrooms w/showers & views of Cortona) are for a single; #32 (large rm. w/2 twin beds or zip & lock king-size bed & bathroom w/shower) is for a single; #19 (corner) & 14 (both classic rms. w/king-size beds, bathrooms w/showers & views of the valley) are for a double; #38 (corner) & 28 (both classic rms. w/2 twin beds or zip & lock king-size bed, bathrooms w/ bathtubs & views of the valley) are for a double; #11 & 23 (both classic rms. w/French double beds, bathrooms w/showers & views of the valley) are for 2 slim people in love; #16 (large classic rm. w/ king-size bed, bathroom w/shower & view of the valley) is for a double but can fit an extra twin bed for a triple; #21 (large classic rm. w/

king-size bed, bathroom w/bathtub & separate shower & view of the valley) is for a double but can fit an extra twin bed for a triple; #31 (huge classic rm. w/2 twin beds or zip & lock king-size bed, bathroom w/bathtub & separate shower & view of the valley) is for a double but can fit an extra twin bed for a triple; #26, 33 & 36 (all large classic rms. w/2 twin beds or zip & lock king-size bed, bathroom w/ showers & views of the valley) are for a double but can fit an extra twin bed for a triple; #15, 27 & 35 (all huge deluxe rms. w/2 twin beds or zip & lock king-size bed, bathrooms w/Jacuzzi bathtubs w/ overhead showers & views of the valley) are for a double but can fit an extra twin bed for a triple; #18, 25 & 37 (all huge deluxe rms. w/ king-size beds, huge bathrooms w/Jacuzzi bathtubs w/overhead showers & views of the valley) are for a double but can fit an extra twin bed for a triple; #20 (corner) & 10 (both huge suites w/king-size beds, sitting rooms, huge bathroom w/triangle-shaped Jacuzzi bathtubs & separate huge shower w/2 marble sinks & views of the valley) are for a double but can fit an extra twin bed for a triple; #30 (huge suite w/ 2 twin beds or zip & lock king-size bed, sitting room w/working fireplace, huge bathroom w/triangle-shaped Jacuzzi bathtub & separate huge shower w/2 marble sinks & view of the valley) is for a double but can fit an extra twin bed for a triple; large bathrooms w/hairdriers & towel heaters, safety boxes, Internet access available, elevator, 2 flrs. 5-min. walk downhill from Piazzale Garibaldi.

This hotel only showed me 2 rooms. The rest of the information was given to me.
ITALIA: Via Ghibellina 5. **Tel:** 0575-630254 or 630564. **Fax:** 0575-605763. **Web site:** http://www.emmeti.it/Hitalia.it.html/ **E-mail:** hotel.italia@technet.it (27 rms., all w/toilet & shower.) 68€ single; 103€ double. Call for triple & quad rates. Buffet breakfast (8-10am) is included in the rates. Air-conditioned. Visa, MC. English spoken (Paola & Gianni), phones, TV, simple 16th-century palace hotel w/ plainly & identically furnished rms. w/no views, tiled flrs., #43, 46 & 20 (all w/twin beds) are for a single; #45 (2 twin beds or zip & lock queen-size bed & small window w/small views of countryside & rooftops) is for a double; #34 (2 twin beds or zip & lock king-size bed, high wood-beamed ceiling & small window w/no view) is for a double; #32 & 31 (both w/queen-size beds) are for a family; charm-

ing breakfast room, interior veranda, rooftop terrace w/magnificent panoramic view, fabulous original underground cave restaurant w/ interior courtyard, elevator. Owned/managed by Dina, Paola & Gianni (grandmother, mother & son). They offer half-board rates. 5-min. walk from Piazza Garibaldi.

SUPERMARKET
Piazza Repubblica. Visa, MC. Hrs. Mon.-Sat. 8am-1:30pm & 4:30pm-8pm. Closed Sun.

RESTAURANT
OSTERIA DEL TEATRO: Via Maffei 5. Tel: 0575-630556.
Web site: http://www.osteria-del-teatro.it/
E-mail: osteria_del_teatro@inwind.it Hrs.: Thurs.-Tues. 12noon-2:30pm & 7pm-9:30pm. Closed Wed. & 2 wks. in Nov. Visa, MC, AX, DC. Reservations required. Wonderful small (12 tables) restaurant that serves delicious food. Owned/managed by chef Emiliano Rossi. Highly recommended by Paolo, Hotel San Michele.

FLORENCE (Firenze)
Tuscany, zip code 50123
Area code 39, city code 055

Firenze Tourist Information Centers
1.) Via Cavour 1r. **Tel:** 055-290832. **Fax:** 055-2760383. **E-mail:** infoturismo@provincia.fi.it Hrs.: Daily 8:30am-7pm. This office is much more helpful & pleasant than the office near the train station. They also have a special counter here dedicated to "Protecting the Rights of the Tourist." Special Tel: 055-2760382. **2.)** Via A. Manzoni 16r., 50121. **Tel:** 055-2330210. **Fax:** 055-2346286. Hrs.: Mon.-Sat. 9am-6pm. **3.)** Piazza Stazione 4. **Tel:** 055-212245. **Fax:** 055-2381226. **E-mail:** turismo3@comune.fi.it Hrs.: Mon.-Sat. 8:30am-7:30pm & Sun. 8:30am-1:30pm. This office **is not** located inside the train station, despite all the misleading signs. It is directly across the street from the train station. **4.)** Florence airport: Via Termine 11. **Tel/Fax:** 055-315874. Hrs.: Daily 8am-3pm.
Web sites: http://www.firenze.turismo.toscana.it/ or http://www.comune.firenze.it/

TRANSPORTATION TIP
There are always long lines at the ticket windows in the front section of Florence's train station. However, if you have your train information and need to purchase tickets, walk straight through the ticket information office, turn left and you will find more ticket windows without lines. It seems travelers (including locals) are not aware of or forgot about these ticket windows.

Florence hotels listed alphabetically

ABACO	CENTRALE
ACCADEMIA	CENTRO
ALDINI	CHIAZZA
ALESSANDRA	CIMABUE
ANNABELLA	COLOMBA
BELLETTINI	CONCORDIA
BERKLEYS	DEI MORI
BURCHIANTI	DESIRÉE
CASCI	ENZA

EUROPA	MAXIM
FERRETTI	NUOVA ITALIA
FIORITA	PERSEO
GINORI	PEZZATI I
GLOBUS	PICCOLO
IL BARGELLINO	SAMPAOLI
IL PORCELLINO	SCALETTA (LA)
JOHANNA	SERENA
JOHLEA I & II	STELLA MARY
KURSAAL-AUSONIA	

In you stay in the center, you may hear the loud church bells ring from 7am-11pm.

HOTELS (Center)
ALESSANDRA: Borgo Santi Apostoli 17, 2nd fl. **Tel:** 055-283438. **Fax:** 055-210619. **Web site:** http://www.hotelalessandra.com/ **E-mail:** info@hotelalessandra.com (27 rms., 20 w/toilet & bath or shower.) 115€ single; 157€ double; 204€ (jr. suite #11) double; 238€ (suite #27) double; 209€ triple; 236€ quad. The rooms without bathrooms are cheaper. Breakfast (7:30-9:30am) is included in the rates & can be served in the room. Air-conditioned. Visa, MC, AX. English spoken (Andrea & Anna), phones, TV w/CNN, wonderful charming renovated 16th-century palace hotel w/beautifully & individually furnished large rms., beautiful wooden flrs., #19 (large twin bed, bathroom w/bathtub & no view), 6 (twin bed & bathroom) & 18 (3rd flr. rm. w/twin bed & private bathroom outside the room) are for a single; #26 (walk one flight up to a special nonsmoking rm. w/2 twin beds or zip & lock queen-size bed, large bathroom w/bathtub & sitting area w/magnificent view of the river) is for a double; #27 (walk one flight up to nonsmoking suite w/2 twin beds or zip & lock queen-size bed, large bathroom w/bathtub & terrace w/magnificent view of the river) is for a double; #15 (huge rm. w/2 twin beds or zip & lock queen-size bed & bathroom w/bathtub) is for a double but can fit an extra twin bed for a triple; #1 (2 twin beds or zip & lock king-size bed & bathroom w/bathtub), 16bis (3rd flr. rm. w/2 twin beds or zip & lock queen-size bed & small bathroom w/shower) & 7 (2 twin beds or zip & lock queen-size bed & small bathroom w/ shower) are for a double; #20 (corner rm. w/3 twin beds or 1 zip &

lock queen-size bed & twin bed, bathroom w/bathtub & no view) & 16 (3rd flr. rm. w/3 twin beds or 1 zip & lock king-size bed & twin bed & bathroom w/bathtub) are for a triple; #21 (3 twin beds or 1 zip & lock queen-size bed & twin bed) & 23 (3 twin beds or 1 zip & lock queen-size bed & twin bed) are for a triple; #11 (huge rm. w/3 twin beds or 1 zip & lock queen-size bed & twin bed, bathroom w/shower & minuscule view of water) is for a triple but can fit an extra twin bed for a family; the 4 rooms w/o bathrooms on the 2nd flr. share 2 communal bathrooms; rms. on the 3rd flr. have high ceilings, modern standard-size bathrooms, lots of character, wonderful location, walk 1 flight up to elevator, 4 flrs. Owned by Arnaldo, Anna & managed by charming & accommodating Andrea Gennarini (father, mother & son). Cross street: Piazza Limbo near Lungarno Acciaioli. Taxi to hotel. (Closed Dec. 9-27.)

ALDINI: Via Calzaiuoli 13, 3rd fl. **Tel:** 055-214752. **Fax:** 055-291621. **Web site:** http://www.pronet.it/hotelaldini/ **E-mail:** hotelaldini@pronet.it (14 rms., all w/toilet & shower.) 90€ single; 145€ double; 185€ triple; 220€ quad. Breakfast (7:30-9:30am) is included in the rates & can be served in the room (1€ extra pp). Air-conditioned. Visa, MC, AX, DC. English spoken (Antonio & Elisabetta), phones, TV, charming hotel w/nicely & identically modern furnished nice-size bright airy rms., red-brick tiled flrs., #111 (nice-size rm. w/twin bed, small bathroom & view of the top of the Duomo & rooftops), 103 & 115 are for a single; #102 (fabulous huge corner rm. w/2 twin beds or zip & lock queen-size bed, standard-size bathroom & window w/partial left view of Duomo) & 105 (fabulous large rm. w/queen-size bed, ceramic nonworking fireplace, standard-size bathroom & 2 windows that face the street) are for a double; #101 (fabulous huge rm. w/2 twin beds or zip & lock queen-size bed, huge bathroom & 2 windows w/partial left view of Duomo) & 108 (large rm. w/2 twin beds or zip & lock queen-size bed, standard-size bathroom & faces the street) are for a double but can fit an extra twin bed for a triple; #107 (2 twin beds or zip & lock queen-size bed, handicapped access bathroom & faces the back) is for a double; #109, 112 & 106 (all w/2 twin beds or zip & lock queen-size bed) are for a double; #110 (3 twin beds or 1 zip & lock queen-size bed & twin bed, standard-size bathroom & 2 windows) is for a triple; #113 (large rm. w/3 twin beds or 1 zip & lock queen-size bed & twin bed, standard-size bathroom & faces the back) is for a triple but can fit an extra twin bed for a family; minibars, wonderful noisy pedestrian location close to the Duomo, elevator, 1 flr. Owned/managed by Antonio & Elisabetta Pio (brother & sister). *10% rm. discount when you show them this book and pay in cash.* Cross street: Via Tosinghi. Taxi to hotel.

CHIAZZA: Borgo Pinti 5, 2nd fl. **Tel:** 055-2480363. **Fax:** 055-2346888. **Web site:** http://www.chiazzahotel.com/ **E-mail:** hotel.chiazza@tin.it (17 rms., 14 w/toilet & shower.) 92€ single; 131€ double; 173€ triple. Call for quad rates. The rooms without bathrooms are cheaper. Breakfast (8-10:30am) is included in the rates & can be served in the room (3€ extra pp). Air-conditioned (10 rms.) Visa, MC, AX, DC. English spoken (Ida & Rosana), phones, cable TV w/CNN (13 rms.), simple hotel w/plainly & identically pinewood furnished not-so-bright rms. w/no views, #4, 13 & 14 (all w/twin beds & bathrooms) are for a single; #11 (huge rm. w/2 twin beds or zip & lock king-size bed & bathroom) is for a double but can fit extra twin beds for a triple or family; #12 (2 twin beds or zip & lock king-size bed & bathroom) is for a double; #7 & 6 (both nice-size rms. w/ 2 twin beds or zip & lock queen-size bed & small bathrooms w/o shower curtains) are for a double; #9 (nice-size rm. w/2 twin beds or zip & lock queen-size bed, small bathroom, faces the interior & no window) is for a double; bar, wonderful location, reception is two steep flights up, no elevator, 1 flr., nearby parking (16€ per day). Owned/managed by charming Mauro Rogai. *10% rm. discount when you show him this book.* Taxi to hotel.

DEI MORI: Via Danta Alighieri 12, 2nd fl. **Tel/Fax:** 055-211438. **Web site:** http://www.bnb.it/deimori/ **E-mail:** deimori@bnb.it (13 rms., 9 w/toilet & shower.) 87€ single; 103€ (standard rms. #3, 6, 7 & 26) double; 128€ (superior rms. #21, 22, 23, 25 & 27) double. Call for triple & quad rates. The rooms without bathrooms are cheaper. Breakfast (8-10am, includes homemade fruit cakes) is included in the rates. Air-conditioned (5€ extra per day). Visa, MC. English spoken (Domenico, Daniele & Franco), phones, no TV, wonderful charming hotel w/beautifully & individually furnished nonsmoking pretty rms. w/no views, #26 (small rm. w/French double bed, wood-beamed ceiling, large bathroom & faces interior) & 3 (small rm. w/French double bed, compact bathroom & faces interior) are for a single; #6 (nice-size rm. w/French double bed, compact bathroom & faces interior) & 7 (nice-size rm. w/French double bed, compact bathroom & faces interior) are perfect for a single or 2 slim people in love; #21 (fabulous bright airy huge rm. w/2 twin beds or zip & lock queen-size bed, convertible sofa, high wood-beamed ceiling, small bathroom & faces the street) & 22 (fabulous bright airy large rm. w/2 twin beds or zip & lock queen-size bed, convertible sofa, high wood-beamed ceiling & compact bathroom) are for a double or triple; #27 (bright airy large rm. w/2 twin beds or zip & lock queen-size bed, high wood-beamed ceiling & faces the side street) & 23 (bright airy large rm. w/2 twin beds or zip & lock queen-size bed, convertible chair/bed & standard-size bathroom) are for a double; #25 (bright airy nice-size rm. w/queen-size bed, wood-beamed ceiling & compact bathroom) is for a double; #2 (French double bed, high arched ceiling, no bathroom & faces interior), 1 (nice-size rm. w/queen-size bed, no bathroom & faces interior), 4 & 5 share 1 communal bathroom, warm ambience, small charming breakfast room w/access to his refrigerator & kitchen (just clean up after yourself), wonderful quiet pedestrian location, reception is two steep flights up, no elevator, 1 flr. Owned/managed by wonderful & charming Domenico, Daniele & Franco. *5% rm. discount when you show them this book.* Cross street: Via Cerchi. Taxi to hotel.

IL PORCELLINO: Piazza Mercato Nuovo 4, 1st flr. **Tel:** 055-282686. **Fax:** 055-218572. **Tel:** 055-2678198. **Web site:** http://www.hotelporcellino.it/ **E-mail:** hotelporcellino@tiscalinet.it (6 rms., all w/toilet & shower.) 74€ single; 77€ (holidays) single; 107€ double; 127€ (holidays) double. Breakfast (8-10:30am) is included in the rates & can be served in the room. Visa, MC, AX, DC. English spoken (Pamela), phones, TV, charming hotel w/nicely & identically hand-painted furnished nice-size rms., #1 (twin bed, red-brick arched wall & faces the square) & 7 (twin bed & faces the back) are for a single; #4 (wonderful large rm. w/2 twin beds or zip & lock king-size bed, small bathroom & balcony that faces the square) is for a double; #5 (2 twin beds or zip & lock queen-size bed & faces the square), 6 (queen-size bed & faces the square) & 3 (queen-size bed, bathroom w/bathtub & faces the back) are for a double; ceiling fans, wonderful noisy pedestrian location, reception is one flight up, no elevator, 2 flrs. Owned/managed by Pamela Nucci. Taxi to hotel. (Closed Aug.)

MAXIM: Via Calzaiuoli 11, 3rd fl. **Tel:** 055-217474. **Fax:** 055-283729. **Web site:** http://www.firenzealbergo.it/home/hotelmaxim/ **E-mail:** hotmaxim@tin.it (26 rms., all w/toilet & bath or shower.) 93€ single; 119€ double; 150€ triple; 185€ quad. Breakfast (8-10am) is included in the rates. Air-conditioned. Visa, MC, AX. English spoken (Virginia, Paolo & Nicolá), phones, no TV, charming sterile hotel w/nicely pinewood furnished bright nice-size rms., mixture of wooden & shiny tiled flrs., #21 (small rm. w/French double bed, cubicle bathroom w/o shower curtain & faces the street w/view of Duomo) is for a single; #24 (small rm. w/French double bed, old-style bathroom & faces the interior courtyard) is for a single or discounted for 2 slim people in love; #15 (small rm. w/double bed, small bathroom & no view) & 12 (small rm.) are for a single or discounted for 2 slim people in love; #28 (fabulous huge rm. w/2 twin beds or zip & lock queen-size bed, high wood-beamed ceiling, large bathroom w/Jacuzzi bathtub & faces the courtyard) is for a double but can fit an extra twin bed for a triple; #18 (2 twin beds or zip & lock queen-size bed & standard-size bathroom) is for a double; #4 (large rm. w/3 twin beds or 1 zip & lock queen-size bed, twin bed, standard-size bathroom & faces the back), 11 & 10 are for a triple; #27 (room near reception w/3 twin beds or 1 zip & lock queen-size bed, twin bed, standard-size bathroom & faces the courtyard) is for a triple; #8 (huge 4th flr. rm. w/4 twin beds or 1 zip & lock queen-size bed & 2 twin beds & standard-size bathroom) & 3 (3rd flr. rm.) are for a family; 3rd flr. rms. #20, 21, 22, 23, 24 & 25 have not been refurbished but are still nice, Internet access available at 3€ per 1/2 hr., wonderful noisy pedestrian location close to the Duomo, elevator only goes to 3rd flr., 4 flrs. Owned/managed by Paolo & Nicolá Maioli (father & son). Cross street: Via Tosinghi. Taxi to hotel.

PERSEO: Via Cerretani 1, 4th fl. **Tel:** 055-212504. **Fax:** 055-288377. **Web site:** http://www.hotelperseo.it/ **E-mail:** info@hotelperseo.it (19 rms., 1 modern studio., 7 w/toilet & shower.) 100€ double; 131€

triple; 157€ quad. Call for quint & studio rates. The rooms without bathrooms are cheaper. Breakfast (7-10am) is included in the rates & can be served in the room (6€ extra pp). Visa, MC, AX. English spoken (Louise, Laura, Susan & Giacinto), phones, no TV, wonderful charming quaint hotel w/nicely furnished large bright airy rms., #36 (wonderful rm. w/2 twin beds or zip & lock king-size bed, small bathroom & faces the back w/partial view of Duomo & rooftops) is for a double; #32 (wonderful huge rm. w/king-size bed, 2 twin beds & bathroom) & 28 (walk one flight up to 2 rms. w/queen-size bed, 2 twin beds, bathroom & wonderful view of Duomo) are for a family; #46 (twin bed & no bathroom) is the only single rm.; #15 (large rm. w/2 twin beds or zip & lock king-size bed & no bathroom) is for a double but can fit an extra twin bed for a triple; #26 (large rm. w/3 twin beds or 1 zip & lock king-size bed & twin bed, no bathroom & faces the back w/rooftops view) is for a triple; #16 (huge rm. w/4 twin beds or 1 zip & lock queen-size bed & 2 twin beds, convertible chair/bed & no bathroom) is for a family or quint; the 12 rooms w/o bathrooms share 3 newly renovated communal bathrooms; high ceilings, floor fans, most w/great views of Florence rooftops, bell tower and the Duomo, lots of character, warm ambience, great artwork on the walls, bar, elevator, 2 flrs. Apt. (Nicely modern furnished 4th flr. studio w/wrought iron frame zip & lock queen-size bed, bathroom w/shower, fully equipped kitchenette w/small dining table & rooftops view.) I stayed in this apt. & loved it. I felt like a local. I made my own breakfast every morning & enjoyed my desserts w/a glass of wine at night. I must point out that you have to be in good physical shape to climb the very steep 4 flights of stairs that take you to & from the apt. This was a perfect way for me to work off my fabulous dinners at night. Owned/managed by wonderful & informative Susan, Louise & Giacinto (mother, daughter & son-in-law). *Rm. discount when you show them this book and pay in cash.* Susan, who is from New Zealand, is an artist. You come to this hotel to experience the family's generous hospitality. They recently took over the Hotel San Giovanni and plan to renovate & maintain it with the same extremely high standards of cleanliness & quality that they have for their Hotel Perseo. Susan is personally making the bedspreads for the hotel. Hotel San Giovanni which is across the street has 9 large rms., 2 w/private bathrooms & 3 communal bathrooms. With the train tracks at your back, exit to the left near track #16, cross the street to McDonald's, cross the street to Piazza Unita Italiana, continue onto Via Panzani which becomes Via Cerretani.

HOTELS (East of SMN train station)
ACCADEMIA: Via Faenza 7. **Tel:** 055-293451. **Fax:** 055-219771.
Web site: http://www.accademiahotel.net
E-mail: info@accademiahotel.net (16 rms., 15 w/toilet & shower.)
137€ single; 153€ double. Call for triple rates. The room without a bathroom is cheaper. Buffet breakfast (7:30-10am) is included in the rates. Air-conditioned. Visa, MC, AX. English spoken, phones, cable TV w/CNN, charming simple 18th-century hotel w/simply furnished pretty rms., marble flrs., #9 (twin bed & private bathroom outside the room) is the only single rm.; #8 (huge rm. w/2 twin beds or zip & lock queen-size bed, large bathroom, sofa & faces the street) is for a double but can fit an extra twin bed for a triple; #7 (faces interior) & 3 (both nice-size rms. w/2 twin beds or zip & lock queen-size bed & small bathrooms) are for a double; #4 (large rm. w/3 twin beds or 1 zip & lock queen-size bed & twin bed, standard-size bathroom & 2 windows) & 5 (nice-size rm. w/3 twin beds or 1 zip & lock queen-size bed & twin bed, standard-size bathroom & 2 windows) are for a triple; #6 (huge rm. w/4 twin beds or 1 zip & lock queen-size bed & 2 twin beds & standard-size bathroom) is for a family; high ceilings, beautiful stained-glass door entrance, charming breakfast room w/ antique ceiling, small indoor patio, quiet location, bar, no elevator, 2 flrs. Owned/managed by Angelo Mari. With the train tracks at your back, exit to the left near track #16, cross the street to McDonald's, cross the street to Piazza Unita Italiana, turn left from the square, walk up Via Sant' Antonio, turn right onto Via Faenza.

ANNABELLA: Via Fiume 17, 2nd fl. **Tel:** 055-281877. **Fax:** 055-2396814. **Web site:** http://www.hotelannabella.it/ **E-mail:** hab@dada.it (8 rms., all w/toilet & shower.) 124€ double; 171€ triple; 199€ quad. Call for single rates. Breakfast (8-10am) at 6€ pp & can be served in the room. Visa, MC, AX. English spoken (Victoria & Sirmone), phones, TV, wonderful beautiful charming hotel w/nicely & identically furnished large bright airy pretty rms., mixture of original antique, shiny tiled & wooden flrs., #7 (nice-size rm. w/2 twin beds or zip & lock king-size bed, standard-size bathroom & balcony w/floor-to-ceiling window that faces the garden) is for a double; #1 & 3 (both large rms. w/2 twin beds or zip & lock king-size bed, standard-size bathrooms & face the street) are for a double; #5 (small rectangular shaped rm. w2 twin beds positioned toe-to-toe, small bathroom & balcony that faces the back) is for a double; #6 (magnificent huge corner rm. w/3 twin beds or 1 zip & lock king-size bed & twin bed, large bathroom w/bathtub & balcony w/2 floor-to-ceiling windows that face the back) is for a triple but can fit an extra twin bed for a family; #4 (large corner rm. w/4 twin beds or 1 zip & lock queen-size bed & 2 twin beds, standard-size bathroom & balcony w/floor-to-ceiling window that faces the street) & 2 (large rm. w/4 twin beds or 1 zip & lock queen-size bed & 2 twin beds, standard-size bathroom & faces the street) are for a family; modern bathrooms w/marble sinks, high ceilings, bar, elevator, 1fl. Owned/managed by wonderful & charming Victoria & Sirmone Becagli (mother & son). Same family manages the charming Hotel Stella Mary in the same bldg. To avoid the crowd on Via Nazionale, with the train tracks at your back, exit to the left near track #16, continue past the taxi stand, cross the island, cross the street, turn left, turn right onto Via Bernardo Cennini, turn right onto Via Fiume.

BELLETTINI: Via Conti 7. **Tel:** 055-213561. **Fax:** 055-283551. **Web site:** http://www.hotelbellettini.firenze.net/ **E-mail:** hotel.bellettini@dada.it (24 rms., all w/toilet & shower.) 98€ (main bldg.: standard rm.) single; 106€ (annex: superior rm.) single; 134€ (main bldg.: standard rm.) double; 162€ (annex: superior rm.) double; 170€ (main bldg.: standard rm.) triple; 208€ (annex: superior rm.) triple; 200€ (main bldg.: standard rm.) quad. Call for quint rates. Buffet breakfast (7:30-10am) is included in the rates & can be served in the room (2€ extra pp). Air-conditioned. Visa, MC, AX, DC. English spoken (wonderful Gina), phones, cable TV w/CNN, wonderful charming renovated 15th-century 2-in-1 hotel. Main bldg. has 19 nicely furnished bright airy nice-size to large pretty rms. w/shiny tiled flrs.: #21 (nice-size rm. w/French double bed, small bathroom & faces the courtyard) & 3 other similar rms. are for a single or discounted for 2 slim people in love; #45 (walk one flight up to charming 2nd flr. rm. w/2 twin beds or zip & lock queen-size bed, sloped ceiling, small bathroom & 4 windows w/wonderful views of Duomo, Medici chapel & rooftops) & 44 (walk one flight up to charming 2nd flr. rm. w/2 twin beds or zip & lock king-size bed, sloped ceiling, standard-size bathroom & balcony w/rooftops views) are for a double; #30 (huge rm. w/3 twin beds or 1 zip & lock king-size bed, 1 step up to standard-size bathroom & 2 windows) & 9 other similar rms. are for a triple; #31 (huge rm. w/2 king-size beds & standard-size bathroom) & 4 other similar rms. are for a family but can fit an extra twin bed for a quint; #24 is considered the worst w/a private bathroom outside the room; you have to walk up one flight to get to the rooms on the hotel's 2nd flr. About 2 blocks away is the annex. If you stay in the annex, you have to walk outside to the main bldg. to have breakfast, but you get 5 newly refurbished & beautifully furnished rms. w/marble flrs. & elevator, tea/coffee makers & minibars (everything in the minibar is free) in each rm., large modern marble bathrooms w/towel heaters & the 2nd telephone inside the bathrooms.: #51 (twin bed, standard-size bathroom & faces courtyard) is the only single rm.; #52 (huge magnificent rm. w/2 twin beds or zip & lock king-size bed, original high frescoed ceiling, marble nonworking fireplace, large marble bathroom & balcony w/view of Medici chapel) & 53 (huge wonderful rm. w/2 twin beds or zip & lock king-size bed, original high frescoed ceiling, large marble bathroom & 2 huge windows) are for a double; #54 (huge corner rm. w/2 twin beds or zip & lock king-size bed, convertible chair/bed, large bathroom w/bathtub & 2 huge windows) is for a double but can fit an extra twin bed for a triple; #55 (huge wonderful rm. w/2 twin beds or zip & lock king-size bed, convertible sofa, large bathroom w/bathtub & 4 floor-to-ceiling windows) is for a double but can fit extra twin beds for a triple or family; there is 24-hr. video surveillance w/direct contact from the annex to the reception room in the main bldg., safety boxes, lots of character, free Internet access available, warm ambience, bar, elevator in both locations but elevator only goes to the hotel's 1st flr. in the main building. Owned/managed by Marzia Naldini. With the train tracks at your back, exit to the left near track #16, cross the street to McDonald's, cross the street to Piazza Unita Italiana, continue onto Via Panzani which becomes Via Cerretani, turn left onto Via Conti.

BERKLEYS: Via Fiume 11, 3rd fl. **Tel:** 055-2382147. **Tel/Fax:** 055-212302. **Web site:** http://www.hotelberkleys.3000.it/ (9 rms., all w/ toilet & shower.) 80€ (small rms. #2 & 4) single; 100€ (small rms. #2 & 4) double; 103€ double; 137€ triple; 152€ quad. Breakfast (8-10am) is included in the rates & can be served in the room (3 € extra pp). Visa, MC. English spoken (Catia & Andrea), phones, TV, charming hotel w/simply to nicely furnished pretty rms., #4 & 2 (small rms. w/double beds & compact bathrooms) is for a single or discounted for a double; #6 (huge rm. w/2 twin beds or zip & lock king-size bed, antique brass headboard, small bathroom & balcony that faces the street) is for a double; #9 (large rm. w/2 twin beds or zip & lock king-size bed, antique brass headboard, small bathroom & faces the back) & 11 (nice-size rm. w/2 twin beds or zip & lock king-size bed, compact bathroom & small window that faces the back) are for a double; #5 (large rm. w/4 twin beds or 1 zip & lock king-size bed & 2 twin beds, compact bathroom & balcony that faces the street) is for a family, high ceilings, fans, bar, elevator, 1 fl. Owned/managed by Pia, Catia & Andrea Andreoli (mother, daughter & son). *Rm. discount when you show them this book.* For directions, see Hotel Annabella. (Closed Aug. 2-20.)

BURCHIANTI: Via Giglio 8, 1st fl. **Tel/Fax:** 055-212796. (11 rms., all w/toilet & bath or shower.) 168€ double. Special price for readers of *"Hello Italy!"* Call for triple, quad & family rates. Breakfast (8-9am) at 5€ pp. Cash only. Owned/managed by Rela Burchianti. This 15th-century palace hotel was in the middle of being renovated when I arrived. It will be completed before this book's publication. Rela gave me a tour of the unfinished rooms while she attempted to describe the furnishings. Limited English spoken (Rela). All 11 air-conditioned beautifully contemporary furnished large rooms will have phones, cable TV w/CNN, BBC & VCR, large windows w/no views, frigobars (5 rms.), 9 of the 11 rms. w/original frescoed ceilings, the 2 singles (both small rms. w/French double beds & bathrooms w/showers) do not have the frescoed ceilings; walk to the back through the glass doors to get to elevator, 2 flrs. With the train tracks at your back, exit to the left near track #16, cross the street to McDonald's, turn left, cross the street to Piazza Unita Italiana, continue onto Via Panzani, turn left onto Via Giglio.

CASCI: Via Cavour 13. **Tel:** 055-211686. **Fax:** 055-2396461. **Web site:** http://www.hotelcasci.com/ **E-mail:** info@hotelcasci.com (25 rms., all w/toilet & bath or shower.) 105€ single; 145€ double; 190€ triple; 240€ quad. Call for quint rates. Buffet breakfast (7:30-9:30am) is included in the rates. Air-conditioned. Visa, MC, AX, DC. English spoken (Paolo & Carla), phones, cable TV w/CNN & Sky News, wonderful charming renovated 15th-century palace hotel w/nicely & identically modern furnished nice-size rms., shiny tiled flrs., #8 (wonderful rm. w/twin bed & 3 steps up to compact bathroom & balcony faces the garden w/partial rooftop view), 27 (French double bed) & 5 (twin bed) are for a single; #20 (bright airy rm. w/2 twin beds or zip & lock king-size bed, convertible chair/bed, 2 steps up to small bathroom & faces the back) is perfect for a double but too snug for a triple; #22 (2 twin beds or zip & lock king-size bed & bathroom w/triangular-shaped bathtub), 6 (2 twin beds or zip & lock queen-size bed, 2 steps up to compact bathroom & faces the garden w/partial rooftop view), 14 (2 twin beds or zip & lock king-size bed & 2 steps up to small bathroom) & 21 (2 twin beds or zip & lock queen-size bed, 2 steps up to small bathroom & faces the interior courtyard) are for a double; #2 (3 twin beds or 1 zip & lock queen-size bed & twin bed, handicapped access bathroom & faces the street) is for a double or triple; #7 (3 twin beds or 1 zip & lock queen-size bed & twin bed, bathroom w/triangular-shaped bathtub & faces the interior courtyard) is for a triple; #23 (4 twin beds or 1 zip & lock king-size bed & 2 twin beds & bathroom w/triangular-shaped bathtub), 26 (bright airy rm. w/4 twin beds or 1 zip & lock king-size bed & 2 twin beds, bathroom w/bathtub & faces the side street) & 24 (bright airy rm. w/4 twin beds or 1 zip & lock king-size bed & 2 twin beds, small bathroom & 2 windows that face the side street) are for a family; #29 (wonderful huge rm. w/5 twin beds or 1 zip & lock queen-size bed & 3 twin beds, bathroom w/triangular-shaped bathtub & faces the side street) & 28 (wonderful huge rm. w/5 twin beds or 1 zip & lock queen-size bed & 3 twin beds, large bathroom w/triangular-shaped bathtub & small window that faces the interior courtyard) are for a family or quint; modern marble bathrooms w/hairdriers & towel heaters, safety boxes, frigobars, free Internet access available (7am-10am), public rms. w/original frescoed ceilings, bar, elevator, 2 flrs., valet parking (28€ per day). Hotel plans to include glass-blocked walls to bring more sunshine into the hotel. Owned/managed by wonderful, accommodating energetic Paolo, Carla & Armando Lombardi (son, mother & father). *10% rm. discount when you show them this book and pay in cash.* With the train tracks at your back, exit to the left near track #16, cross the street to McDonald's which is near the corner of Via Nazionale, walk up Via Nazionale about 5 blocks, turn right onto Via Guelfa for about 4 blocks, turn right onto Via Cavour. (Closed last 2 wks. in Jan.)

CENTRALE: Via Conti 3, 2nd fl. **Tel:** 055-215761. **Fax:** 055-215216. **Web site:** http://www.pensionecentrale.it/ **E-mail:** info@pensionecentrale.it (18 rms., 12 w/toilet & shower.) 99€ single; 122€ double; 158€ triple; 187€ quad. The rooms without bathrooms are cheaper. Buffet breakfast (8-10am) is included in the rates & can be served in the room (1 € extra pp). Visa, MC, AX, DC. English spoken (Franco), phones, TV, charming renovated 14th-century hotel w/simply to old-fashioned antique furnished large bright pretty rms., wooden flrs., #3 (wonderful large rm. w/2 twin beds or zip & lock queen-size bed, standard-size bathroom & view of Medici chapel), 19 (huge rm. w/2 twin beds or zip & lock queen-size bed, standard-size bathroom w/bathtub & view of Medici chapel) & 20 (nice-size rm. w/2 twin beds or zip & lock queen-size bed, convertible chair/bed, standard-size bathroom & view of Medici chapel) are for a double but can fit an extra twin bed for a triple; #2 (nice-size rm. w/2 twin beds or zip & lock queen-size bed, high decorative ceiling, standard-size bathroom & view of Medici chapel) is for a double; #16 & 15 (both huge rms. w/3 twin beds or 1 zip & lock queen-size bed & twin bed, compact bathrooms & face the back) are for a triple but can fit an extra twin bed for a family; #5 & 12 (both w/ 3 twin beds or 1 zip & lock queen-size bed & twin bed & private bathrooms) are for a triple; #11 (fabulous huge rm. w/2 twin beds, convertible sofa, 2 convertible chair/beds, no bathroom & 2 huge windows that face the back), 6, 8 & 14 share 3 communal bathrooms; warm ambience, bar, elevator only goes to the hotel's 1st flr., 2 flrs. Owned/managed by charming Franco who has spent a lot of time in the U.S. For directions, see Hotel Bellettini.

CENTRO: Via Ginori 17. **Tel:** 055-2302901 or 2302902. **Fax:** 055-212706. **Web site:** http://www.hotelcentro.net/ **E-mail:** centro@pronet.it (16 rms., 12 w/toilet & shower.) 98€ single; 141€ double; 195€ triple; 230€ quad. Call for quint rates. The rooms without bathrooms are cheaper. Breakfast (7:30-11am) is included in the rates & can be served in the room (5 € extra pp). Air-conditioned (6 rms. at 10€ extra per day). Visa, MC, AX, DC. English spoken (Rudina, Tiziana, Sandra & Andrea), phones, cable TV w/CNN, charming renovated palace hotel w/modern contemporary & identically furnished rms., mixture of new red-carpeted & shiny tiled flrs., #209 (small rm. w/French double bed & large bathroom) is perfect for a single but too snug for a double; #206 (2 twin beds & standard-size bathroom) is for a single or double; #203 (large rm. w/2 twin beds, red-carpeted flr., standard-size bathroom & faces the street) is for a double but can fit an extra twin bed for a triple; #211 (2 twin beds or zip & lock queen-size bed, red-carpeted flr., small bathroom & tiny balcony faces the back w/small rooftops view) & 207 (2 twin beds or zip & lock queen-size bed, red-carpeted flr., standard-size bathroom & faces the back) are for a double; #104 (3 twin beds or 1 zip & lock queen-size bed & twin bed, red-carpeted flr., high ceiling w/fan, small bathroom & faces the back) is for a triple but can fit an extra twin bed for a family; #201 (super huge rm. w/4 twin beds or 1 zip & lock queen-size bed & 2 twin beds, tiled flr., small bathroom & 2 windows that face the street) is for a family but can fit an extra twin bed for a quint; #208 has 2 twin beds or zip & lock queen-size bed & private bathroom outside the room; #202 has private bathroom outside the room; there is 1 communal bathroom for rooms #102 (French double bed) & 103 (twin bed) to share; modern bathrooms w/ hairdriers, fans, elevator starts from the 1st flr., 3 flrs. Owned/managed by Andrea Vendali. *5% rm. discount when you show her this book.* Cross street: Via Taddea. With the train tracks at your back, exit to the left near track #16, cross the street to McDonald's (20-min. walk.), walk up Via Nazionale about 5 blocks, turn right onto Via Guelfa, turn right onto Via Ginori.

CIMABUE: Via Benifacio Lupi 7. **Tel:** 055-471989 or 475601. **Fax:** 055-4630906. **Web site:** http://www.hotelcimabue.it/ **E-mail:** hotelcimabue@tin.it (16 rms., all w/toilet & shower.) 99€ single;

140€ double; 180€ triple; 213€ quad. Buffet breakfast (8-9:30am, includes cereals, fruit, assorted breads, jams, juices & freshly ground coffee) is included in the rates. Visa, MC, AX, DC. English spoken (Igino, Danièle & Regis), phones, TV, fabulous wonderful charming 19th-century palace hotel w/nicely to beautifully old-fashioned Venetian style furnished pretty rms., shiny tiled flrs., #10 (2 steps into ground-flr. rm. w/twin bed, bathroom w/bathtub & faces the interior) & 2 other rms. are for a single; #14 (large ground-flr. rm. w/2 twin beds or zip & lock queen-size bed, curved original frescoed ceiling, prefabricated shower in the middle of the room, small bathroom w/ toilet & faces the street) & 16 (large ground-flr. rm. w/2 twin beds or zip & lock queen-size bed curved original ceiling, prefabricated shower in the middle of the room, small bathroom w/toilet & faces the street) are for a double; #22 (beautiful huge 1st flr. rm. w/2 twin beds or zip & lock queen-size bed, convertible sofa, magnificent high original frescoed ceiling, compact bathroom & 2 huge windows), 28 (beautiful 1st flr. rm. w/magnificent high original frescoed ceiling) & 30 (beautiful 1st flr. rm. w/magnificent high original frescoed ceiling) are for a double, triple or family; 10 ground-flr. rms., 6 first flr. rms., hairdriers, digital safety boxes, floor fans, quiet location, no elevator, 1 flr. *Show the wonderful & accommodating owners/managers Igino Rossi, Danièle Dinau (Belgium) & Regis Rossi (husband, wife & son) this book and get a complimentary aperitif.* Cross street: Via Zara. Taxi to hotel. (Closed 3 wks. in Dec. including Christmas.)

COLOMBA: Via Cavour 21, 1st fl. **Tel:** 055-289139 or 2654562. **Fax:** 055-284323. **Web site:** http://www.hotelcolomba.com/ **E-mail:** info@hotelcolomba.com (14 rms., all w/toilet & shower.) 140€ double; 189€ triple; 255€ quad. Breakfast (8-9:30am) is included in the rates & can be served in the room. Air-conditioned. Visa, MC, AX, DC. English spoken (Rosanna), phones, cable TV w/CNN, wonderful charming simple hotel w/nicely & identically modern pinewood furnished bright airy rms., shiny tiled flrs., #203 (large private 3rd flr. rm. w/2 twin beds or zip & lock queen-size bed, nonworking fireplace, access to the family's private living room, bathroom w/ large shower stall w/bidet inside, wonderful rooftops view) is for a double; #15 (nice-size rm. w/2 twin beds or zip & lock queen-size bed, convertible chair/bed, small bathroom & faces the back w/partial rooftops view) is perfect for a double but too snug for a triple; #16 (nice-size rm. w/2 twin beds or zip & lock queen-size bed, huge handicapped access bathroom & faces the back w/partial rooftops view) & 8 (nice-size rm. w/2 twin beds or zip & lock king-size bed & handicapped access bathroom) are for a double; #14 (nice-size rm. w/2 twin beds or zip & lock king-size bed, small bathroom w/large shower stall w/bidet inside, faces the back w/no view) is for a double; #6 (huge rm. near reception w/3 twin beds or 1 zip & lock king-size bed & twin bed, bathroom w/large shower stall w/bidet inside, terrace that faces the back w/partial rooftop view) & 1 (nice-size corner rm. w/3 twin beds or 1 zip & lock king-size bed & twin bed, compact bathroom & 2 windows that face the back w/no view) are for a triple; #5 (nice-size rm. w/3 twin beds or 1 zip & lock king-size bed & twin bed, futon convertible chair/bed, compact bathroom) is for a triple; #3 (huge rm. w/3 twin beds or 1 zip & lock king-size bed & twin bed, futon convertible chair/bed, standard-size bathroom w/large shower stall w/bidet inside, faces the street) & 1 (huge rm. w/3 twin beds or 1 zip & lock king-size bed & twin bed, futon convertible chair/bed, small bathroom & faces the street) are for a triple or family; #7 (cubicle bathroom); minibars, hairdriers, digital safety boxes, noisy location, fans, bar, elevator, 1 fl. Owned/managed by Michele Rossi & wonderful charming Rosanna Caporale (husband & Australian wife). Cross street: Via Guelfa. With the train tracks at your back, exit to the left near track #16, cross the street to McDonald's, walk up Via Nazionale about 5 blocks, turn right onto Via Guelfa for about 4 blocks, turn left onto Via Cavour. 20-min. walk. (Closed Nov.-March.)

CONCORDIA: Via Amorino 14, 1st fl. **Tel:** 055-213233. **Fax:** 055-213337. **Web site:** http://www.albergoconcordia.it/
E-mail: info@albergoconcordia.it (16 rms., all w/toilet & shower.) 65€ single; 112€ double; 145€ triple. Call for quad rates. Buffet breakfast (8-10am) is included in the rates & can be served on the terrace in warm weather. Air-conditioned (5 rms.). Visa, MC, AX, DC. English spoken (Fabrizio, Pierre & Grazia), phones, TV, wonderful charming modern hotel w/nicely & identically pinewood furnished modern rms. w/no views, #6 (nice-size air-conditioned rm. w/twin bed & 2 windows that face the street), 18 (nice-size rm. w/twin bed), 32 (nice-size rm. w/twin bed & standard-size bathroom)

& 1 other rm. are for a single; #2 (large rm. w/2 twin beds or zip & lock queen-size bed, futon convertible chair/bed, original frescoed ceiling & faces the interior) is for a double; #5 (nice-size rm. w/2 twin beds or zip & lock king-size bed, antique armoire, wood-beamed ceiling & small bathroom) is for a double but can fit an extra twin bed for a triple; #28 (nice-size air-conditioned rm. w/2 twin beds or zip & lock queen-size bed, bathroom w/bathtub & faces the interior) & 22 (air-conditioned rm.) are for a double; #10, 16 & 30 (all nice-size rms. w/2 twin beds or zip & lock queen-size bed & standard-size bathrooms) are for a double; #20 (small air-conditioned rm. w/2 twin beds or zip & lock queen-size bed, small bathroom & faces the interior) & 24 (small rm. w/2 twin beds or zip & lock queen-size bed, small bathroom & faces the interior) are for a double; #8 (nice-size air-conditioned rm. w/3 twin beds or 1 zip & lock king-size bed & twin bed, futon convertible chair/bed, small bathroom where you cannot use the shower & toilet at the same time & faces the interior) & 26 (walk down 6 steps into large rm. w/3 twin beds or 1 zip & lock queen-size bed & twin bed & standard-size bathroom) are for a triple; 1st flr., terrace, noisy location, no elevator, 2 flrs. Owned/managed by Fabrizio Romeo. With the train tracks at your back, exit to the left near track #16, cross the street to McDonald's, cross the street to Piazza Unita Italiana, turn left onto Via San Antonio, turn right onto Via Amorino.

DESIRÉE: Via Fiume 20, 2nd fl. **Tel:** 055-2382382. **Fax:** 055-291439. **Web site:** http://www.desireehotel.com/
E-mail: hoteldesiree@tin.it (19 rms., all w/toilet & shower.) 84€ single; 131€ double; 168€ triple; 205€ quad. Breakfast (7:30-9am) is included in the rates. Visa, MC, AX, DC. English spoken (Aluizio), phones, TV, wonderful charming hotel w/simply furnished pretty rms. The rooms will be totally refurbished before this book's publication. #121 (wonderful nice-size bright airy rm. w/2 twin beds or zip & lock king-size bed, small bathroom & small balcony w/partial view of the top of the Duomo & rooftops) & 125 (wonderful nice-size corner rm. w/king-size bed & decorative antique headboard, sofa, antique armoire, antique stained-glass window, small bathroom & 2 windows) are for a double; #127 (small rm. w/2 twin beds or zip & lock king-size bed, small bathroom & antique stained-glass window

that faces the street) is for a double; #123 (huge bright airy rm. w/3 twin beds or 1 zip & lock king-size bed & twin bed, standard-size bathroom w/large shower stall & balcony w/2 windows w/rooftops view & the back) & 124 (huge bright airy rm. w/3 twin beds or 1 zip & lock king-size bed & twin bed, standard-size bathroom & balcony that faces the street) are for a double; #135 (huge rm. w/4 twin beds or 1 zip & lock king-size bed & 2 twin beds, standard-size bathroom & small balcony that faces the street) & 133 (large rm. w/4 twin beds or 1 zip & lock king-size bed & 2 twin beds) are for a double; charming breakfast room w/small terrace w/rooftops view, safety boxes, high ceilings, arched stained-glass windows, hairdriers, elevator, 1 flr. Owned by Moreno Bruni & managed by Aluizio Costa. For directions, see Hotel Annabella. (Closed Aug.)

ENZA: Via San Zanobi 45. **Tel:** 055-490990. **Fax:** 055-473672. **Web site:** http://www.hotelenza.it/ **E-mail:** info@hotelenza.it (16 rms., 8 w/toilet & shower.) 58€ single; 87€ double; 108€ triple; 160€ quad. The rooms without bathrooms are cheaper. Italian or American/English breakfast (8:30-10:30am) at 7€ pp. Air-conditioned (6 rms. at 8€ extra per day). Visa, MC, AX, DC. English spoken (Tatyana & Katia), no phones, no TV, charming hotel w/nicely & identically pinewood modern furnished rms. which vary in size, beautiful red-carpeted flrs., #22 (nice-size air-conditioned rm. w/twin bed, compact bathroom & faces the interior) & 23 (2nd flr. air-conditioned rm. w/ twin bed, private bathroom w/o shower curtain outside the room & faces the interior) are for a single; #21 (2nd flr. air-conditioned rm. w/2 twin beds or zip & lock queen-size bed, small bathroom & faces the street) & 6 (large 1st flr. rm. w/2 twin beds or zip & lock queen-size bed, compact bathroom & faces the interior) are for a double but can fit an extra twin bed for a triple; #7 (2 steps up to large 1st flr. rm. w/2 twin beds or zip & lock queen-size bed, standard-size bathroom w/bathtub & faces the interior) & 25 (2nd flr. air-conditioned rm. w/ 2 twin beds or zip & lock queen-size bed, small bathroom w/o shower curtain & faces the back) are for a double; #24 (2nd flr. air-conditioned rm. w/2 twin beds or zip & lock queen-size bed, private bathroom outside the room & faces the back) is for a double; #10 (large rm. w/2 twin beds or zip & lock queen-size bed, freestanding prefabricated shower in the middle of the room, no toilet & faces the back) is for a double; #20 (large 2nd flr. air-conditioned rm. w/3 twin beds or 1 zip & lock queen-size bed & twin bed, standard-size bathroom & faces the street) & 26 (air-conditioned loft rm. w/2 twin beds on the upper level, 2 twin beds or zip & lock queen-size bed on the lower-level, small bathroom & faces the back w/no view) are for a triple but can fit an extra twin bed for a family; the 6 rooms w/o private bathrooms share 2 communal bathrooms; fans, noisy location, lots of stairs, no elevator, 2 flrs. Newly (2000) owned/managed by Emiliano Concilio. *5% rm. discount when you show him this book.* Cross street: Via Ventisette (XX) Aprile. Taxi to hotel.

EUROPA: Via Cavour 14, 2nd fl. **Tel/Fax:** 055-210361.
Web site: http://www.webhoteleuropa.com/
E-mail: firenze@webhoteleuropa.com (13 rms., all w/toilet & bath or shower.) 102€ single; 142€ double; 184€ triple; 205€ quad. Breakfast (7:30-9:30am, yogurt, assorted breads, cheese, self-serve cappuccino) is included in the rates & can be served in the room (3€ extra pp). Air-conditioned. Visa, MC, AX, DC. English spoken (Miriam & Gassim), phones, cable TV w/CNN, wonderful charming nice hotel w/simply (3rd flr.) to nicely (2nd flr.) furnished nice-size rms., #48 (small rm. w/2 twin beds, small bathroom & wonderful view of the top of the Duomo) & 43 (nice-size rm. w/French double bed, small bathroom & faces the street) are for a single or discounted for 2 slim people in love; #42 (small rm. w/twin bed, small bathroom & faces the back) is for a single; #47 (wonderful 2nd flr. rm. w/2 twin beds or zip & lock king-size bed, small bathroom & small balcony that faces the back w/partial view of the top of the Duomo), 52 (walk up one flight to huge 3rd flr. rm w/2 twin beds or zip & lock king-size bed, bathroom w/bathtub & wonderful view of the top of the Duomo) & 46 (2nd flr. rm. w/2 twin beds) are for a double; #53 (walk up one flight to large 3rd flr. rm w/3 twin beds or 1 zip & lock queen-size bed & twin bed, standard-size bathroom & partial view of the tip of the Duomo) is for a triple; #49 (bright airy rm. w/3 twin beds or 1 zip & lock queen-size bed & twin bed, small bathroom & wonderful view of the top of the Duomo) & 50 (bright airy rm. w/3 twin beds or 1 zip & lock queen-size bed & twin bed, convertible chair/bed, small bathroom & wonderful view of the top of the Duomo) are for a triple but can fit an extra twin bed for a family; hairdriers,

frigobars, charming breakfast room w/16th-century frescoed ceiling, elevator only goes to 2nd flr., 2 flrs. Owned/managed by wonderful charming & adorable Gassim (Somalian), Maria & Miriam Abicar (husband, wife & daughter) for more than 30 years. *10% rm. discount when you show them this book.* They are quite proud of the fact that their hotel was written up favorably by the N.Y. Times. For directions, see Hotel Casci.

FIORITA: Via Fiume 20, 3rd fl. **Tel:** 055-283189. **Fax:** 055-2728153. **Web site:** http://www.hotelfiorita.com/ **E-mail:** htlfior@tin.it (13 rms., 11 w/toilet & shower.) 83€ single; 134€ double; 169€ triple; 200€ quad. The rooms without bathrooms are cheaper. Breakfast (7:15-10am) is included in the rates & can be served in the room. Air-conditioned. Visa, MC, AX, DC. English spoken (Massimo & Roberto), phones, cable TV w/CNN, charming nice hotel w/nicely & identically furnished nice-size to large rms., #2 (nice-size rm. w/ twin bed & standard-size bathroom) is the only single rm.; #10 & 4 (both large rms. w/2 twin beds or zip & lock queen-size bed, standard-size bathrooms & face the street) are for a double; #8 (nice-size rm. w/2 twin beds or zip & lock queen-size bed & small bathroom) is for a double; #3 (wonderful huge corner rm. w/3 twin beds or 1 zip & lock queen-size bed & twin bed, high decorative antique ceiling, large bathroom & 2 windows) is for a triple; #1 (huge rm. w/4 twin beds or 1 zip & lock queen-size bed & 2 twin beds & compact bathroom) is for a family; there is one 4th flr. communal bathroom & two 3rd flr. communal bathrooms for the two 4th flr. rooms (#18 & 19) to share; rooms w/bathrooms have hairdriers & frigobars, high ceilings, charming breakfast room w/small terrace, bar, elevator, 2 flrs., parking (14€ per day). Owned/managed by delightful & accommodating Massimo & Roberto Maselli. *10% rm. discount when you show them this book.* For directions, see Hotel Annabella.

GINORI: Via Ginori 24, 2nd fl. **Tel:** 055-218615.
Tel/Fax: 055-211392. (7 rms., all w/toilet & shower.)
Web site: http://www.hotelginori.com/ **E-mail:** hotelginori@dada.it 115€ double; 155€ triple; 195€ quad. Breakfast (8-10am) is included in the rates. Air-conditioned. Visa, MC. English spoken (Clara & Ann), phones, cable TV w/CNN, charming hotel w/simply & iden-

tically modern pinewood furnished rms., #22 (nice-size 2nd flr. rm. near reception w/2 twin beds or zip & lock queen-size bed, small bathroom w/shower over toilet & faces the interior), 28 (nice-size 3rd flr. rm. w/2 twin beds or zip & lock queen-size bed, 5 steps up to compact bathroom & faces the interior), 32 (nice-size 3rd flr. rm. w/ 2 twin beds or zip & lock queen-size bed, small bathroom w/shower over toilet & faces the interior) & 23 (2nd flr. rm. w/double bed & faces the interior) are for a double; #21 (huge 2nd flr. rm. near reception w/3 twin beds or 1 zip & lock queen-size bed & twin bed, small bathroom w/shower over toilet & faces the street) & 24 (2nd flr. rm. w/3 twin beds or 1 zip & lock queen-size bed, standard-size bathroom & faces the interior) are for triple; #25 (nice-size 2nd flr. rm. w/2 twin beds, double bed, standard-size bathroom & faces the street) is for family; quaint breakfast room w/2 wooden benches & sloped wood-beamed ceiling, bar, lots of stairs, reception is two steep flights up, no elevator, 3 flrs. Owned/managed by Ann Elsasser. *5% rm. discount when you show her this book.* Cross street: Via Taddea. With the train tracks at your back, exit to the left near track #16, cross the street to McDonald's which is near the corner of Via Nazionale, walk up Via Nazionale about 5 blocks, turn right onto Via Guelfa, turn right onto Via Ginori. (Closed 1 wk. in Aug. & 2 wks. in Dec.)

GLOBUS: Via S. Antonio 24, 1st fl. **Tel:** 055-211062. **Fax:** 055-2396225. **Web site:** http://www.hotelglobus.com/
E-mail: info@hotelglobus.com (23 rms., all w/toilet & bath or shower.) 74€ single; 124€ double; 152€ triple; 178€ quad. Call for quint rates. Breakfast (7:30-10am) is included in the rates & can be served in the room (11€ extra pp). Air-conditioned. Visa, MC, AX. I didn't look at any of the rooms because they were in the middle of renovations which made it impossible to describe them. This wonderful charming hotel will be totally refurbished before this book's publication. English spoken (Serena, Michele, Nicholas & Andrea), phones, cable TV w/CNN, #309 (large rm. w/view of church) is for a double; #101 (2 rms. w/4 twin beds or 1 zip & lock queen-size bed & 2 twin beds) is for a family but can fit an extra twin bed for a quint; modern bathrooms w/hairdriers, 2 rms. have handicapped access, Internet access available at 6€ per 1/2 hr., bar, one flight up (equipped w/mobile chair) to elevator, 4 flrs. Owned by Serena Forzieri & man-

aged by Michele Piccione. *10% rm. discount when you show them this book.* From the station, walk straight to Piazza Unita Italiana, turn left onto Via San Antonio. (Closed 2 wks. in Dec.)

IL BARGELLINO: Via Guelfa 87. **Tel:** 055-2382658. **Fax:** 055-2382698. **Web site:** http://www.ilbargellino.com/
E-mail: carmel@ilbargellino.com (10 rms., 5 w/toilet & shower.) 79€ single; 84€ double; 115€ triple; 147€ quad. The rooms without bathrooms are cheaper. No breakfast served. Visa, MC. English spoken (Carmel), no phones, no TV, quaint pleasant hotel w/mixture of modern to old-fashioned antique furnished bright nice-size pretty rms., original marble flrs., #6 (walk one flight up to large rm. w/king-size bed, huge bathroom w/bathtub & faces the street) is for a double but can fit an extra twin bed for a triple; #9 (walk one flight up to rm. w/ 2 twin beds or zip & lock queen-size bed & small bathroom) & 5 (walk one flight up to rm. w/2 twin beds or zip & lock queen-size bed, small bathroom w/o shower curtain & faces the street) are for a double; #9 (see above), 10 (walk one flight up to rm. w/double bed, freestanding prefabricated shower in the middle of the room & no toilet), 7 & 8 are large rooms that open up onto a wonderful large garden public terrace but with no private windows, high ceilings, hairdriers (5 rms.), frigobars (5 rms.), quiet location, no elevator, 2 flrs. Owned/managed by wonderful & charming Pino & Carmel Gallo. Carmel is originally from the U.S. With the train tracks at your back, exit to the left near track #16, cross the street to McDonald's, walk up Via Nazionale, turn left onto Via Guelfa. 15-min. walk. Cross street: Via Pratello. It might be easier to take a taxi because of the amount of people you have to go through to walk to the hotel. (Closed Christmas wk.)

JOHANNA: Via Bonifacio Lupi 14, 1st fl. **Tel:** 055-481896. **Fax:** 055-482721. **Web site:** http://www.johanna.it/
E-mail: lupi@johanna.it (11 rms., 9 w/toilet & shower.) 52€ single; 85€ double. Instant prepared breakfast is included in the rates & already in the room. Cash only. English spoken (Stephanie), no phones, no TV, wonderful charming 19th-century palace hotel w/nicely & identically furnished nice-size pretty rms., #1 (fabulous rm. w/wrought iron French double bed & private bathroom outside the rm.) & 4 (twin bed & private bathroom outside the rm. & faces the garden) are for a

single; #2 (queen-size bed & standard-size bathroom), 3, 5, 6, 7, 8, 9 & 10 are for a double; high ceilings, reception desk closes at 7pm, quiet residential location, elevator, 1 fl. Owned/managed by Evelyne Arriahi & Lea Gulmanelli. Lea also owns/manages the wonderful Hotel Johlea I & II. Cross street: Via Zara. Taxi to hotel.

JOHLEA I & II: Via San Gallo 80, 3rd fl. **Tel:** 055-4633292. **Fax:** 055-4634552. **Web site:** http://www.johanna.it/ **E-mail:** johlea@johanna.it (15 rms., all w/toilet & shower.) 75€ (standard) single; 94€ (superior) single; 99€ double; 109€ (superior) double; 120€ (suite) double. Call for triple rates. Instant prepared breakfast is included in the rates. Air-conditioned. Cash only. English spoken (Paola), phones, TV, 2-in-1 renovated 19th-century new (2001) hotel w/nicely to beautifully furnished nice-size pretty rms., original tiled flrs., Johlea 1 (7 rms.): #3 (standard rm. w/French double bed, small bathroom & faces the garden) is for a single; #4 (superior rm. w/ double bed on lower-level, wooden stairs up to loft w/convertible sofa) is for a single; #1 (standard rm. w/2 twin beds or zip & lock queen-size bed, standard-size bathroom & faces the garden) & 2 (standard rm. w/2 twin beds or zip & lock queen-size bed, small bathroom & faces the garden) are for a double; #7 (2 twin beds or zip & lock queen-size bed & standard-size bathroom) when it becomes available will be for a double; #5 (superior rm. w/2 twin beds or zip & lock queen-size bed on lower-level, wooden stairs up to loft w/convertible sofa, large bathroom w/bathtub & faces the side street) & 6 (large superior rm. w/king-size bed, sitting area w/convertible chair/ bed, small bathroom & faces the street) is for a double; modern bathrooms w/towel heaters, high ceilings, safety boxes, access to communal refrigerator, reception desk closes at 8pm, small narrow circular staircase to rooftop terrace w/magnificent panoramic view, quiet residential location, 6 steps up to elevator, 1 fl. Johlea II (8 rms.): Located 2 doors down at Via San Gallo 76, 1st fl. I did not see these rooms but I was told that the 8 rooms are as nicely furnished as the rooms in Johlea 1. #8 (standard rm.) is for a single; #4, 5 & 7 (all standard rms.) are for a double; #2 & 6 (both superior rms.) are for a double; #1 (suite) is for a double. Owned/managed by Lea Gulmanelli. Cross street: Via Salvestrina. Taxi to hotel.

KURSAAL-AUSONIA: Via Nazionale 24, 2nd fl. **Tel:** 055-496324. **Fax:** 055-4626615. **Web site:** http://www.kursonia.com/ **E-mail:** info@kursonia.com (30 rms., 19 w/toilet & shower.) 70€ (standard rm. #14) single; 89€ (superior) single; 110€ (standard rm. #12 & 31) double; 128€ (superior) double; 138€ (standard rm. #13) triple; 160€ (superior) triple; 170€ (standard rm. #13) quad; 192€ (superior) quad. The rooms without bathrooms are cheaper. Breakfast (8-10am) is included in the rates & can be served in the room (5€ extra pp). Air-conditioned (16 superior rms.), Visa, MC. English spoken (Paola & Celeste), phones, cable TV w/CNN (16 superior rms.), wonderful charming hotel w/nicely furnished bright airy nice-size rms, mixture of carpeted & shiny tiled flrs., superior (16 air-conditioned) rms.: #28 (small superior rm. near reception w/double bed, carpeted flr. & small bathroom) is for a single or 2 slim people in love; #37 (large superior honeymoon rm. w/2 twin beds or zip & lock queen-size bed, large bathroom & large balcony w/rooftops view) is for a double; #35 (fabulous large superior rm. w/2 twin beds or zip & lock king-size bed, red-brick tiled flr., convertible chair/bed, standard-size bathroom w/large shower stall & small window w/view of the top of the Duomo), 34 (fabulous huge superior rm. w/2 twin beds or zip & lock king-size bed, red-brick tiled flr., convertible chair/bed, standard-size bathroom w/large shower stall & faces the street) & 25 (large superior corner rm. w/2 twin beds or zip & lock queen-size bed, convertible sofa, red-brick tiled flr., compact bathroom & window w/rooftops view) are perfect for a double but too snug for a triple; #27 (superior rm. w/2 twin beds or zip & lock queen-size bed, carpeted flr., small bathroom & balcony w/rooftops view), 36 (nice-size superior rm. w/2 twin beds or zip & lock queen-size bed, standard-size bathroom & small window w/view of the top of the Duomo), 29 (large superior rm. near reception w/2 twin beds or zip & lock queen-size bed, carpeted flr. & standard-size bathroom), 6 (superior rm. w/2 twin beds or zip & lock queen-size bed, tiled flr., standard-size bathroom w/circular shower stall & faces the street), 7 (superior rm. w/2 twin beds or zip & lock queen-size bed, tiled flr., standard-size bathroom & faces the side street), 32 (superior rm. w/2 twin beds or zip & lock queen-size bed, marble flr., small bathroom w/o shower curtain & faces the street) & 33 (superior rm. w/2 twin beds or zip & lock queen-size bed, marble flr., small bathroom w/o shower curtain & faces the street) are for a double; #10 (large superior corner rm. w/3 twin beds or 1 zip & lock king-size bed & twin bed, tiled flr., small bathroom & faces the side street), 5 (large superior rm. w/ 3 twin beds or 1 zip & lock queen-size bed & twin bed, futon convertible chair/bed, tiled flr., standard-size bathroom & faces the street) & 4 (large superior rm. w/3 twin beds or 1 zip & lock queen-size bed & twin bed) are for a triple; all the rooms on the right side of the 3rd flr. are superior except for the wonderful rm. #31; standard rms. have no TV & minibars: #14 (walk one flight up to nice-size standard rm. w/twin bed, wood-beamed ceiling, small bathroom w/o shower curtain & view of the top of the Duomo) is for a single; #31 (wonderful standard small air-conditioned rm. near the breakfast room w/2 twin beds or zip & lock queen-size bed, red-brick tiled flr., frigobar, small bathroom w/o shower curtain & faces the street) is for a double; #12 (wonderful standard rm. w/2 twin beds positioned toe-to-toe, tiled flr., small bathroom & window w/view of the top of the Duomo & rooftops) is for a double; #13 (wonderful standard rm. w/3 twin beds or 1 zip & lock queen-size bed & twin bed, futon convertible chair/ bed, small bathroom & faces the back) is for a triple; there is 1 handicapped access bathroom on each floor, minibars (16 superior rms.), hairdriers (16 superior rms.), high ceilings, Internet access available at 4€ per 1/2 hr., bar, small outside terrace, elevator, 2 flrs. Owned/ managed by Giovanpaolo & warm Paola Angelini (husband & wife). *5% rm. discount when you show them this book.* You can receive free E-mail messages at the hotel. With the train tracks at your back, exit to the left near track #16, cross the street to McDonald's which is near the corner of Via Nazionale.

NUOVA ITALIA: Via Faenza 26. **Tel:** 055-268430 or 287508. **Fax:** 055-210941. **Web site:** http://www.hotelnuovaitalia.com/ **E-mail:** hotel.nuova.italia@dada.it (20 rms., all w/toilet & shower.) 92€ single; 129€ double; 160€ triple; 192€ quad. Rates are 8% cheaper if you pay in cash. Breakfast (7-10am) is included in the rates & can be served in the room (3€ extra pp). Air-conditioned. Visa, MC, AX. English spoken (Luciano, Eileen, Daniela & Madeleine), phones, cable TV w/CNN, wonderful charming 17th-century renovated bldg. w/ nicely furnished bright rms., beautiful carpeted flrs., #10 (French double bed & small bathroom) is for a single or discounted for 2 slim people in love; there are 4 other rooms similar to #10; #18 (nice-size rm. w/2 twin beds or zip & lock king-size bed & large bathroom) is for a double but can fit an extra twin bed for a triple; #14 (nice-size corner rm. w/3 twin beds or 1 zip & lock king-size bed & twin bed, high ceiling, small bathroom & 2 windows) & 15 (nice-size rm. w/3 twin beds or 1 zip & lock king-size bed & twin bed, high ceiling, small bathroom & 2 windows) are for a triple but can fit an extra twin bed for a family; Luciano takes great pride in the original paintings & posters that hang on the walls of the rooms, mosquito window screens, bar, no elevator, 2 flrs. Owned/managed by wonderful, charming & informative Luciano & Eileen (Canadian) Vita (husband & wife). *8% rm. discount when you show them this book and pay in cash.* They try very hard to please their guests. With the train tracks at your back, exit to the left near track #16, cross the street to McDonald's, walk up Via Nazionale, turn right onto Via Faenza. (Closed Dec.)

PEZZATI I DANIELA: Via San Zanobi 22, 2nd fl. **Tel:** 055-291660. **Fax:** 055-287145. **Web site:** http://www.soggiornopezzati.it/ **E-mail:** 055287145@iol.it (6 rms., all w/toilet & shower.) 53€ single; 85€ double; 110€ triple. No breakfast served. Air-conditioned (9€ extra per day). Visa, MC. English spoken (Daniela), charming hotel w/modern pinewood furnished nice-size bright airy rms., #4 (twin bed & compact bathroom) is for a single; #3 (2 twin beds or zip & lock queen-size bed & small bathroom w/o shower curtain), 1 & 2 are all air-conditioned rooms for a double; #6 (room near reception w/2 twin beds, compact bathroom & faces the side street) is for a double; #5 (2 twin beds or zip & lock king-size bed, dining area & compact bathroom) is for a double but can fit an extra twin bed for a triple; frigobars, windows w/mosquito screens, fans, reception is two flights up, no elevator, 2 flrs. Owned/managed by Daniela Pezzati. *5% rm. discount when you show her this book.* Daniela's family also manages Hotel Pezzati II (which I did not see) across the Arno river. Taxi to hotel.

PICCOLO: Via San Gallo 51. **Tel:** 055-475519. **Fax:** 055-474515. **Web site:** http://www.piccolohotelfirenze.com/ **E-mail:** info@piccolohotelfirenze.com (10 rms., all w/toilet & shower.) 99€ single; 137€ double; 173€ triple; 205€ quad. Breakfast (8-9:30am) at 6€ pp can be served in the room (3€ extra pp). Visa, MC, AX,

DC. English spoken (Silvia, Sandra & Duccio), phones, cable TV w/ CNN, Eurosport & CNBC, charming renovated hotel w/nicely pinewood furnished rms. w/no views, wooden & carpeted flrs., #5 (French double bed, worn carpeted flr. & standard-size bathroom) is for a single or discounted for 2 slim people in love; #4 (large 1st flr. rm. w/2 twin beds or zip & lock king-size bed, wooden flr., standard-size bathroom & balcony that faces the garden), 2 (nice-size 1st flr. rm. w/2 twin beds or zip & lock queen-size bed, wooden flr., large bathroom & faces the back), 3 (1st flr. rm. w/2 twin beds or zip & lock queen-size bed, worn carpeted flr. & faces the garden) & 1 (1st flr. rm. w/2 twin beds or zip & lock queen-size bed, worn carpeted flr. & small bathroom) are for a double; #8 (large 2nd flr. rm. w/2 twin beds or zip & lock queen-size bed, wooden flr., small bathroom & faces the back) & 7 (2nd flr. rm. w/2 twin beds or zip & lock queen-size bed, worn carpeted flr., 2 steps up to small bathroom & faces the back) are for a double; #9 (large 2nd flr. rm. w/3 twin beds or 1 zip & lock queen-size bed & twin beds, worn carpeted flr., original nonworking fireplace, small bathroom & 2 windows that face the back) is for a triple; #6 (large 2nd flr. rm. w/4 twin beds or 1 zip & lock queen-size bed & 2 twin beds, worn carpeted flr., standard-size bathroom w/bathtub w/hand-held shower & 2 windows that face the street) is for a family; floor fans, quiet location, lots of stairs, no elevator, 2 flrs. Owned/managed by Silvia Angeloni. Cross street: Via Ruote. Taxi to hotel.

SAMPAOLI: Via San Gallo 14. **Tel:** 055-284834. **Tel/Fax:** 055-282448. **Web site:** http://www.hotelsampaoli.it/ **E-mail:** hotelflorence@inwindit (12 rms., 6 w/toilet & shower.) 59€ single; 97€ double; 128€ triple; 150€ quad. Call for quint rates. The rooms without bathrooms are cheaper. No breakfast served. Visa, MC, AX, DC. English spoken (Floriana), no phones, no TV, charming hotel w/ nicely old-fashioned furnished rms., #7 (1st flr. rm. w/French double bed, 1 step up to large handicapped access bathroom & small balcony that faces the back w/rooftops view) is for a single or discounted for 2 slim people in love; #6 (2 twin beds or zip & lock queen-size bed, 1 step up to bathroom w/o shower curtain & faces the interior), 13 (2nd flr. 2 twin beds or zip & lock queen-size bed, standard-size bathroom w/o shower curtain & small window that faces the interior) & 5 (1st flr. rm. near reception w/2 twin beds or zip & lock queen-size bed, 1 step up to handicapped access bathroom w/o shower curtain & faces the interior) are for a double; #8 (small rm. w/2 twin beds or zip & lock queen-size bed, sometimes can have a private bathroom w/o shower curtain outside the room & faces the street) is for a double; #3 (wonderful antique furnished 1st flr. rm. near reception w/3 twin beds or 1 zip & lock king-size bed & twin bed, antique flr., original red-brick nonworking fireplace, lots of character, standard-size bathroom w/o shower curtain & 2 windows that face the street) is for a triple; #11 (huge 2nd flr. rm. w/4 twin beds or 1 zip & lock king-size bed & 2 twin beds, convertible chair/bed, bathroom & 2 small windows) is for a family or quint; the 6 rooms w/o bathrooms share 4 communal bathrooms, access to communal refrigerator, free Internet access available, warm ambience, no elevator, 2 flrs. Newly (2001) owned/managed by wonderful Valentino Camastro & Morar Genssler (husband & American wife), Leonardo Caponi & Francesca Mele. *10% rm. discount when you show them this book.* With the train tracks at your back, exit to the left near track #16, cross the street to McDonald's, walk up Via Nazionale, turn right onto Via Guelfa, turn left onto Via San Gallo.

SERENA: Via Fiume 20, 1st fl. **Tel:** 055-213643. **Fax:** 055-280447. **Web site:** http://www.emmeti.it/aserena/ **E-mail:** thserena@dada.it (8 rms., all w/toilet & shower.) 90€ double; 123€ triple. Call for quad rates. Breakfast (7:30-9:30am) at 6€ pp. Visa, MC, AX. English spoken (Antonella), phones, cable TV w/CNN, wonderful plain hotel w/simply furnished bright airy rms. & wooden flrs. The rooms will be totally refurbished before this book's publication. #4 (wonderful large corner rm. w/2 twin beds or zip & lock king-size bed, standard-size bathroom & balcony w/2 huge windows that face the street) is for a double; #3 (large rm. w/2 twin beds or zip & lock king-size bed & standard-size bathroom) & 1 (large rm. w/2 twin beds or zip & lock king-size bed, standard-size bathroom & faces the street) are for a double but can fit an extra twin bed for a triple; #5 (wonderful large rm. w/3 twin beds or 1 zip & lock king-size bed & twin bed, standard-size bathroom & balcony that faces the back) is for a triple; hairdriers, high ceilings, stained-glass French doors, elevator, 1 flr. Owned/managed by wonderful charming Giovanni &

Maria Bigazzi (husband & wife). *15% rm. discount when you show them this book.* For directions, see Hotel Annabella.

STELLA MARY: Via Fiume 17, 2nd fl. **Tel:** 055-281877 or 215694. **Fax:** 055-264206. **Web site:** http://www.stellamary.3000.it/ **E-mail:** smh@dada.it (7 rms., all w/toilet & bath or shower.) 124€ double; 171€ triple; 199€ quad. Call for single rates. Breakfast (8-10am) is included in the rates & can be served in the room. Air-conditioned. Visa, MC, AX. English spoken (Sirmone & Victoria), phones, TV, wonderful simple hotel w/nicely furnished large bright airy rms., wooden flrs., #26 (large rm. w/2 twin beds or zip & lock king-size bed, standard-size bathroom w/shower & balcony w/floor-to-ceiling window that faces the garden) & 23 (huge rm. w/2 twin beds or zip & lock king-size bed, standard-size bathroom w/bathtub & faces the back) are for a double but can fit an extra twin bed for a triple; #24 (nice-size rm. w/2 twin beds or zip & lock king-size bed, standard-size bathroom w/bathtub & faces the square) & 27 (nice-size rm. w/ 2 twin beds or zip & lock king-size bed, standard-size bathroom w/ shower & faces the garden) are for a double; #21 (huge rm. w/3 twin beds, standard-size bathroom w/bathtub & faces the street) is for a triple but can fit an extra twin bed for a family; #25 (large rm. w/3 twin beds or 1 zip & lock king-size bed & twin bed, standard-size bathroom w/shower & faces the square) is for a triple; hairdriers, high ceilings, bar, elevator, 1fl. Owned/managed by friendly & charming Victoria & Sirmone Becagli (mother & son). Same family manages the wonderful Hotel Annabella in the same bldg. For directions, see Hotel Annabella.

HOTEL (Oltrarno, south of the Arno river)
SCALETTA (LA): Via Guicciardini 13, 2nd fl. **Tel:** 055-283028 or 214255. **Fax:** 055-289562. **Web site:** http://www.lascaletta.com/ **E-mail:** info@lascaletta.com (15 rms., 11 w/toilet & bath or shower.) 100€ single; 120€ (small rm. #31) double; 142€ double; 163€ triple; 188€ quad. The rooms without bathrooms are cheaper. Buffet breakfast (8-9:30am, cereals, cheese, assorted breads) is included in the rates & can be served in the room (4€ extra pp). Air-conditioned (8 rms.) Visa, MC. English spoken (Manfredo & Matteo), phones, cable TV w/CNN on request (extra cost per day), wonderful charming reno-

vated palace hotel w/nicely old-fashioned furnished rms., most w/ original flrs., #25 (twin bed & bathroom w/shower) is the only single rm.; #30 (walk one flight down to wonderful large rm. w/2 twin beds or zip & lock king-size bed, high ceiling, compact bathroom & large window w/no view) & 20 (large rm. w/2 twin beds or zip & lock queen-size bed, compact bathroom & small window w/rooftops view) are for a double; #31 (small rm. w/2 twin beds or zip & lock queen-size bed, compact bathroom & faces the street) is for a double; #21 (wonderful huge rm. w/3 twin beds or 1 zip & lock queen-size bed & twin bed, standard-size bathroom & w/magnificent rooftops view), 27 (huge rm. w/3 twin beds or 1 zip & lock queen-size bed & twin bed, 2 steps down to large bathroom w/bathtub & no view) & 29 (huge rm. w/3 twin beds or 1 zip & lock queen-size bed & twin bed, nonworking fireplace, small bathroom & faces the street) are for a triple; #32 (wonderful huge rm. w/4 twin beds or 1 zip & lock queen-size bed & 2 twin beds, marble nonworking fireplace, high ceiling, compact bathroom & 2 large windows w/no views) is for a family; hairdriers, lots of character, wonderful ambience, small terrace where snacks & wine are served, rooftop terrace w/magnificent panoramic view, bar, walk toward the back to the left & up 5 steps to elevator, 2 flrs. Owned/managed by wonderful charming chef Manfredo who claims to be a fabulous cook. *5% rm. discount when you show him this book.* Cross street: Piazza Pitti. Taxi to hotel.

HOTELS (West of SMN train station)
ABACO: Via Banchi 1, 2nd fl. **Tel:** 055-2381919. **Fax:** 055-282289. Bruno's mobile: 3356078310. **Web site:** http://www.abaco-hotel.it/ **E-mail:** abacohotel@tin.it (8 rms., 3 w/toilet & shower.) 70€ single; 99€ double; 125€ triple; 155€ quad. Rates for the rooms without bathrooms & if you pay cash are cheaper. Breakfast (8-10:30am) at 6€ pp & can be served in the room. Visa, MC, AX. English spoken (Bruno), phones, TV, charming simple hotel w/old-fashioned furnished large rms. that are named after artists shown in the gallery, wooden flrs., #7/Raffaello (2 twin beds or zip & lock king-size bed, compact bathroom & faces the street) is for a double; #1/Botticelli (corner rm. w/2 twin beds or zip & lock king-size bed, convertible chair/bed, compact bathroom & faces the street) is for a double or triple; #6/Michelangelo (3 twin beds & bathroom) is for a triple; #4/

Leonardo DaVinci (2 twin beds or zip & lock queen-size bed, compact shower, no toilet & faces the street), 2/Tiziano (compact shower & no toilet) & 3/Giotto (freestanding prefabricated compact shower in the middle of the room & no toilet) are for a double; #5/Caravaggio & 8/Masaccio both have no bathrooms; high wood-beamed ceilings w/fans, quaint breakfast room w/wooden benches, access to refrigerator to store your food, coin operated laundry machine, free Internet access available, warm ambience, bar, reception is one steep flight up, no elevator, 2 flrs. Owned/managed by wonderful, charming & accommodating Bruno Serratore who is good friends with Luciano, Hotel Ferretti. *5% rm. discount when you show him this book.* Let Bruno know when you are coming or ring the hotel bell so he can help you up the steep steps with your luggage. You come to this hotel to experience Bruno's generous hospitality. With the train tracks at your back, exit to the left near track #16, cross the street to McDonald's, cross the street to Piazza Unita Italiana, continue onto Via Panzani to where it intersects Via Tornabuoni and Via Banchi.

FERRETTI: Via Belle Donne 17. **Tel:** 055-2381328.
Fax: 055-219288. **Web site:** http://www.emmeti.it/Hferretti/ **E-mail:** pensioneferretti@pronet.it (16 rms., 6 w/toilet & shower.) 62€ single; 103€ double; 132€ triple; 152€ quad. The rooms without bathrooms are cheaper. Breakfast (7:30-10am) is included in the rates & can be served in the room. Visa, MC, AX, DC. English spoken (Luciano, Susy & Ermin), phones, no TV, charming simple hotel w/plainly furnished odd-shaped rms., original flrs., #8 (nice-size 1st flr. rm. w/ large twin bed, compact bathroom & faces the side street) is for a single; #6 (large 1st flr. rm. w/2 twin beds or zip & lock queen-size bed, convertible chair/bed, small bathroom & 2 windows that face the side street) & 10 (nice-size 1st flr. rm. w/2 twin beds or zip & lock queen-size bed, standard-size bathroom & faces the interior) are for a double; #3 (nice-size 1st flr. rm. near reception w/2 twin beds or zip & lock queen-size bed, futon convertible chair/bed, compact bathroom & faces the street) is for a double & triple; #1 (nice-size 1st flr. rm. near reception w/2 twin beds or zip & lock queen-size bed, 2 futon convertible chair/beds, compact bathroom & faces the interior) is for a double or triple; #24 (bathroom) is for a double; #9 (nice-size 1st flr. rm. near reception w/French double bed, no bath-

room & faces the interior) is for a single; #2 (nice-size 1st flr. rm. near reception w/2 twin beds, no bathroom & faces the interior) is for a double; #21 (nice-size 2nd fl. rm. w/3 twin beds or 1 zip & lock queen-size bed & twin bed, no bathroom & faces the interior) is for a triple; #11 (3 twin beds or 1 zip & lock queen-size bed & twin bed, futon convertible chair/bed, freestanding prefabricated shower in the middle of the room, no toilet & 2 windows that face the interior) is for a triple or family; #22 (huge 2nd flr. rm. w/4 twin beds, no bathroom & faces the interior) is for a family; #12 has freestanding prefabricated shower in the middle of the room & no toilet; the 10 rooms w/o bathrooms share 4 communal bathrooms; high ceilings, fans, lots of character, warm ambience, free Internet access available, bar, noisy location, no elevator, 3 flrs. Owned/managed by wonderful charming Luciano & Susy Michel (husband & Scottish/South African wife) who are good friends with Bruno, Hotel Abaco. *5% rm. discount when you show them this book.* Luciano is quite experienced in accommodating tourists. He had been a manager at a 4-star hotel for more than 20 years. The hotel itself is quite simple. It is Luciano's attentive & warm personality that makes your stay at this hotel memorable. He goes out of his way to make you feel comfortable and to make sure all your needs are met. He keeps plenty of journals with kind notes from his guests. If you stay at his hotel for 7 nights, Luciano treats you to dinner. With the train tracks at your back, exit to the left near track #16, cross the street to McDonald's, cross the street to Piazza Unita Italiana, continue onto Via Panzani, turn right onto Via Rondinelli, turn right onto Via Trebbio which intersects w/Via Belle Donne.

The perfect way to discover Florence.
Walking Tours of Florence: Piazza Santo Stefano 2, mezzanine level. Tel: 055-2645033. Hrs.: Mon.-Sat. 8am-6pm & Sun. morning. Mobile: 329-6132730. Web site: http://www.artviva.com/ E-mail: staff@artviva.com Hrs.: Daily 8am-8pm. Visa, MC, AX. This company offers a variety of tours from exploring the Uffizi Gallery, downtown Florence, to riding a bike in the countryside. Owned/managed by Pier & Rose (Italian husband & Australian wife) for 4 years. The tours are led by native English-speaking students of American history. Minimum 2 people, maximum 20 people. Reservations required

for all tours. One of the advantages of using this service is for an extra 20€ pp, you can avoid the long lines at the Uffizi Gallery, get an English tour guide & stay a little longer to enjoy the exhibits. I have to thank Giacinto & Louise Bianchi & Susan (Louise's mother), who manage the wonderful charming simple Hotel Perseo (see above). for telling me about this great service.

LAUNDROMATS (Lavanderia)
Daily 8am-10pm. Internet access available at 2€ per 1/2 hr. at all locations.
Near the train station: Wash & Go: Via Guelfa 55r; Wash & Dry: Via Nazionale 129r; Wash & Dry: Via Sole 29/R; Wash & Dry: Via Scala 52/54r; Wash & Dry: Via Scala 30r; Wash & Go: Via Faenza 26r. **Convenient for hotels near Duomo:** Wash & Dry: Via Servi 105r; **convenient for Hotels Dei Mori & Chiazza:** Wash & Dry: Via Ghibellina 143r; **convenient for Hotel La Scaletta:** Wash & Dry: Via Serragli 87r.

TAXI
Tel: 055-4242; Tel: 055-4390; Tel: 055-4499; Tel: 055-4798.

BOOKSTORES
Web site: http://www.feltrinelli.it/ Feltrinelli: Via Cerretani 30/32 Tel: 055-2382652. Fax: 055-288482. Hrs.: Mon.-Sat. 9am-7:30pm. Closed Sun. Visa, MC, AX, DC. Feltrinelli: Via Cavour 12r. Tel: 055-292196. Fax: 051-282183. Hrs.: Mon.-Sat. 9am-7:30pm. Closed Sun. Visa, MC, AX, DC.

INTERNET CAFE
The Netgate has several locations. Train Station. Tel: 055-2399541; Via S.Egidio 14r. Tel: 055-2347967; Via Nazionale 156r. Tel: 055-4628925; Via Cimatori 17r. Tel: 055-219491; Via S.Spirito 14. Tel: 055-2398274; Via Bardi 58r. Tel: 055-214502; Via Martelli 4. Tel: 055-2654510. Web site: http://www.thenetgate.it/

SUPERMARKETS
Conrad: Via Panzani 31. Visa, MC. Hrs. Tues.-Sat. 8:30am-9pm & Mon 2pm-9pm, Closed Sun. & Mon. morning. Near train station;

Standa: Via Pietrapiana 42/44. Visa, MC. Hrs. Mon. 2pm-9pm & Tues.-Sat. 8:30am-9pm. Closed Sun. & Mon.

RESTAURANTS

All the restaurants listed below were selected by Giacinto & Louise Bianchi. They are a wonderful Italian-New Zealand couple, who along with Susan (Louise's mother) manage the wonderful charming simple Hotel Perseo (see above). They compiled a list of many tried and proven affordable restaurants in the heart of Florence. With the help of my Italian menu reader *Eating & Drinking in Italy* (see books recommended), and Louise & Giacinto's tips, I experienced some good eating at great prices.

ANITA (DA): Via Vinegia16r. Tel: 055-218698. Hrs.: Mon.-Sat. 12noon-2:30pm & 7pm-9:45pm. Closed Sun. Visa, MC, AX. Specialty: Meat. Small quaint restaurant that serves delicious food. Cross street: Via Parlascio. Also highly recommended by Hotel Dei Mori.

ANTICA MESCITA SAN NICCOLÒ: Via San Niccolò 60r. Tel: 055-2342836. Reservations advised. Hrs.: Mon.-Sat. 12noon-3pm & 7:30pm-12midnight. Closed Sun. & Aug. Cash only. Casual residential neighborhood restaurant with an outdoor street terrace that serves delicious homemade food to locals. Located near Church San Niccolò. Also highly recommended by Hotel Alessandra.

BENVENUTO (DA): Via Mosca 16R. Tel: 055-214833. Mon.-Sat. Hrs.: 12noon-2:30pm & 7pm-10:30pm. Closed Sun. Visa, MC, AX. Reservations required. Specialty: Meat. They do offer a limited selection of fresh fish. Wonderful quaint restaurant that serves delicious food. It continues to be my favorite restaurant. Owner/waiter Giuseppe who speaks English will take wonderful care of you. Just ask him what you should order. It is one of the few restaurants I know of that doesn't have a 2-people minimum on ordering *risotto*. I usually travel alone and am not always able to order it. *Show Giuseppe this book and he will give you a complimentary after-dinner drink.* From the Duomo walk down Via Calzaiuoli to Piazza Signoria, walk through the square, turn left onto Via Ninna near Palazzo Vecchio, which becomes Via Neri. Located on the corner of Via Neri & Via Mosca.

CASALINGA (LA): Via Michelozzi 9r. Tel: 055-218624. Fax: 055-2679143. Hrs.: Mon.-Sat. 12noon-2:30pm & 7pm-9:30pm. Closed Sun., Aug., Sat. & Sun. Visa, MC, AX. Near Piazza Santo Spirito. Also highly recommended by Hotel Abaco.

MASTRO CILIEGIA: Via Matteo Palmieri 30r. Tel: 055-293372. Fax: 055-354811. Hrs.: Wed.-Mon. 12noon-3pm & 7pm-12midnight. Closed Tues. Visa, MC, AX. Casual neighborhood restaurant with an outdoor street terrace that serves delicious homemade food to locals. I had a fabulous time at this restaurant.

PALLOTTINO: Via Isola Stinche 1r. Tel/Fax: 055-289573. Hrs.: Mon.-Sat. 12noon-2:30pm & 6:30pm-9:45pm. Closed Sun. Visa, MC, AX, DC. Simple local restaurant that serves delicious homemade food. The only problem I have is straining to hear an Italian accent. The place is filled with tourists.

PALLE D'ORO: Via Sant'Antonio 43-45r. Tel: 055-288383. Tel/Fax: 055-354811. Web site: http://www.paginegialle.it/palledoro/ Hrs.: Mon.-Sat. 12noon-2:30pm & 6:30pm-9:45pm. Closed Sun. Visa, MC, AX. This charming small restaurant can easily become one of my favorite restaurants. The food was delicious, the ambience casual & warm and the staff most attentive. Luca's family has been managing & cooking at this restaurant since 1860.

13 GOBBI: Via Porcellana 9r. Tel: 055-284015. Hrs.: Mon.-Sat. 12noon-2:30pm & 7:30pm-11pm. Closed Sun. & Aug. Visa, MC, AX. Reservations required. Specialty: Meat. Wonderful huge restaurant that caters to the locals. Owned/managed by Enrico Verrecchia.

ZÀ ZÀ: Piazza Mercato Centrale 26r. Tel: 055-215411. Fax: 055-210756. Hrs.: Mon.-Sat. 11:30am-2:30pm & 6:45pm-11pm. Closed Sun. & major holidays. Visa, MC, AX, DC. Reservations advised. Specialty: Meat. Wonderful large restaurant with street terrace that caters to the locals. Make sure you try their Zà Zà pizza which is unbelievably delicious. Also highly recommended by Hotels Stella Mary & Annabella.

SANDWICHES
I FRATELLINI: Via Cimatori 38r. Tel: 055-2396096. Hrs.: Daily 8am-8pm. Closed Sun. in Feb. & Nov. Cash only. If you want to eat wonderful fresh sandwiches like the locals, try this place. If it weren't for the crowd of locals standing in front of this fabulous small hole in the wall, you might pass it. Locals line up in front and squeeze their way up to the bar to order sandwiches & drinks. You order your food & drinks from the menu hanging on the left side of the bar, just look for the number next to the sandwich, stand in the street to enjoy it and then squeeze your way back to the bar and try to pay. It was great. Owned/managed by the charming Armando & Michele. Let them know if you have any problems trying to order; they both speak English. Cross street: Via Calzaiuoli.

NORCINERIA: Via Sant'Antonio 19/21r Tel: 055-294859. Web site: http://www.lanorcineria.it/ E-mail: mail@lanorcineria.it Hrs.: Mon.-Sat. 8am-8pm & Sun. 9:30am-7:30pm. Cash only. You can't miss the place. There is a table w/a red-&-white checked tablecloth and 4 stuffed pigs sitting at it ready to eat. They serve delicious sandwiches. Perfect for taking on train rides. The only problem is Emanuele, who works behind the counter. He doesn't seem to have much patience if you don't speak Italian. He can be extremely impolite but don't let that stop you from enjoying his sandwiches. (5-min. walk from the train station.)

LUCCA
Tuscany, zip code 55100
Country code 39, city code 0583

TOURIST OFFICE
Vecchia Porta San Donato, Piazzale Verdi. **Tel:** 0583-583150. **Fax:**
0583-312581. Hrs.: Daily 9:30am-5:30pm. Longer hours in summer.
Web site: http://www.comune.lucca.it/ **E-mail:** aptlucca@lunet.it or
aptlucca.info@lunet.it

TRANSPORTATION TIP
It is a 1 1/2-hr. train ride (5€) from Florence to Lucca. There is a
small convenience store at the train station where you can purchase a
map of Lucca. 10-min. walk to the center.

HOTELS
ALLA CORTE ANGELI: Via Angeli 23. **Tel:** 0583-469204. **Fax:**
0583-99189. **Web site:** http://www.allacortedegliangeli.com/ **E-mail:**
info@allacortedegliangeli.com (10 rms., all w/toilet & bath or shower.)
149€ (annex) double; 170€ (main bldg.) double. Call for triple, quad
or quint rates. Buffet breakfast (8-11am, includes ham, cheese & fresh
fruit) is included in the rates (main bldg. rooms only). Air-conditioned. Visa, MC, AX, DC. English spoken (Roberto & Pietro), phones
(main bldg. only), TV, fabulous wonderful charming new (2001) 2-
in-1 renovated 16th-century palace hotel w/beautifully & individually furnished nice-size to large rms. that are named after flowers,
wooden flrs., main bldg. (7 rms.): Paolina (large corner rm. w/2 twin
beds or zip & lock queen-size bed, convertible sofa, large bathroom
w/Jacuzzi bathtub & 3 windows) & Papavero (standard rm. w/2 twin
beds or zip & lock queen-size bed & bathroom w/Jacuzzi bathtub)
have connecting doors but can be rented separately or together as one
family or quint rm.; Rododendro (large rm. w/2 twin beds or zip &
lock king-size bed, bathroom w/Jacuzzi bathtub & faces the back w/
rooftops view), Campanula (ground flr. rm. w/2 twin beds or zip &
lock queen-size bed, large bathroom w/Jacuzzi bathtub & faces the
interior), Strelizia (large standard rm. w/2 twin beds or zip & lock
queen-size bed & bathroom w/Jacuzzi bathtub), Ibisco (2 twin beds
or zip & lock queen-size bed & bathroom w/shower) & Erika (walk

up narrow steep staircase to smallest rm. w/2 twin beds or zip & lock queen-size bed, sloped ceiling & bathroom w/shower) are for a double; Annex (3 beautiful ground flr. rms. w/no phones): Girasole (wonderful huge rm. w/2 twin beds or zip & lock king-size bed, high wood-beamed ceiling & huge bathroom w/shower & marble flr.) & Glicine (wonderful huge rm. w/2 twin beds or zip & lock king-size bed, high arched red-bricked ceiling & huge bathroom w/shower & marble flr.) have connecting doors but can be rented separately as a double or together as one family or quint rm.; Campanelia (wonderful huge rm. w/2 twin beds or zip & lock king-size bed, 2 steps up to sitting area w/convertible sofa, 2 TVs, high arched red-bricked ceiling & huge bathroom w/shower & marble flr.) is for a double, triple or family; modern bathrooms w/hairdriers, bedroom slippers, bathrobes & telephones, frigobars, breakfast room w/fireplace, if you stay in the annex, you have to walk outside to the main bldg. to have breakfast at an extra cost pp, bar, fabulous location, elevator (main bldg. only), parking (11€ per day.). Owned/managed by a young & charming Pietro Bonino. Taxi to hotel. (Closed Dec. 24-26.).

DIANA: Via Molinetto 11. **Tel:** 0583-492202. **Fax:** 0583-467795. **Web site:** http://www.albergodiana.com/
E-mail: info@albergodiana.com (15 rms., 13 w/toilet & shower.) 76€ (annex) single; 75€ (main bldg.) double; 105€ (annex) double; 102€ (main bldg.) triple; 134€ (annex) triple; 116€ (main bldg.) quad; 160€ (annex) quad. The rooms without bathrooms are cheaper. Breakfast (7:30-9:30am) at 6€ pp. Air-conditioned (6 annex rms.). Visa, MC, AX, DC. English spoken (Giovannni & Ivan), phones, cable TV w/CNN, BBC & Sky News (6 annex rms.), wonderful charming 2-in-1 hotel w/simply (main bldg.) to beautifully modern (annex) furnished rms. w/no views, main bldg. (9 ground-flr. rms. w/standard-size bathrooms): #12 & 16 (both w/2 twin beds or zip & lock queen-size bed) are for a double; #20 (one step up to large rm. w/3 twin beds or 1 zip & lock queen-size bed & twin bed & 2 small windows) is for a triple; #18 & 14 (both large rms. w/3 twin beds or 1 zip & lock queen-size bed & twin bed) are for a triple but can fit an extra twin bed for a family; #22 & 24 (both ground-flr. rms. w/entrances off the street & 2 twin beds or zip & lock queen-size bed) share 1 communal bathroom; annex (6 beautiful air-conditioned newly refurbished nonsmok-

ing rms. w/huge modern marble bathrooms w/large shower stalls): #30 (8 steps up to a large ground-flr. rm. w/French double bed, huge bathroom & faces the garden) is for a single; #38 (large 2nd flr. rm. w/2 twin beds or zip & lock queen-size bed, sitting area w/convert-ible sofa, huge bathroom & faces the garden) is for a double; #32 (8 steps up to a ground-flr. rm. w/2 twin beds or zip & lock queen-size bed & huge bathroom) is for a double; #34 (large 1st flr. rm. w/2 twin beds or zip & lock queen-size bed, convertible chair/bed, huge bath-room w/balcony & faces the garden), 36 (large 1st flr. rm. w/2 twin beds or zip & lock queen-size bed, sitting area & huge bathroom) & 40 (large 2nd flr. rm. w/2 twin beds or zip & lock queen-size bed, sitting area & huge bathroom) are for a double; hairdriers, frigobars (6 annex rms.), safety boxes (6 annex rms.), fabulous location, no elevator, 2 flrs. (annex). Owned/managed by Dino, Giovanni & Ivan (father & sons). Cross street: Piazza Martino. Taxi to hotel.

LUNA (LA): Corte Compagni 12. **Tel:** 0583-493634. **Fax:** 0583-490021. **Web site:** http://www.hotellaluna.com/ **E-mail:** laluna@onenet.it (28 rms., 2 suites, all w/toilet & shower.) 72€ single; 109€ double; 177€ (suite #242 & 130) double; 137€ triple; 186€ (suite #242 & 130) triple; 155€ quad. Call for quint rates. Buffet breakfast (7:30-10am, includes ham, cheese & cereals) at 11€ pp can be served in the room (3€ extra pp). Air-conditioned. Visa, MC, AX, DC. English spoken, phones, cable TV w/CNN, wonderful charming renovated 15th-century 2-in-1 hotel w/nicely modern pin-ewood (annex) to nicely to beautifully (main bldg.) furnished rms. w/no views, shiny tiled flrs., main bldg. (15 rms.): #126 (French double bed, wood-beamed ceiling & large bathroom) & 1 other rm. are for single; #241 (super huge beautifully furnished 2nd flr. rm. w/ king-size bed, 2 convertible chair/beds, magnificent 16th-century fres-coed ceiling, standard-size bathroom & 1 huge window) is for a double, triple or family; #240 (huge beautifully furnished corner 2nd flr. rm. w/king-size bed, 16th-century frescoed ceiling, standard-size bathroom & 2 huge windows) is for a double but can fit an extra twin bed for a triple; #239 (large 2nd flr. rm. w/2 twin beds or zip & lock queen-size bed, standard-size bathroom & small balcony that faces the street) is for a double; #122 (nice-size rm. w/2 twin beds or zip & lock queen-size bed & large bathroom w/bathtub) & 125 (2 twin beds or zip & lock queen-size bed, standard-size bathroom & faces the back) are for a double; #242 (super huge fabulous beautifully furnished 2nd flr. suite w/king-size bed, 2 convertible chair/beds, magnificent 16th-century frescoed ceiling, decorative nonworking fireplace & huge bathroom w/Jacuzzi shower) is for a double, triple, family or quint; #130 (large suite w/2 twin beds or zip & lock queen-size bed, living room w/2 convertible chair/beds & separate shower & toilet) is for a double, triple or family; annex (15 rms.): #211 (large twin bed & standard-size bathroom), 212 (large twin bed & standard-size bathroom) & 4 other rms. are for single; #319 (2 twin beds, 2 convertible chair/beds, standard-size bathroom & small window w/tiny view of tower) is for a double; #318, 316 & 209 (all w/2 twin beds or zip & lock queen-size bed & standard-size bathrooms) are for a double; if you stay in the annex, you have to walk outside to the main bldg. to have breakfast; modern bathroom w/hairdriers & towel heaters, minibars, bar, lots of stairs, fabulous location, no elevator (main bldg. 2 flrs.), elevator (annex. 3 flrs.), parking (11€ per day.) Owned/managed by Nino & Nedo Barbieri (brothers). Cross street: Via Fillungo. Taxi to hotel. (Closed Jan. 6-Feb. 2.)

PICCOLO PUCCINI: Via Poggio 9. **Tel:** 0583-55421 or 55239. **Fax**: 0583-53487. **Web site:** http://www.hotelpuccini.com/ **E-mail:** info@hotelpuccini.com (14 rms., all w/toilet & shower.) 62€ single; 92€ double. Breakfast (8-11am) at 4€ pp. Visa, MC, AX, DC. English spoken, phones, TV, wonderful charming hotel w/nicely & identically modern furnished rms. w/no views, carpeted flrs., #53 & 51 (nice-size rms. w/double beds & compact bathrooms) are for a single; #22 (large twin bed & small bathroom) is for a single; #54 (corner rm. w/standard-size bathroom) is for a double; #21 & 30 (both w/2 twin beds or zip & lock queen-size bed & small bathrooms) are for a double; high ceilings w/fans, safety boxes, warm ambience, bar, fabulous location, no elevator, 1 flr., parking (17€ per day.) Owned/managed by Paolo Mancini. Taxi to hotel.

TAXI
Tel: 0583-492691. Tel: 0583-494190. Tel: 0583-581305.

LAUNDROMAT (Lavanderia)
Niagara: Via Rosi 26. Hrs.: Daily 8am-10pm.

MENAGGIO
Lake Como, zip code 22017
Country code 39, city code 0344

TOURIST OFFICE
Piazza Garibaldi 4. **Tel/Fax:** 0344-32924. Hrs.: Mon.-Sat. 9am-12noon & 3pm-6pm. Closed Sun. Longer hours in summer. **Web site:** http://www.menaggio.com/ **E-mail:** infomenaggio@tiscalinet.it

TRANSPORTATION TIP
Before purchasing individual boat tickets to see the different towns, look into the all-day ticket (7€ pp). They are great; you can hop on & off the boats to the various towns. Visa, MC. **Web site:** http://www.navigazionelaghi.it/ **E-mail:** navicomo@navigazionelaghi.it

HOTEL
IL VAPORE: Piazza Grossi 3. **Tel:** 0344-32229. **Fax:** 0344-34850. **Web site:** http://www.italiaabc.com/ (10 rms., all w/toilet & shower.) 35€ (rm. #27) single; 57€ (no view) double; 62€ (view) double. Call for triple rates. Breakfast (8-10am) at 7€ pp. Cash only. No English spoken, phones, no TV, charming simple hotel w/plainly & identically furnished rms., #27 (small rm. that faces the back w/no view) is for a single; #25 (corner rm. w/2 twin beds or zip & lock queen-size bed) & 26 (queen-size bed) both large rms. w/balconies that face the square w/views of water & are for a double; #28 (3rd flr. corner rm. w/queen-size bed & tiny balcony that faces the square w/ small view of water) & 21 (2 twin beds or zip & lock queen-size bed & patio door that faces the square w/view of water) are for a double; #29 (3rd flr. corner rm. w/2 twin beds or zip & lock queen-size bed, convertible sofa & tiny balcony that faces the square w/small view of water) & 22 (2 twin beds or zip & lock queen-size bed, convertible sofa & window that faces the square w/view of water) are for a double, triple or family; #20, 23 & 24 (all w/2 twin beds or zip & lock queen-size bed & face the back w/no views) are for a double; wooden ceilings, small bathrooms, restaurant, wonderful location in a square behind the tourist office, no elevator, 3 flrs. Owned/managed by wonderful, warm & accommodating Gigi, Pinuccia & Simone (father, mother & son). Taxi to hotel. (Closed Nov. & 20 days in Feb.)

TAXI
Piazza Garibaldi. Tel: 0344-31244.

SUPERMARKET
Super Cappa: Via IV Novembre 87. Hrs.: Mon.-Sat. 8am-12:30pm & 3:30pm-7:30pm. Closed Sun. Opposite the boat dock.

RESTAURANT
VECCHIA MENAGGIO: Via al Lago 13. Tel: 0344-32082. Fax: 0344-30141. Visa, MC. Hrs.: Wed.-Mon. 12noon-2pm & 6:30pm-10pm. Closed Tues. Visa. MC. Specialty: Pizza. Located around the corner from the tourist office. Highly recommended by Pinuccia, Hotel Il Vapore.

MILAN (Milano)
Lombardy, zip code 20121
Country code 39, city code 02

Milan's Tourist Information Centers

1.) Piazza Duomo/Via Marconi 1 **Tel:** 02-72524301. **Fax:** 02-72524350. Located to the right as you face the church. Hrs.: Mon.-Fri. 8:45am-1pm & 2pm-6pm; Sat. & Sun. 9am-1pm. & 2pm-5pm. Longer hours in summer. **2.**) Train station: **Tel:** 02-72524360. Hrs.: Mon.-Sat. 9am-6:30pm; Sun. 9am-12:30pm. & 1:30pm-5pm. Located on the top level facing away from the tracks. **E-mail:** apt.info@libero.it

TRANSPORTATION FROM MALPENSA AIRPORT TO CENTER

Airport Web site: http://www.sea-aeroportimilano.it/
Tel: 02-74852200.
You can either catch an airport shuttle bus, the Malpensa express train or a taxi from the Malpensa airport to the center. I have only used the airport express shuttle bus. However, I was able to get detailed information on the Malpensa express train from the tourist office. The **airport express shuttle bus** departs approximately every 1/2 hr. in the morning & every hour until late evening from Milan's Malpensa airport for 1-hr. ride (6€ pp) to the Milan's Central train station. Tickets can be purchased at the shuttle bus ticket office at the airport. When you exit through the doors from customs, walk straight, then walk to your right to the ticket office where you buy your shuttle bus ticket to the Central station. Exit the airport & get in the line for the bus to "Centrale Station." The **Malpensa Express train** departs every 1/2 hr. until late evening from Malpensa airport for 40-min. ride (10€ pp, cheaper for Alitalia passengers) to the Milan's Cadorna North Railways train/metro station which is more convenient & much closer to the the Duomo than Milan's Central train station. Look for the signs to direct you down the stairs to the Malpensa Express ticket office. Malpensa Express train: http://www.malpensaexpress.com/

TRANSPORTATION TIP

Purchase your tram or metro ticket at the newsstand or bar inside the train station. The bathrooms (no charge) are next to track #21, inside Milan's Central train station.

Milan hotels listed alphabetically
ANTICA LOCANDA MERCANTI
AURORA
KENNEDY
LONDON
MALTA
PROMESSI SPOSI
SAN FRANCISCO
SPERONARI
STAR

HOTELS
ANTICA LOCANDA MERCANTI: Via San Tommaso 6, 2nd fl. **Tel.** 02-8054080. **Fax:** 02-8054090. **Web site:** http://www.locanda.it/ **E-mail:** locanda@locanda.it (16 rms., all w/toilet & shower.) 146€ (8 standard rms.) double; 172€ (4 master rms.) double; 224€ (4 terraced rms.) double. Call for triple rates. Buffet breakfast (7-10:30am) at 10€ pp is served in the room. Air-conditioned (4 terraced rms.) Visa, MC, AX. English spoken (Bruce, Greta & Nicole), phones, no TV, fabulous wonderful charming renovated 19th-century hotel w/nicely & individually furnished pretty rms. that have names Donna Nives degli Accattaits (wonderful large standard rm. w/2 twin beds or zip & lock king-size bed, white wood-beamed ceiling w/fan, standard-size bathroom & faces the street) is for a double; Jvisconti (wonderful large standard rm. w/2 twin beds or zip & lock king-size bed, ceiling fan, small bathroom & faces the back) is for a double; Donna Laura dei Mori (standard rm. w/2 twin beds or zip & lock queen-size bed, ceiling fan, standard-size bathroom & faces the interior courtyard w/no view) is for a double; J. Malaspina (2 steps down into small standard rm. w/2 twin beds or zip & lock queen-size bed, white wood-beamed ceiling w/fan, small bathroom & faces the street) is for a double; La Baronessa (2 steps down into master rm. w/ 2 twin beds or zip & lock king-size bed, convertible sofa, white wood-beamed ceiling w/fan, standard-size bathroom & 2 windows that face the street) is for a double or triple; Standa dei Bamboo Al Vento (wonderful huge bright airy terraced air-conditioned rm. w/canopy

queen-size bed, wooden flr., standard-size bathroom & garden terrace) is for a double; modern bathrooms w/hairdriers & towel heaters, fresh flowers are put into each room every day, 2 nonsmoking
rms. available, warm atmosphere, wonderful quiet location, elevator,
2 flrs. This hotel is not family-owned but managed by Ora Paola,
Bruce Scott & Alex (mother, father & son), a wonderful & attentive
family. **Metro:** Cairoli. Catch Malpensa Express train from airport
to Cadorna train/metro station. Taxi to hotel.

AURORA: Corso Buenos Aires 18, 1st fl. **Tel:** 02-2047960. **Fax:**
02-2049285. **Web site:** http://www.hotelitaly.com/hotels/aurora/ **E-
mail:** hotel.aurora@tiscalinet.it (16 rms., 12 w/toilet & shower.) 64€
single; 102€ double; 111€ triple; 130€ quad. The room without a
bathroom is cheaper. Breakfast (8-10am) at 5€ pp can be served in
the room. Air-conditioned (7 rms.). Visa, MC, AX, DC. English spoken (Donato, Angelo, Anna & Elia), phones, TV, wonderful charming simple hotel w/nicely & identically furnished modern bright airy
nice-size rms. w/no views, shiny tiled flrs., #110 (air-conditioned
rm. w/twin bed, futon convertible chair/bed & faces the street) is for
a single or double; #101 (French double bed & faces the street) &
103 (French double bed, small bathroom & faces the street) are for a
single or discounted for 2 slim people in love; #108 (rm. near reception area w/twin bed) is for a single; #112 (air-conditioned rm. w/2
twin beds or zip & lock queen-size bed & faces the interior courtyard) is for a double; #111 (air-conditioned rm. w/queen-size bed &
faces the street) & 113 (air-conditioned rm. w/queen-size bed & faces
the interior courtyard) are for a double; #102 (large rm. w/queen-size
bed, futon convertible chair/bed & faces the street) & 106 (2 twin
beds, futon convertible chair/bed & faces the street) are for a double
or triple; #114 (large air-conditioned rm. w/queen-size bed & twin
bed & faces the street) is for a double or triple; #107 (large rm. near
reception area w/2 twin beds or zip & lock queen-size bed, convertible sofa, small bathroom & faces the street) is for a double, triple or
family; #104 (double bed, small bathroom & faces the street) is for a
double; #105 (double bed, freestanding prefabricated shower in the
middle of the room, private toilet outside the rm. down the hall &
faces the street) is for a double; #116, 115 (both air-conditioned rms.
w/twin beds, freestanding prefabricated showers in the middle of the
rooms, no toilets & face the interior courtyard) & 109 (air-condi-

tioned rm. w/French double bed, no bathroom & faces the interior courtyard) share 1 communal bathroom & are for a single; newly remodeled bathrooms w/hairdriers, wonderful location, walk through the open courtyard to the elevator, 1 fl., parking (12€ per day). Owned/ managed by Donato & Anna Casella (husband & wife). *5% rm. discount when you show them this book.* Donato's son Gerry owns/manages the Hotel Promessi Sposi. I used to stay at this hotel but I switched to Hotel Promessi Sposi because they have TV w/CNN. This feature is important to me because it keeps me in touch with the U.S. From Milan's Central train station, taxi or catch tram #5 to hotel. Tram stop: San Francesca Romana. Cross street: Via Omboni.

KENNEDY: Via Tunisia 6, 6th fl. **Tel:** 02-29400934. **Fax:** 02-29401253. **Web site:** http://www.kennedyhotel.it/ **E-mail:** hotelkennedy@galactica.it (10 rms., 5 w/toilet & shower.) 103€ double; 126€ triple; 168€ quad. The rooms without bathrooms are cheaper. Breakfast (8-10am) at 4€ pp can be served in the room. Visa, MC, AX, DC. English spoken (Rafaello), phones, TV, wonderful charming hotel w/nicely & identically furnished rms., shiny tiled flrs., #21 (bright airy rm. w/2 twin beds or zip & lock queen-size bed, compact bathroom & small terrace that faces street w/rooftops view) & 13 (2 twin beds or zip & lock queen-size bed, compact bathroom & large terrace that faces the back) are for a double; #18 (bright airy rm. w/3 twin beds or 1 zip & lock queen-size bed & twin bed, compact bathroom & 2 windows that face the street) & 14 (bright airy rm. w/3 twin beds, bathroom & small balcony that faces street) are for a triple; #16 (bright airy rm. w/4 twin beds or 1 zip & lock queen-size bed & 2 twin beds, compact bathroom & 2 windows that face the street) is for a family; the 5 rooms (3 singles & 2 doubles) w/ o bathrooms share 2 communal bathrooms; bar, wonderful quiet location, 2 elevators. Owned by Andrea Giacobbe and managed by Raffaello Bianchi. *Free breakfast when you show them this book.* From Milan's Central train station, taxi or catch metro to hotel. **Metro:** Porto Venezia. From metro stop, walk up Buenos Aires (odd numbers going up), turn left onto Via Tunisia. Cross streets: Corso Buenos Aires & Via Tadino.

LONDON: Via Rovello 3. **Tel.** 02-72020166. **Fax:** 02-8057037. **Web site:** http://www.traveleurope.it/hotellondon.htm/ **E-mail:**

hotel.london@traveleurope.it (30 rms., 25 w/toilet & shower.) 95€ single; 147€ double; 194€ triple. The rooms without bathrooms are cheaper. Breakfast (8-10am) at 8€ pp can be served in the room. Air-conditioned. Visa, MC. English spoken (Licia, Tanya, Paolo & Safar), phones, cable TV w/CNN, wonderful charming hotel w/nicely & identically dark wood modern furnished bright nice-size rms. w/no views, #30 (French double bed, compact bathroom & faces the street) is for a single or 2 slim people in love; #34 & 14 (both w/twin beds, compact bathrooms & face the street) are for a single; #38 & 18 (both w/twin beds & compact bathrooms) are for a single; #56 (3rd flr. rm. w/twin bed, freestanding prefabricated shower in the middle of the room, compact bathroom w/toilet & balcony w/rooftops view) is for a single; #8 (2 balconies) & 28 (both corner rms. w/3 twin beds or 1 zip & lock queen-size bed & twin bed, standard-size bathrooms & floor-to-ceiling windows that face the side street) are perfect for a double but snug for a triple; #58 (3rd flr. rm. w/2 twin beds or zip & lock queen-size bed, small bathroom & 2 balconies that face the back) is for a double; #22 (faces the interior), 44 (faces the interior), 36 (faces the street) & 24 (all w/2 twin beds or zip & lock queen-size bed & compact bathrooms) are for a double; #42 (3rd flr. rm. w/twin bed, no bathroom & balcony) is for a single; #40 (2nd flr. rm. w/2 twin beds or zip & lock queen-size bed, freestanding prefabricated shower in the middle of the room, no toilet & faces the interior) & 26 (2nd flr. rm. w/no bathroom) share a communal bathroom; #20 (1st flr. rm. w/2 twin beds or zip & lock queen-size bed, freestanding prefabricated shower in the middle of the room, no toilet & faces the interior) & 6 (1st flr. rm. w/no bathroom) share a communal bathroom; #46 (3rd flr. rm. w/2 twin beds or zip & lock queen-size bed & no bathroom) has a communal bathroom outside the room; hairdriers, bar, wonderful quiet location, elevator, 3 flrs. Owned/managed by Francesco Gambino. *Free breakfast when you show him this book* **Metro:** Cairoli. Catch Malpensa Express train from airport to Cadorna train/metro station. Taxi to hotel. (Closed Aug. & Christmas wk.)

PROMESSI SPOSI: Piazzale Oberdan 12. **Tel.** 02-29513661. **Fax:** 02-29404182. **Web site:** http://www.hotelpromessisposi.com/ **E-mail:** prosposi@tin.it (31 rms., all w/toilet & shower.) 90€ single; 137€ double; 173€ triple; 189€ quad. Breakfast (7-10:30am) is included in the rates & can be served in the room. Air-conditioned.

Visa, MC, AX, DC. English spoken (Gerry, Carmelo, Rocco & Luca), phones, cable TV w/CNN, wonderful charming hotel w/nicely & identically furnished modern rms., #331 (compact rm. w/cubicle bathroom) & 330 (both 3rd flr. rms. w/twin beds & face the back) are for a single; #221 (compact rm. w/cubicle bathroom) & 220 (both 2nd flr. rms. w/twin beds & face the back) are for a single; #332 (huge bright 3rd flr. corner rm. w/2 twin beds or zip & lock queen-size bed, convertible chair/bed, standard-size bathroom & 2 windows) is for a double or triple; #222 (corner rm.) & 204 (both 2nd flr. rms. w/2 twin beds or zip & lock queen-size bed & small balconies that face the street) are for a double; #334 (3rd flr. rm. w/2 twin beds or zip & lock queen-size bed & faces the street) & 224 (2nd flr. rm. w/2 twin beds or zip & lock queen-size bed & faces the street) are for a double; #339 (3rd flr. rm. w/double bed & faces the back) & 229 (2nd flr. rm. w/double bed & faces the back) are for a double; #336 (3rd flr. rm. w/2 twin beds & faces the street) is for a double; #335 (nice-size 3rd flr. rm. w/3 twin beds or 1 zip & lock queen-size bed & twin bed & faces the street) & 225 (2nd flr. rm. w/3 twin beds or 1 zip & lock queen-size bed & twin bed & faces the street) are for a triple; #338 (nice-size 3rd flr. rm. w/3 twin beds or 1 zip & lock queen-size bed & twin bed & faces the back) & 228 (2nd flr. rm. w/double bed, twin bed & faces the back) are for a triple; rooms that face the street are brighter but noisier; rooms that face the back are quieter, wonderful noisy location, modern bathrooms w/hairdriers, bar, garden, elevator, 3 flrs. Owned/managed by Gerry & Donato Casella (son & father). *5% rm. discount when you show them this book.* Donato also owns/manages the Hotel Aurora. I love staying at this hotel because of Gerry, his wonderful staff's (Carmelo, Rocco & Luca) generous hospitality, the hotel's location and the fact that I can use my Italian calling card to make phone calls. I also love it because it is an easy metro ride or 30-min. wonderful walk to the Duomo and there is a supermarket & laundromat less than two blocks away from the hotel. The tram from the train station drops you off a block from the hotel. **Metro:** Porta Venezia. From Milan's Central train station, taxi or catch tram #9 to hotel. Tram stop: Piazzale Oberdan.

SPERONARI: Via Speronari 4. **Tel.** 02-86461125. **Fax:** 02-72003178. **E-mail:** hotelsperonari@inwind.it (32 rms., 22 w/toilet & bath or shower.) 69€ single; 116€ double; 157€ triple; 178€

quad. The rooms without bathrooms are cheaper. Breakfast (7am-12noon) costs extra pp. Visa, MC. English spoken (John Paolo & Carla), phones, TV, charming plain hotel w/simply & identically white pinewood furnished nice-size rms, shiny tiled flrs., there are 4 rooms w/private bathrooms for a single; there are 3 rooms w/showers but no toilets for a single; #230 (bright 3rd flr. rm. w/2 twin beds or zip & lock queen-size bed, standard-size bathroom, ceiling fan & balcony that faces the street) is for a double; #230 (large bright 3rd flr. rm. w/4 twin beds or 1 zip & lock queen-size bed & 2 twin beds, standard-size bathroom, ceiling fan & faces the street), 214 & 225 are all large rooms for a family; the 10 rooms w/o bathrooms share 5 communal bathrooms; rooms that face the street are brighter, ceiling fans, they do not reserve specific rooms, wonderful location close to the Duomo where you can hear the bells through the very thin walls, lots of stairs, no elevator, 4 flrs. Owned/managed by John Paolo Isoni & his family who usually offer a complimentary cappuccino upon your arrival. **Metro:** Duomo. Catch Malpensa Express train from airport to Cadorna train/metro station. Taxi to hotel.

STAR: Via Bossi 5. **Tel.** 02-801501. **Fax:** 02-861787. **Web site:** http://www.starhotel.it/ **E-mail:** information@starhotel.it (30 rms., all w/toilet & bath or shower.) 111€ single; 116€ (sauna shower) single; 162€ double; 167€ (Jacuzzi bathtub &/or sauna shower) double. Buffet breakfast (7:30-9:30am, includes hard-boiled eggs, yogurt, cereals & assorted breads) is included in the rates. Air-conditioned. Visa, MC, AX, DC. English spoken, phones, cable TV w/CNN & Eurosport, wonderful charming modern hotel w/contemporary & identically furnished modern nice-size not-so-bright rms. w/no views, #25 & 27 (both w/twin beds & bathrooms w/sauna showers) are for a single; #9 (2 twin beds or zip & lock queen-size bed & bathroom w/Jacuzzi bathtub & sauna shower) is for a double; #23 (2 twin beds or zip & lock queen-size bed & bathroom w/bathtub & sauna shower) & 22 (2 twin beds or zip & lock queen-size bed & bathroom w/sauna shower) are for a double; modern standard-size bathrooms w/hairdriers, towel heaters & telephones, handicapped access bathroom in hall, minibars, bar, wonderful quiet location, 1 step up to elevator. Owned/managed by David & Bruno Ceretti. **Metro:** Cordusio or Cairoli. Cross street: Via Broletto. Catch Malpensa Express train from airport to Cadorna train/metro station. Taxi to hotel.

HOTELS AWAY FROM THE TOURIST AREA

These hotels are not convenient to either the train station or the Duomo. They are located in a safe, residential area in the University district. You have to taxi or catch a metro to the Duomo unless you don't mind a 40-min. walk.

MALTA: Via Ricordi 20. **Tel:** 02-2049615. **Fax:** 29521210. **Web site:** http://www.hotelmalta.it/ **E-mail:** hotelmalta@hotmail.com (15 rms., all w/toilet & shower.) 60€ single; 91€ double. No breakfast served. Visa, MC, DC. English spoken (AnnaMaria & Antonio), phones, TV, wonderful charming simple hotel w/nicely & identically furnished nice-size rms., #12 (1st flr. rm. w/twin bed, compact bathroom & small balcony that faces the garden) & 10 (1st flr. rm. w/ twin bed, compact bathroom & small balcony that faces the street) are for a single; #20 (2nd flr. rm. w/twin bed, compact bathroom & small balcony that faces the garden) & 18 (2nd flr. rm. w/twin bed, compact bathroom & faces the street) are for a single; #26 (3rd flr. rm. w/twin bed & faces the street) & 28 (3rd flr. rm. w/twin bed & faces the garden) are for a single; #14 (1st flr. rm. queen-size bed, small bathroom & terrace that faces the garden) & 16 (2nd flr. rm. w/ 2 twin beds or zip & lock queen-size bed, small bathroom & balcony that faces the street) are for a double; #4 (walk 1 flight up to ground-flr. rm. w/2 twin beds or zip & lock queen-size bed, bathroom w/ bathtub w/hand-held shower & faces the garden), 6 (walk 1 flight up to ground-flr. rm. w/2 twin beds or zip & lock queen-size bed, standard-size bathroom & faces the garden) & 2 (walk 1 flight up to ground-flr. rm. w/2 twin beds & small bathroom) are for a double; #8 (1st flr. rm. w/2 twin beds, standard-size bathroom & faces the street) is for a double; #22 (2nd flr. rm. w/2 twin beds or zip & lock queen-size bed & faces the garden), 24 (3rd flr. rm. w/2 twin beds & faces the street) & 30 (3rd flr. rm. w/2 twin beds & faces the garden) are for a double; modern bathrooms w/sinks that are part of the rooms, hairdriers, pretty garden, quiet residential location, walk one flight down to reception, lots of stairs, no elevator, 3 flrs. *10% rm. discount when you show owners/managers AnnaMaria & Antonio Del Gaudio (wife & husband) this book.* **Metro:** Loreto. Cross street: Via Pecchio. From Milan's Central train station, taxi or catch tram #33 to hotel. Tram stop: Piazza Aspromante.

SAN FRANCISCO: Viale Lombardia 55. **Tel:** 02-2361009. **Fax:** 02-26680377. **Web site:** http://www.hotel-sanfrancisco.it/ **E-mail:** sf@hotel-sanfrancisco.it (31 rms., all w/toilet & shower.) 71€ single; 112€ double; 153€ triple. Breakfast (7-10am) is included in the rates. Air-conditioned. Visa, MC, AX, DC. English spoken (Pino, Dario & Luca), phones, cable TV w/CNN, CNBC & BBC, charming modern hotel w/nicely & identically furnished not-so-bright modern rms., carpeted flrs., there are 17 rooms for a single: 1/2 of the singles have a French double bed & 1/2 have a twin bed; #64 (French double bed, small bathroom & huge terrace w/rooftops view), 26 (French double bed & balcony) & 10 (French double bed) are for a single or discounted for 2 slim people in love; #62 (queen-size bed, large bathroom & interior balcony) is for a double; #14 (large rm. w/2 twin beds & faces the street) is for a double; #24 (queen-size bed & twin bed, small bathroom & balcony that faces the garden) is for a triple; most w/standard-size bathrooms, garden, bar, elevator, 3 flrs. Owned/ managed by Gianfranco, Pino & Cicco Volante. **Metro:** Loreto. Cross streets: Via Porpora & Via Vallazzee. From Milan's Central train station, taxi or catch tram #33 to hotel. Tram stop: Porpara-Ampere.

LAUNDROMATS (Lavanderia)
Lavanderia Gettoni Adriana: Via Tadino 4. Cross streets: Via Castaldi & Via Palazzi. Daily 7:30am-9:30pm; Lava e Lava: Via Melzo 24. Cross street: Via Malpighi. Daily 8am-10pm; Lavanderia Automatica: Corso Porta Vittoria 51. Daily 8am-10pm; Minola: Via San Vito 5. Daily 8am-10pm.

TAXI
Tel: 02-6767 or 02-8383 or 02-5353.

INTERNET CAFE
The Netgate: Via Aselli, 23. Tel: 02-70006248.
Web site: http://www.thenetgate.it/

BOOKSTORES
Feltrinelli: Corso Buenos Aires 20. Tel: 02-29400731. Fax: 02-29406842. Hrs.: Mon.-Sat. 9am-7:30pm; Sun. 10am-1:30pm & 3:30pm-7:30pm; Feltrinelli: Via Alessandro Manzoni 12. Web site: http://www.feltrinelli.it/ Touring Club Italiano: Corso Italia 10. Tel:

02-8526304. Fax: 02-8526493. Visa, MC. Hrs.: Mon.-Sat. 9am-7pm. Great for maps & guidebooks. Web site: http://www.touringclub.it/ American Bookstore: Largo Cairoli/Via Camperio 16. Metro: Cairoli. Tel:02-878920. Fax: 02-72020030. Hrs.: Tues.-Sat. 10am-7pm; Mon. 1pm-7pm. Closed Sun. & Mon. morning. Great place to exchange or sell your used paperback books.

SUPERMARKETS
Sigma: Located on the street level in the Milan train station, near the entrance opposite the tram depot. Hrs.: Daily 8am-11pm. Visa, MC.; Esselunga: Viale Piave 38b. Hrs.: Mon.-Sat. 7:30am-1pm & Tues.-Sat. 3pm-7:30pm. Closed Sun. Visa, MC.

RESTAURANTS
AZZURA GRILL: Via San Gregorio 11. Tel/Fax: 02-29406115. Hrs.: 12noon-3pm & 7pm-12midnight. Closed Sat. afternoon & Sun. Visa, MC, AX. Specialty: Fresh fish & seafood. This wonderful family-owned restaurant has been owned/managed by Matteo, Tina & Franco Fabrizio (father, mother & son) since 1988. Large restaurant w/wonderful fresh fish, delicious pizzas and homemade pastas. This continues to be one of my favorite restaurants in Milan. Put yourself in good hands and ask Franco who speaks great English what to order. He takes it from there. *Show Franco or the family the book and they will give you a complimentary Vinassa or limoncello.* Metro: Lima. Highly recommended by Donato & Anne, Hotel Aurora.

CALALUNA: Viale Piave 38. **Tel**. 02-29401982. Hrs.: Tues.-Sun. 12noon-2:30pm & 7:30pm-12midnight. Closed Mon. Specialty: Fresh seafood & fish. It is one of the few restaurants I know of that doesn't have a 2-people minimum on ordering *risotto*. I usually travel alone and am not always able to order it. Metro: Porta Venezia. Highly recommended by Carmelo, Hotel Promessi Sposi.

MARUZZELLA: Piazzale Oberdan 3. **Tel**. 02-29525729 or 29516418. Web site: http://www.ristorantemaruzzella.it/ Hrs.: Thurs.-Tues. 12noon-2:30pm & 6pm-12midnight. Closed Wed. Metro: Porta Venezia. Highly recommended by Rocco & Luca, Hotel Promessi Sposi.

NAPLES (Napoli)
Country code 39, city code 081
zip code 80142

Naples Tourist Information Centers
1.) Piazza Martiri 58, scala B. **Tel:** 081-405311. **Fax:** 081-401961.
Hrs.: Mon.-Fri. 9am-2pm. **2.)** Stazione Centrale. **Tel:** 081-268779.
Fax: 081-206666. Hrs.: Mon.-Sat. 9am-7pm & Sun. 9am-1pm. Hours
listed above are not etched in stone.
Web site: http://www.ept.napoli.it/ **E-mail:** ept@netgroup.it or
osservatorio@comune.napolo.it

TRANSPORTATION TIPS
Naples to Sorrento by train
Naples Centrale Stazione is the main train station facing Piazza
Garibaldi. On the lower level of this station is where you can catch
the independent local *Ferrovia Circumvesuviana* commuter trains to
Sorrento, Herculaneum and Pompei. Tel: 081-7722444. When you
arrive at the Naples Centrale station, look for the large blue signs
"*Circumvesuviana.*" Follow the signs, walk downstairs, buy your
ticket at the *Circumvesuviana* window. Walk to the far left of the
turnstiles, insert your ticket into the machine and walk downstairs to
the tracks. Naples to Sorrento: 70-min. train ride. 3€ one way. No
rail passes accepted. (There are no toilets on these local trains.)

Naples to Sorrento by boat
CA.RE.MAR: Tel: 081-5513882. Hydrofoil 8€ one way. 35-min.
Cash only. Don't assume the boats run every day in high season. The
condition of the weather dictates their schedule. Always check the
day before departure.

Naples to Capri
Buy a tram/bus ticket (.80€ pp) at the tobacco shop or newsstand
inside the Centrale Stazione. Exit train station, walk straight through
Piazza Garibaldi, continue walking past the waiting buses to the other
end. Look for the tram tracks and catch tram (electric bus) #1 to the
port (Molo Beverello). **Navigazione Libera Golfo:** Tel: 081-5527209.
CA.RE.MAR: Tel: 081-5513882. Naples to Capri: 11€ pp. Cash only.

35 min. Departure time to Capri: Approx. every hour until 6pm. Example: I arrived at the Rome airport around 9:45am, caught the train from Rome to Naples and was able to catch the 2:40pm ferry to Capri.

Naples hotels listed alphabetically
ALLOGGIO VASSATTI
BELLA CAPRI
CASANOVA
DONNAREGINA
DUOMO
GINEVRA
MANCINI

HOTEL (In the monument area near port)
BELLA CAPRI: Via Melisurgo 4, 6th fl. **Tel:** 081-5529494. **Fax:** 081-5529265. **Alfredo's mobile:** 3396344412/3284736334. **Web site:** http://www.bellacapri.it/ **E-mail:** info@bellacapri.it (9 rms., 8 w/toilet & shower.) 63€ single; 84€ double; 103€ triple; 126€ quad. The room without a bathroom is cheaper. Breakfast (7-11am, coffee & pastry) is included in the rates. Air-conditioned (11€ extra per day). Visa, MC, AX, DC. English spoken (Gerardo, Luca, Alfredo, Merlino & Pietro), phones, TV, wonderful charming warm hotel w/ nicely furnished airy rms., #9 (twin bed & faces back w/no view) is for a single but can fit an extra twin bed for a double; #3 & 4 (nice-size rms. w/queen-size beds & balconies w/wonderful views of Capri, Pompei, Vesuvius, Sorrento & port) are for a double; #8 (large queen-size bed & interior balcony w/side views of Vesuvius, castle & port) is for a double but can fit an extra twin bed for a triple; #5 (queen-size bed & balcony w/wonderful view of Capri, Pompei, Vesuvius, Sorrento & port) is for a double; #7 (queen-size bed & interior balcony w/side views of Vesuvius, castle & port) is for a double; #6 (3 twin beds or 1 zip & lock queen-size bed & twin bed, shower inside the room, communal bathroom down the hall & window w/wonderful view of Capri, Pompei, Vesuvius, Sorrento & port) is for a triple; #1 (queen-size bed & twin bed & balcony that faces back) is for a triple; #2 (fabulous large rm. w/queen-size bed & twin bed, compact shower stall & terrace w/wonderful view of Capri, Pompei, Vesuvius, Sorrento & port) is for a triple but has a futon convertible chair/bed

for a family; fluffy towels, rooms that face the street are bright & airy but can be noisy at night, ceiling fans, free luggage storage, Internet access available at 3€ per 1/2 hr., you eat your breakfast (coffee & pastry) at a local cafe across the street from the hotel (at least you know it is fresh coffee) wonderful location, coin-operated elevator, 1 flr., parking (14€ per day). Owned/managed by Gerardo Giacobbe. *10% rm. discount when you show him this book.* Alfredo who works here also owns Hotel Mancini near the train station. He is wonderful, accommodating, generous & well informed and goes out of his way to make sure you are comfortable and safe in Naples. Don't bother wasting your time waiting on the long lines at the Naples tourist offices. They have lots of information on Naples at each of their hotels. Alfredo will help you hire private trustworthy drivers to see the major sights in Naples & Sorrento, book sightseeing tours & boat trips to various islands. He selected the restaurants for this chapter. It is because of Alfredo that I had the best time I ever had in Naples. Located on corner of Cristofor Colombo, across the street from the port. You can catch bus #152 (every 20 min.), bus #R2 (more frequent) or the well-known "pickpocket tram" #1. Bus #152 goes along the waterfront. Ask bus driver for the port (Molo Beverello) stop. It drops you off across the street from the hotel. Bus #R2: Ask bus driver for *secondo fermato* (2nd stop) which is Via Depretis, cross the street and walk onto Via Melisurgo; enter the courtyard, look to your left for the guard in the glass booth, ask him for a coin to use the elevator (not necessary on holidays), enter bldg. B, walk up the stairs and catch the elevator to the 6th floor. Don't judge the hotel by its exterior appearance.

HOTELS (Historical center)

DUOMO: Via Duomo 228. **Tel/Fax:** 081-265988. **E-mail:** lacentral1@interfree.it (9 rms., all w/toilet & shower.) 84€ double; 105€ triple; 126€ quad. Call for quint rates. Breakfast (8-10am) at 6€ pp & can be served in the room (3€ extra pp). Cash only. English spoken (Enrico, Luigi & Salvatore), phones, TV, charming hotel w/ simply furnished large airy rms., shiny tiled flrs., #105 (2 steps down into large rm. w/queen-size bed) is for a double but can fit an extra twin bed for a triple; #107 (2nd flr. rm. w/queen-size bed & faces back w/no view) is for a double but can fit an extra twin bed for a triple; #104 (wonderful huge rm. w/queen-size bed & twin bed, original art deco ceiling & faces back w/no view) is for a triple; #102 (large rm. w/queen-size bed & twin bed, original art deco arched ceiling & small window faces back) is for a triple but can fit an extra twin bed for a family; #108 (large rm. w/queen-size bed & twin bed & faces side street w/no view) is for a triple; #101 (large rm. w/ queen-size bed & twin bed & faces interior) & 106 (2 steps down into large rm. w/queen-size bed & twin bed) are for a triple but can fit extra twin beds for a family or quint; high ceilings w/fans, fabulous location not far from the Museum National, no elevator, 1 fl. Owned/managed Enrico, Luigi & Salvatore Lacentra (brothers) for more than 10 years. *5% rm. discount when you show them this book.* Don't judge the hotel by its exterior appearance. From the train station, walk straight ahead through Piazza Garibaldi, bear left onto Corso Umberto, walk up Corso Umberto (10 min.) to Piazza Nicola Amore, turn right onto Via Duomo (20-min. walk) or catch any of the buses to Piazza Nicola Amore, walk up Via Duomo (away from the water and up). Bus #42 does pass the hotel on Via Duomo but I don't know the stop.

The following 2 B&Bs contacted me after I left Naples.
They are both located in the historical center. They each wrote me wonderful letters and their establishments look good on the Web site.

ALLOGGIO VASSATTI: Via Donnalbino 56. **Tel/Fax:** 081-5515118. **Web site:** http://www.bandbnapoli.it/
E-mail: info@bandbnapoli.it (5 rms., all w/toilet & shower.) 99€ single; 130€ double; 178€ (rm. #10) triple. Breakfast is included in the rates. Air-conditioned. Visa, MC, AX. English spoken (Lisa), phones, TV. I did not get a chance to see this bed & breakfast hotel.

DONNAREGINA: Via Luigi Settembrini 80, 4th fl. **Tel:** 081-446799. **Mobile:** 0339-7819225 or 03381831773.
Web site: http://www.discovernaples.net/
E-mail: info@discovernaples.net (4 rms., all w/toilet & shower.) 105€ double. Breakfast is included in the rates & served in the kitchen. Visa, MC, AX, DC. Former nunnery of Donnaregina Vecchia, a 14th-century monumental complex. I did not get a chance to see this bed & breakfast hotel.

HOTELS (Near the train station)
CASANOVA: Corso Garibaldi 333/Via Venezia 2.
Tel/Fax: 081-268287. **Tel/Fax:** 081-269792.
Web site: http://www.hotelcasanova.3000.it/
E-mail: hcasanov@tin.it (18 rms., 12 w/toilet & shower.) 58€ double;
79€ triple; 94€ quad. The rooms without bathrooms are cheaper.
Breakfast (8-11am) at 5€ pp & can be served on the terrace in warm
weather. Visa, MC, AX, DC. English spoken (Giuseppe & Vittorio),
phones, TV (not all rms.), charming plain hotel w/plainly furnished
nice-size rms., #13 (not-so-bright corner rm. w/queen-size bed, bathroom, frigobar & faces street), 23 (not-so-bright rm. w/queen-size
bed, bathroom w/shower but no curtain, frigobar & no view), 19 (not-
so-bright rm. w/2 twin beds or zip & lock queen-size bed, bathroom
w/shower but no curtain, frigobar & no view) & 9 (not-so-bright
small rm. w/double bed, frigobar, bathroom w/shower but no curtain
& faces street) are for a double; #14 & 16 (both w/3 twin beds or 1
zip & lock queen-size bed & twin bed, leather sofas, bathrooms,
frigobars & face street) are for a triple; #20 (large rm. w/4 twin beds
or 1 zip & lock queen-size bed & 2 twin beds, small bathroom & no
view) is for a family; #8 is a nice-size rm. w/private bathroom outside the room; #11 & 12 both have private showers but no toilets; #4,
7, 24 & 25 all have no bathrooms, tiny narrow circular staircase to
rooftop terrace w/bar service in the summer, ivy-covered front, quiet
location, bar, no elevator, 1 flr. Owned by charming Vittorio Arzillo
& managed by Giuseppe Arzillo. *10% rm. discount when you show
them this book.* I prefer the more attractive entrance on Via Venezia.
From the train station, walk bearing to your right through Piazza
Garibaldi, take the 3rd right onto Via Milano, turn left onto Via
Venezia, walk to the end of the street. Vittorio's daughter manages
another hotel which I did not see. Hotel Zara: Via Firenze 81. Tel:
081-287125. Fax: 081-268287. **Web site:** http://www.hotelzara.it/ **E-
mail:** hotelzara@tin.it

GINEVRA: Via Genova 116, 2nd flr. **Tel/Fax:** 081-283210. **Tel/Fax:**
081-5541757. **Web site:** http://www.mds.it/ginevra/ **E-mail:**
hgineva@tin.it (15 rms., 6 w/toilet & shower.) 60€ double; 85€ triple;
100€ quad. The rooms without bathrooms are cheaper. Breakfast (8-
10am) at 4€ pp is served in the room. Visa, MC, AX, DC. English
spoken (Lello & Bruno), phones, TV (6 rms.), wonderful charming

hotel w/simply furnished bright nice-size airy rms., shiny tiled flrs., #24 (newly furnished nice-size rm. w/2 twin beds or zip & lock queen-size bed, bathroom & tiny balcony that faces side street), 19 (large rm. w/2 twin beds or zip & lock queen-size bed, bathroom & tiny balcony that faces side street), 23 (newly furnished small rm. w/queen-size bed, bathroom & tiny balcony that faces side street) & 20 (romantic small rm. w/double bed, bathroom & faces backyard) are for a double; #22 (large rm. w/3 twin beds or 1 zip & lock queen-size bed & twin bed, bathroom & window that faces side street) is for a triple; #18 (large rm. w/4 twin beds or 1 zip & lock queen-size bed & 2 twin beds, bathroom & faces the back) is for a family; rms. facing the back are quieter, cheerful warm ambience, free luggage storage, no elevator, 2 flrs. Owned/managed by the wonderful Bruno, Anna & Lello Lorenzo (father, mother & son). *10% rm. discount when you show them this book.* Bruno's family tries hard to make your stay enjoyable. Call ahead if you have lots of luggage and they will meet you downstairs to help you. Sometimes in the summer evenings they have sing-alongs w/guitar. It has been in this family for more than 40 years. Bruno & his family are close friends of Alfredo, owner of Hotels Bella Capri & Mancini. Bruno trained Alfredo in the hotel management business. In 2003 they will have 5 brand-new air-conditioned rooms (rms. #25-29) that will have new furnishings & bathrooms. From the train station, turn right onto Corso Novara, walk under an elevated road for two blocks, turn right onto Via Genova.

MANCINI: Via Mancini 33, 2 fl. **Tel:** 081-5536731. **Fax:** 081-5546675. **Alfredo's mobile:** 3396344412/3284736334.
Web site: http://www.hostelpensionemancini.com/
E-mail: alfredocefalo@hotmail.com (6 rms., 4 w/toilet & shower.) 55€ double; 81€ triple; 108€ quad; 119€ (rm. #5) quint. The rooms without bathrooms are cheaper. Breakfast is included in the rates. Cash only. English spoken (Marguerita & Alfredo), no phones, no TV, wonderful plain hotel w/simply furnished nice-size rms., #4 (nice-size bed w/2 twin beds or zip & lock queen-size bed, newly renovated bathroom & faces back) is for a double but can fit an extra twin bed for a triple; #2 (bright airy large rm. w/2 twin beds, newly renovated bathroom & small balcony that faces the square/market place) is for a double but can fit extra twin beds for a triple or family; #3

(bright airy large rm. w/5 twin beds, large bathroom & balcony that faces the square/market) can be booked in advance for a family or quint otherwise it is rented out as a public dormitory; #5 (nice-size rm. w/twin bed & no bathroom) & 6 (small rm. w/small double bed, no bathroom & faces back) are for a single; the 4 rooms w/o bathrooms share 1 communal bathroom w/hotel staff; free luggage storage, Internet access available at 3€ per 1/2 hr., noisy location, coin-operated elevator, 2 flrs. Owned/managed by the wonderful, accommodating, generous & well informed Marguerita & Alfredo Cefalo (wife & husband). They both go out of their way to make sure you are comfortable and safe in Naples. Don't bother wasting your time waiting on the long lines at the Naples tourist offices. There is lots of information on Naples at the hotel. Alfredo will help you hire private trustworthy drivers to see the major sights in Naples & Sorrento, book sightseeing tours & boat trips to various islands. There is a daily noisy crowded permanent market located in front of the hotel. Located within a 5-min. walk from the train station. From the train station, walk bearing to your right through Piazza Garibaldi, turn left onto Corso Umberto, turn right onto Via Ranieri, turn right onto Via Mancini. If you don't feel like walking up the 2 flights of stairs, buzz hotel so they can bring down a coin for the elevator.

TAXI
Tel: 081-5564444. Make sure the driver turns the meter on when you get into the taxi.

SUPERMARKET
Centro Citta: Via Mancini 33. Hrs.: Mon.-Sat. 8:30-1pm & 5pm-8pm. Closed Sun. Near Hotel Mancini.

RESTAURANTS
AL FARETTO: Via Marechiaro. Tel: 081-5750407. Tues.-Sun. Hrs.: 12:30-5:30pm & 8pm-2am. Closed Mon. Visa, MC, AX, DC. Reservations required. Wonderful contemporary restaurant that serves some of the best food in Naples along with a fabulous view of Naples. It is the small inexpensive side of the upscale & expensive restaurant Al Faro. There are no tourists here, only Neapolitans who reserve way in advance to eat here. Walk down 2 flights of stairs to the restaurant.

This is the only affordable restaurant located in the expensive restaurant section of Marechiaro, on top of Naples. *Show owners Davide, Patrizio & Lello Rosiello & Salvatore Parrrotti this book and they will give you a complimentary after-dinner drink.* Highly recommended by Alfredo, Hotel Bella Capri.

TAVERNA E ZI CARMELA: Via Nicolo Tommaseo 11-12. Tel: 081-7643581. Tues.-Sun. Hrs.: 12noon-2am. Closed Mon. Visa, MC, AX, DC. Charming local restaurant that serves delicious homemade food. Owned/managed by Gianni & Carmela Ciano. Giuseppe does the cooking. Highly recommended by Alfredo, Hotel Bella Capri.

DAY TRIPS FROM NAPLES
Castellammare (hot springs), Pozzuoli (birthplace of Sophia Loren), Ercolono, Pompei & Sorrento.

ORVIETO
Southern Umbria, zip code 05018
Country code 39, city code 0763

Orvieto Tourist Information Center
1.) Piazza Duomo 24. **Tel:** 0763-341772/341911. **Fax:** 0763-344433.
Hrs.: Mon.-Fri. 8:15am-1:50pm & 4pm-7pm; Sat. 10am-1pm & 4pm-
7pm; Sun. & holidays 10am-12pm & 4pm-6pm. Located opposite
the Duomo. Longer hours in summer. The orange shuttle bus from
Piazza Cahen drops you in front of the tourist office. This is where
you buy tickets for the Duomo & Orvieto Underground. Hrs.: 10am-
1pm & 4pm-6pm. **Web sites:** http://www.comune.orvieto.tr.it/ or
http://www.umbria2000.it/ **E-mail:** info@iat.orvieto.tr.it

TRANSPORTATION TIP
From the train station, it is 1 1/2 miles up a winding steep road to the
Piazza Duomo (center of town). Buy your funicular/orange shuttle
bus ticket (1€ pp) at the train station tobacco shop. Save yourself
some time and buy round-trip tickets. Walk out the train station, cross
the street to the funicular, which takes you to Piazza Cahen (top of the
hill), a transportation hub at the entrance to the hilltop town. From
Piazza Cahen, walk out immediately to the waiting orange shuttle bus
to Piazza Duomo. (Confirm it is the correct bus to the Duomo.) The
bus will drop you off in front of the tourist office in the Piazza Duomo.
To walk (15 min.) from Piazza Cahen to the Duomo, walk straight
down Corso Cavour, turn left onto Via Duomo to the Piazza Duomo.

HOTELS
CORSO: Corso Cavour 343. **Tel/Fax:** 0763-342020. **Web site:**
http://www.argoweb.it/hotel-corso/ **E-mail:** hotelcorso@libero.it
(18 rms., all w/toilet & shower.) 65€ single; 92€ double; 121€
triple; 245€ quad. Buffet breakfast (7-10:30am) at 7€ pp can be
served in the room & on the terrace in warm weather. Air-conditioned. Visa, MC, AX, DC. English spoken (Carla), phones, cable
TV w/CNN, wonderful charming renovated hotel w/nicely furnished
modern bright airy nice-size rms., shiny tiled flrs., #8 (nice-size
rm. w/double bed, small bathroom & balcony that faces the back),
12, 20 & 21 are for a single; #23 (5 steps up to large rm. w/3 twin

beds or 1 zip & lock queen-size bed & twin bed, small bathroom, wood-beamed ceiling & faces the back), 16 (large rm. w/3 twin beds or 1 zip & lock queen-size bed & twin bed, large bathroom & small balcony that faces back) & 18 are for a double or triple; #24 (wonderful rm. w/loft bedroom & 2 balconies w/views of Duomo) is for a double; #14 (huge rm. w/3 twin beds or 1 zip & lock king-size bed & twin bed, large handicapped access bathroom, minibar & faces the street) is for a triple but can fit an extra twin bed for a family; modern bathrooms, minibars (6 rms.), terrace, bar, wonderful location, elevator, 2 flrs., parking (14€ per day). Owned/managed by charming & accommodating Carla Caponeri. *10% rm. discount when you show them this book and pay in cash.* From Piazza Cahen where the funicular drops you off, walk (5 min.) down Corso Cavour. (Closed Dec. 26 & 27.)

MAITANI: Via Lorenzo Maitani 5. **Tel:** 0763-342011. **Fax:** 0763-342012. **Web site:** http://www.argoweb.it/hotelmaitani/ **E-mail:** infoargo@argoweb.it (39 rms., all w/toilet & bath or shower.) 79€ single; 132€ double; 155€ jr. suite; 176€ superior suite. Visa, MC, AX, DC. Continental breakfast (8-10am) at 10€ pp can be served in the room (3€ extra pp). Air-conditioned. English spoken, rotary phones, cable TV w/CNN & BBC, wonderful charming 19th-century grand hotel w/beautifully & identically darkwood furnished nice-size to large rms., carpeted halls, wooden flrs., #80 (large rm. w/twin bed & convertible chair/bed) is for a single; #32 (2nd flr. rm. w/king-size bed & faces the Duomo) & 10 (1st flr. rm. w/king-size bed & faces the Duomo) are for a double; #158 (3rd flr. rm. w/king-size bed, sitting area w/green cushion chairs & wonderful view of the countryside) & 160 (3rd flr. rm. w/2 twin beds or zip & lock king-size bed, chandelier & wonderful view of the countryside) are for a double; #144 & 146 (both w/views of the countryside) are for a double; #50 (large rm. w/2 twin beds or zip & lock king-size bed, sitting area & faces the interior), 62 (2 twin beds & large bathroom), 82 (king-size bed), 152 (king-size bed & faces the interior) & 72 (balcony that faces the garden) are for a double; #26 (huge rm. w/king-size bed, convertible chair/bed, 2 bathrooms w/showers & faces street) & 4 (large rm. w/king-size bed, convertible chair/bed & 2 bathrooms w/ bathtub & shower) are for a double or triple; they have only 2 rms. (#26 & 4) that can accommodate more than 2 people. You have to get rooms with connecting doors and rent them as one triple or family room, like: #74 (single) & 76 (double) which can be rented together as one triple or family rm.; #86 (single rm. w/twin bed, convertible chair/bed & faces the garden) & 88 (2 twin beds or zip & lock king-size bed & faces the garden) can be rented together as one triple or family rm.; #148 (large unusual shaped jr. suite w/king-size bed, sitting area & faces the interior), 28 (large jr. suite w/king-size bed, sitting area & faces the street) & 36 (large jr. suite w/2 twin beds, sitting area & faces the interior) are for a double; #8 (large superior suite w/2 twin beds or zip & lock king-size bed, large bathroom, sitting area & balcony that faces the Duomo & street) & 78 (large superior suite w/king-size bed, sitting area w/green cushion chairs, beautiful huge bathroom & blue glass door & faces garden) are for a double; rms. face the Duomo, countryside, garden or interior; all the singles have bathrooms w/showers, all the doubles have bathrooms w/bathtubs, some beds have old-fashioned brass or wooden headboards, hairdriers, minibars, terrace w/magnificent view of the Duomo, wonderful ambience, bar, fabulous location near the Duomo, 2 elevators, 3 flrs., parking (14€ per day). Owned/managed by the wonderful charming & accommodating Dino & Giuseppe Morino (brothers). Their business card has chocolate candy attached to it. (Closed Jan.)

PALAZZO PICCOLOMINI: Piazza Ranieri 36. **Tel:** 0763-341882 or 341743. **Fax:** 0763-391046 or 343797. **Web site:** http://www.hotelpiccolomini.it/ **E-mail:** piccolomini.hotel@orvienet.it (31 rms., all w/toilet & shower.) 97€ single; 144€ double; 185€ triple; 229€ suite. Breakfast (8-10am) is included in the rates. Visa, MC, AX, DC. Air-conditioned. English spoken, phones, cable TV w/CNN & BBC, wonderful charming renovated 12th-century grand hotel w/ nicely & identically modern darkwood furnished large rms.,#3 (ground-flr. rm. w/queen-size bed) is for a double; #101 (3 twin beds or 1 zip & lock king-size bed & twin bed) is for a triple; #202 (fabulous large rm. w/king-size bed on lower-level, circular wrought iron staircase that takes you up to a loft bedroom w/wrought iron 4-poster 2 twin beds & faces the street) is for a family; #206 (4 twin beds) & 306 (4 twin beds) are for a family but can fit an extra twin bed for a quint; minibars, wonderful quiet location, elevator. This hotel is not family-owned but managed by Roberto Mazzolai.

VIRGILIO: Piazza Duomo 5/6. **Tel:** 0763-341882. **Fax:** 0763-343797. **Web site:** http://www.hotelvirgilio.com/ **E-mail:** info@hotelvirgilio.com (13 rms., all w/toilet & bath or shower.) 69€ single; 97€ double; 128€ triple; 159€ quad. Breakfast (7-10am) at 6€ pp can be served in the room. Visa, MC. English spoken (Paola & Peiro), phones, TV, charming modern palazzo hotel w/nicely furnished bright airy small pretty rms., #25 & another room that faces the Duomo are for a single; #26 (nice-size rm. w/2 twin beds or zip & lock queen-size bed & face the Duomo) is for a double but can fit an extra twin bed for a triple; #15 (bathroom w/bathtub) & 24 (both face the Duomo) are for a double; #6 & 18 face the Duomo, bar, elevator, parking (8€ per day). Owned/managed by Vladmiro Belcapo. I am sorry neither Paola & Peiro were around when I got to the hotel to get the updated information. Mr. Belcapo is a grumpy, rude man who has a wonderful hotel in a fabulous location facing the Duomo. I have received complaints about his attitude but not about the hotel itself. (Closed Jan.-mid-Feb.)

TAXI
Piazza Matteoti. Tel: 0763-301903. Near train station.

RESTAURANT
GROTTE FUNARO: Via Ripa Serancia 41.
Tel: 0763-343276. Fax: 0763-342898.
Web site: http://www.argoweb.it/ristorante_grottedelfunaro/ Hrs.: Tues.-Sun. 12:30-2:30pm & 7:30pm-10pm. Closed Mon. Visa, MC, AX, DC. Reservations required for dinner. Delicious food served in a wonderful atmosphere. The restaurant is built inside a cave. Carlo, the waiter, speaks great English which helps because there is no Italian menu. I just surrendered to his expertise and had one of my best meals ever in Orvieto. Highly recommended by Carla, Hotel Corso. Carla also suggested restaurants Buca di Baco & Al Pozzo Estrusca. I did not have an opportunity to eat at either one. Buca di Baco: Corso Cavour 299-301. Tel/Fax: 0763-344792. Closed Tues.; Al Pozzo Estrusca: Piazza Ranieri 1a. Tel/Fax: 0763-344458. Closed Tues.

PERUGIA
Northern Umbria, zip code 06123
Country code 39, city code 075

Perugia Tourist Information Center
Piazza IV Novembre 3. **Tel:** 075-5736458. **Fax:** 075-5739386. Hrs.:
Mon.-Sat. 8:30am-1:30pm & 3:30-6:30pm, Sun. 9am-1pm. Located
in Palazzo Priori, in the back of the Duomo at the end of Corso
Vannucci, the historic center's main avenue. **Web site:** http://
www.umbria2000.it/ **E-mail:** info@iat.perugia.it

TRANSPORTATION TIPS
Stazione Fontivegge, Perugia's main train station, is inconveniently
located in Piazza Vittorio Veneto (suburbs), a challenging 5km downhill below the town, outside the center. It is too far and too steep to
walk from the train station to the center. Catch buses #6, 7, 9, 11, 13
or 15 in front of the train station to the right at the orange sign. Just
look for the buses with the destination "Piazza Italia" on the front
(20-min. ride). Purchase your bus ticket (7€ pp) at the La Repubblica
newsstand before you leave the train station. For your convenience,
buy enough bus tickets to get you to & from the station. Escalia Mobila
Pellini (escalator/mobile stairs) hrs.: 6:45am-2am.

Perugia hotels listed alphabetically
ALLA RESIDENZA DOMUS MINERVAE
ANNA
EDEN
ETRURIA
EUROPA
FORTUNA PERUGIA
PRIORI

HOTELS
ALLA RESIDENZA DOMUS MINERVAE: Viale Pompeo Pellini
19. **Tel/Fax:** 075-5732238. **Web site:** http://www.domusminervae.it/
E-mail: info@domusminervae.it (8 rms., 1 apt., 6 w/toilet & bath or
shower.) 50€ single; 67€ double; 94€ triple; 105€ quad. Breakfast
(8-11am) is included in the rates & can be served in the room. Visa,

MC. English spoken (Catia), phones, TV (5 rms.), wonderful charming Italian hotel w/old-fashioned & individually furnished large rms., #7 (wonderful huge bright airy rm. w/2 twin beds or zip & lock queen-size bed, sitting area, TV, bathroom w/shower & view of countryside) & 8 (bathroom w/shower) are for a double & have access to a fully equipped small kitchenette; #3 & 4 (both large rms. w/2 twin beds or zip & lock queen-size bed, TV, small bathrooms w/showers & balconies w/views of countryside) are for a double; #2 (view & bathroom); #1 (bathroom); #5 (large corner rm. w/queen-size bed, no bathroom & balcony that faces the parking lot & side street); #6 (no bathroom); walk one flight up from elevator to apt. (fabulous huge bright airy 2-bedroom corner apt. w/4 twin beds or 2 zip & lock queen-size beds, 3 steps up to large bathroom w/bathtub, TV, fully equipped kitchen, terrace & 3 windows w/views of countryside) is for 2-4 people w/no minimum nights required; garden, elevator, 2 flrs., parking (6€ per day). I stayed at this hotel and loved it. Owned/managed by Catia Mugnani (daughter, Emma, Hotel Anna). *5% rm. discount when you show her this book.* The family organizes Italian language, culture and cooking courses. Catia's brother Giacomo with his American wife Michela also manage Hotel Europa in the same bldg. Bus #6 or 7. Bus stop: Piscina Pellini, on the corner the hotel's street, just in front of an escalator (escalia mobile) that links Viale Pompeo Pellini to the historic center.

ANNA: Via Priori 48, 1st fl. **Tel/Fax:** 075-5736304.
E-mail: annahotel@jumpy.it (14 rms., 10 w/toilet & bath or shower.) 47€ single; 74€ double; 94€ triple; 105€ quad. The rooms without bathrooms are cheaper. No breakfast served. Visa, MC. English spoken, phones, TV, charming 17th-century hotel w/simple old-fashioned & individually furnished rms., #15 (small rm. w/French double bed, standard-size bathroom & faces the interior) & 14 (twin bed, cubicle bathroom & no view) are for a single; #1 (2 twin beds or zip & lock queen-size bed, small bathroom & faces back) is for a double; #3 (nice-size rm. w/3 twin beds or 1 zip & lock queen-size bed & twin bed, small bathroom & interior balcony w/rooftops view), 4 (huge rm. w/3 twin beds or 1 zip & lock queen-size bed & twin bed, small bathroom & interior balcony/sitting area w/rooftops view) & 5 (3 twin beds or 1 zip & lock queen-size bed & twin bed, compact

bathroom & rooftops view) are for a double or triple; #8 (fabulous huge rm. w/3 twin beds or 1 zip & lock queen-size bed & twin bed, beautiful 17th-century decorative high ceiling & small bathroom) is for a triple but can fit an extra twin bed for a family; #2 (4 twin beds or 1 zip & lock queen-size bed & 2 twin beds, small bathroom & faces street w/no view) is for a family; #9 (fabulous massive rm. w/3 twin beds or 1 zip & lock queen-size bed & twin bed, beautiful 17th-century decorative high ceiling, small bathroom & faces parking lot) is for a triple but can fit extra twin beds for a family or quint; #6 (3 twin beds or 1 zip & lock queen-size bed & twin bed, no bathroom & rooftops view) & 10 (nice-size rm. w/2 twin beds or zip & lock queen-size bed, no bathroom & small window w/rooftops view) share a bathroom; #11 (twin bed, no bathroom & faces side street) shares a bathroom with another room; high ceilings, lots of character, 3 flights of steep stairs up to 1st fl., no elevator, 2 flrs. Owned/managed by Marcelo & Emma Citti. *5% rm. discount when you show them this book.* Their son Giacomo & daughter Catia own/manage Hotels Europa & Alla Residenza Domus Minervae. The family organizes Italian language, culture and cooking courses. From Piazza Italia, walk straight down Corso Vannucci to Piazza Repubblica, turn left onto Via Priori (behind the Palazzo Priori) & walk 2 1/2 blocks down the steep street to the hotel.

EDEN: Via Cesare Caporali 9. **Tel:** 075-5728102. **Fax:** 075-5720342. (20 rms., all w/toilet & shower.) 43€ single; 68€ double; 95€ triple; 127€ quad.Visa, MC, AX, DC. Breakfast (8-10am) at 6€ pp can be served in the room (3€ extra pp). Limited English spoken, phones, TV, wonderful charming renovated 14th-century hotel w/nicely & identically furnished modern rms., #14, 15, 21 & 23 (all w/twin beds & small bathrooms) are for a single; #24 (large rm. w/king-size bed, small bathroom & view of countryside & rooftops), 11 (king-size bed & faces the back w/rooftops view), 20 (2 twin beds or zip & lock queen-size bed), 25 (small rm. w/queen-size bed, small bathroom, arched ceiling & view of countryside & rooftops) & 12 (2 twin beds & faces back) are for a double; 6 fabulous large rms. that Maximo calls apts.: #204 (2 twin beds or zip & lock king-size bed, original stone wall, wood-beamed ceiling, sitting area, large modern bathroom & wooden flrs.) & 309 (huge rm. w/2 twin beds or zip & lock king-size bed, high wood-beamed ceiling & small balcony that faces back w/no view) are for a double; #203 (3 twin beds or 1 zip & lock queen-size bed & twin bed, high wood-beamed ceiling, modern bathroom, wooden flrs. & faces the interior) & 308 (balcony) are for a triple; #310 is for a triple; #201 (large apt. w/4 twin beds or 1 zip & lock king-size bed & 2 twin beds, high wood-beamed ceiling, modern bathroom, wooden flrs. & huge terrace/garden w/no view) & 202 (large apt. w/4 twin beds or 1 zip & lock king-size bed & 2 twin beds, high wood-beamed ceiling, modern bathroom & wooden flrs.) is for a family; great location near Piazza Italia, elevator, 3 flrs., free nearby permit street parking w/prior arrangement. Owned/managed by warm & accommodating Maximo & Vera (husband & wife). From Piazza Italia, look for Banco Italia, walk to the right of the bank down the steps, turn left on Via Luigi Bonazzi, turn right around the corner to Via Cesare Caporali. (Closed Dec. 23-29.)

ETRURIA: Via Bella Luna 21. **Tel:** 075-5723730. (8 rms., 5 w/toilet & shower.) 58€ double. The rooms without bathrooms are cheaper. Cash only. English spoken (Louisa & Maria), no phones, no TV, charming medieval 13th-century cave-like basic hotel w/simple individually old-fashioned furnished rms., #7 (large rm. w/2 twin beds, large new bathroom, high ceiling & wonderful view of countryside), 5 (nice-size bright airy rm. w/queen-size bed, bathroom & wonderful view of countryside) & 4 (small bright rm. w/2 twin beds, small bathroom & view of countryside) are for a double; #8 (large rm. w/king-size bed, bathroom & no view) & 2 (small rm. w/king-size bed, bathroom & faces the interior) are for a double; #6 (queen-size bed, high arched ceiling, private bathroom outside the room & rooftops view) is for a double; #3 (large rm. w/twin bed, no bathroom & view of countryside) & 1 (twin bed, no bathroom & faces the back) are for a single; charming 16th-century cave-like lounge, wonderful simple Italian ambience, 12midnight curfew, fabulous quiet location, no elevator, 1 fl. Owned/managed by Louisa, Antonetta & Maria (sisters), who are extremely interesting women. Kimbo is the hotel's small black poodle mascot. From Piazza Italia, walk straight down Corso Vannucci to Piazza Repubblica, turn left on Via Bella Luna (the 1st arched portal next to the pharmacy), walk down the steep steps to the hotel.

EUROPA: Viale Pompeo Pellini 19. **Tel:** 075-5726883. **Fax:** 075-5736304. **Web site:** http:/www.hoteleuropa-pg.com/ **E-mail:** info@hoteleuropa-pg.com (14 rms., all w/toilet & shower.) 53€ single; 74€ double; 100€ triple; 113€ quad. Breakfast (8-10am) is included in the rates & can be served in the room (3€ extra pp). Visa, MC. English spoken (Michelle), phones, TV, wonderful charming 19th-century Italian hotel w/old-fashioned & individually furnished large rms., some w/shiny tiled, carpeted or authentic flrs., #24 (fabulous bright airy rm. w/king-size bed, antique headboard, small bathroom & balcony w/wonderful view of countryside), 28 (Giacomo's favorite rm. w/king-size bed, cut-glass windows w/unusual shutters, wooden flr. & faces the parking lot), 3 (large rm. w/king-size bed, handicapped access bathroom & balcony w/view of countryside) & 4 (large rm. w/king-size bed & large bathroom) are for a double; #25 (romantic large corner rm. w/2 twin beds or zip & lock queen-size bed, compact bathroom, authentic floor & balcony that faces the street w/no view), 5 (romantic large rm. w/2 twin beds or zip & lock queen-size bed, small bathroom & faces flowerless garden) & 6 are for a double; #21 (wonderful corner rm. w/3 twin beds or 1 zip & lock queen-size bed & twin bed, standard-size bathroom, authentic floor & 3 windows that face the parking lot w/view of countryside), 27 (romantic large rm. w/3 twin beds or 1 zip & lock queen-size bed & twin bed, small bathroom, authentic floor & faces the street w/no view), 22 (nice bright airy rm. w/3 twin beds or 1 zip & lock queen-size bed & twin bed, standard-size bathroom & view of countryside), 26 (3 twin beds or 1 zip & lock queen-size bed & twin bed, compact bathroom, authentic floor & faces the street w/no view) & 2 (3 twin beds or 1 zip & lock king-size bed & twin bed & faces the parking lot w/view of countryside) are for a triple; #1 (wonderful huge rm. w/4 twin beds or 1 zip & lock king-size bed & 2 twin beds, high ceiling & faces the parking lot w/view of countryside) is for a quad; hairdriers, high ceilings, wonderful Italian ambience, elevator, 2 flrs., parking (6€ per day). Owned/managed by Giacomo Mugnani & Michelle McCarthy (husband & wife & son of Emma, Hotel Anna). Giacomo's sister owns/manages the Hotel Alla Residenza Domus Minervae in the same building. The family organizes Italian language, culture and cooking courses. Bus #6 or 7. Stop: Piscina Pellini. For directions, see Hotel Alla Residenza Domus Minervae.

FORTUNA PERUGIA: Via Luigi Bonazzi 19. **Tel:** 075-5722845. **Fax:** 075-5735040. **Web site:** http://www.umbriahotels.com/ **E-mail:** fortuna@umbriahotels.com (32 rms., all w/toilet & bath or shower.) 84€ single; 124€ double; 160€ (rm. #309) double; 160€ triple; 190€ quad. Buffet breakfast (7:30-10am, includes cold cuts, cheese, assorted breads, cereals, juices, yogurt & hard-boiled eggs) is included in the rates & can be served in the room (3€ extra pp) or on the terrace in warm weather. Air-conditioned. Visa, MC, DC. English spoken (Dina, Lorenzo & Valeria), phones, cable TV w/CNN, wonderful beautiful 12th-century provincial hotel w/contemporary & identically furnished rms., #206 (walk up 1 flight to large rm. w/French double bed, 1 step up to small bathroom, near breakfast room & faces back w/no view) & 308 are for a single; #502 (fabulous romantic corner rm. w/queen-size bed, arched doorway & terrace w/view of countryside & rooftops) is for a double; #211 (wonderful bright corner rm. w/queen-size bed, small bathroom & balcony w/fabulous rooftop view) & 209 (queen-size bed, small bathroom & balcony w/fabulous rooftop view) are for a double; #215 (huge rm. w/queen-size bed, sitting area, bathroom w/Jacuzzi shower & balcony w/fabulous view of countryside) is for a double but can fit an extra twin bed for a triple; #205 (queen-size bed, high ceiling, original stone wall, fabulous bathroom w/Jacuzzi bathtub, shower & no view) & 204 (huge rm. w/3 twin beds or 1 zip & lock king-size bed & twin bed & large bathroom w/shower) have an outside common door & can be rented together as one family rm. or separately as a double; #218 & 216 (walk up 1 flight to both large rms. w/2 twin beds or zip & lock queen-size bed, arched ceilings & wonderful views of countryside & rooftops) are for a double; #208 (huge rm. w/2 twin beds or zip & lock queen-size bed, large bathroom w/Jacuzzi bathtub & balcony that faces the back) is for a double but can fit an extra twin bed for a triple; #101 (walk up 1 flight to huge 1st flr. rm. w/2 twin beds or zip & lock queen-size bed & high ceiling) is for a double; #408 (walk 1/2 flight up to a large corner 5th flr. rm. w/2 twin beds or zip & lock queen-size bed & 3 windows w/fabulous view of countryside & rooftops) is for a double; #501 (large rm. w/2 twin beds, bathroom w/bathtub & view) is for a double but can fit an extra twin bed for a triple; #309 (Executive large 3rd flr. rm. w/king-size bed, bathroom w/bathtub, frescoed ceiling & near the communal lounge) is priced higher for a double; #407 (large rm. w/3 twin beds or 1 zip & lock queen-size bed

& twin bed, leather sofa, sitting area, bathroom w/large shower stall & balcony w/fabulous view of countryside) is for a triple; #302 (French double bed & twin bed) is for a double but discounted for a triple; #403 is a combination of two rooms: #404 (2 twin beds or zip & lock queen-size bed & view of countryside & rooftops) & 405 (single/ double & view of countryside & rooftops) which are rented together as one family room w/small bathroom that parallels both rooms; all the following rooms extend off the communal lounge on the 3rd flr. & are the last to go: #308 (single), 307 (large double), 305 (double), 304 (small rm. w/2 twin beds or zip & lock queen-size bed) & 306 (small 3rd flr. rm. w/2 twin beds or zip & lock queen-size bed & faces the street); hairdriers, minibars, 13th-century lounge w/nonworking fireplace, frescoed ceiling & terrace w/view on 3rd flr., beautiful veranda terrace w/fabulous panoramic view, wonderful ambience, free Internet access (8pm-12midnight), wonderful location, bar, elevator only goes to 4th flr., 5 flrs., free nearby permit street parking w/prior arrangement or garage parking (16€ per day). They offer half- and full-board rates. Owned/managed by the wonderful charming Valeria Hencaroni who prefers a young energetic staff. From Piazza Italia, look for Banco Italia, walk to the right of the bank down the steps to Via Luigi Bonazzi, hotel is on the right.

PRIORI: Via Priori/Vermiglioli 3. **Tel:** 075-5723378. **Fax:** 075-5723213. **Web site:** http://www.perugia. com/hotelpriori/ **E-mail:** hotelpriori@perugia.com (64 rms., all w/toilet & shower.) 65€ single; 95€ double; 130€ triple; 155€ quad. Breakfast (7:15-10:30am) is included in the rates & can be served in the room (3€ extra pp) or in the garden in warm weather. Air-conditioned (rms. #103-108 at 20€ extra per day). Visa, MC, AX, DC. English spoken (Raffaele, Marzia & Franziska), phones, cable TV w/CNN (25 rms.), wonderful charming renovated modern 18th-century hotel w/contemporary & identically furnished large bright airy pretty rms., #265 (large corner rm. w/view of rooftops & countryside) & 105 (air-conditioned rm. w/2 twin beds) are for a double; #128 & 129 (both lower-level rms. w/2 twin beds or zip & lock queen-size bed) are for a double; #353 (large rm. w/3 twin beds or 1 zip & lock queen-size bed & twin bed & view of countryside) is for a triple; #108 & 104 (both air-conditioned rms. w/2 twin beds or zip & lock queen-size bed, bunk beds & terraces that face the back w/no views) are for a family; #103 (huge air-conditioned rm. w/3 twin beds or 1 zip & lock king-size bed & twin bed, bunk beds & faces the back) is for a family or quint; #105 &107 (both air-conditioned pretty rms. w/5 twin beds & terraces that face the back w/no views) are for a family or quint; #351 (single), 352 (double) & 353 (triple) all have views of the valley; #261, 264 & 265 (all w/queen-size beds & bunk beds & w/views of the valley) are for a family; #251, 252, 263 & 355 all have views of the valley; fabulous terrace w/no view, bar, wonderful location, no elevator, 4 flrs., garage parking (13€ per day). Owned/managed by Raffaele Stoppini. His two friendly boxers stand guard behind the reception desk.

TAXI
Tel: 075-5004888.

INTERNET CAFE
Web site: http://www.thenetgate.it/ The Netgate: Via Cesare Battisti 19. Tel: 075-5716000.

LAUNDROMATS (Lavanderia)
Ondablu: Corso Bersaglieri 2/4. Hrs.: Daily: 8am-10pm. Located on the corner of Via Pinturicchio. Not conveniently located in town; Lava e Lava: Via Mario Angeloni 32a. Hrs.: Daily: 8am-10pm. Located near train station.

SUPERMARKET
Delicie: Piazza Matteotti 15. Hrs.: Mon.-Sat. 9am-8pm. There is also a supermarket located across the street from the train station.

RESTAURANTS
IL FALCHETTO: Via Bartolo 20. Tel: 075-5731775. Fax: 075-5729057. Hrs.: Tues.-Sun. 12:30pm-3:30pm & 7:30pm-12midnight. Closed Mon. in winter & last 2 wks. in Jan. Visa, MC, AX, DC. Specialty: Meats.

OSTERIA DEL GHIOTONE: Via Cesare Caporali 12. Tel: 075-5727788. Hrs.: Wed.-Mon. 1pm-3pm & 7:30pm-11pm. Closed Tues. Visa, MC. Specialty: Umbricelli Casalinga. Wonderful new restaurant owned/managed by Aldo Cimarelli (husband/trained French chef) & Monica Silvestrini (wife/salad chef/waitress).

POSITANO
Amalfi Coast, zip code 84017
Country code 39, city code 089

Positano Tourist Information Center
Via Saraceno 4. **Tel:** 089-875067. **Fax:** 089-875760. Hrs.: Mon.-Fri. 8:30am-2pm; Sat. 8am-1pm. Hours are not etched in stone. With your back to the Duomo, look straight down to the bldg. w/red doors. **E-mail:** positano.aacst@interbusiness.it

TRANSPORTATION TIPS
Positano by bus: The SITA buses are blue and they travel only the exterior of Positano. There are only two SITA scheduled bus stops in Positano: "Sponda" & "Chiesa." As you leave Sorrento, "Chiesa" is Positano's main bus stop at the Bar Internazionale which is located at the top of the village on the main road. This stop is not convenient for any of the hotels listed below. The "Sponda" bus stop is on the same side as Amalfi near the top of Via Cristoforo Colombo. Make sure you purchase your bus ticket before trying to board the blue bus. 35-min. bus ride (sit on the left side for a spectacular coastline view) to Sorrento. 50-min. bus ride (sit on the right side for a spectacular coastline view) to Amalfi. The bus/taxi depot is near Hotel Bougainville on Via Cristoforo Colombo. The *tabacchio* (tobacco) shop near Bar Mulino Verde (not far from Hotel Bougainville) on the first landing is where you can buy your bus tickets.

Positano by boat: As you arrive by boat, walk down the stairs to your right past the restaurants (Chez Black, Tre Sorelle, etc.), then walk up the narrow road to the stairs on your right towards the Duomo, pass the Duomo and continue up the stairs onto the cobblestone road with the vendors displaying their wares on your left side, continue walking straight up the hill, past the Bank Napoli. If you have a lot of luggage, I suggest you look for the baggage handlers/porters near the port before you take the strenuous 20-min. walk uphill. Porters Tel: 089-875310. Positano to Sorrento (via Capri): 9€ one-way ticket (hydrofoil); 8€ one-way ticket (ferry). Positano to Amalfi: 4€ one-way ticket (ferry). Cash only. Don't assume the boats run every day in high season. The condition of the weather dictates their schedule. Always check the day before departure. **TRA.VEL.MAR:** Tel: 089-873190. Fax: 089-872950.

Within Positano

Local orange buses travel only in the interior of Positano. They make a counter clockwise circle from the main road and go down Via Marconi to Viale Pasitea, then the bus climbs back up Viale Pasitea where the name changes to Via Colombo as it continues to climb back up to the main road.

Positano hotels listed alphabetically

BOUGAINVILLE
CALIFORNIA
CASA GUADAGNO
REGINELLA (LA)
TAVOLOZZA (LA)
VILLA MARIA LUISA
VILLA LA TARTANA
VILLA ROSA

HOTELS

Spiaggia Grande side of Positano

BOUGAINVILLE: Via Cristoforo Colombo 25. **Tel:** 089-875047. **Fax:** 089-811150. **Web site:** http://www.bougainville.it/ **E-mail:** hotel@bougainville.it (14 rms., all w/toilet & bath or shower.) 64€ single; 85€ (no view) double; 100€ (sea view) double; 138€ triple. Continental buffet breakfast (8-10am, includes homemade cake) at 6€ pp can be served on the terrace in warm weather. Visa, MC, AX, DC. English spoken (Carlo & Luisa), phones, no TV, charming simple hotel w/simply furnished rms., shiny tiled flrs., #14 (nice-size rm. w/ twin bed & small window w/no view) is the only single rm.; #10 (2 twin beds or zip & lock king-size bed & large l-shaped shared terrace that faces the street) is for a double; #26, 24 & 20 (all w/2 twin beds or zip & lock king-size bed & balconies w/wonderful sea & mountainside views) are for a double; #18 (nice-size rm. w/2 twin beds or zip & lock king-size bed & window that faces the street w/ views of rooftop & sea) is for a double; #12 (small rm. w/2 twin beds or zip & lock double bed, no sun & no view) is for a double; #36, 30, 28, 22 & 16 (all w/2 twin beds or zip & lock queen-size bed & small windows near the ceiling w/no views) are for a double; #34 & 32 (both large nonsmoking rms. w/3 twin beds or zip & lock king-size bed &1 twin bed, balconies w/wonderful sea & mountainside views) are for a triple; solar-heated water, small terrace (seats 4) w/sea & mountainside view, reception is one flight up, no elevator, 1 fl. Owned/ managed by Carlo Cuomo. *Free breakfast when you show him this book.* Ask bus driver for Sponda bus stop. Walk down Via Cristoforo Colombo to hotel. (Closed Nov. 15-March 15.)

CALIFORNIA: Via Cristoforo Colombo 141. **Tel:** 089-875382. **Fax:** 089-812154. **Web site:** http://www.hpe.it/california/
E-mail: albergocalifornia@tiscalinet.it (17 rms., all w/toilet & bath) 163€ (sea view) double; 179€ (Jacuzzi bathtub & sea view) double. Call for triple & quad rates. The 5 rooms that face the back w/no views are cheaper. Breakfast (7:30-10:30am) is included in the rates & can be served in the room (6€ extra pp) or on the terrace in warm weather. Visa, MC, AX, DC. English spoken (Antonio, Franco, Maria & John), phones, no TV, fabulous wonderful charming pretty 18th-century renovated palazzo hotel w/beautifully hand-made chestnut furnished newly renovated large to huge rms., shiny tiled flrs. & high curved ceilings, #62 (huge rm. furnished w/Maria's grandmother's antique furniture, decorative ceiling w/chandelier & 17th-century antique flr.), 60 (romantic lighting), 59, 53 & 52 (all w/2 twin beds or zip & lock king-size bed & small balconies w/magnificent sea & mountainside views) are for a double; #57 (huge rm.) & 56 (large rm.) both w/terraces w/magnificent sea & mountainside views are for a double; #61 (Jacuzzi bathtub) & 51 (both are fabulous huge corner rms. w/2 twin beds or zip & lock queen beds & small balconies w/magnificent sea & mountain views) are for a double; #58 (huge honeymoon corner rm. w/king-size bed, Jacuzzi bathtub, 2 small balconies w/magnificent sea & mountainside view) is for a double; #54 (huge fabulous suite w/2 twin beds or zip & lock queen bed & faces the terrace w/magnificent sea view) is for a double but can fit an extra twin bed for a triple; #55 (huge fabulous suite w/2 twin beds or zip & lock king-size bed, sitting rm., chandelier, Jacuzzi bathtub & huge terrace w/magnificent view of sea & mountainside view) is for a double but can fit 2 extra twin beds for a family; all rooms have newly renovated beautifully hand-painted tiled large bathrooms w/ bathtubs & hand-held showers, towel heaters, frigobars & hairdriers, bar, large terrace w/wonderful view, great location, no elevator, 3 flrs., free parking. If you are on a budget they have 5 old-fashioned furnished rooms that face the back with small windows near the ceil-

ing w/old-fashioned bathrooms, no views & no frigobars. They are #63 (top-flr. large rm.), 64 (top-flr. large rm.), 68 (top-flr. large rm.), 69 & 70. Owned by the wonderful, warm accommodating and energetic Antonio, Maria & John Cinque (husband, wife & son) and Franco Cinque. *5% rm. discount when you show them this book.* Antonio & Franco Cinque (brothers) were raised in New York City, USA. Maria spent about 10 years in NYC. I absolutely love this hotel. The family speaks great English and they go out of their way to make sure all your needs are met. For directions, see Hotel Bougainville. (Closed Nov. 15-March.)

REGINELLA (LA): Via Pasitea 154. **Tel/Fax:** 089-87524. **Web site:** http://www.reginellahotel.it/ **E-mail:** lareginella@libero.it (8 rms., 1 apt., all w/toilet & bath or shower.) 118€ double; 150€ triple; 178€ quad; 200€ quint. Continental breakfast at 3€ pp is served in the room. Visa, MC. English spoken, no phones, TV, wonderful beautiful new (2001) hotel w/nicely furnished large rms. that all have balconies w/spectacular sea views, shiny tiled flrs., #28 also known as "Angel room" (huge honeymoon rm. w/double bed, sitting rm., fabulous huge bathroom w/shower & high ceiling) & 22 are for a double; #21 (bathroom w/bathtub), 24 (bathroom w/shower) & 26 (bathroom w/shower) all have 3 twin beds or 1 zip & lock king-size bed & twin bed are for a double or a triple; #23 (large rm. w/4 twin beds or 1 zip & lock king-size bed & 2 twin beds & bathroom w/ bathtub) is for a family; apt. (2 bedrooms,1 bathroom & balcony w/ spectacular view) is for a family or a quint; wonderful fabulous new bathrooms w/towel heaters; no elevator, 3 flrs., parking arrangements available. Owned by the accommodating Tonino, Rosy & Giovanni Maresca (husband, wife & son). Giovanni personally decorated some of the rooms. The family has plans to build a reception area & bar on the street level in another year. Bus stop: Punta Reginella which is located in front of the hotel near restaurant Vincenzo.

TAVOLOZZA (LA): Via Colombo 10. **Tel/Fax:** 089-875040. **E-mail:** celeste.dileva@tiscalinet.it (8 rms., all w/toilet & bath or shower.) 90€ double; 115€ (small apt.) double; 170€ triple; 225€ quad. Call for quint, sextet & septet rates. Breakfast (8am-12noon) at 8€ pp is served in the room. Cash only. English spoken (Anna), phones, TV (apts. only), wonderful charming hotel w/nicely furnished bright airy rms., shiny tiled flrs., #6 (lower-level rm. w/2 twin beds or zip & lock king-size bed, large bathroom w/bathtub & hand-held shower & huge terrace) & 1 (king-size bed, 3 steps up to the bathroom w/shower & balcony) both w/magnificent sea & mountain views are for a double; #5 & 4 (both lower-level rms. w/2 twin beds or zip & lock king-size bed, private bathrooms outside the rooms & terraces w/magnificent sea & mountain views) are for a double; #8 (small lower lower-level 2-rm. apt. w/king-size bed, twin bed, small fully equipped kitchen & large balcony w/magnificent sea & mountain view) is for triple but an extra twin bed for a family; #7 (small lower lower-level apt. w/queen-size bed, twin bed, nice-size fully equipped kitchen, bathroom w/ bathtub & balcony w/side sea view) is for double or a triple; #2 (huge 1 bedroom apt. w/private bathroom down the hall, no TV & huge fully equipped kitchen/dining area) & 3 (large bathroom w/bathtub) share a small balcony w/magnificent sea, mountain & church views and have connecting doors but can be rented separately or together as one apt. for a family of 4, 5 or 6 people; no elevator. Owned/managed by the wonderful & charming Celeste & Anna (sisters). Contact Anna via e-mail for detailed transportation information. For directions, see Hotel Bougainville. (Closed Nov.-Feb.)

VILLA ROSA: Via Cristoforo Colombo 127. **Tel:** 089-811955. **Fax:** 089-812112. **Web site:** http://www.villarosapositano.it/ **E-mail:** info@villarosapositano.it (13 rms., all w/toilet & shower.) 147€ double; 179€ triple; 209€ quad; 273€ (rm. #24) quad. Breakfast (8-10am) is included in the rates & is served in the room or on their terraces. Air-conditioned. Visa, MC, AX, DC. English spoken (Francesco), phones, cable TV w/CNN, wonderful charming beautiful hotel w/beautifully furnished large rms., #22, 21, 20 & 18 (large rms. w/2 twin beds or zip & lock king-size bed & terraces w/wonderful sea views) are for a double but can fit extra twin beds for a triple; #15, 14 13, 12 & 11 (lower-level nice-size rms. w/2 twin beds or zip & lock king-size bed & terraces w/view of mountainside) are for a double; #27 & 28 (lower lower-level nice-size rms. w/2 twin beds or zip & lock king-size bed & terraces) are for a double; #24 (large rm. w/2 twin beds or zip & lock king-size bed & terrace w/wonderful sea view, huge living rm. w/2 twin beds & large dining rm.) is for a family; #23 (terrace & private bathroom outside the room) is for a double; well-known for its characteristic Mediterranean architecture, terrace, charming lobby w/magnificent view of mountainside, reception is 3 flights up, no elevator, 4 flrs. Owned/managed by Francesco (Franco)& Virginia Caldiero (husband & wife) who also own Hotel Villa Tartana. Call ahead for assistance if you are traveling with a lot of luggage. (Closed Nov.-March.)

VILLA LA TARTANA: Via Vicolo Vito Savino 6/8. **Tel:** 089-812193. **Fax:** 089-8122012. **Web site:** http://www.villalatartana.it/ **E-mail:** info@villalatartana.it (12 rms., all w/toilet & bath or shower.) 158€ (standard rm.) double; 179€ (jr. suite) double; 211€ triple; 241€ quad. Breakfast (8-10am) is included in the rates & is served in the room. Air-conditioned. Visa, MC, AX, DC. English spoken (Carmela & Franco), phones, cable TV w/CNN, wonderful charming beautiful new (1998) typical Positanasian renovated house w/ beautifully furnished large bright rms., shiny tiled flrs., #48, 49 & 51 (all standard rms. w/2 twin beds or zip & lock king-size bed, bathrooms w/showers, large balconies w/magnificent sea views) are for a double; #54 (bathroom w/bathtub & large balcony), 52 (bathroom w/bathtub) & 53 (bathroom w/shower) all are 4th-flr. rms. w/2 twin beds or zip & lock king-size bed & tiny balconies w/magnificent sea views for a double; #44 & 43 (both lower-level large standard rms. w/3 twin beds or zip & lock king-size bed & 1 twin bed, bathrooms w/bathtub & balconies w/no views) are for a double or triple; #45 (large jr. suite w/2 twin beds or zip & lock king-size bed, bathroom w/shower, large living rm. w/convertible sofa & magnificent sea view) & 42 (huge rm. w/4 twin beds or zip & lock king-size bed & 2 twin beds, convertible sofa, large bathroom w/bathtub & small balcony w/partial sea view) are for a family; minibars, hairdriers, many of the original architectural features remain & have been enhanced, fabulous location 5-min. walk from Spiaggia Grande beach, no elevator, 3 flrs. & reception. Owned/managed by Francesco (Franco) & Virginia Caldiero (husband & wife) who also own Hotel Villa Rosa. (Closed Nov.-Easter.)

HOTELS
Fornillo side of Positano
CASA GUADAGNO: Via Fornillo 22. **Tel:** 089-875042. **Fax:** 089-811407. (10 rms., all w/toilet & bath or shower.) 106€ double; 121€ triple; 136€ quad. Breakfast (8-10am) is included in the rates & can

be served in the room or on the terrace in warm weather. Cash only. English spoken (Guadagno), phones (10 rms. in the main bldg.), no TV, wonderful charming plain hotel w/nicely furnished nice-size bright airy rms. that all face the sea, shiny tiled flrs., #2 (bathroom w/ bathtub), 3 (bathroom w/bathtub), 4 & 5 (all have 2 twin beds or zip & lock queen-size bed, & balconies w/wonderful sea & mountain views) are for a double; #10 (double bed & small balcony w/wonderful sea & mountain view) is for a double; #6 (3 twin beds or zip & 1 lock queen-size bed & twin bed & huge terrace), 9 (queen-size bed & 1 twin bed) & 8 (3 twin beds & terrace) all w/magnificent sea & mountainside views are for a triple; #7 (2 twin beds, queen-size bed, huge shared terrace w/magnificent sea & mountainside view) is for a family; minibars, terrace, bar, no elevator, 3 flrs. The annex (5-min. walk) has 4 rms. (which I did not see) w/bathrooms & terraces w/sea views. If you stay in the annex, you have to walk outside to the main bldg. to have breakfast. Owned/managed by Guadagno. Catch the local orange bus. Stop: Grotto Fornillo. Via Fornillo is to the right off Viale Pasitea. As you exit the bus, with the sacred miniature churches carved in the hill to your back, look to your right and turn right onto Via Fornillo to your hotel.

VILLA MARIA LUISA: Via Fornillo 40. **Tel/Fax:** 089-875023. (10 rms., all w/toilet & bath or shower.) 74€ (rms. 1, 2 & 7) double; 79€ double. Call for triple & quad rates. No breakfast is served. Automatic coffee machine. Cash only. English spoken (Carlo), plain homey charming hotel w/old-fashioned simply furnished bright rms., #5 & 6 (both w/2 twin beds or zip & lock queen-size bed & terraces w/magnificent sea views) are for a double; #1 & 2 (2 twin beds or zip & lock queen-size bed & faces the back w/mountainside view) is for a double; #7 (2 twin beds or zip & lock queen-size bed, compact bathroom & window w/mountainside view) is for a double; #13 & 14 (both lower-level rms. w/2 twin beds or zip & lock queen-size bed & face the back w/mountainside views) are for a double; #4 (large rm. w/2 twin beds or zip & lock queen-size bed & terrace w/magnificent sea view) is for a double but can fit an extra twin bed for a triple; #3 (huge rm. w/2 twin beds or zip & lock queen-size bed, unusual bathroom layout & terrace w/magnificent sea view) is for a double but can fit extra twin beds for a triple or a family; #9 (huge rm. w/3 twin beds or 1 zip & lock queen-size bed & twin bed, large bathroom

& tiny balcony w/mountainside view) is for a triple but can fit an extra twin bed for a family; spectacular panoramic view from rooftop terrace, access to refrigerator, nearby restaurant, no elevator, 3 flrs. Owned/managed by the charming Carlo Giovanni Milo for more than 30 years. Carlo will supply you with towels for use at the beach. For directions, see Hotel Casa Guadagno. (Closed Dec. & Jan.)

LAUNDROMAT (Lavanderia)
Via Colombo 175. (Near Hotel California.) Tel: 089-811144. Hrs.: Mon.-Sat: 8:30am-1pm. & 3:15pm-8pm. Closed Sun. Drop-off & pick-up only.

PARKING
Anna Russo: Via Pasitea 173A. Tel: 089-875737.

RESTAURANTS
DA VINCENZO: Viale Pasitea 172/178. Tel: 089-875128 or 875852. Hrs.: Tues. 7pm-12midnight; Wed.-Sun. 1pm-3pm & 7pm-12midnight. Closed Mon. & Tues. Lunch. Visa, MC, AX, DC. Reservations required. Vincenzo started cooking for artists in 1958. His sons Giosue & Vito now manage the restaurant, along with Giosue's wife, Marcella, who does the cooking & Giosue's son, Vincenzo. Noisy crowded well-priced restaurant that serves unbelievably delicious food such as zucchini flowers (fried in yeast batter), *pizza scarola*, wonderful sausages, *pasta e ceci*, *pasta e fagioli* and everything fresh daily from the Sorrento market. Highly recommended by my good friends Geovanni Brewer & Jeffrey Fischgrund and Maria, Hotel California.

DA COSTANTNO: Via Montepertuso 107/Via Corvo 95. **Tel:** 089-875738. Hrs.: Thurs.-Tues. 1pm-3pm & 7pm-12midnight. Closed Wed. Visa, MC, AX, DC. Huge noisy crowded well-priced restaurant that serves delicious homemade food along with a spectacular view of Positano, Montepertuso & Nocelle. Try to get a window seat. Located on top of the mountain overlooking Positano. Have your hotel make the reservations and the restaurant will send a bus to pick you up at your hotel. The bus will have about 0-12 passengers from various hotels. Owned/managed by the charming Luigi. Highly recommended by Maria, Hotel California.

RIVA DEL GARDA
Lake Garda. zip code 38066
Country code 39, city code 0464

Riva del Garda's Tourist Information Center
Giardini Porta Orientale 8. **Tel:** 0464-554444. **Fax:** 0464-520308.
Hrs.: Mon.-Fri. 9am-12pm & 3pm-5:30pm. Closed Sun. Longer hours
& Saturdays in summer. Located opposite the castle. **Web site:** http:/
/www.gardatrentino.it/ **E-mail:** info@gardatrentino.com

TRANSPORTATION TIPS
From the north by rail: Catch a train to the Roverto train station,
which is the nearest train station to Riva del Garda. Purchase your
bus ticket (3€) to Riva del Garda inside the train station at the same
window that sells train tickets. The bus stop is in front of the train
station to the right. It is a 45-min. ride from the Roverto train station
to Riva del Garda. Viale Roverto is the main highway that goes through
the town.

From the south by rail: Catch a train to the Desanzano del Garda
train station, but don't look for a bus station there-there isn't any.
Purchase your bus ticket (6€) to Riva del Garda at the bar inside the
train station. Walk across the street to Bar Olympia, where there should
be some bus drivers hanging out. Ask them for the departure times to
Riva del Garda. It is a 2-hr. bus ride from the Desanzano train station
to Riva del Garda. Or you can walk (15 min.) or taxi to Desanzano's
port to catch (April-Oct.) a 3-hr. catamaran or a 6-hr. ferry boat ride
to Riva del Garda. If you arrive by boat, the port is right in the middle
of the center. Don't assume the boats run every day in high season.
The condition of the weather dictates their schedule. Always check
the day before departure. Navigazione Lago di Garda Tel: 800-551801.
Note: You can also catch a train to Peschiera train station. The problem I had was finding a place to purchase my bus ticket to Riva del
Garda. It was an exhausting challenge.

To leave Riva del Garda by bus: Pick up bus schedule at the tourist
office. Depending on where you want to go, you can purchase your
bus ticket at one of the following locations: Tabaccheria Edicola:

Viale Dante 46; Bar Celtic Dragon: Viale Martiri 6d; Agenzia Viaggi Benacus: Viale Rovereto 47. There is a service charge if you purchase your ticket on the bus.

Riva del Garda hotels listed alphabetically
ANCORA
BELLARIVA
GIGLIO
LUISE
PORTICI
VENEZIA

HOTELS
ANCORA: Via Montanara 2. **Tel:** 0464-522131. **Tel/Fax:** 0464-550050. **Web site:** http://www.rivadelgarda.com/ancora/ **E-mail:** hotelancora@rivadelgarda.com (14 rms., all w/toilet & shower.) 65€ single; 102€ double; 136€ triple; 172€ quad; 188€ (3-bedroom) quad/quint. Buffet breakfast (7:30-10:30am) is included in the rates. Visa, MC, AX, DC. Limited English spoken (Loredana), phones, TV, wonderful charming quaint hotel w/nicely & identically furnished nice-size rms., carpeted flrs., #10 & 11 (both large 3rd flr. bright airy rms. w/2 twin beds or zip & lock king-size bed, futon convertible chair/bed, small bathrooms & balconies that face the street) are for a double or triple; #5 & 6 (large 1st flr. rm. w/2 twin beds or zip & lock king-size bed, futon convertible chair/bed & small bathrooms) are for a double or triple; #4 (huge 1st flr. corner rm. w/king-size bed, convertible sofa, standard-size bathroom & 2 windows) is for a double, triple or family; #6 (2nd flr. rm. w/king-size bed, small bathroom & faces the street) & 8 (2nd flr. rm. w/king-size bed) are for a double; large 3-bedroom (walk 1 flight up to 3 rooms w/2 twin beds or zip & lock king-size bed in 1 bedroom, twin bed in 1 bedroom, 2 twin beds or zip & lock king-size bed & convertible sofa in 1 bedroom & standard-size bathroom) is for a family or quint; warm ambience, many of the original features remain, bar, wonderful location on the pedestrian walkway, not far from the lake, restaurant w/1st flr. terrace, elevator, 4 flrs. Newly (2001) owned/managed by Ivano Targhini.

BELLARIVA: Via Franz Kafka 13/Viale Roverto 58. **Tel:** 0464-553620. **Fax:** 0464-556633. **Web site:** http://www.rivadelgarda.com/bellariva/ **E-mail:** bellariva@rivadelgarda.com (29 rms., all w/toilet & bath or shower.) 79€ single; 126€ double. Call for triple or quad rates. Breakfast (7am) is included in the rates & can be served in the room. Air-conditioned. Visa, MC, AX, DC. Limited English spoken, phones, cable TV w/CNN, charming hotel w/nicely & identically furnished modern nice-size rms., carpeted flrs., you have to be specific when you ask for a room, such as whether you want 2 twin beds or queen-size bed, because many of the rooms have French double beds; balcony w/view of the lake & mountain because some rooms face the pedestrian walkway, the higher the rm., the better the view but you may not want to climb the stairs (about 10 ground-flr. rms.), if you are 3 people or more make sure you get a room w/a real twin bed because the rooms w/futon convertible chair/beds are snug for a triple; #102 (ground-flr. rm. w/double bed & bathroom w/handicapped access) is for a double; #204 (large rm. w/2 twin beds or zip & lock queen-size bed, futon convertible chair/bed & shares huge terrace w/other rms.) is for a double; standard-size modern marble bathrooms w/hairdriers & towel heaters, minibars, warm ambience, Internet access available, garden, bar, restaurant w/terrace facing the water, wonderful peaceful location across from the lake, marble staircase, no elevator, 3 flrs., free parking. Owned/managed by Giulio Boniotti. They offer half- and full-board rates. Ask the bus driver for bus stop: Viale Roverto. (Closed Oct.-March.)

GIGLIO: Via Disciplini 23. **Tel:** 0464-552674. **Fax:** 0464-521069. (13 rms., 7 w/toilet & shower.) 50€ single; 81€ double; 111€ triple; 129€ quad. The rooms without bathrooms are cheaper. Breakfast (8-10am) is included in the rates. Visa, MC, AX, DC. Limited English spoken (Leda), phones, TV, simple hotel w/plainly pinewood furnished nice-size bright rms., shiny tiled flrs., #103 (small 1st flr rm. w/French double bed & large bathroom) is perfect for a single but too snug for a double; #101 (1st flr rm. w/2 twin beds or zip & lock queen-size bed) & 201 (2nd flr. rm. w/2 twin beds or zip & lock queen-size bed) is for a double; #202 (2nd flr. rm. w/queen-size bed & futon convertible chair/bed) is for double or triple; #401 (large 4th flr. bright rm. w/3 twin beds & large bathroom) is for a triple; #102 (large 1st flr rm. w/3 twin beds or 1 zip & lock queen-size bed & twin bed & futon convertible chair/bed) is for a triple or family; there is 1 communal bathroom for 1st flr. rms. #104 (twin bed) & 105 (2 twin beds) to share; there is 1 communal bathroom for 2nd flr. rms. #204 (2 twin beds) & 205 (2 twin beds) to share; there is 1 communal bathroom for 3rd flr. rms. #304 (2 twin beds) & 305 (2 twin beds) to share; standard-size bathrooms w/towel heaters, no ambience, bar, wonderful location, restaurant, elevator, 4 flrs. They offer half- and full-board rates. This 3-star hotel is furnished more like a 1-star hotel. Owned/managed by Franco & Leda Lazzarotto.

LUISE: Viale Roverto 9. **Tel**: 0464-552796. **Fax:** 0464-554250. **Web site:** http://www.hotelluise.com/ **E-mail:** luise@hotelluise.com (69 rms., all w/toilet & bath or shower.) The following rates are charged in the highest time of the season. They drop dramatically at different times throughout the year. 87€ (Margherita) single; 97€ (Gardenia) single; 107€ (Orchidea) single; 150€ (Margherita) double; 160€ (Gardenia) double; 170€ (Orchidea) double; 186€ (3 jr. suites) double; 198€ (suite La Terrazza) double. Call for triple, quad or quint rates. Normally I do not include large hotels like the Luise. However, I love this hotel because of the amenities, the warmth of the staff, the location & because of their prices it is one of the rare 4-star hotels I can afford. It is also one of the few hotels that remain open all year in Riva del Garda. Buffet breakfast (7-10:30am, includes cereals, assorted pastries, scrambled & hard-boiled eggs, cheese, ham, bacon, juices & croissants) is included in the rates. Air-conditioned. Visa, MC, AX, DC. English spoken, phones, cable TV w/CNN, CNBC, BBC & Eurosport, wonderful charming modern large grand hotel w/ nicely pinewood (Margherita) to contemporary (Gardenia) to beautifully (Orchidea) & identically furnished modern nice-size to large rms., carpeted flrs., #121, 120 119, 118, 117 & 116 (all 1st flr. Margherita rms. w/2 twin beds or zip & lock queen-size bed & balconies that face the street w/wonderful mountain views) are for a double; #110 (bathroom w/mini-bathtub w/hand-held shower), 114, 112, 115 & 109 (all 1st flr. Margherita rms. w/2 twin beds or zip & lock queen-size bed & face the back w/mountain views) are for a double; #108 (large 1st flr. Margherita rm. w/double bed, large bathroom w/bathtub w/hand-held shower & faces the back w/mountain view) is for a double; #319 (large 3rd flr. Gardenia rm. w/2 twin beds or zip & lock king-size bed, bathroom w/bathtub & faces the street w/wonderful mountain view) is for a double; #311 (large 3rd flr. Gardenia rm. w/king-size bed, twin bed, bathroom w/bathtub & faces the back w/mountain view) is for a double or triple; #303 (3rd flr. Orchidea rm. w/king-size bed, twin bed, convertible chair/bed, bathroom w/shower & faces the street w/wonderful mountain view) is for a double or triple; #304 (3rd flr. Orchidea rm. w/2 French double beds, bathroom w/shower & faces the back w/mountain view) is for a double; #51-61 (all large newly remodeled unusually shaped wonderful rms.): #58 (king-size bed, futon convertible chair/bed, large bathroom w/shower & faces the back) is for a double; #59 (huge rm. w/2 queen-size beds, huge bathroom w/bathtub & faces the back) is for a double; modern bathrooms w/hairdriers, there are bathrooms w/handicapped access in the halls, minibars, 19 rms. w/balconies that face the front have wonderful mountain views, Internet access available at 4€ per 1/2 hr., mountain bikes available, swimming pool, tennis, pingpong, garden w/sunbeds, children's play area, bar, restaurant, 2 elevators, free parking. They offer half-board rates. *5% rm. discount when you show both the wonderful & accommodating owner Stella Bertolini or director Fausto Franzoi this book.*

PORTICI: Piazza III Novembre 19. **Tel**: 0464-555400. **Fax:** 0464-555453. (45 rms., 13 apts., all w/toilet & shower.) 59€ single; 115€ double. Call for triple, quad, quint & apt. (3-night minimum) rates. Buffet breakfast (8-10am) is included in the rates. Visa, MC. English spoken, phones, cable TV w/Sky News, wonderful charming modern hotel w/simply & identically pinewood furnished rms., carpeted flrs., main bldg.: #110, 210, 310 & 504 (all w/twin beds) are for a single; #202 (corner rm. w/2 twin beds, roll-out twin bed & balcony that faces the square) & 203 (2 twin beds, roll-out twin bed & balcony that faces the square) are for a double; #204 (large rm. w/2 twin beds, roll-out twin bed & faces the square) is for a double or triple; the following information is for the apts. (3-night minimum): apt. #8 (tiny apt. w/convertible sofa, sloped wood-beamed ceiling, fully equipped kitchenette & faces the back) is for a double; apt. #4 (small 2nd flr. studio apt. w/convertible sofa, wooden flrs., fully equipped kitchenette & faces the square) is for a double; apt. #3 (2nd flr. studio apt. w/convertible sofa, futon convertible chair/bed, original nonworking fireplace, antique ceiling, wooden flrs., fully equipped kitchenette & faces the square) is for a double or triple; apt. #5 (small studio apt. w/convertible sofa, futon convertible chair/bed, wood-beamed ceiling, fully equipped kitchenette & faces the back) is for a double or triple; apt. #6 (studio attic apt. w/convertible sofa, 2 futon convertible chair/beds, sloped wood-beamed ceiling, wooden flrs., fully equipped kitchenette & faces the back) is for a double, triple or family; apt. #7 (studio attic apt. w/convertible sofa, 2 futon convertible chair/beds, sloped wood-beamed ceiling, wooden flrs., fully equipped kitchenette & small window that faces the back) is for a double, triple or family; apt. #12 (3rd flr. attic apt. w/convertible sofa, 2 futon convertible chair/beds, wood-beamed ceiling, fully equipped kitchenette & no view) is for a double, triple or family; apt. #2 (nice-size 1st flr. apt. w/queen-size bed, 2 futon convertible chair/beds, convertible sofa, living room w/fully equipped kitchenette & faces the back) is for a family; apt. #13 (3rd flr. attic apt. w/queen-size bed, convertible sofa, futon convertible chair/bed, wood-beamed ceiling, fully equipped kitchenette & no view) is for a family; apt. #1 (huge 1st flr. apt. w/queen-size bed, 2 roll-out beds, convertible sofa, huge living room, dining table, fully equipped kitchenette, washing machine, large bathroom & faces the square) is for a family or quint; wonderful location near the lake, bar, pizzeria/restaurant, original 13th-century staircase (apts.), elevator (main bldg. only), 5 flrs. They offer half- and full-board rates. Owned/managed by Giuliano Bertoldi. Piero works in the restaurant and according to him makes the best pizza in Riva del Garda. (Closed Oct.-April.)

VENEZIA: Via Franz Kafka 7/Viale Roverto 62. **Tel**: 0464-552216. **Fax:** 0464-556031. **Web site:** http://www.rivadelgarda.com/venezia/ **E-mail:** venezia@rivadelgarda.com (24 rms., all w/toilet & bath or shower.) 57€ single; 114€ double; 157€ triple. Breakfast (7-10:30am) at 9€ pp can be served in the room or on the terrace in warm weather. Visa, MC, AX. English spoken (Archille, Nicoletta & Andrea), phones, cable TV w/CNN & Eurosport, charming modern hotel w/nicely & identically pinewood furnished modern nice-size rms., #43 (3rd flr. rm.), 44 (3rd flr. rm), 36 (2nd flr. rm.), 35 (2nd flr. rm.), 28 (1st flr. rm.) & 27 (1st flr. rm.) all w/twin beds are for a single; #41 & 42 (both 3rd flr. corner rms. w/2 twin beds or zip & lock queen-size bed, bathrooms w/bathtubs w/hand-held showers & balconies w/fabulous views of lake & mountains) are for a double; #37 & 38 (both 3rd flr. rms. w/2 twin beds or zip & lock queen-size bed, convertible chair/bed & views) are perfect for a double but too snug for a triple; the rooms on the 3rd flr. have views, standard-size bathrooms w/hairdriers, bar, rooftop terrace w/magnificent panoramic view, wonderful peaceful location near the lake, no elevator, 3 flrs., free parking. Owned/managed by Archille, Nicoletta & Andrea La-sagna (father, mother & son). They plan to add an elevator soon. Call & confirm. Ask the bus driver for bus stop Viale Roverto. (Closed Nov.-Easter.)

SUPERMARKETS
Orvea Mercati: Giardino Verdi 12. Hrs.: Mon. 8:30am-12:30pm; Tues.-Sat. 8:30am-12:30pm & 3pm-7pm. Closed Sun & Mon. after-noon. Visa, MC. Cross street: Viale San Francisco; Mercati Trentini: Viale Roverto 41. Visa, MC. Hrs.: Mon.-Fri. 9am-1pm & 3:30pm-7:30pm; Sat. 9am-7:30pm. Closed Sun.

RESTAURANT
AL VOLT: Via Fiume 73. Tel: 0464-552570. Web site: http://www.gardatopline.com/ Hrs.: 12noon-2pm & 7pm-10pm. Closed Mon. & Feb. 15-March 15. Reservations required. Visa, MC. Quaint totally nonsmoking restaurant that serves fabulous food. Wonderful romantic atmosphere. Highly recommended by Hotel Luise.

ROME (Roma)
Latium, zip code 00186
Country code 39, city code 06

Rome Tourist Information Centers
1.) Termini (main train station) **Tel:** 06-4871270/4824078. Hrs.: Daily 8am-9pm. Located in front of tracks #4 & 5. **2.)** Via Parigi 5. **Tel:** 06-36004399. **Fax:** 06-48899238/4819316/4741647. Hrs.: Walk-ins. Mon.-Fri. 9am-1pm. This office is about a 10-min. walk from the front of the train station diagonally to the left, cross the huge Piazza Cinquecento, bear left near Piazza Repubblica's large fountain. Via Parigi begins on the other side of the church. **3.)** Leonardo da Vinci Airport, just outside customs to your left. **Tel:** 06-65954471. Hrs.: Mon.-Sat. 8:30am-7:00pm. **Web site:** http://www.romaturismo.com/ **E-mail:** editoria@apt-roma.it

TRANSPORTATION TO AND FROM AIRPORT
Termini Train station: Catch the **Termini line,** an air-conditioned express train (every hr.) from Rome's Leonardo da Vinci (Fiumicino) airport for 30-min. ride (9€ pp) to the Termini train station. Hrs.: 7:30am-9pm. Simply follow the signs to your left for Stazione FS/ Railway Station also labeled "Treno." Right after you walk through customs, when you leave the arrivals building, you'll see the train station about 40 feet in front of you across the street and up the ramp. If you plan to take the train back to the airport, purchase all your tickets at the same time. It will save you a lot of time when you get ready to leave Rome. Also, pick up a train schedule when you purchase your train ticket. Trains run from Termini to the airport every half-hour from track #22. Hrs.: 6:50am-9:15pm. Then take a bus, metro or taxi from Termini to your hotel. Look under the individual hotels for more transportation details. **Taxi:** Airport to center (45 min.) is approximately 90,000L including luggage. Airport Shuttle: airportshuttle@tiscalinet.it Tel: 06-42014507. Fax: 06-42014511. **ATM**: As you pass the Customs office, there is a Bank de Roma with an ATM on your left side (right side of the baggage claim.)

TRANSPORTATION TIPS
If you plan on using your railpass immediately after landing at Rome airport, you can get it validated at the train station office located at

the airport. (This way you can use it for the express airport train that takes you from Rome airport to the train station.) **Termini train station**: The train information office is located next to the United Colors of Benetton clothing store. Hrs.: Daily 7am-9:45pm. It is not the office that shares a space with the tourist office. I made the mistake of going into the office next to the tourist office after waiting for my number to be called, only to find out that they are a travel agency and charge for their services. As soon as you enter the train information office, pull a number from the machine and wait for it to be called. The wait could be very long which is the reason I emphasize getting the *Thomas Cook European Timetable*. See books recommended in "Before You Leave Home."

Rome hotels listed alphabetically

ALIMANDI	LEALE
ARENULA	LYDIA-VENIER
BROTZKY	MARCUS
CAMBRIDGE	MARGUTTA
CAMPO DE' FIORI	NARDIZZI AMERICANA
CONTILIA	NAVONA
CONTINENTALE	OCCHIO DI TREVI
CORALLO	OCEANIA
CORONET	ORLANDA
COROT	PAPA GERMANO
DODGE	PARLAMENTO
DOLOMITI	PLANET 29
ERCOLI	PRIMAVERA
ERDARELLI	ROMAE
FENICIA	SAN PANTALEO
FIORINI	SOLE
FIRENZE	SWEET HOME
GABRIELLA	TETI
HOLLYWOOD STELLA	ZANARDELLI
LAZZARI	

HOTELS (In the historic center)
ARENULA: Via Santa Maria Calderari 47. **Tel:** 06-6879454. **Fax:** 06-6896188. **Web site:** http://www.hotelarenula.com/ **E-mail:** hotel.arenula@flashnet.it (50 rms., all w/toilet & shower.) 97€ single;

132€ double; 160€ triple; 185€ quad. Buffet breakfast (7-10am) is included in the rates & can be served in the room (3€ extra pp). Air-conditioned (20 rms. at 11€ extra per day). Visa, MC. English spoken (Rosanna & Paolo), cable TV w/CNN, charming renovated palace hotel w/modern identically furnished shiny tiled flrs., the best rms. are on the 4th flr. because they are brighter, larger, airier & have rooftop views, but there is no elevator, #407 (French double bed & compact bathroom w/shower) is for a single; they have 10 single rooms; #411 (wonderful corner rm. w/2 twin beds or zip & lock queen-size bed, small bathroom w/shower, high ceiling & 2 windows) is for a double; 1st flr. rms.: #107 (newly renovated rm. w/2 twin beds or zip & lock queen-size bed, standard-size bathroom & tiny balcony that faces the street), 112 (2 twin beds or zip & lock queen-size bed, standard-size bathroom & faces the interior) & 105 (2 twin beds or zip & lock queen-size bed, small bathroom & tiny balcony that faces the street) are for a double; #106 (2 twin beds & tiny balcony that faces the street) is for a double but can fit an extra twin bed for a triple; #110 & 208 are for a family; hairdriers, bar, wonderful noisy location, white marble & wrought iron oval staircase, no elevator, 4 flrs. (You'd better be in good physical shape to walk up & down the stairs.) Owned/managed by Paolo Chiodi. Located near Piazza Campo de' Fiori. **Bus:** #64. Stop: Largo Torre Argentina. Start walking west, in the same direction that the bus is going, along Corso Vittorio Emanuele II, turn left onto Via Torre Argentina, which becomes Via Arenula when you walk straight through Largo Arenula & Piazza Cairoli, turn left onto Via Santa Maria Calderari.

CAMPO DE' FIORI: Via Biscione 6. **Tel:** 06-68806865 or 6874886. **Fax:** 06-6876003. **Web site:** http://www.hotelcampodefiori.com/ **E-mail:** campofiori@inwind.it (27 rms., 8 apts., 9 rms. w/toilet & bath or shower.) 160€ double; 195€ triple; 275€ quad; 305€ quint (same for apts.) The rooms without bathrooms are cheaper. Breakfast (7:30-10am) is included in the rates. Visa, MC. English spoken (Edith & Andy), no phones, no TV, charming picturesque cozy hotel w/nicely & individually furnished pretty rms. which vary in size from claustrophobic to nice-size rms., the 9 rooms that have bathrooms are the following: #602 (6th flr. romantic attic rm. w/canopy bed, bathroom & balcony w/rooftop view) is for a double but can fit an extra twin

NOISY

bed for a triple; #601 (6th flr. small attic rm., bathroom & balcony w/ rooftop view) is for a double; #106 (nice-size rm. w/2 twin beds & bathroom) & 305 (3rd rm. w/bathroom & faces the back) are for a double but can fit an extra twin bed for a triple; #105 (small romantic rm. w/2 twin beds or zip & lock queen-size bed, red-brick wall, high wood-beamed ceiling, compact bathroom w/shower & faces the square) is for a double; #104 (small rms. w/2 twin beds & bathroom) is for a double; #102 & 103 (both small 1st flr. rms. w/French double beds, bathrooms & face street) are for 2 slim people in love; #101 (tiny romantic not-so-bright 1st flr. rm. w/French double bed, standard-size bathroom w/shower & faces back w/no view) is for 2 slim people in love; split-level rooftop garden terrace w/wonderful panoramic view of Rome, fabulous noisy location near Piazza Campo de' Fiori, no elevator, 6 flrs. (You'd better be in good physical shape if you want to stay at this hotel & enjoy the rooftop view.) They have 8 wonderful beautifully furnished large private apts.: no phones, no TV, fully equipped regular-size kitchens, no elevator & no minimum nights required. If you stay in the apts. & don't feel like making your own breakfast, you'll have to walk outside to the hotel to have breakfast. This hotel is not family-owned but managed by the charming & accommodating Edith. **Bus:** #64. Stop: Piazza San Pantaleo. Located around the corner from Piazza Paradiso. From Piazza San Pantaleo, cross the street, walk down Via Baullari, turn left at the clothing store, walk down the street, turn left into Piazza Teatro Pompeo, turn left past the barbershop to hotel.

CORONET: Piazza Grazioli 5, 3rd fl. **Tel:** 06-6790653. **Tel/Fax:** 06-69922705. **Web site:** http://www.hotelcoronet.com/ **E-mail:** hotelcoronet@tiscalinet.it (13 rms., 10 w/toilet & bath or shower.) 140€ single; 160€ double; 206€ triple; 236€ quad. Call for quint rates. The rooms without bathrooms are cheaper. Breakfast (7:30-9:30am) is included in the rates & can be served in the room (3€ extra pp). Visa, MC, AX. English spoken (Sirmone, Marco & Alex), phones, no TV, wonderful charming renovated 17th-century grand old palace hotel w/fabulously old-fashioned & individually furnished large to massive pretty rms., some w/wooden or carpeted flrs., #45 (huge rm. w/2 twin beds or zip & lock queen-size bed, futon convertible chair/bed, compact bathroom w/shower & faces the private gardens) is for a double but can fit an extra twin bed for a triple; #44 (huge rm. w/2 twin beds or zip & lock queen-size bed, 2 chairs, compact bathroom w/shower & faces the private gardens) is for a double but can fit an extra twin bed for a triple; #38 (huge rm. w/2 twin beds or zip & lock queen-size bed, standard-size bathroom w/shower & faces the busy street) is for a double but can fit an extra twin bed for a triple; #41 (large rm. w/2 twin beds or zip & lock queen-size bed, futon convertible chair/bed, compact bathroom w/shower & faces the private gardens) is for a double or triple; #33 (massive rm. w/2 twin beds or zip & lock queen-size bed, convertible sofa, huge bathroom w/bathtub & huge window that faces the busy street) is for a double but can fit extra twin beds for a triple or family; #34 (massive rm. w/3 twin beds or 1 zip & lock queen-size bed & twin bed, convertible sofa, 2 armchairs, huge bathroom w/bathtub & hand-held shower, chandelier & window that faces the busy street) is for a triple but can fit extra twin beds for a family, quint or sextet; #40 (massive rm. w/3 twin beds or 1 zip & lock queen-size bed & twin bed, mini-chandelier & compact bathroom w/shower) is for a triple but can fit extra twin beds for a family, quint or sextet; #35 (huge rm. w/2 twin beds or zip & lock queen-size bed, no bathroom & faces the street), 36 (huge rm. w/2 twin beds or zip & lock queen-size bed, rocking chair, carpeted flr., no bathroom & faces the private gardens) & 37 (huge rm. w/2 twin beds or zip & lock queen-size bed, no bathroom, wooden flr. & faces the street) share 3 communal bathrooms; antique wooden doors, hairdriers, high wood-beamed ceilings, wonderful warm Italian ambience & environment, fabulous noisy location near Piazza Venizia, elevator, 1 flr. Owned/managed by the wonderful & charming Sirmone Teresi & her family for more than 35 years. The palace itself belongs to Princess Doria Pamphili & the royal family who still live on the premises. **Bus:** #64. Stop: Piazza Venezia. From Piazza Venezia, take Via Plebiscito, turn right onto Via Astalli into Piazza Venezia. Located inside the Palazza Doria.

NAVONA: Via Sediari 8. **Tel:** 06-68211391. **Tel/Fax:** 06-68803802. **Web site:** http://www.hotelnavona.com/
E-mail: info@hotelnavona.com (20 rms., all w/toilet & shower.) 90€ single; 121€ double; 165€ triple; 220€ quad. The rooms without bathrooms are cheaper. Breakfast (8:15-9:15am) is included in the

rates. Air-conditioned (19€ extra per day). Cash only. English spoken (Patricia & Corry), no phones, no TV, charming 15th-century Roman style hotel w/simply & identically furnished bright rms., #11 (nice-size rm. w/twin bed & faces the street) is for a single; #13 (corner rm. w/2 twin beds or zip & lock queen-size bed & small window that faces the street) is for a double; #13a & 13b (both large 2nd flr. rms. w/2 twin beds or zip & lock queen-size bed, wood-beamed ceilings & face the street) are for a double; #15c & 15d (both w/2 twin beds, arched wood-beamed ceilings & face the side street) are for a double; #15e (wonderful corner rm. w/2 twin beds or zip & lock queen-size bed, futon convertible chair/bed, arched wood-beamed ceiling & 2 windows) & 12c (large rattan furnished rm. w/2 twin beds or zip & lock queen-size bed, futon convertible chair/bed, wood-beamed ceiling, original stone showing in wall & faces the street) are for a double or triple; #15a (2 twin beds & 2 futon convertible chair/beds) is for a double, triple or family; #14 (large rm. w/3 twin beds or 1 zip & lock queen-size bed & twin bed & tiny balcony w/no view) is for a triple; #5 & 3 (both w/3 twin beds) are for a triple; #4 (large rm. w/4 twin beds & faces the street) is for a family; #12b (small rm. w/wood-beamed ceiling & faces the side street) & 12a (large rm.) have connecting doors but can be rented separately as a double or together as one family rm., all bathrooms are small & identically designed with pretty Versace tiles & towel heaters; high ceilings, wonderful location near Piazza Navona, hotel was built on top of a Roman bath, no elevator, 3 flrs. Owned/managed by charming & accommodating Patricia & Corry (sister & brother) who are Australian-Italian architect & antique dealers. Ask about the posted rules before making reservations such as: Pay in advance, no washing laundry, no guests and you must leave your room every day by 10am. Let them know in advance if you are on your honeymoon. **Bus:** #70 or 492. Stop: Corso Rinascimento. From Corso Rinascimento, turn right at Largo Sapienza, walk straight through onto Via Sediari. The same family owns & manages the Hotel Zanardelli Residence.

OCCHIO DI TREVI (Eye of the Trevi): Via Crociferi 26.
Tel/Fax: 06-4460634. **Tel/Fax:** 06-44704335.
Web site: http://www.hotelhollywoodroma.com/
E-mail: hotelhollywoodstella@libero.it (7 rms., 5 w/toilet & shower.)

128€ double; 160€ triple; 191€ quad. The rooms without bathrooms are cheaper. Self-service breakfast is included in the rates. Owned/managed by the wonderful, accommodating Marco Hazinah & Maria Gourbanpour (husband & wife) who also own Hotel Hollywood Stella. This hotel was in the middle of being built when I arrived. It will be completed before this book's publication. Marco gave me a tour of the unfinished rooms while Maria described the furnishings. English spoken (Marco & Maria). All 7 rooms will have air-conditioning, mobile cell phones, cable TV w/CNN & VCR and frigobars (5 rms). The rooms will be beautifully furnished in contemporary style. Marco will have someone to help with the luggage because there is no elevator and the rooms are on the 3rd & 4th flrs. There are 4 rms. on the 3rd floor: one room will have a queen-size bed, bathroom & small balcony that faces the interior; one room will have 2 twin beds or zip & lock queen-size bed & private bathroom outside the room; one room will have 2 twin beds or zip & lock queen-size bed that is for a double but can fit an extra twin bed for a triple; one room will have 4 twin beds, bathroom & 3 windows that face the street. There are 3 not-so-bright 4th flr. attic rms.: one room will have a twin bed, no bathroom & tiny window in arched ceiling which is for a single; one room will have a French double bed, no bathroom & tiny window in arched ceiling which is for a single or 2 slim people in love, one room will have 3 twin beds, no bathroom & face interior; they all share 1 communal bathroom and will access to common kitchen, fabulous location near the Trevi fountain. Call ahead and Marco will provide free transportation from the train station to the hotel.

PRIMAVERA: Piazza San Pantaleo 3, 1st fl. **Tel:** 06-68803109. **Fax:** 06-6869265. (16 rms., 12 w/toilet & shower.) 134€ double; 165€ triple; 193€ quad. The rooms without bathrooms are cheaper. Buffet breakfast (8:30-9:30am) is included in the rates. Air-conditioned (6€ extra per day). Cash only. English spoken (Serena & Victorio), no phones, cable TV w/CNN, wonderful charming simple 19th-century hotel w/simply & identically furnished large airy bright rms., shiny tiled flrs., #18 (large rm. w/small bathroom) & 19 (both 5th flr. rms. w/2 twin beds or zip & lock king-size bed, bathrooms, high ceilings & face back w/right side views of Duomo) are for a double; #9 & 8 (both w/2 twin beds or zip & lock king-size bed, small bathrooms &

face the interior) are for a double; #13, 14, 15 & 16 (all wonderful large 5th flr. rms. w/3 twin beds or 1 zip & lock king-size bed & twin bed, bathrooms, high ceilings & small windows w/wonderful right views) are for a triple; #5 (2 steps up & 2 steps down into wonderful large rm. w/3 twin beds or 1 zip & lock king-size bed & twin bed & small bathroom) & 6 are for a triple but can fit an extra twin bed for a family; #4 (4 twin beds or 1 zip & lock queen-size bed & 2 twin beds, small bathroom & faces side street) is for a family; #11 (5th flr. rm. w/2 twin beds, no bathroom & wonderful view) & 12 (no bathroom & wonderful view) share1 communal bathroom; #3 (1st flr. rm. w/ double bed, 2 twin beds & no bathroom) & 1 (1st flr. rm. w/no bathroom) share1 communal bathroom; hairdriers, terrace, magnificent entrance, charming Italian ambience, wonderful location near Piazza Navona, marble staircase, elevator, 2 flrs. Owned/managed by warm, accommodating & generous family Maria, Serena & Michael (grandmother, mother & grandson). **Bus:** #64. Stop: Piazza San Pantaleo.

SAN PANTALEO: Piazza San Pantaleo 3, 4th flr. **Tel:** 06-6832345. **Fax:** 06-6868073. **Web site:** http://www.residenzasanpantaleo.com/ **E-mail:** info@residenzasanpantaleo.com (5 rms., 1 suite, all w/toilet & or shower.) 84€ single; 110€ double; 155€ (suite) double; 130€ triple; 181€ (suite) triple; 173€ quad; 212€ (suite) quad. Call for quint rates. Breakfast (8:30-9:30am) is included in the rates & served in the room. Visa, MC, DC, AX. Air-conditioned. English spoken (Carlo, Serena & Chiara), no phones, cable TV w/CNN, wonderful charming hotel w/beautifully furnished pretty rms., shiny tiled flrs., #1 (large rm. w/2 twin beds or zip & lock queen-size bed & small balcony that faces the interior) is for a double; #2 (large rm. w/ 2 twin beds or zip & lock queen-size bed, futon convertible chair/bed & faces the interior) is for a double or triple; #3 (small quaint rm. w/ double bed, small bathroom & faces the interior) is for a double; #4 (step down into rm. w/3 twin beds or 1 zip & lock queen-size bed & twin bed & window which looks out to Piazza Campo de' Fiori) is for a triple; #5 (large bright airy rm. w/3 twin beds or 1 zip & lock queen-size bed & twin bed, convertible sofa & huge window which looks out to Piazza Campo de' Fiori) is for a triple or family; wonderful suite (beautiful antique furnished 3rd flr. large bedroom w/2 twin beds or zip & lock queen-size bed, huge living rm. w/convertible sofa, 18th-century decorative high ceiling, dining table, bathroom w/bathtub & hand-held shower that parallels both rooms & faces the street) is for a family or quint; wonderful location near Piazza Navona, elevator, 1 flr. Owned/managed by warm & accommodating Carlo, Serena & Chiara Sbisa (husband, wife & daughter) for 4 years. **Bus:** #64. Stop: Piazza San Pantaleo.

SOLE: Via Biscione 76. **Tel:** 06-68806873 or 6879446. **Fax:** 06-6893787. **Web site:** http://www.solealbiscione.it/ **E-mail:** info@solealbiscione.it (60 rms., 32 w/toilet & shower.) 95€ single; 145€ double. Call for triple, quad & quint rates. The rooms without bathrooms are cheaper. No breakfast is served. Cash only. English spoken (Paolo & Piera), phones, cable TV w/CNN, old (oldest hotel in Rome) pleasant hotel w/old-fashioned furnished bright large rustic rms., #419 (wonderful 5th flr. attic rm. w/2 twin beds or zip & lock queen-size bed, arched wood-beamed ceiling, bathroom w/bathtub) & 418 (wonderful 5th flr. large attic rm. w/3 twin beds or 1 zip & lock queen-size bed & twin bed, arched wood-beamed ceiling & bathroom w/shower) share a terrace w/rooftops view & are for a double; #421 (5th flr. attic rm. w/queen-size bed, bathroom, arched wood-beamed ceiling & view of St. Andrews & rooftops) & 420 (5th flr. attic rm. w/queen-size bed, arched wood-beamed ceiling & bathroom) are for a double; #408 (4th flr. rm. w/bathroom & terrace) is for a double; #303 (small quaint 3rd flr. rm. w/2 twin beds or zip & lock queen-size bed, large bathroom w/round shower stall & faces the interior garden) is for a double; #222 (double rm. & bathroom), 223 (queen-size bed, twin bed, bathroom & faces the street) & 224 (queen-size bed, twin bed, bathroom & faces the street) extend off a communal living rm.; #416 (large 4th flr. rm. w/3 twin beds or 1 zip & lock queen-size bed & twin bed, bathroom w/large shower stall & faces street) & 204 (queen-size bed, twin bed, small bathroom & opens into the communal interior garden) are for a triple; #417 (4th flr. rm. w/4 twin beds & bathroom) is for a family; #415 (large 4th flr. rm. w/5 twin beds or 1 zip & lock queen-size bed & 3 twin beds, huge bathroom & faces street) is for a family or quint; ceiling fans, inner courtyard garden, 2 communal bathrooms on each flr., lots of communal areas to relax; all the rooms (except 1) on the 3rd floor have been renovated & have bathrooms; rooftop terrace w/magnificent panoramic view, fabulous noisy location near Piazza Campo de' Fiori, walk one flight up to elevator, 5 flrs., garage parking (29€ per day). Look out for Cleopatra the hotel's black mascot cat. This hotel was built on the structures of the ancient Pompeo theater. They do not reserve specific rooms. Managed by Piera. **Bus:** #64. Stop: Piazza San Pantaleo. For directions, see Hotel Campo Fiori.

ZANARDELLI: Via Zanardelli 7. **Tel:** 06-68211392. **Tel/Fax:** 06-68803802. **Web site:** http://www.hotelnavona.com/ **E-mail:** info@hotelnavona.com (7 rms., all w/toilet & shower.) 126€ single; 152€ double; 173€ triple; 215€ quad. Breakfast (8:30-9:30am) is included in the rates & served in a small quaint family room. Air-conditioned. Visa, MC, AX, DC. English spoken (Patricia & Corry), phones, cable TV w/CNN, wonderful charming palazzo hotel w/nicely & identically darkwood furnished romantic bright pretty rms., shiny iled flrs., #6 & 7 (both nice-size rms. w/2 twin beds or zip & lock ing-size bed, small bathrooms, ceilings w/round stucco designs & ace side street w/view of museum) are for a double; #4 (large corner m. w/2 twin beds or zip & lock king-size bed, gold-leaf frames, .iton convertible chair/bed & faces the street), 3 (nice-size rm. w/2 vin beds or zip & lock king-size bed, futon convertible chair/bed, andard-size bathroom) & 2 (large rm. w/2 twin beds or zip & lock ing-size bed, futon convertible chair/bed, small bathroom & floor-.ɔ-ceiling window that faces the street) are for a double or triple; #5 (large rm. w/3 twin beds or 1 zip & lock queen-size bed & twin bed, standard-size bathroom & faces the side street) is for a triple but can fit an extra twin bed for a family; 18th-century doors w/original medieval frames, high ceilings, wonderful location near Piazza Navona, elevator, 1 fl. Owned/managed by charming & accommodating Patricia & Corry (sister & brother) who are Australian-Italian architects & antique dealers. Let them know in advance if you are on your honeymoon. **Bus:** #70 or 87. Stop: Napoleonico Museum Via Zanardelli. The same family owns & manages Hotel Navona.

HOTELS (Near Piazza Spagna & Piazza Popolo)
BROTZKY: Via Corso 509, 3rd fl. **Tel/Fax:** 06-3612339. **Tel:** 06-3236641. (25 rms., 20 w/toilet & shower.) 75€ single; 123€ double; 155€ triple; 188€ quad; 220€ quint; 253€ sextet. The rooms with-

out bathrooms are cheaper. Breakfast (8-11am) at 6€ pp can be served in the room. Visa, MC. English spoken (Marco & Eleonora), no phones, TV, plain hotel w/plainly furnished rms. that are named after famous painters, PD (small rm. w/2 twin beds, low wood-beamed ceiling, bathroom & communal terrace that faces side street) is for a double; walk up 2 narrow flights of stairs to rm. Van Gogh 2 (small rm. w/2 twin beds, arched wood-beamed ceiling & bathroom) is for a double; Leonardo (large rm. w/3 twin beds or 1 zip & lock queen-size bed & twin bed, small bathroom & balcony that faces busy pedestrian street) is for a triple; Cezanne (3 twin beds or 1 zip & lock queen-size bed & twin bed, small bathroom & faces side street) is for a triple; Caravaggio 4 (double bed, twin bed & bathroom) is for a triple; Mantegna 11 (faces interior) & Fattori 8 (both large rms. w/3 twin beds or 1 zip & lock queen-size bed & twin bed & small bathrooms) are for a triple but can fit an extra twin bed for a family; walk up 2 narrow flights of stairs to rm. Toulouse P3 (huge rm. w/6 twin beds, arched wood-beamed ceiling w/small window, small bathroom w/o shower curtain & no view) is for a family, quint or sextet; #10 has a bathroom & balcony that faces busy pedestrian street; #13A/13B both w/bathrooms & balconies that face the busy pedestrian street; charming old-fashioned furnished breakfast room w/balcony that faces the busy pedestrian street, hairdriers (5 rms.), magnificent panoramic view from rooftop terrace, hotel attracts lots of students, wonderful noisy pedestrian location near Piazza Popolo, walk to inner courtyard to catch elevator, 2 flrs. Owned/managed by Marco & Eleonora (sister & brother). **Metro:** Flaminio. Walk through the large Roman arch (Porta Popolo), continue straight across Piazza Popolo to Via Corso (the middle street).

DODGE: Via Due Macelli 106, 4th fl. **Tel:** 06-6780038. **Tel/Fax:** 06-6791633. (18 rms., all w/toilet & shower.) 100€ single; 144€ double; 169€ triple; 183€ quad. Breakfast (8-10am) is included in the rates & can be served in the room. Air-conditioned. Visa, MC, AX. Limited English spoken (Romano, who is wonderful), phones, TV, charming simple hotel w/plainly furnished airy rms., shiny tiled flrs., there are 4 rooms for a single; #4 (corner rm. w/2 twin beds or zip & lock queen-size bed & faces back) is for a double; #8 (corner rm. w/3 twin beds or 1 zip & lock queen-size bed & twin bed & 2 steps up to a small balcony) is for a triple; #10 (large rm. w/2 twin beds or zip & lock queen-size bed, futon convertible chair/beds & 3 steps up to a tiny balcony that faces street) is for a double, triple or family; small bathrooms, hairdriers, bar, fabulous location, 7 steps up to elevator, 2 flrs. Entrance located through a retail sports store. **Metro:** Spagna. Turn left onto Piazza Spagna, walk out onto Via Macelli. Cross street: Via Di Capo Le Case.

ERDARELLI: Via Due Macelli 28. **Tel:** 06-6791265 or 6784010. **Fax:** 06-6790705. **Web site:** http://www.venere.com/it/roma/erdarelli/ **E-mail:** erdarelli@italyhotel.com (28 rms., 18 w/toilet & bath or shower.) 98€ single; 131€ double; 173€ triple; 200€ quad. The rooms without bathrooms are cheaper. Breakfast (7:30-9:30am) is included in the rates & can be served in the room. You can order American/English breakfast at an extra charge. Air-conditioned (11€ extra per day). Visa, MC, AX, DC. English spoken (Franco & Katia, father & daughter), phones, no TV, simple hotel w/plainly old-fashioned furnished not-so-bright rms., #16, 12, 13, 8 & 9 (all large rms. w/twin bed, compact bathrooms w/showers & face street) are for a single; #20 & 10 (both large rms. w/2 twin beds, bathrooms w/showers & face street) are for a double but can fit an extra twin bed for a triple; #6 & 3 (nice-size rms. w/2 twin beds or zip & lock queen-size bed, bathrooms w/showers & face back) are for a double; #33 (large rm. w/3 twin beds & bathroom w/shower) is for a triple; high ceilings, rooms on the inner courtyard are more quiet, fabulous location, ground-floor reception, elevator, 5 flrs. Owned/managed by Franco Erdarelli. *10% rm. discount when you show him this book.* **Metro:** Spagna. For directions, see Hotel Dodge. Cross street: Via Di Capo Le Case.

FIRENZE: Via Due Macelli 106. **Tel:** 06-6797240 or 6794988. **Fax:** 06-6785636. **Web site:** http://www.hotelfirenzeroma.it/ (27 rms., all w/toilet & bath or shower.) Call for single rates. 160€ double; 201€ triple. Breakfast (8-10am) at 6€ pp can be served on the terrace in warm weather. Air-conditioned (11€ extra per day). Visa, MC, AX. English spoken, phones, cable TV w/CNN, wonderful charming hotel w/nicely & identically furnished nice-size rms., #8 (large rm. w/queen-size bed & bathroom w/shower) is for a double but can fit an extra twin bed for a triple; #14 (large rm. w/2 twin beds, roll-out bed, bathroom w/bathtub & faces street) is for a double or triple; #16 (large rm. w/2 twin beds or zip & lock queen-size bed, roll-out bed, compact bathroom w/shower & faces street) is for a double or triple; hairdriers, minibars, fabulous location, walk 1 flight up to hotel's reception, elevator. **Metro:** Spagna. Turn left onto Piazza Spagna, walk out onto Via Macelli. Cross street: Via Di Capo Le Case.

LYDIA-VENIER: Via Sistina 42. **Tel:** 06-6791744. **Fax:** 06-6797263. **Web site:** http://www.IHZ.it/lydia/ **E-mail:** lydia@IHZ.it (28 rms., 6 w/toilet & shower.) 108€ single; 165€ double; 196€ triple. Call for quad & quint rates. The rooms without bathrooms are cheaper. Continental buffet breakfast (8-10am, includes cereals, juices, assorted breads & cakes) is included in the rates & can be served in the room. Visa, MC, AX, DC. English spoken (Catrine, Antonio, Ismaili & Giuseppina), phones, TV, renovated simple 18th-century hotel w/nicely furnished modern rms., shiny tiled flrs., #310 (nonsmoking rm. w/ French double bed, bathroom w/shower & faces back) is for a single; #309 (small rm. w/2 twin beds or zip & lock queen-size bed, bathroom w/shower & 2 balconies that face the back) is for a double; #201 (large rm. w/2 twin beds or zip & lock queen-size bed, roll-out bunk beds, bathroom w/shower & faces street) is for a double, triple or family; #316 (double bed, roll-out bunk beds, bathroom w/shower & faces back) is for a double, triple or family; #307 (large rm. w/2 twin beds or zip & lock queen-size bed, roll-out bunk beds, bathroom w/shower & faces back) is for a double, triple, family or quint; #308 (huge rm. w/double bed, 2 roll-out bunk beds, bathroom w/shower & faces back) is for a double, triple, family, quint or sextet, sterile atmosphere but fabulous location, elevator, 3 flrs. This hotel is not family-owned but managed by Catrine Zintel-Branco. *10% rm. discount when you show her this book.* Located near Piazza Trinità Monti.

MARCUS: Via Clementino 94, 2nd fl. **Tel:** 06-68300320 or 6873679. **Fax:** 06-68300312. **Web site:** http://www.hotelmarcus.com/ **E-mail:** solemarco@hotmail.com (17 rms., 16 w/toilet & bath or shower.) 95€ single; 158€ double; 184€ triple; 220€ quad. The room without a bathroom is cheaper. Breakfast (7:30-10am) is included in the rates & can be served in the room. Air-conditioned (11€ extra per day). Visa, MC, AX. English spoken (Salvatore & Marco), phones,

Bad Review on Trip Advisor

cable TV w/CNN, wonderful charming 16th-century palace hotel w/ simple individually old-fashioned furnished nice-size pretty rms., carpeted flrs., #13 (2 steps up to rm. w/French double bed & small bathroom) is for a single or discounted for 2 slim people in love; #8 (corner rm. w/twin bed & private bathroom outside the room) is for a single; #4 & 5 (small rms. w/queen-size beds, high ceilings w/ceiling fans, compact bathrooms & face street) are for a double; #3 (wonderful large rm. w/2 twin beds or zip & lock queen-size bed, convertible chair/bed, high ceiling w/ceiling fan, compact bathroom & faces street) is for a double or triple; #12 (nice-size rm. w/2 twin beds or zip & lock queen-size bed, convertible chair/bed, compact bathroom & balcony that faces interior) is for a double or triple; #9 (3 twin beds or 1 zip & lock queen-size bed & twin bed & 1 step up to compact bathroom) & 6 (16th-century fireplace) are for a triple; hairdriers, minibars, great ambience, bar, fabulous quiet location, walk up 9 steps to elevator, 2 flrs. Owned by Salvatore DeCaro & managed by Marco Sole (godfather & godson). *5% rm. discount when you show them this book.* Marco mentioned they have plans to renovate some rooms & add a suite w/huge bathroom w/Jacuzzi bathtub. **Metro:** Spagna. From Piazza Spagna, turn left, then right onto Via Condotti, follow this street which becomes Via Fontanella Borghese and eventually becomes Via Clementino. Cross streets: Via Scrofa & Via Ripetta.

MARGUTTA: Via Laurina 34. **Tel:** 06-3223674. **Fax:** 06-3200395. (24 rms., all w/toilet & bath or shower.) 114€ double; 147€ (rms. #50 & 52) double; 157€ (rm. #54) double; 155€ triple; 173€ (rm. #50) triple; 178€ (rm. #54) triple; 175€ quad; 193€ (rm. #54) quad. Breakfast (7-10am) is included in the rates & can be served in the room. Visa, MC, AX, DC. English spoken (Francesco, who is wonderful), phones, no TV, charming simple hotel w/simply & identically furnished small rms., shiny tiled flrs., #44 (nice-size ground-flr. rm. w/2 twin beds or zip & lock king-size bed & compact bathroom w/shower) & 46 (ground-flr. rm.) are for a double; #48 (ground-flr. rm.) & 14 (both nice-size rms. w/2 twin beds or zip & lock queen-size bed, convertible chair/beds, large bathrooms w/showers & face interior) are for a double or triple; #10 (small rm. w/2 twin beds or zip & lock queen-size bed, small bathroom w/shower & faces interior) is for a double; walk up 20 steps up to 3 more expensive wonderful rms.: #50 (2 twin beds, bathroom w/bathtub & shares terrace w/rm. #52) is for a double; #52 (large rm. w/2 twin beds, bathroom w/bathtub & shares terrace w/rm. #50) is perfect for a double but too snug for a triple; #54 (bathroom w/bathtub & balcony w/rooftop view) is perfect for a double but too snug for a triple; hairdriers, ground-flr. reception, fabulous location near Piazza Popolo, elevator, 4 flrs. This hotel is not family-owned but managed by Carlo Alberto Rosati. **Metro:** Flaminio. Cross streets: Via Babuino & Via Corso.

PARLAMENTO: Via Convertite 5, 3rd fl. **Tel:** 06-6792082 or 69941697. **Fax:** 06-69921000.
Web site: http://www.hotelparlamento.it/
E-mail: hotelparlamento@libero.it (23 rms., all w/toilet & bath or shower.) 109€ single; 129€ double; 155€ (rm. #82) double; 165€ triple; 217€ quad. Rates are 20% more during Christmas week. Breakfast (7:30-10:30am) is included in the rates & can be served in the room or in the garden in warm weather. Air-conditioned (15 rms. at 11€ extra per day). Visa, MC, AX, DC. English spoken (Tiziano, George, Plinio & Andrea), phones, cable TV w/CNN, wonderful charming hotel w/nicely to beautifully furnished pretty rms., shiny tiled flrs., #109 (walk up 12 narrow stairs to a delightful unusual shaped rm. w/French double bed, 5 steps down to bathroom, wood-beamed ceiling & small window w/view of rooftops) is for a single; #78, 90 & 92 (all w/French double beds, compact bathrooms w/showers & face interior) are for a single; #106, 104 & 107 (all large rms. w/2 twin beds or zip & lock queen-size bed & open out onto the communal rooftop terrace) are for a double; #74 (large rm. w/2 twin beds or zip & lock queen-size bed, small bathroom w/bathtub & located near the reception) is for a double; #76 (large rm. w/2 twin beds or zip & lock queen-size bed, chandelier, sofa & small bathroom w/shower) is for a double but can fit an extra twin bed for a triple; #108 (wonderful large rm. w/2 twin beds or zip & lock queen-size bed, convertible chair/bed, small bathroom w/shower & balcony w/wonderful rooftop view) is for a double, triple or family; #82 (grand old rm. w/3 twin beds or 1 zip & lock queen-size bed & twin bed, bathroom w/shower & faces street) is for a triple; hairdriers, Internet access available at 6€ per 1/2 hr., wonderful ambience, flowered rooftop garden terrace, walk up 15 steps to elevator, 2 flrs. Owned/

managed by the wonderful Plinio Chini & his family. Located between Piazza Colonna and the Spanish steps. **Metro:** Spagna. From Piazza Spagna, walk down Via Condotti, turn left onto Via Corso, walk about 4 blocks, turn left onto Via Convertite.

HOTEL (Near Citta Vaticano/Vatican City)
ALIMANDI: Via Tunisi 8, **Tel:** 06-39723948/39726300. **Fax:** 06-39723943. **Web site:** http://www.alimandi.org/ **E-mail:** alimandi@tin.it (35 rms., all w/toilet & bath or shower.) 96€ single; 160€ double; 185€ triple; 200€ quad. Buffet breakfast (8-10am) is included in the rates & served on the covered rooftop terrace. Air-conditioned. Visa, MC, AX, DC. English spoken, phones, cable TV w/ CNN & movie channels, wonderful charming modern hotel w/nice contemporary & identically furnished nice-size to large airy bright rms., shiny tiled flrs., #201 (large ground-flr. rm. w/2 twin beds or zip & lock queen-size bed) & 202 (ground-flr. rm. w/queen-size bed) are for a double; #212 (1st flr. rm. w/handicapped-access bathroom) is for a double; #233 (faces the street w/view of the top of the Vatican Museum) & 235 (both nice-size rms. w/3 twin beds & bathrooms w/showers) are for a triple; #134, 136 & 138 (all nice-size rms. w/3 twin beds & bathrooms w/bathtubs) are for a triple; #123, 135 & 221 (all w/4 twin beds or 1 zip & lock queen-size bed & 2 twin beds & bathrooms w/bathtubs) are for a family; modern nice-size to large bathrooms & most of them have bathtubs, hairdriers, safety boxes, beautiful piano in a wonderful lounge, spectacular panoramic view from rooftop garden/terrace, enjoy the rooftop view, pool room, bar, handicapped-access ramp, wonderful quiet location just down the steps off Viale Vaticano in front of the Vatican Museum, 2 elevators, 3 flrs., free parking. Owned/managed by Enrico, Paolo, Luigi Alimandi (brothers) and their nieces & nephews. *5% rm. discount when you show them this book and pay in cash.* This bldg. has been in the family for years. There are 7 brothers and 4 sisters in the family. Their mother was born on the 3rd fl. of the hotel. The family tries to make sure all your needs are met. Guests from all over send back special plates that hang on the walls of the hotel. If you call in advance, they can arrange to have you catch their free scheduled bus to and from the airport. If you want your own schedule then you'll have to pay. Laundromat: There are 2 nearby the hotel. **Metro:** Cipro-Musei Vaticani. (Closed Jan.)

HOTELS (Right of Stazione Termini, exit near track 1)
CAMBRIDGE: Via Palestro 87. **Tel:** 06-4456821. **Fax:** 06-49384917. **Web site:** http://www.hotel-cambridge.it/ **E-mail:** hcambrrm@tin.it (40 rms., 34 w/toilet & bath or shower.) 95€ single; 120€ double; 145€ triple; 180€ quad. The rooms without bathrooms are cheaper. Breakfast (7:30-9:30am) is included in the rates & served in a charming room w/mural ceiling. Air-conditioned (29 rms. at 11€ extra per day). Visa, MC, AX, DC. English spoken, phones, TV w/ CNN, wonderful charming beautiful hotel w/nicely to beautifully furnished rms., shiny tiled flrs. This hotel has 40 rooms, I only saw some of the newly renovated rms. described below. I had the feeling they had rooms I did not see that were not renovated. #117 (small rm. w/double bed, Jacuzzi bathtub, mural ceiling & faces busy street) is perfect for a single but too snug for a double; #116 (large not-so-bright corner rm. w/queen-size bed, beautiful glass-blocked walled bathroom w/Jacuzzi bathtub & 2 sinks & balcony that faces interior) & 115 (large not-so-bright rm. w/queen-size bed, mural wall, high ceiling, Jacuzzi bathtub & faces interior) are for a double; #112 (queen-size bed, high ceiling modern bathroom & faces street) & 113 (huge rm. w/queen-size bed, modern small bathroom & faces street) are for a double; #26 (nice-size rm. w/2 twin beds or zip & lock queen-size bed & high mural ceiling) & 104 (small rm. w/queen-size bed, cubicle bathroom & faces busy street) are for a double; #114 (large rm. w/queen-size bed, roll-out bunk beds, Jacuzzi bathtub, high ceiling & faces street) is for a double or triple; #102 (3 twin beds, chandelier, small bathroom & faces busy street) & 22 (nice-size rm. w/3 twin beds, standard-size bathroom & high mural ceiling) are for a triple; #24 (nice-size rm. w/2 twin beds or zip & lock queen-size bed, roll-out bunk beds, small bathroom, large-screen TV & high mural ceiling), 103 (queen-size bed & roll-out bunk beds) & 109 (2 twin beds or zip & lock queen-size bed & roll-out bunk beds) are for a family; hairdriers, minibars (20 rms.), nonsmoking rms. available, the rms. that face the interior are quieter but not-so-bright, Internet access available at 2€ per 1/2 hr., bar, elevator, 4 flrs. Owned/ managed by Vincenzo Fuggetta. *10% rm. discount when you show him this book*. **Metro:** Termini. Exit the train station to the right, walk up Via Marghera, turn right onto Via Palestro.

CONTINENTALE: Via Palestro 49. **Tel:** 06-4450382/4462855. **Fax:** 06-4452629. **Web site:** http://www.hotel-continentale.com/ **E-mail:** info@hotel-continentale.com (25 rms., all w/toilet & bath or shower.) 126€ double; 142€ triple; 157€ quad. Breakfast (7-9:30am) at 6€ pp. Air-conditioned. Visa, MC, AX, DC. English spoken (Stephania, Iorlanda & Tiziana), phones, cable TV w/CNN & BBC, simple hotel w/nicely & identically furnished not-so-bright nice-size rms., shiny tiled flrs., #230 (2 twin beds or zip & lock queen-size bed) is for a double; #256, 258 & 260 (all w/double beds, small to cubicle bathrooms & small balconies that face the noisy street) are for a double; #344 (2 twin beds, cubicle bathroom & faces side street) is for a double; #262 (large rm.) is for a double or triple; #220 (4 twin beds or 1 zip & lock queen-size bed & 2 twin beds, cubicle bathroom & faces back) & 346 are for a family; small to cubicle bathrooms, hairdriers, bar, wonderful location, elevator, 2 flrs. Owned by Stephanie Restivo (mother) & managed by Iolanda & Tiziana Mascelloni (Stephanie's daughters). *15% rm. discount when you show them this book.* Their grandmother, Maria Pada, is a wonderful & delightful Sicilian woman full of personality. From Termini train station, exit right and walk up Via Marghera (4 blocks), turn left onto Via Palestro. **Metro:** Castro Pretorio.

CORALLO: Via Palestro 44, 6th fl. **Tel/Fax:** 06-4456340. **Web site:** http://www.hotelcorallo-roma.com/ **E-mail:** info@hotelcorallo-roma.com (12 rms., 11 w/toilet & shower.) 75€ single; 105€ double; 123€ triple; 141€ quad. The room without a bathroom is cheaper. Breakfast (8-10am) is included in the rates & can be served in the room. Cash only. English spoken (Andrea & Giuseppe), no phones, TV, charming plain hotel w/simply furnished rms. w/no views, shiny tiled flrs., #6 (twin bed, cubicle bathroom & access to hotel's balcony) is for a single; #3 (bright small rm. w/2 twin beds or zip & lock double bed, roll-out bed, 2-steps up to small bathroom & small interior balcony) is perfect for a double but too snug for a triple; #2 (bright rm.), 1 & 8 (all w/double beds, small bathrooms & small interior balconies) are for a double; #11 & 10 (both rectangular shaped small rms. w/2 twin beds & standard-size bathrooms) are for a double; #12 (bright nice-size corner rm. w/double bed, twin bed, roll-out bed & balcony that faces street & has rooftop view) is perfect for a triple but too snug for a family; #7 (double bed, shares the 1 communal bathroom w/staff & access to hotel's balcony) is for a double; small bathrooms, ceiling fans, bar, wonderful location, walk to the back of the bldg. to catch elevator to 6th flr. *10% rm. discount when you show owners/managers Andrea & Giuseppe Celestino (uncle & nephew) this book.* From Termini train station, exit right and walk up Via Marghera (4 blocks), turn left onto Via Palestro. **Metro:** Castro Pretorio.

COROT: Via Marghera 15-17. **Tel:** 06-44700900. **Fax:** 06-44700905. **Web site:** http://www.hotelcorot.it **E-mail:** info@hotelcorot.it (28 rms., all w/toilet & bath or shower.) 105€ single; 145€ double; 170€ triple; 200€ quad. Breakfast (7-10am) is included in the rates & can be served in the room (3€ extra pp). Air-conditioned. Visa, MC, AX, DC. English spoken (Mario, Luciano, Francesco & Rocco), phones, cable TV w/CNN & BBC, wonderful charming modern hotel w/contemporary & identically furnished rms., wooden flrs., #101 (1st flr. large rm. w/twin bed & wood-beam ceiling), 201, 301 & 302 are for a single; #106 (large rm. w/2 twin beds, handicapped-access bathroom w/Jacuzzi bathtub & located near the ground flr. reception) is for a double; #104 & 103 (both 1st flr. rms. w/Jacuzzi bathtubs & wood-beam ceilings) are for a double; #209 (nice-size rm. w/2 twin beds & large bathroom), 212 (2 twin beds) & 303 (2 twin beds) are for a double; #204 (large rm.) 202 & 203 (all w/2 twin beds or zip & lock queen-size bed) are for a double; #105 (1st flr. large rm. w/ queen-size bed, twin bed, Jacuzzi bathtub, wood-beam ceiling & faces street) is for a triple; #305 (2 twin beds or zip & lock queen-size bed, convertible chair/bed) & 210 are for a triple; #304 (large rm. w/queen-size bed, twin bed, convertible chair/bed & faces street) is for a triple or family; all the rooms & bathrooms were renovated in 2001, there are telephones in the bathrooms on the 2nd & 3rd flr., minibars, digital safety boxes, modern bar, newly carpeted staircase, elevator, 3 flrs. They have a ramp for the four stairs in front of the hotel. Owned by Mario Pazienza & managed by Luciano Palmieri. *10% rm. discount when you show them this book.* It is Luigi (mornings) & Giuseppe (afternoons) who keep the hotel running. **Metro:** Termini. One block from the train station.

DOLOMITI: Via San Martino Battaglia 11, 1st fl. **Tel:** 06-4957256/ 491058. **Fax:** 06-4454665. **Web site:** http://www.hotel-dolomiti.it/ **E-mail:** dolomiti@hotel-dolomiti.it (31 rms., 27 w/toilet & shower.) 74€ single; 100€ double; 142€ triple; 157€ quad. Call for quint rates. The rooms without bathrooms are cheaper. Continental breakfast (8-10:30am, includes ham & cheese) at 7€ pp. Air-conditioned (14€ extra per day). Visa, MC. English spoken (Sabrina & Franco), phones, cable TV w/CNN & BBC, wonderful charming newly renovated hotel w/beautifully & identically furnished nice-size pretty rms., #208 (faces street) & 210 (both 2nd flr. rms. w/twin beds) are for a single; #416 (4th flr. & bathroom w/bathtub) & 207 (2nd flr.) both large bright corner rms. w/2 twin beds or zip & lock queen-size bed & 2 windows are for a double but can fit an extra twin bed for a triple; #204, 205 & 206 (all 2nd flr. rms. w/queen-size beds & balconies that face street) are for a double; #403 (4th flr.) & 209 (2nd flr.) have 2 twin beds or zip & lock queen-size bed & are for a double; #405 (bathroom w/bathtub) & 413 (both 4th flr. large rms. w/queen-size beds & face busy street) are for a double; #412 & 411 (both 4th flr. large rms. w/2 twin beds or zip & lock queen-size bed & face busy street) are for a double but can fit an extra twin bed for a triple; #218 (2nd flr. large rm. w/queen-size bed, convertible chair/bed & faces interior) is for a double or triple; #414 & 417 (both 4th flr. small rms. w/queen-size beds & face busy street) are for a double; #203 (2nd flr. rm. w/3 twin beds or 1 zip & lock queen-size bed & twin bed & faces street) is for a triple; #406 (4th flr. large corner rm. w/queen-size bed, twin bed & faces side street) is for a triple; #407 (4th flr. rm. w/3 twin beds or 1 zip & lock queen-size bed & twin bed & convertible chair/ bed) is for a triple or family; #410 (4th flr. huge rm.) & 201 (2nd flr. large rm. that faces interior) both w/queen-size beds & 2 twin beds are for a family but can fit an extra twin bed for a quint; my least favorite rooms because they are located near the reception & breakfast areas are: #104 (1st flr. rm. w/twin bed, no minibar & balcony w/ no view) is for a single; #103 (1st flr. rm. w/queen-size bed, no minibar & no view) is for a double; #101 (large 1st flr. rm. w/2 twin beds, no minibar & no view) & 102 (1st flr. rm. w/3 twin beds or 1 zip & lock queen-size bed & twin bed, no minibar & no view) are for a triple; #409 (4th flr. single rm. w/twin bed & no bathroom), 404 (4th flr. double rm. w/2 twin beds or zip & lock queen-size bed & no bathroom), 408 (4th flr. triple rm. w/queen-size bed, convertible chair/bed & no bathroom) & 401 (4th flr. large corner rm.) share 2 communal bathrooms; all the rms. on the 2nd & 4th flrs. (except #401, 404, 408 & 409) are beautifully & identically furnished & have newly tiled marbled bathrooms, the rooms on the 4th flr. have longer beds than than any of the other rms., hairdriers, minibars (all rms. except #101-104, 401, 408, 408 & 409), Internet access available at 3€ per 1/2 hr., fabulous location, bar, elevator stops in between flrs., 3 flrs. Owned/managed by Gaetano & Sabrina Ensabella & their family for more than 35 years. From Termini train station, exit right and walk 3 blocks up Via Marghera, turn left onto Via Varese, walk up 2 blocks to Piazza Indipendenza, turn right onto Via San Martino Battaglia. **Metro:** Castro Pretorio. I stayed at this hotel on my last trip. I love its location because it is between the historic center and the train station. It is only a 10-min. walk to the train station which is convenient if you are using Rome as a base to do day trips. You can catch the express bus #40 from the train station straight to the Vatican or catch bus #492 which stops in front of the hotel at the Trevi fountain & Piazza Navona. You can also catch the metro to Piazza Spagna. It is a 45-min. walk from the hotel to the historic center. There is a laundromat around the corner and a supermarket across the street.

ERCOLI: Via Collina 48, 3rd fl. **Tel/Fax:** 06-4745454. **Tel/Fax:** 06-4744063. **Web site:** http://www.hotelercoli.com/ **E-mail:** hotelercoli@hotelercoli.com (14 rms., all w/toilet & shower.) 80€ single; 117€ double; 158€ triple; 179€ quad. Breakfast (7:30-9:30am) is included in the rates & can be served in the room. Air-conditioned. Visa, MC. English spoken (Flavio & Giorgio), phones, TV, wonderful charming modern hotel w/nicely contemporary & identically furnished nice-size pretty rms., shiny tiled flrs., #13 (twin bed) is the only single rm.; there are 6 rms. like #9 (2 twin beds or zip & lock queen-size bed) that are for a double; there are 4 rms. like #3 (2 twin beds or zip & lock queen-size bed, convertible chair/bed & faces street) that are for a double or triple; #11 (2 twin beds or zip & lock queen-size bed, 2 convertible chair/beds & large bathroom) is for a family; beautiful bathrooms w/hairdriers, lots of ambience, wonderful quiet location, elevator, 1 fl. Owned/managed by the wonderful & accommodating Flavio & Giorgio Biasotti (brothers). From Termini train station, go diagonally left across Piazza Cinquecento (in front of station) to Piazza Repubblica, walk to the right around Piazza Repubblica, walk down Via Vitt. Emanuele Orlando, turn right onto Via Venti (XX) Settembre, turn left onto Via Aureliana, turn right onto Via Flavia, turn right onto Via Collina. **Metro:** Repubblica. Flavio & Giorgio also own/manage Hotel Piave. The hotel will be totally refurbished before this book's publication. It will have 11 air-conditioned rms., all w/bathrooms and priced the same as Hotel Ercoli. Hotel Piave is a couple of blocks away. **Hotel Piave:** Via Piave 14. **Tel:** 4743447. **Fax:** 06-4873360.

FENICIA: Via Milazzo 20. **Tel/Fax:** 06-490342. **Web site:** http:// www.hotelfenicia.it/ **E-mail:** hotelfenicia@tiscalinet.it (15 rms., all w/toilet & shower.) 61€ single; 105€ double; 130€ triple; 150€ quad. Breakfast (7-9am) at 7€ pp can be served in the room. Air-conditioned (11€ extra per day). Visa, MC, AX, DC. English spoken (Rosalea & Anna), phones, TV, wonderful charming hotel w/nicely to beautifully furnished nice-size bright rms., wooden & shiny tiled flrs., #24 (wonderful huge 2nd flr. rm. w/queen-size bed & wooden flr.) is for a double but can fit an extra twin bed for a triple; #23 (large 2nd flr. rm. w/queen-size bed & faces street), 22 (small 2nd flr. rm. w/queen-size bed & small bathroom w/shower) & 25 are for a double; #21 (balcony) & 16 (both are small 4th flr. rms w/queen-size beds, small bathrooms & face back) are for a double; #20 (large nicely furnished 4th flr. rm. w/3 twin beds or 1 zip & lock queen-size bed & twin bed & small balcony that faces street) is for a triple; #18 (large nicely furnished 4th flr. rm. w/3 twin beds or 1 zip & lock queen-size bed & twin bed & balcony that faces street) is for a triple but can fit an extra twin bed for a family; hairdriers, minibars, the 5 rms. on the 2nd flr. (#22, 23, 24, 25 & 26) are beautifully furnished rms., they plan to refurnished the larger rooms on the 4th flr. before this book's publication to resemble the rooms on the 2nd flr., the rooms on the 1st floor are cheaper because they are older, no elevator, 3 flrs. (1st, 2nd & 4th flrs.), parking (22€ per day). Owned/managed by wonderful & accommodating Anna & Giorgio Brancadoro (wife & hisband) & Rosalea (Anna's mother). *5% rm. discount when you show them this book.* Upon request, the hotel will organize a sightseeing tour. I have stayed at this hotel on past trips and loved it.

It is close to the train station and there are lots of people (of all colors) including tourists hanging out but I never felt threatened in any way. **Metro:** Termini. Exit station, turn right onto Via Marsala, turn left onto Via Milazzo. Two blocks from the train station.

GABRIELLA: Via Palestro 88, 1fl. **Tel:** 06-4450120. **Fax:** 06-4450252. **Web site:** http://www.gabriellahotel.com/ **E-mail:** reservations@gabriellahotel.it (23 rms., all w/toilet & bath or shower.) 98€ single; 124€ double; 169€ triple; 216 € quad. Breakfast (7-9:30am) is included in the rates. Air-conditioned (3rd flr. rms. at 12€ extra per day). Visa, MC, AX, DC. English spoken (Barbara, Bruna, Romolo, Francesca & Nicola), phones, cable TV w/CNN & BBC, wonderful charming hotel w/simply furnished pretty rms., shiny tiled flrs., #28, 30 32 34, 36 38 & 40 (all nonsmoking rms., double beds, minibars & face busy street) are for a double; #26 (2 twin beds or zip & lock queen-size bed & mini-bathtub w/hand-held shower) is for a double; #22 (huge corner rm. w/3 twin beds, beautiful antique armoire, large bathroom w/shower & faces interior) is for a triple but can fit an extra twin bed for a family; the 7 rooms on the 2nd flr. are not air-conditioned, hairdriers, bar, nice location, elevator, 2 flrs., parking (20€ per day). Owned/managed by Barbara, Bruna, Romolo, Francesca & Nicola Nardelli. *5% rm. discount when you show them this book.* **Metro:** Termini. Exit the train station to the right, walk up Via Marghera, turn right onto Via Palestro.

LAZZARI: Via Castelfidardo 31, 3rd fl. **Tel:** 06-4464638. **Fax:** 06-4941378. **Web site:** http://www.hotelcastelfidardo.com/ (35 rms., 18 w/toilet & shower.) 58€ single; 79€ double; 102€ triple; 126€ quad. The rooms without bathrooms are cheaper. No breakfast served. Visa, MC, AX. English spoken (Luisella, Mario & Sandro), phones, cable TV (10 rms.), charming simple hotel w/nicely pinewood furnished airy rms., shiny tiled flrs., #513 (5th flr. rm. w/private bathroom outside the room) is for a single; #514 (wonderful 5th flr. honeymoon rm. w/2 twin beds or zip & lock queen-size bed, small bathroom & terrace w/rooftop view) & 412 (wonderful 4th flr. rm. w/queen-size bed, large bathroom & faces interior) are for a double; #509 (balcony) & 508 (both 5th flr. rms. w/2 twin beds or zip & lock queen-size bed & bathrooms) are for a double; #408 & 409 (both are 4th flr. nice-size

rms. w/2 twin beds or zip & lock queen-size bed, small bathrooms w/
o shower curtains & face street) are for a double; #301 (3rd flr. large
rm. w/queen-size bed, compact bathroom w/o shower curtain & faces
street) & 308 (3rd flr. rm. w/2 twin beds or zip & lock double bed,
compact bathroom w/o shower curtain & faces street) are for a double;
#512 (5th flr. rm. w/2 twin beds, compact bathroom & faces interior)
& 411 (4th flr. small rm. w/2 twin beds or zip & lock double bed,
standard-size bathroom & faces interior) are for a double; #204 (2nd
flr. huge rm. w/3 twin beds or 1 zip & lock queen-size bed & twin
bed, small bathroom & faces street), 304 (3rd flr. large rm. w/3 twin
beds or 1 zip & lock queen-size bed & twin bed, small bathroom &
faces street), 310 (3rd flr. nice-size rm. w/3 twin beds or 1 zip & lock
queen-size bed & twin bed, compact bathroom & faces street) & 410
(4th flr. rm. w/3 twin beds or 1 zip & lock queen-size bed & twin bed,
compact bathroom & faces street) are for a triple; #510 (huge rm. w/
bathroom) is for a triple or family; the 16 rooms w/o bathrooms share
4 communal bathrooms; most of the doors have the original finish on
them, high ceilings (2nd & 3rd flrs.), the rooms that face the street are
brighter but noisier, elevator, 4 flrs. Owned/managed by Luisella
Lazzari. *10% rm. discount when you show her this book.* **Metro:** Termini. Exit the train station to the right, walk up Via Marghera, left on
Via Varese which becomes Via Vittorio Bachelet when you cross Via
Vicenza, continue straight as it becomes Via Castelfidardo.

LEALE: Via Milazzo 4. **Tel:** 06-4455661. **Fax:** 06-4462965/
233204381. **Web site:** http://www.hotel-leale.net/ **E-mail:**
hotel_leale@yahoo.com (7 rms., all w/toilet & bath or shower.) 85€
single; 130€ double; 170€ triple. Breakfast (8-9am) is included in
the rates & is served in the room. Air-conditioned. Visa, MC, AX,
DC. English spoken (Maria), phones, TV, wonderful charming modern hotel w/nicely furnished pretty rms., shiny tiled flrs., #105 (French
double bed) is for a single; #106 (corner rm. w/queen-size bed, standard-size bathroom, high ceiling & 2 large windows) is for a double;
#103 & 104 (both nice-size rms. w/queen-size beds, high ceilings &
face street) are for a double; #101 (large rm. w/2 twin beds or zip &
lock queen-size bed, small bathroom, high ceiling & faces street) is
for a double; #107 (large rm. w/3 twin beds or 1 zip & lock queen-
size bed & twin bed, cubicle bathroom & high ceiling) is for a triple

but can fit an extra twin bed for a family; only rms. #101, 103, 104 & 105 have hairdriers & safety boxes; Maria has added a brand new wing called Hotel Michelangelo that has 9 air-conditioned newly furnished rms. w/phones, TV, frigobars & new bathrooms w/ hairdriers. Here are the details: #9 (twin bed & small bathroom w/ shower) & 4 are for single; #5 (corner rm. w/queen-size bed, large bathroom w/shower & small window) is for a double; #1 & 8 (both w/2 twin beds or zip & lock queen-size bed & bathrooms w/showers) are for a double; #3 (large rm. w/2 twin beds or zip & lock queen-size bed & bathroom w/bathtub) is for a double but can fit an extra twin bed for a triple; #7 (3 twin beds or 1 zip & lock queen-size bed & twin bed & bathroom w/bathtub) is for a triple; #2 (large rm. w/3 twin beds or 1 zip & lock queen-size bed & twin bed & bathroom w/ bathtub) is for a triple; #6 (large rm. w/4 twin beds & bathroom w/ bathtub) is for a family, elevator, 4 flrs. *10% rm. discount when you show owner/manager Maria Quagliarella Concentta this book*. Maria is also adding 7 more rooms to Hotel Leale. They will be identical to the new rooms (newly furnished air-conditioned rms. w/phones, TV, frigobars & new bathrooms w/hairdriers) in the Hotel Michelangelo. The rooms were in the middle of renovations which made it impossible to describe them. They will be completed before this book's publication. **Metro:** Termini. Exit station, turn right onto Via Marsala, then left onto Via Milazzo. One block from the train station.

PAPA GERMANO: Via Calatafimi 14a. **Tel:** 06-486919. **Fax:** 06-47825202. **Web site:** http://www.hotelpapagermano.it/ **E-mail:** info@hotelpapagermano.it (18 rms., 8 w/toilet & shower.) 69€ single; 89€ double; 108€ triple; 126€ quad. The rooms without bathrooms are cheaper. No breakfast served. Visa, MC, DC, AX. English spoken (Gino & Claudio), phones, cable TV w/CNN, wonderful charming plain hotel w/simply furnished nice-size airy rms., shiny tiled flrs., #108 (2 twin beds or zip & lock queen-size bed & compact bathroom) is for a double; #107 (2 twin beds or zip & lock queen-size bed, futon convertible chair/bed, compact bathroom w/o shower curtain & faces street) is for a double or triple; #117 (3 twin beds or 1 zip & lock queen-size bed & twin bed, frigobar, small bathroom & faces street) is for a triple; #110 (nice-size rm. w/3 twin beds or 1 zip & lock queen-size bed & twin bed, standard-size bathroom & faces interior)

& 109 are for a triple but can fit an extra twin bed for a family; hairdriers, good location, no elevator, 2 flrs., parking (16€ per day). Owned/managed by wonderful, generous & accommodating Gino Tomasso. *10% rm. discount when you show him this book.* I promised Gino that I would quote him. According to him, he is not only handsome & charming but he will make sure your stay at his hotel is the best time you will ever have in Italy. He speaks great English & has been successfully hosting tourists for more than 30 years. All you have to do is read his guest sign-in books that go back 20 yrs. **Metro:** Termini. Exit station, turn right onto Via Marsala, which becomes Via Volturno; turn right onto the backward L-shaped Via Calatafimi.

PLANET 29: Via Gaeta, 29. **Tel:** 06-486520. **Fax:** 06-484141. **Web site:** http://www.mclink.it/com/travel/ **E-mail:** cristina@mclink.it **Cell phone:** 3405747638. (10 rms., all w/toilet & bath or shower.) 58€ single; 84€ double; 105€ triple; 120€ quad. Breakfast (8-9am) at 3€ pp is available only on request. Visa, MC, AX, DC. English spoken (Cristina, Olimpia & Adriana), phones, no TV, wonderful charming plain hotel w/simply furnished nice-size rms., shiny tiled flrs., #201 (small rm. w/twin bed, bathroom w/shower & small balcony w/no view) is for a single; #103 (2 twin beds or zip & lock queen-size bed, mural wall, ceiling fan, small bathroom w/bathtub & faces street) & 102 (2 twin beds or zip & lock queen-size bed, mural wall & bathroom w/bathtub) are for a double; #118 (2 twin beds or zip & lock queen-size bed, bathroom w/bathtub, fully equipped tiny kitchenette w/hot stove & faces street), 120 (2 twin beds or zip & lock queen-size bed, bathroom w/bathtub, fully equipped tiny kitchenette w/hot plate & faces the back) & 119 (2 twin beds or zip & lock queen-size bed, bathroom w/shower, fully equipped tiny kitchenette w/hot plate & faces the back) are for a double; #202 (large rm. w/2 twin beds, bathroom w/shower & small interior balcony w/no view) is for a double but can fit an extra twin bed for a triple; #203 (large rm. w/3 twin beds or 1 zip & lock queen-size bed & twin bed, frigobar & bathroom w/shower) is for a triple; good location, no elevator, 2 flrs. Owned/managed by warm & accommodating Cristina Pignataro for 4 years. *Free breakfast when you show her this book.* The murals were painted by Helga (Cristina's mother). **Metro:** Castro Pretorio. Corner of Via Volturno & Via Gaeta.

ROMAE: Via Palestro 49. **Tel:** 06-4463554. **Fax:** 06-4463914. **Web site:** http://www.hotelromae.com/ **E-mail:** info@hotelromae.com (32 rms., all w/toilet & shower.) 119€ single; 150€ double; 179€ triple; 212€ quad. Call for quint & sextet rates. Buffet breakfast (7:30-10am, includes hot beverages, cereals, hard-boiled eggs, yogurt, juices & jams) is included in the rates & served in a charming warm room decorated w/fresh flowers on each table. Air-conditioned. Visa, MC, AX, DC. English spoken (Marco, Kris, Mariella, Lucy, Valeria & Federicao), phones, cable TV w/CNN, wonderful charming pretty hotel w/nicely & identically furnished nice-size rms., mixture of wooden or shiny tiled flrs., #312 (corner rm. w/small balcony) & 310 (2 twin beds or zip & lock double bed, wooden flr. & faces street) are for a double; #309 (2 twin beds, convertible sofa that turns into bunk beds, bathroom w/bathtub, wooden flr., high ceiling & small window that faces street) is for a double, triple or family; #304 (bright huge rm. w/ double bed, roll-out bunk beds, tiled flr. & faces courtyard) is for a family; #103 & 106 (both w/double beds, roll-out bunk beds & face the street) are for a family; #108 (huge corner rm. w/double bed, twin bed & roll-out bunk beds) is for a family or a quint; #311 (huge rm. w/ double bed, 2 sets of roll-out bunk beds & wooden flr.) is for a family, quint or sextet; fruit basket in each rm., they prefer nonsmoking guests, hairdriers, minibars, safety boxes, 1 rm. has handicapped access but you have to climb stairs to get to it, great atmosphere, free Internet access available, bar, wonderful location, elevator, 4 flrs. Owned by Francesco Boccaforno & Lucy Baumhauer (husband & wife) & managed by Marco Coppola. *10% rm. discount when you show them this book.* Lucy has worked very hard to make this a special & warm hotel as seen from her individual touches throughout the hotel. From Termini train station, exit right and walk up Via Marghera (4 blocks), turn left onto Via Palestro. **Metro:** Castro Pretorio.

APTS.

On Via Villa Franca, around the corner form Hotel Dolomiti, Vincenzo's son Paolo (see Vincenzo's restaurant below for phone number) has built 6 new fabulous air-conditioned modern bright large apts. w/phones, cable TV w/CNN, queen-size beds, full-size fully equipped kitchens w/dishwashers, washing machines & modern bathrooms w/towel heaters. Visa, MC, AX, DC. 5 of the 6 apts. are on the

6th flr. & 1 is on the 7th flr. The building has an elevator. Large 1-bedroom apt. (queen-size bed, living room w/convertible chair/bed & connecting terrace from the bedroom to the kitchen w/view of rooftops) is for a double or triple; 1-bedroom apt. (queen-size bed & living room w/convertible sofa) is for a double; triple or family; small 1-bedroom apt. is for a double; 2-bedroom apt. (2 queen-size beds, living rm. w/convertible sofa & huge terrace w/fabulous view of rooftops) is for a family, quint or sextet; 7th-flr. 1-bedroom apt. w/huge terrace. Paolo is working on building a rooftop apt. that will have a spectacular view of Rome.

HOTELS (Front of Stazione Termini)
NARDIZZI AMERICANA: Via Firenze 38, 4th fl. **Tel:** 06-4880368. **Fax:** 06-4880035. **Web site:** http://www.hotelnardizzi.it/ **E-mail:** info@hotelnardizzi.it (22 rms., all w/toilet & shower.) 69€ single; 116€ double; 152€ triple; 184€ quad. Call for quint & sextet rates. Breakfast (7:30-9:30am) is included in the rates & can be served in the room or on the terrace in warm weather. Air-conditioned. Visa, MC, AX, DC. English spoken (Nik, Sammy & Mario), phones, cable TV w/CNN, beautiful charming renovated 19th-century palace hotel w/beautifully dark wooden furnished bright airy rms., beautiful wooden flrs., there are 7 rms. similar to #402 (small rm. w/2 twin beds & large bathroom) which are perfect for a single but too snug for a double; #406 (large rm. w/2 twin beds or zip & lock queen-size bed, high ceiling & faces street) is for a double; #404 & 411 (both wonderful large corner rms. w/3 twin beds or 1 zip & lock queen-size bed & twin bed & 2 windows that face the street) are for a double or triple; there are 5 rms. similar to #416 (large rm. w/3 twin beds or 1 zip & lock queen-size bed & twin bed) that are for a triple; #413 (large rm. w/4 twin beds or 1 zip & lock queen-size bed & 2 twin beds) is for a family but can fit an extra twin bed for a quint; #415 & 419 (both huge rms. w/4 twin beds or 1 zip & lock queen-size bed & 2 twin beds) is for a family but can fit extra twin beds for a quint or sextet; #414 has an interior balcony; modern bathrooms w/hairdriers & towel heaters, all the rms. w/2 twin beds can be made into a zip & lock queen-size bed, elegant Roman-style decor w/columns, halls that conveniently light up when you walk through them, rooms facing the front are noisy, 8 nonsmoking rms. available, safety boxes, bar, rooftop terrace w/spectacular panoramic view, wonderful loca-

tion not far from the American Embassy & opposite the Ministry of Defense, elevator, 2 flrs., parking (11€ per day). Owned/managed by Fabrizio & Stefano Tarquini. *15% rm. discount when you show them this book.* **Metro:** Repubblica. From Termini train station, go diagonally left across Piazza Cinquecento (in front of station), turn left onto Via Viminale, turn right onto Via Firenze and walk up the steep hill to the hotel which is on the left side of the street. Located 1/ 2 block from Via Venti (XX) Settembre. It is a 25-min. walk from the hotel to the historic center.

OCEANIA: Via Firenze 38, 3rd fl. **Tel:** 06-4824696/4820852. **Fax:** 06-4885586. **Web site:** http://www.hoteloceania.it/ **E-mail:** hoceania@tin.it (9 rms., all w/toilet & shower.) 120€ single; 145€ double; 200 € triple; 230€ quad. Call for quint & sextet rates. Breakfast (8-9:30am) is included in the rates & can be served in the room (6€ extra pp). Air-conditioned. Visa, MC, AX, DC. English spoken (Stephano & Simone), phones, cable TV w/CNN, wonderful charming quaint renovated 19th-century palace hotel w/beautifully old-fashioned furnished large pretty rms., carpeted flrs., #6 (large corner rm. w/2 twin beds or zip & lock queen-size bed & 2 floor-to-ceiling windows that face the street) is for a double; #7 (large rm. w/2 twin beds & faces street) & 2 (large rm. w/2 twin beds or zip & lock queen-size bed & faces back) are for a double but can fit an extra twin bed for a triple; #3 (huge rm. w/2 twin beds or zip & lock queen-size bed & faces back), 4 (huge rm. w/queen-size bed) & 1 (small rm. w/queen-size bed) are for a double; #5 (large rm. w/3 twin beds or 1 zip & lock queen-size bed & twin bed & faces side street) is for a triple but can fit an extra twin bed for a family; #8 (wonderful huge rm. w/4 twin beds or 1 zip & lock queen-size bed & 2 twin beds & faces street) is for a family but can fit an extra twin bed for a quint; #9 (wonderful huge rm. w/2 twin beds or zip & lock queen-size bed, convertible sofa & faces street) is for a family but can fit extra twin beds for a quint or sextet; high ceiling, small old bathrooms w/hairdriers, bar, wonderful location not far from the American Embassy & opposite the Ministry of Defense, elevator, 1 flr. Owned/managed by Stefano Loreti & Luisa Armando. *10% rm. discount when you show them this book.* They plan to add 7 more rooms. **Metro:** Repubblica. For directions, see Hotel Nardizzi Americana. It is a 25-min. walk from the hotel to the historic center.

HOTELS (Left of Stazione Termini, exit near track 22)
CONTILIA: Via Principe Amedeo 81. **Tel:** 06-4466942/4466887.
Fax: 06-4466904. **Web site:** http://www.hotelcontilia.com/ **E-mail:**
contilia@tin.it (41 rms., all w/toilet & shower.) 98€ single; 126€
double; 146€ triple; 178€ quad. Buffet breakfast (7:30-10am, includes hot beverages, cheese, ham, butter, assorted pastries, cereals,
juices & jams) at 8€ pp can be served in the room (6€ extra pp) & on
the indoor patio in warm weather. Air-conditioned. Visa, MC, AX,
DC. English spoken (Stepania, Emanuela, Franco & Nicola), phones,
cable TV w/CNN, wonderful charming beautiful modern hotel w/
beautifully & identically furnished large rms., shiny tiled flrs., #505
(2 twin beds or zip & lock king-size bed, decorative ceiling, chandelier & small bathroom w/Jacuzzi shower), 507 (2 twin beds or zip &
lock king-size bed & bathroom w/bathtub) are for a double; #207 &
208 (both w/2 twin beds or zip & lock queen-size bed, bathrooms w/
bathtubs & near the handicapped bathrooms) are for a double; 20
rms. w/balconies, hairdriers, minibars (5 rms.), 2 handicapped-access
bathrooms in the halls, 2 nonsmoking rms. available, halls that conveniently light up when you walk through them, interior patio, charming American hotel type huge lobby, bar, elevator, 5 flrs., parking
(22€ per day). Owned by Gennaro Simeone & managed by Stefania
Simeone but it was Nicola who impressed me with his hospitality. *5%
rm. discount when you show them this book.* They offer half- and full-
board rates w/nearby restaurant. **Metro:** Termini. Exit the train station near track 22, turn left, walk down Via Giovanni Giolitti, turn
right onto Via Gioberti for 2 blocks, turn left onto Via Principe Amedeo.

FIORINI: Via Principe Amedeo 62, 5th fl. **Tel:** 06-4885065. **Fax:**
06-4882170. **Web site:** http://www.hotelfiorini.com/ **E-mail:**
info@hotelfiorini.com (15 rms., 14 w/toilet & bath or shower.) 98€
single; 131€ double; 189€ triple. Call for quad rates. Breakfast (7:30-
9:30am) at 11€ pp can be served in the room. Air-conditioned (portable unit @11€ extra per day). Visa, MC, AX, DC. English spoken
(Khan & Aurelia), phones, cable TV w/CNN, wonderful charming
simple hotel w/simply furnished airy nice-size rms., shiny tiled flrs.,
#518 (French double bed & compact bathroom w/shower) is for a
single; #502 (twin bed & no bathroom) is for a single; #526 & 528
(both w/2 twin beds or zip & lock queen-size bed & face street) are

for a double; #512 (2 twin beds or zip & lock queen-size bed & bathroom w/bathtub w/hand-held shower) is for a double; 516 (2 twin beds & bathroom w/shower), 532 (2 twin beds & bathroom w/ bathtub w/hand-held shower) are for a double; #530 (1 step down into small quaint rm. w/older type bathroom w/shower & mural wall) is for a double; #510 & 514 are for a double; #520 (3 twin beds), 522 (3 twin beds) & 524 (3 twin beds & older type bathroom w/shower) are for a triple; hairdriers, bar, elevator, 1 fl. Owned/managed by Anna Grazia de Chicchis. *15% rm. discount when you show her this book.* They offer half-board rates at a nearby restaurant. **Metro:** Termini. Exit the train station near track 22, turn left, walk down Via Giovanni Giolitti, turn right onto Via Gioberti for 2 blocks, turn right onto Via Principe Amedeo.

HOLLYWOOD STELLA: Via Principe Amedeo 79a, 3rd fl. **Tel/Fax:** 06-4460634. **Tel/Fax:** 06-44704335. **Web site:** http://www.hotelhollywoodroma.com/ **E-mail:** hotelhollywoodstella@libero.it (12 rms., 1 apt., 8 w/toilet & bath or shower.) 90€ single; 116€ double; 146€ triple; 175€ quad. Apt.: 225€ family, quint or sextet. The rooms without bathrooms are cheaper. Breakfast (8-10am) at 6€ pp can be served in the room or on the roof garden in warm weather. Air-conditioned (5 rms.). Visa, MC. English spoken (Marco & Maria), phones, TV (4 rms.), wonderful charming simple hotel w/nicely & individually furnished nice-size pretty rms. that all face the interior w/no views, shiny tiled flrs., #6 (double bed, TV, high ceiling, chandelier & small bathroom), 3 (2 twin beds or zip & lock queen-size bed & small bathroom), 8 (small corner rm. w/queen-size bed, TV, cubicle bathroom & small balcony), 9 (2 twin beds or zip & lock queen-size bed, TV & cubicle bathroom) & 1 (small quaint rm. w/double bed & cubicle bathroom) are for a double; #2 (small quaint rm. w/double bed & outside private bathroom near room) is for a double; #7 (air-conditioned rm. w/2 twin beds or zip & lock queen-size bed, roll-out bunk beds, TV, small bathroom & balcony) is perfect for a double but too snug for a family; #4 (double bed, no bathroom & balcony) & 5 (double bed & no bathroom) share a bathroom; #13 (single rm.), 12 (double bed) & 11 (double bed & twin bed) have connecting doors so they can be rented out together as 1 apt. which comes w/a small fully equipped kitchen w/dining table & 1 bathroom. Otherwise the 3 separate rooms have to share the one bathroom; apt. (air-conditoned @11€ extra per day); all rms. face the inner courtyard and are quiet, rooftop terrace in front of the 6th flr. apt., hairdriers (8 rms.), elevator, 3 flrs., parking (14€ per day). Owned/managed by the wonderful, accommodating Marco Hazinah & Maria Gourbanpour (husband & wife). They also own/manage the newly opened Hotel Occhio di Trevi. *10% rm. discount when you pay in cash.* **Metro:** Termini. For directions, see Hotel Contilia. Take the stairs on the right side of the courtyard at 79a.

ORLANDA: Via Principe Amedeo 76, 3rd fl. **Tel:** 06-4880124/ 4880637. **Fax:** 06-4880183. **Web site:** http://www.traveleurope.it/ h24htm/ **E-mail:** hotelorlanda@traveleurope.it (23 rms., 18 w/toilet & shower.) 84€ single; 152€ double; 204€ triple. Call for quad rates. The rooms without bathrooms are cheaper. Air-conditioned (rms. #306-318). Continental breakfast (8-11am) is included in the rates & can be served in the room (6€ extra pp). Visa, MC, AX, DC. English spoken (Amadeo), phones, TV, wonderful charming hotel whose rooms are divided into two sections: left side (#312-318) have newly renovated & furnished air-conditioned rms.: #312 (air-conditioned rm. w/twin bed) is for a single; #314 (air-conditioned rm. w/2 twin beds or zip & lock queen-size bed, large shower stall & faces street) is for a double; #313, 315 & 318 (all air-conditioned rooms) are for a double; #316 (huge corner air-conditioned rm. w/3 twin beds or 1 zip & lock king-size bed & twin bed, large shower stall & 2 windows that faces street) is for a triple but can fit an extra twin bed for a family; rooms (#301-311) on the right side were renovated in 1999: #306-11 are air-conditioned rms.; #301-305 are not air-conditioned rms.; #303 (large rm. w/twin bed) is for a single; #306 & 310 (both air-conditioned rms.) are for a double; #309 (air-conditioned rm.) & 305 (both large rms. w/ 2 twin beds or zip & lock queen-size bed) are for a double but can fit an extra twin bed for a triple; hairdriers, bar, elevator, 2 flrs., parking (15€ per day). Owned/managed by Marco & Paolo Policheni. **Metro:** Termini. For directions, see Hotel Fiorini. Walk into inner courtyard, bear to your right and walk the flight up to the elevator.

SWEET HOME: Via Principe Amedeo 47, 1st fl. **Tel:** 06-4880954. **Fax:** 06-4817613. **Web site:** http://www.homesweethome.it/ **E-mail:** homesweet@tin.it (11 rms., 8 w/toilet & bath or shower.) The rooms without bathrooms are cheaper. 85€ single; 105€ double; 145€ triple; 170€ quad. Call for quint rates. Breakfast (8:30-10:30am) is included in the rates & can be served in the room (6€ extra pp). Visa, MC, AX, DC. English spoken (Daniele), phones, TV, wonderful charming very Italian hotel w/old-fashioned furnished not-so-bright nice-size rms., most w/authentic wooden flrs., #30 (1st flr. rm w/2 twin beds or zip & lock queen-size bed, small bathroom w/shower & faces street) & 32 (1st flr. rm w/2 twin beds or zip & lock queen-size bed, compact bathroom w/shower & faces interior) are for a double; #12 (not-so-bright quaint 2nd flr. small corner rm. w/2 twin beds, standard size bathroom w/shower & faces interior) is for a double; #10 (delightful 2nd flr. huge rm. w/double-size bed, leather sofa, 2 arm chairs, high ceiling, old-style bathroom w/o shower curtain & faces interior) is for a double but can fit an extra twin bed for a triple; #33 (1st flr. large rm. w/3 twin beds or 1 zip & lock queen-size bed & twin bed, standard size bathroom & faces street) is for a triple but can fit an extra twin bed for a family; #11 (delightful 2nd flr. huge rm. w/queen-size bed, twin bed, leather sofa, 2 arm chairs, high ceiling & standard size bathroom w/bathtub w/hand-held shower) is for a triple but can fit an extra twin bed for a family; #31 (1st flr. wonderful huge rm. w/3 twin beds or 1 zip & lock queen-size bed & twin bed, leather sofa, sitting area & standard size bathroom w/bathtub w/hand-held shower) is for a triple but can fit extra twin beds for a family or quint; #7 (huge rm. & no bathroom) is for a single; #9 (delightful 2nd flr. huge rm. w/2 twin beds, high ceiling, no bathroom & faces street) is for a double; quaint small breakfast room, homey atmosphere, ceiling fans, elevator, 2 flrs. Owned/managed by the very warm & accommodating Ryad & Luana (father & mother) & Augusto, Daniele & Massimo (sons). **Metro:** Termini. For directions, see Hotel Fiorini.

TETI: Via Principe Amedeo 76, 2nd fl. **Tel/Fax:** 06-48904088. **Web site:** http://www.hotelteti.it/ **E-mail:** hotelteti@iol.it (12 rms., all w/ toilet & bath or shower.) 78€ single; 124€ double; 149€ triple; 186€ quad. Breakfast (8-10am) at 6€ pp can be served in the room (8€ extra pp). Air-conditioned (11€ extra per day). Visa, MC, AX, DC. English spoken (Sergio, Mario, Gianni, Tony & Carlo), phones, cable TV w/CNN, modern hotel w/nicely & identically furnished nice-size rms., shiny tiled flrs., #5 (faces back), 10 & 9 are for a single;

#1, 4 & 6 (all w/2 twin beds or zip & lock queen-size bed & face back) are for a double; #2 & 3 (both w/2 twin beds & face back) are for a double; #11 (2 twin beds) & 12 (2 twin beds or zip & lock queen-size bed) are for a double; #7 (large rm. w/2 twin beds or zip & lock queen-size bed & faces back) is for a double but can fit an extra twin bed for a triple; #8 (large bright corner rm. w/3 twin beds or 1 zip & lock queen-size bed & twin bed, small bathroom & face street) is for a triple but can fit an extra twin bed for a family; all w/ compact bathrooms, rooms that face the back are not so bright but quieter; walk up one flight to elevator, 1 fl. Owned/managed by Sergio Trotta. *10% rm. discount when you show him this book.* **Metro:** Termini. For directions, see Hotel Fiorini. Walk into inner courtyard, bear to your left and walk the flight up to the elevator.

LAUNDROMATS (Lavanderia)
Right of the train station
Internet access available at 2€ per 1/2 hr. at all locations.
Acqua & Sapone: Via Montebello 66. Daily 8am-10pm; Laundromat: Via Montebello 11. Daily 8am-10pm; Bolle Blu2: Via Palestro 59/61. Daily 8am-10pm; Bolle Blu2: Via Milazzo 20. Daily 8am-12midnight; Bolle Blu2: Via Milazzo 20b. Daily 8am-12midnight; Laundromat: Via Vicenza 50. Daily 8am-11pm; Oblo: Via Vicenza 50. Daily 8am-11pm; Splashnet: Via Varese 33. Daily 9am-10pm.

South of the train station
Daily 8am-10pm. Internet access available at 2€ per 1/2 hr. at all locations. Bolle Blu2: Via Principe Amedeo 116/118; Onda Blu: Via Principe Amedeo 70b.

BOOKSTORES
Economy Book & Video Center: Via Torino 136. Tel: 06-4746877. Fax: 06-483661. E-mail: books@booksitaly.com Hrs.: Mon.-Sat. 8am-8pm. Visa, MC, AX, DC. Great place to exchange or sell your used paperback books. Managed by Barbara Goldfield, who relocated to Italy from U.S.; Feltrinelli: Largo Argentina 5a-6a. Tel: 06-68803248. Fax: 06-6893121. Web site: http://www.feltrinelli.it/ Feltrinelli: Via V. Emanuele Orlando 84. Tel: 06-4870171. Fax: 06-4815502. Hrs.: Mon.-Sat. 10am-8pm; Sun. 10am-1:30pm & 4pm-7:30pm; Libreria Rizzoli Roma: Largo Chigi 15. Tel: 06-6796641. Hrs.: Mon.-Sat. 9am-

7:30pm; Sun. 10am-1:30pm & 4pm-8pm; Lion Bookshop: Via Greci 33/36. Tel: 06-32654007 or 32650437. Fax: 06-32651382. Hrs.: Tues.-Sun. 10am-7:30pm & Mon. 3:30pm-7:30pm.

INTERNET CAFES

Easy Everything: Piazza Barberini/Via Barberini 2. Web site: http://www.easyeverything.com/ Visa, MC (5€ min.); The Net Gate: Lower-level of the train station. Tel: 06-87406008. Hrs.: Daily 6am-11:30pm. Cash only. Take escalator inside the train station one level down; The Net Gate Pantheon: Piazza Firenze 25. Tel: 06-6893445; The Net Gate also plans on opening up a location at Campo De Fiori. Tel: 06-68192812. Web site: http://www.thenetgate.it/

SUPERMARKETS

Conad: Lower-level of the train station. Hrs.: Daily 6am-midnight. Visa, MC, AX. Take escalator inside the train station one level down. Alimentari Market: Via Marsala 52. Between Via Marghera & Via Milazzo. Hrs.: Mon.-Sat. 8:15am-1:30pm & 4:30pm-8pm; Sun. 9am-1pm. Visa, MC, AX. Located across the street from the train station. Exit near track 1. Pam: Via San Martino Battaglia 18/20. Hrs.: Mon.-Sat. 8am-8pm & Sun. 8:30am-1pm. Visa, MC, AX. Located opposite Hotel Dolomiti.

RESTAURANTS

If you are staying near the train station and plan to bus to the restaurants in/near the historic center, make sure you purchase the bus tickets ahead of time. It is very difficult to buy bus tickets after 8pm. I stayed at Hotel Dolomiti and found the buses convenient for me to eat in the historic center in the evenings, especially because I was too tired to walk back to the hotel.

Near train station (right side)

REATINA (LA): Via S. Martino Battaglia 17. Tel: 06-4940768. Hrs.: 12noon-3pm & 6:30pm-11pm. Closed Sat., Dec. 25-Jan. 10. Cash only. Specialty: Meat. Truly a local homey restaurant which is owned/managed by five brothers for more than 35 years. None of the brothers speak English. Each brother has his assigned task to ensure the restaurant serves delicious food. Carmine prepares the 1st dish (appetizer or pasta dish), Mario prepares the 2nd dish (entree), Franco bakes the desserts (cakes) and Benito & Felicia are the waiters. If you can't make up your mind on the desserts you can order half/half at an additional cost. Casual atmosphere. Located near Hotel Dolomiti. Highly recommended by Sabrina, Hotel Dolomiti.

VINCENZO: Via Castelfidardo 4-6. Tel: 06-484596. Fax: 06-4870092. Mon.-Sat. Hrs.: 12pm-3pm & 7pm-11pm. Closed Sun., holidays & Aug. Visa, MC, AX, DC. Reservations recommended. Extensive menu in English. English spoken (Rita & Paolo). It is truly a challenge to find a restaurant near the train station that serves delicious food as good as this one does. It continues to be one of my favorites. This restaurant specializes in fresh fish (including fabulous well-priced lobster) but they also serve meat dishes and homemade desserts. *Show owners/managers Vincenzo, Rita & Paolo (father, daughter & son) this book and they will give you a complimentary limoncello or sambucca.* Exit the train station to the right, walk up Via Marghera, left onto Via Varese which becomes Via Vittorio Bachelet when you cross Via Vicenza, continue straight as it becomes Via Castelfidardo. Located just before you reach Via Venti (XX) Settembre.

Historical center
AL CHIANTI: Via Ancona 17-19. **Tel:** 06-44250242 or 44291534. Web site: http://www.paginegialle.it/alchianti/ Hrs.: Mon.-Sat. 12noon-3pm & 7pm-11pm. Closed Sun. & Aug. Visa, MC, AX, DC. Reservations recommended. Specialty: Meat (pheasant, deer, rabbit, steak, veal & lamb). They do offer a limited selection of fresh fish. If you desire they can bring the fish out to your table to show how fresh it is. Wonderful decorated restaurant with a great ambience. The place was filled with only locals. Owned/managed by three charming brothers & their wives. Alvaro & Cesariuia (husband & wife), Piero & Giuseppina (husband & wife), Rino & Carlo (father & son). Highly recommended by Gino, Hotel Papa Germano.

GABRIELLE: Via Crociferi 25. Tel: 06-6794348. Hrs.: Mon.-Sat. 12noon-4pm & 6:30pm-10pm. Closed Sun. Cash only. Reservations recommended. Specialty: Meat & salted cod. Small quaint restaurant that serves delicious homemade food made by a wonderful family. Alfredo (father/waiter), Rita (wife/evening chef), Alexandro (son/

waiter who speaks English) & Giancarlo (Alexandro's uncle/daytime chef). Homey atmosphere. Highly recommended by Marco, Hotels Hollywood Stella & Occhio Trevi. Located near Trevi fountain.

GINO: Vicolo Rosini 4. Tel: 06-6873434. Hrs.: Mon.-Sat. 1pm-2:45pm & 8pm-11:30pm. Closed Sun., Aug. & Dec. 25. Cash only. Reservations required. Owned/managed by Gino & his family for more than 40 years. Gino, Emma (husband & wife), Fabrizio (son) & Elizabeth (Fabrizio's wife). Elizabeth, who speaks great English, will help you select your dishes. Delicious food. Highly recommended by Plinio, Hotel Parlamento. Located on the corner of Parlament square.

PIERLUIGI: Piazza Ricci 144. Tel: 06-6861302 or 6868717. Fax: 06-68807879. Web site: http://www.ristorante-pierluigi.com/ Hrs.: Tues.-Sun. 1pm-2:45pm & 8pm-11:30pm. Closed Mon. Visa, MC, AX, DC. Specialty: Fresh fish & seafood. Large restaurant w/in an impersonal environment but they serve great fish that you can select from the water tank. Located near Campo de' Fiori.

SAGRESTIA: Via Seminario 89. Tel: 06-6797581. Fax: 06-6990885. Hrs.: Thurs.-Tues. 12noon-3pm & 7pm-12midnight. Closed Wed. Visa, MC, AX, DC. D'Annunzio is co-owner & chef & has been here since 1957. D'Annunzio had a restaurant in Miami but left because of the hot weather. Thank goodness he came back to this restaurant and works with a fabulous staff: Claudio (co-owner), Elizabeth (D'Annunzio's daughter, Julio (Claudio's son) and Maurizo & Sergio (waiters who speak English). Together they serve delicious food presented in a wonderful, energetic ambience. Highly recommended by Sirmone, Hotel Coronet & Corry, Hotels Navona & Zanardelli. Located near Pantheon.

3 AMICI: Via Rotonda 7-9. Tel: 06-6875239. Hrs.: Daily 12noon-3:30pm & 7pm-12midnight. Small quaint restaurant that serves delicious homemade food made by a wonderful family. Alfio, Vincenza, Rodolfo & Nina Schiafone (husband, wife, son & daughter). They always keep one table reserved daily for the workers in the Parliament building. Highly recommended by Marco, Hotels Hollywood Stella & Occhio Trevi. Located near Pantheon.

SANTA MARGHERITA
Italian Riviera, zip code 16038
Country code 39, city code 0185

Santa Margherita's Tourist Information Center
Via XXV Aprile 4. **Tel:** 0185-2921. **Fax:** 0185-290222. Hrs.: Mon.-
Sat. 9am-12:30pm & 2:30pm-5:30pm; Sun. 9:30am-12:30pm. Longer
hours in summer. From train station, turn right, walk down Via Trieste
which becomes Via Roma, turn right onto Via XXV Aprile.
Web site: http://www.apttigullio.liguria.it/
E-mail: infoapt@apttigullio.liguria.it

Santa Margherita hotels listed alphabetically
CONTE VERDE
EUROPA
FASCE
JOLANDA
MINERVA
TERMINUS

HOTELS
CONTE VERDE: Via Zara 1. **Tel:** 0185-287139. **Fax:** 0185-284211.
(33 rms., 28 w/toilet & bath or shower.) 105€ single; 126€ double;
142€ triple; 162€ quad. The rooms without bathrooms are cheaper.
Breakfast (8-11am) is included in the rates & can be served in the
room or in the garden in warm weather. Visa, MC, AX, DC. English
spoken (Alessandro, Ornella & Davide), phones, cable TV w/CNN,
charming hotel w/nicely & identically furnished nice-size modern rms.
w/no views, carpeted flrs., #5 (1st flr. rm. w/queen-size bed & bathroom w/shower) is perfect for a single but too snug for a double; #25
(large 3rd flr. rm. w/2 twin beds or zip & lock queen-size bed, sitting
area, bathroom w/mini bathtub w/hand-held shower & balcony w/
rooftops view) & 24 (large 3rd flr. rm. w/2 twin beds or zip & lock
queen-size bed, futon convertible chair/bed, frigobar, large bathroom
w/shower & large terrace w/rooftops view) are for a double or triple;
#26 (large 3rd flr. rm. w/queen-size bed & bathroom w/shower) is for
a double; #6 (1st flr. corner rm. w/queen-size bed, twin bed, futon
convertible chair/bed & bathroom w/bathtub w/hand-held shower) is

for a double, triple or family; #1 & 2 (both 1st flr. rms. w/queen-size beds, bathrooms w/showers & huge terrace) are for a double; #30 & 31 (both w/2 twin beds or zip & lock queen-size bed & bathrooms w/ showers) are for a double; #21 (corner rm. w/2 twin beds or zip & lock queen-size bed, bathroom w/shower, needs new carpet & 2 windows) is for a double; #18A (double rm. w/2 twin beds or zip & lock queen-size bed & no bathroom) & 18B (single rm. w/twin bed & no bathroom) share a bathroom, have a common door & can be rented together as one triple rm.; #19A (double rm. w/bunk beds & no bathroom) & 19B (double rm. w/2 twin beds or zip & lock queen-size bed & bathroom w/bathtub w/hand-held shower) have a common door & can be rented together as one family rm.; I prefer the newly furnished rooms on the 3rd flr., hairdriers, garden, bar, elevator, 5 flrs., parking (11€ per day). Owned/managed by charming & attentive Alessandro Pizzi. From train station, turn right, walk down Via Trieste which becomes Via Roma, turn right onto Via Zara. (Closed Nov.-Dec.)

EUROPA: Via Trento 5. **Tel:** 0185-287187. **Fax:** 0185-280154. **E-mail:** hoteuro@tin.it (18 rms., all w/toilet & shower.) 113€ double; 126€ triple; 147€ quad. Breakfast (8-9:30am) is included in the rates. Visa, MC, DC. English spoken (Stefano, Marina & Adriana), phones, TV, charming plain hotel w/simply & identically furnished not-so-bright nice-size rms. w/no views, #31 (twin bed) is for a single; #27 (corner rm. w/2 twin beds or zip & lock queen-size bed & L-shaped balcony) is for a double; #28 (large rm. w/3 twin beds or 1 zip & lock queen-size bed & twin bed) is for a triple; #22 (2 twin beds or zip & lock queen-size bed & bunk beds) & 3 other similar rooms are for a family; 14 rms. w/balconies, Internet access available at 6€ per 1/2 hr., wonderful quiet location, bar, no elevator, 2 flrs., free street parking, private parking (6€ per day, confirm in advance). Owned/managed by wonderful Nicosia, Stefano & Marina Pierluigi (father, son & daughter). Stefano assured me that all the rooms will have a private bathroom inside the room by this book's publication. Taxi to hotel. (Closed Dec.-Feb.)

FASCE: Via Luigi Bozzo 3. **Tel:** 0185-286435. **Fax:** 0185-283580. **Web site:** http://www.hotelfasce.it/ **E-mail:** hotelfasce@hotelfasce.it (16 rms., all w/toilet & shower.) 84€ single; 99€ double; 134€ triple;

167€ quad. Breakfast (8-9:30am) is included in the rates & can be served in the room (6€ extra pp) or on the terrace in warm weather. Visa, MC, AX, DC. English spoken (Jane & staff), phones, cable TV w/CNN, NBC, BBC & Movie Channel, wonderful charming hotel, quiet location, no elevator, 3 flrs., parking (16€ per day). Owned/ managed by husband and wife, Aristide Fasce (Italian) & Jane McGuffie (Scottish). Jane was unable to show me around the hotel the way I usually like. Because of this I am unable to give a detailed description of the hotel or the rooms. I prefer to see at least 5 or more rooms. Perhaps on my next visit to Italy, I will have the opportunity to see more of the hotel. Taxi to hotel. (Closed Dec. 9-Feb.) Jane recently opened a new 4-star hotel in Chianti. Hotel Radda: Tel/Fax: 0577-73511. Web site: http://www.hotelradda.it/ E-mail: hotelradda@hotelradda.it

JOLANDA: Via Luisito Costa 6. **Tel:** 0185-287512. **Fax:** 0185-284763. **Mobile:** 335 5850668. **Web site:** http://www.hoteljolanda.it/ **E-mail:** desk@hoteljolanda.it (50 rms., all w/toilet & bath or shower.) 83€ single; 132€ (standard rm. & corner rms. w/o sofas) double; 142€ (large corner rms. w/sofas) double; 157€ (suite) double; 165€ triple; 194€ quad. Buffet breakfast (8-10am) is included in the rates & can be served in the room (3€ extra pp). Air-conditioned. Visa, MC, AX, DC. English spoken (Giuseppe, Mariana & Viviana), phones, cable TV w/CNN, wonderful charming beautiful hotel w/ beautifully & identically furnished modern pretty rms., mixture of carpeted & wooden flrs., #512 (large 5th flr. rm. w/mini-canopy bed), 304 (3rd flr. rm.) & 3 other similar rooms are for a single; #213 (small 2nd flr. rm. w/2 twin beds or zip & lock queen-size bed & small balcony that faces the garden) is discounted for a double in low season; #208 (large 2nd flr. standard rm. w/2 twin beds or zip & lock queen-size bed, bathroom w/shower & faces the street) & 206 (large 2nd flr. standard rm. w/2 twin beds or zip & lock king-size bed, decorative ceiling, small bathroom w/shower & faces the street) are for a double; #513 (5th flr. corner rm. w/2 twin beds or zip & lock king-size bed, bathroom w/shower & L-shaped balcony w/fabulous views of countryside & rooftops) & 510 (5th flr. corner rm.) are for a double; #311 (3rd flr. corner rm. w/2 twin beds or zip & lock queen-size bed, bathroom w/shower & L-shaped balcony) & 205 (2nd flr. corner rm.

w/2 twin beds or zip & lock queen-size bed, small bathroom w/shower & L-shaped balcony) are for a double; #305 (3rd flr. corner rm. w/2 twin beds or zip & lock queen-size bed, convertible chair/bed, wooden flr. & L-shaped balcony), 406 (4th flr. rm. w/2 twin beds or zip & lock queen-size bed & convertible chair/bed) & 506 (5th flr. rm. w/2 twin beds or zip & lock queen-size bed & convertible chair/bed) are for a double or triple; #104 (corner rm.) & 105 (walk one flight up to both 1st flr. rms. w/2 twin beds or zip & lock king-size bed, carpeted flrs., bathrooms w/showers & face the street) are for a double; #212 (huge rm. w/3 twin beds or 1 zip & lock queen-size bed & twin bed, wooden flr., large bathroom w/shower & balcony that faces the street) is for a triple; #514 (fabulous 5th flr. suite w/mini-canopy 2 twin beds or zip & lock king-size bed, small sitting area w/convertible sofa, large bathroom w/bathtub, wooden flr. & 2 large windows) & 306 (fabulous 3rd flr. suite w/2 twin beds or zip & lock king-size bed, small sitting area w/convertible sofa, huge bathroom w/shower, decorative ceiling, wooden flr. & 2 large windows) are for a double, triple or family; modern standard-size bathrooms w/hairdriers & towel heaters, minibars, 22 rms. w/balconies (most of the corner rooms have balconies), the higher the floor the better the view, 10 nonsmoking rms. available, free small fitness rm., sauna (extra charge), bar, restaurant, wonderful quiet location, elevator doesn't go to 1st flr., 5 flrs., parking (16€ per day). Owned/managed by wonderful & charming Giuseppe Pastine & his family for more than 50 years. *5% rm. discount when you show them this book.* This 3-star hotel could easily be a 4-star hotel but Giuseppe prefers not to change the hotel's rating. They offer half- and full-board rates. Taxi to hotel. (Closed Nov. & Dec.)

MINERVA: Via Maragliano 34d. **Tel:** 0185-286073. **Fax:** 0185-281697. **Web site:** http://www.hminerva.it/ **E-mail:** info@hminerva.it (28 rms., all w/toilet & bath or shower.) 81€ single; 112€ (double bed) double; 132€ double; 163€ (suite) double; 168€ triple; 198€ quad. Buffet breakfast (7:30-9am) is included in the rates & can be served in the room or in the garden in warm weather. Air-conditioned. Visa, MC, AX, DC. English spoken (Franco), phones, cable TV w/ CNN, wonderful charming hotel w/contemporary & identically furnished nice-size modern pretty rms., #109 (large rm. w/twin bed, large handicapped-access bathroom w/shower & small window) is for a single but can fit an extra twin bed for a double; #401 (4th flr. rm. w/twin bed, bathroom w/shower & opens out to the communal rooftop terrace) is for a single; #204 (double bed & balcony w/view of countryside) & 207 (double bed & small bathroom w/shower) are for a single or discounted for a double; #110 (double bed, large handi-capped-access bathroom w/shower & interior patio w/no view) is for a single or discounted for a double; #203 (2 twin beds or zip & lock king-size bed, small bathroom w/shower & balcony w/rooftops view) is for a double; #301 (2-rm. suite w/2 twin beds or zip & lock king-size bed, sitting room w/convertible sofa, bathroom w/bathtub w/ hand-held shower & large terrace w/fabulous views of countryside & rooftops) is for a double, triple or family; #304 (huge suite w/2 twin beds or zip & lock queen-size bed, sitting area w/convertible sofa, bathroom w/bathtub w/hand-held shower & large terrace w/ fabulous views of countryside & rooftops) is for a double, triple or family; 14 rooms w/balconies, most w/views of the sea or surround-ing hills, modern bathrooms w/hairdriers & towel heaters, minibars, pool table, Internet access available at 6€ per 1/2 hr., rooftop so-larium/terrace w/magnificent panoramic view, bar, restaurant, won-derful quiet location, 2 elevators, 4 flrs., parking (14€ per day). Charming & attentive assistant manager Franco Grisolia. Taxi to hotel.

TRAIN STATION
TERMINUS: Piazza Raul Nobili 4. **Tel:** 0185-286121. **Fax:** 0185-282546. (24 rms., 20 w/toilet & bath or shower.) 66€ single; 103€ double; 131€ triple; 168€ quad. The rooms without bathrooms are cheaper. Huge delicious buffet breakfast (7:30-10am, includes cere-als, cheese, assorted cold cuts, assorted fruit, yogurt, juices) is in-cluded in the rates & can be served in the room (3€ extra pp) or on the terrace in warm weather. Visa, MC, AX, DC. English spoken (Angelo & Valentina), phones, TV, wonderful charming simple hotel w/plainly & identically furnished nice-size bright airy rms., #222 & 220 (both w/double beds, small bathrooms w/o shower curtains & wonderful views of water) are for a double; #120 (corner rm. w/double bed, compact bathroom & wonderful view of water), 122 (corner rm. w/double bed, small bathroom & wonderful view of water) & 224 (double bed, compact bathroom & faces the garden) are for a double;

#116 & 216 (both w/2 twin beds or zip & lock king-size bed, small bathrooms & balconies that face the train station) are for a double; #126 & 226 (both w/3 twin beds or 1 zip & lock queen-size bed & twin bed, compact bathrooms & face the garden) are for a triple; #102 (large rm. w/2 twin beds or zip & lock king-size bed, bunk beds, large bathroom w/bathtub & faces the garden) is for a family; #106 (2-rm. corner w/2 sets of bunk beds, bathroom w/bathtub & faces the garden) is perfect for a group of young people; #114 & 214 (both w/ French double beds, no bathrooms & no views) are for a single; the 4 rooms w/o bathrooms share 2 communal bathrooms; Angelo personally cleans the hotel's carpet 3 times a year (it has been blackened by the sun), garden terrace, bar, restaurant, no elevator, 2 flrs., parking (6€ per day). Owned/managed by the wonderful and charming chef Angelo Caló. The hotel itself is quite simple. It is Angelo's attentive & warm personality that makes your stay at this hotel memorable. He goes out of his way to make you feel comfortable and to make sure all your needs are met. If you have an early train, it is Angelo that rises early to make sure you have your coffee or tea before you leave his hotel. He even helps carry your luggage to the train station. From Feb.-Sept., around 7pm, Angelo brings out buffet appetizers and his own wine (which comes from his vineyards in the south of Italy). I have received many e-mail messages regarding his wonderful hospitality. It's less than a 2-min. walk from the train station. Turn left as you exit the train station straight to hotel. 10-min. walk to the waterfront. The hotel is very convenient for making day trips.

TAXI
Train station: Tel. 286508. Via Pescino. Tel 287998.

INTERNET CAFE
Via Giuncheto 39. Tel: 0185-293092. E-mail: liguriacom@tigullio.it
Hrs.: Daily 9am-9pm. Owned/managed by Jane, Hotel Fasce.

SUPERMARKET
Co-op: Corso Matteotti 9e. Hrs.: Mon.-Fri. 8:15am-1pm & 3:30pm-7:30pm, Sat. 3:30pm-8pm. Closed Sat. morning & Sun. Visa. MC.

RESTAURANTS

CAMBUSA (LA): Via Bottaro, 1. Tel: 0185-287410. Hrs.: Fri.-Wed. 12noon-3:30pm & 7:50pm-11:30pm. Closed Thurs. Visa, MC. Reservations required in season. Delicious food served in a great location close to the water. Highly recommended by Stefano, Hotel Europa & Giuseppe, Hotel Jolanda.

DAL BAFFO: Corso Matteotti 56-58. Tel: 0185-288987. Hrs.: Wed.-Mon. 12noon-3pm & 7pm-12midnight. Closed Tues. & Nov. 5-Nov. 28. Visa. MC. Specialty: Delicious food. If you call the day before for lunch or the morning for dinner, you can order fresh fish. You can even order homemade apple pie & ice cream for dessert. Highly recommended by Giuseppe, Hotel Jolanda.

IL FARO: Via Maragliano 24a. Tel: 0185-284867 or 286867. Fax: 0185-283975. Visa, MC. Hrs.: Wed.-Mon. 12noon-2:30pm & 7:30pm-10:30pm. Closed Tues. Specialty: Pasta w/seafood & pizza. Reservations recommended in the summer. Wonderful simple restaurant that serves delicious food. Owned/managed by Luigi (chef/father), Margherita (wife) & Roberto (waiter/son) Fabbro. Luigi is known for opening up almost every restaurant in Santa Marguerita. This could easily become my favorite restaurant. Highly recommended by Jane, Hotel Fasce.

SANTA LUCIA: Piazza Martiri Libertà 42. Tel: 0185-287163. Hrs.: Tues.-Sun. 12noon-3pm & 6pm-12midnight. Closed Mon. & Jan. Visa, MC. Specialty: Pizza. Delicious food served in a great location close to the water. I really enjoyed the family & the food. Owned/managed by chef Mario, Chianna & Emilio (father, mother & son). Highly recommended by Jane, Hotel Fasce.

SIENA
Central Tuscany, zip code 53100
Country code 39, city code 0577

Siena Tourist Information Centers
1.) Piazza II Campo 56. **Tel:** 0577-280551. **Fax:** 0577-270676. Hrs.:
Mon.-Sat. 8:30am-7:30pm; Sun. 9am-3pm. Longer hours in sum-
mer. **2.)** Via Città 43. **Tel:** 0577-42209. **Fax:** 0577-281041. Hrs.: Mon.-
Fri. 9am-1pm. **3.)** Train station. Hrs.: Mon.-Fri. 9am-1pm and 4pm-
7pm. **Web site:** http://www.siena.turismo.toscana.it/ **E-mail:**
aptsiena@siena.turismo.toscana.it

TRANSPORTATION TIPS
Most people arrive in Siena by bus from Florence. I prefer taking the
train from Florence to Siena because there are no toilets on the buses.
However, Siena's train station is inconveniently located in Piazza
Fratelli Rosselli, a challenging 2km downhill below the town, outside the center. It is too far and too steep to walk from the train station
to the center. If you arrive by train to Siena with luggage, I recommend you taxi (9€) to your hotel. The taxi stand is in front of the bus
stop, to your right as you exit the train station. To catch a bus, cross
the street to the bus stop, to your right as you exit the train station.

Siena hotels listed alphabetically
ALEX
BERNINI
CANNON D'ORO
CENTRALE
CHIUSARELLI
DUOMO
IL GIARDINO
LEA
PALACE DUE PONTI
PICCOLO ETRURIA

HOTELS (In the center)

BERNINI: Via Sapienza 15. **Tel/Fax:** 0577-289047. **Web site:** http://www.albergobernini.com/ **E-mail:** hbernin@tin.it (9 rms., 4 w/toilet & shower.) 89€ double; 121€ triple; 141€ quad. The rooms without bathrooms are cheaper. Breakfast (8-10am) at 7€ pp can be served on the terrace in warm weather. Air-conditioned (2 rms. at 6€ extra per day). Cash only. English spoken (Alessandro & Mauro), no phones, no TV, charming simple hotel w/simply old-fashioned furnished bright airy nonsmoking rms., #10 (small air-conditioned rm. w/compact bathroom & view of San Domenico church) is the most popular rm. for a double; #4 (wonderful large rm. w/2 twin beds or zip & lock queen-size bed, small bathroom & no view) is for a double; #8 (large air-conditioned rm. w/king-size bed, convertible chair/bed, small bathroom, high ceiling & partial side view) & 2 (huge rm. w/ queen-size bed, antique headboard, convertible chair/bed, small bathroom, decorative high ceiling & no view) are for a double or triple; #11 (wonderful huge rm. w/2 French double beds, twin bed, no bathroom & magnificent view of Siena) is for a triple or slim family; #7 (queen-size bed, wood-beamed ceiling, no bathroom & faces the street), 6 (rectangular shaped rm. w/2 twin beds, no bathroom & no view), 1 (small quaint rm. w/no bathroom & no view) & 5 share 3 communal bathrooms; charming communal room, rooftop terrace w/magnificent panoramic view (only used during the day), 12midnight curfew, wonderful location, no elevator, 1 fl. Owned/managed by wonderful, attentive & accommodating Mauro, Nadia & Alessandro Saracini (father, mother & son). Mauro loves to be asked to play his accordion, which he does with a passion. Cross street: Costa San Antonio. (Closed Dec.)

CANNON D'ORO: Via Montanini 28. **Tel:** 0577-44321. **Fax:** 0577-280868. **Web site:** http://www.svpm.it/ **E-mail:** cannondoro@libero.it (30 rms., all w/toilet & shower.) 77€ single; 96€ double; 123€ triple; 144€ quad. Breakfast (8-10am) at 7€ pp can be served in the room. Visa, MC, AX. English spoken (Maurizo, Deborah, Chiara & Rodrigo), phones, cable TV w/CNN, BBC, CNBC & Sky News, wonderful charming simple hotel w/simply & identically furnished large rms., combination of shiny tiled & original antique flrs., #37 (the most popular rm. w/view of countryside) is for a double; #35 (2 twin beds or zip & lock queen-size bed

& standard-size bathroom w/shower) & 26 (2 twin beds, small bathroom w/shower & faces the street) are for a double; #12 & 14 (both w/queen-size beds, standard-size bathrooms w/showers & face the interior w/no views) are for a double; #29 (3 twin beds or 1 zip & lock queen-size bed & twin bed, decorative iron headboard, bathroom w/bathtub & faces the street) is for a double or triple; #22 (3 twin beds or 1 zip & lock queen-size bed & twin bed, standard-size bathroom w/shower & faces side street), 10, 32, 15 & 25 are for a double or triple; #30 (large rm. w/king-size bed, 2 twin beds, stone wall bathroom w/shower, charming quaint area w/arched wood-beamed ceiling & faces the street) is for a family; midnight curfew, warm ambience, wonderful quiet location near the end of Via Montanini, original stone staircase, no elevator, 2 flrs. Owned by Luca Buccianti & managed by Maurizo, who is very attentive & accommodating. *10% rm. discount when you show them this book.* Cross street: Via Vallerozzi.

CENTRALE: Via Cecco Angiolieri 26, 3rd fl. **Tel:** 0577-280379 **Fax:** 0577-42152. (7 rms., 6 w/toilet & shower.) 78€ double; 80€ (rms. #41 & 42) double; 100€ triple; 122€ quad. The room without a bathroom is cheaper. Breakfast (8-10am) at 6€ pp & is served in the room. Visa, MC. English spoken (Lucia), phones, TV, simple hotel w/plainly furnished nice-size rms., #41 (large rm. w/2 twin beds or zip & lock queen-size bed, bathroom & terrace w/no view) & 42 (terrace w/no view) are for a double; #35 & 37 (both w/views of tower) are for a double; #38 (4 twin beds or 1 zip & lock queen-size bed & 2 twin beds & no view) is for a double, triple or family; #36 (no bathroom) is for a double or triple; hairdriers, frigobars, no ambience, wonderful quiet location a block from Piazza Il Campo, rooms are on the 3rd. floor, lots of stairs, no elevator, 3 flrs. New ownership will take over sometime this year. (Closed Christmas & 10 days in Jan.)

CHIUSARELLI: Viale Curtatone 15. **Tel:** 0577-280562. **Fax:** 0577-271177. **Web site:** http://www.chiusarelli.com/
E-mail: info@chiusarelli.com (49 rms., all w/toilet & bath or shower.) 92€ single; 123€ double; 165€ triple; 205€ quad. Buffet breakfast (7:30-10:30am, includes ham, cheese, assorted cakes & hard-boiled eggs) is included in the rates & can be served in the room (3€ extra pp). Air-conditioned. Visa, MC, AX. English spoken (Barbara),

phones, cable TV w/CNN, charming simple hotel w/simply & identically furnished modern nice-size rms., shiny tiled flrs., #8 (2 twin beds or zip & lock queen-size bed, large bathroom w/shower & balcony w/view of soccer stadium) & 55 (3 steps up to rm. w/2 twin beds or zip & lock king-size bed & bathroom w/bathtub) are for a double; #51 (3 twin beds or 1 zip & lock king-size bed & twin bed, bathroom w/shower & balcony w/view of soccer stadium) is for a triple; #38 (large rm. w/3 twin beds or 1 zip & lock king-size bed & twin bed, convertible chair/bed, small bathroom w/shower & faces the back w/no view) is for a triple or family; #20 (queen-size bed & 2 twin beds or zip & lock queen-size bed) is for a family; 7 rms. have balconies w/views of the soccer stadium, the rooms w/views of the San Domenico church are also noisy, the rooms that face the back are the quietest, hairdriers, 85% of rms. have bathtubs, huge breakfast room, veranda garden, bar, restaurant, noisy location across from the Piazza Domenico (bus station), no elevator, 2 flrs., free parking. They offer half- and full-board rates. Owned/managed by Carlo Rosi.

DUOMO: Via Stalloreggi 38. **Tel:** 0577-289088. **Fax:** 0577-43043. **Web site:** http://www.hotelduomo.it/
E-mail: booking@hotelduomo.it (23 rms., 22 w/toilet & shower.) 111€ single; 141€ double; 189€ triple; 209€ quad. Call for quint rates. Buffet breakfast (7:30-10am, includes ham, cheese, assorted breads, cereals & juices) is included in the rates & can be served in the room (6€ extra pp). Air-conditioned. Visa, MC, AX, DC. English spoken (Ute), phones, cable TV w/CNN, Sky News & Eurosport, wonderful charming 17th-century mansion hotel w/nicely modern & identically furnished nice-size rms., wooden flrs., #55 (walk outside through terrace up one flight to small rm. w/French double bed, 3 steps up to compact bathroom & large windows w/fabulous views of countryside & rooftops) is for a single; #50 (walk one flight up to small rm. w/French double bed, private bathroom outside the room & view of tower & rooftops) & 53 (walk one flight up to small rm. w/French double bed, compact bathroom & small window w/no view) are for a single; #45 (twin bed, compact bathroom w/shower & rooftops view) is for a single; #61 (large bathroom) & 62 (both wonderful large rms. w/2 twin beds or zip & lock king-size bed & terraces w/fabulous views of countryside & rooftops) are for a double; #52 (walk up one flight to rm. w/2 twin beds or zip & lock queen-size

bed, small bathroom & balcony w/fabulous views of countryside & rooftops), 63 (wonderful large bright airy rm. w/2 twin beds or zip & lock queen-size bed, small bathroom & view of countryside & rooftops) & 54 (walk outside through terrace up one flight to corner rm. w/queen-size bed, compact bathroom & 4 windows w/fabulous views of countryside & rooftops) are for a double; #51 (walk up one flight to rm. w/2 twin beds or zip & lock queen-size bed, small bathroom & view of the square) & 46 (large rm. w/2 twin beds or zip & lock queen-size bed, compact bathroom & rooftops view) are for a double; #43 & 44 (2 twin beds or zip & lock queen-size bed, small bathroom & rooftops view) are for a double; #48 (large rm. w/2 twin beds or zip & lock king-size bed, large bathroom w/circular shower stall & faces the interior w/no view), 58 (2 twin beds or zip & lock king-size bed, large bathroom w/large shower stall & faces the interior w/no view) & 47 (queen-size bed, compact bathroom w/shower & faces the interior w/no view) are for a double; #60 & 59 (both large rms. w/ 3 twin beds or 1 zip & lock queen-size bed & twin bed, large bathrooms w/large shower stalls & no views) are for a triple; #49 (large rm. w/2 twin beds or zip & lock king-size bed, convertible chair/bed, large bathroom w/circular shower stall & faces the interior w/no view) is for a triple; #57 (huge rm. w/3 twin beds or 1 zip & lock king-size bed & twin bed, high ceiling, large bathroom & no view) is for a triple but can fit an extra twin bed for a family; #56 (huge rm. w/3 twin beds or 1 zip & lock king-size bed & twin bed, high ceiling, huge bathroom w/bathtub & no view) is for a triple but can fit extra twin beds for a family or quint, hairdriers, downstairs breakfast room, wonderful rooftop terrace w/magnificent panoramic view, fabulous quiet location, bar, elevator, 2 flrs., free parking near Piazza Il Campo. The hotel is not family-owned but is managed by Adriano Davitti & Ute. Ute (who has worked at the hotel for more than 11 years) is wonderful & accommodating. I stayed here and loved it.

PICCOLO ETRURIA: Via Donzelle 3. **Tel:** 0577-288088 or 283685. **Fax:** 0577-288461. **E-mail:** hetruria@tin.it (13 rms., 12 w/toilet & shower.) 50€ single; 84€ double; 113€ triple; 140€ quad. The room without a bathroom is cheaper. Breakfast (8-10:30am) at 6€ pp can be served in the room. Visa, MC, AX, DC. English spoken (Lucia), phones, TV, charming simple 2-in-1 hotel w/plainly furnished rms. w/ no views, main bldg. (9 rms. w/a 12:30am curfew): #1 (twin bed &

bathroom) is for a single; #2 (2 twin beds or zip & lock queen-size bed & small bathroom) is for a double; #3 (nice-size rm. w/4 twin beds & bathroom w/o shower curtain) is for a family; annex (4 nice rms. w/o a curfew): #13 (5 steps down into large rm. w/2 twin beds or zip & lock queen-size bed, high ceiling & bathroom) is for a double; #11 & 12 (both w/2 twin beds or zip & lock queen-size bed & bathrooms) are for a double; if you stay in the annex, you have to walk outside to the main bldg. to have breakfast; hairdriers, wonderful noisy location, no elevator, 3 flrs. Owned/managed by friendly & accommodating Paolo, Giorgia & Lucia Fattorini (father, mother & daughter).

Note: Gianni Mazzini, owner of Hotel Toscana, made it perfectly clear to me that he is not fond of Americans or our guidebooks.

HOTEL (near Forte Santa Barbara)
LEA: Viale XXIV Maggio/Ventiquattro Maggio 10. **Tel/Fax:** 0577-283207. **Web site:** http://www.digilander.iol.it/hotellea/lea.htm/ **E-mail:** hotellea@libero.it (11 rms., 10 w/toilet & shower.) 57€ single; 97€ double; 121€ triple. The room without a bathroom is cheaper. Breakfast (7:30-10:30am) is included in the rates & can be served in the room (6€ extra pp). Visa, MC, AX, DC. English spoken (Arianna), phones, TV (10 rms.), charming simple 18th-century villa hotel w/ plainly & identically furnished bright airy nice-size rms., original tiled flrs., #6 (1st flr. rm. w/twin bed, no bathroom, no TV & balcony) is for a single; #11 (large 1st flr. rm. w/2 twin beds or zip & lock queen-size bed & wonderful view of Duomo, tower & rooftops) is for a double; #9 (large 1st flr. rm. w/2 twin beds or zip & lock queen-size bed & no view), 10 (view), 8, 3 & 5 are for a double; #20 (ground flr. rm. near reception w/2 twin beds or zip & lock queen-size bed, futon convertible chair/bed & large bathroom), 12 (view) & 7 are for a double or triple; there is 1 communal bathroom for room #6 & staff to share; homey atmosphere, rooftop terrace w/magnificent panoramic view, garden, bar, quiet location in nice residential neighborhood about a 25-min. walk to the Piazza Il Campo, no elevator, 2 flrs., street parking. Owned/managed by Arianna & Federica Sandrucci (sisters) who also own the inconveniently located Palace Hotel Due Ponti. Bus #9 or 10. Bus stop: Via Trieste & Viale XXIV Maggio.

HOTELS (Outside the walls)

ALEX: Via Girolamo Gigli 5. **Tel:** 0577-282338. **Fax:** 0577-288776. (14 rms., all w/toilet & shower.) 90€ single; 103€ double; 136€ triple; 162€ quad. Breakfast (8-9:30am) is included in the rates & can be served in the room (6€ extra pp). Air-conditioned. Visa, MC. English spoken (Maurizio), phones, cable TV w/CNN & BBC, wonderful charming hotel w/nicely old-fashioned & individually furnished pretty rms., shiny tiled flrs., #8 (lower-level large corner rm. w/2 twin beds or zip & lock queen-size bed, 3 steps down to small bathroom w/circular shower stall, new frescoed ceiling & faces the interior) is for a double; #7 (lower-level rm. w/2 twin beds or zip & lock queen-size bed, compact bathroom & partial view of countryside) & 9 (walk 4 steps up to a rm. w/2 twin beds or zip & lock double bed, freestanding prefabricated shower in the middle of the room, wood-paneled ceiling & small window w/garden view) are for a double; #6 & 5 (large rms. w/2 twin beds or zip & lock queen-size bed, brass headboards & face the street w/no views) are for a double; #13 (lower-level rm. w/2 twin beds or zip & lock king-size bed & small bathroom) is for a double; #10 (walk upstairs to loft bedroom w/2 twin beds or zip & lock queen-size bed on the top level, convertible sofa & small bathroom on the 1st level & faces the street w/no view) & 1 (3 twin beds or 1 zip & lock queen-size bed & twin bed, freestanding prefabricated shower in the middle of the room & faces the street w/ no view) are for a triple or family; hairdriers, minibars, 1 rm. has handicapped access, terrace, reception is one flight up but the stairs are equipped w/mobile handicapped-access chair, bar, quiet location about a 15-min. walk to the Piazza Il Campo, no elevator, 2 flrs., parking (11€ per day). Owned/managed by Fracassi Chiara. *10% rm. discount when you show him this book.* Catch bus #17 from train station. Bus stop: Porta Pispini. (Closed Dec. 15-March.)

IL GIARDINO: Via Baldassarre Peruzzi 35. **Tel/Fax:** 0577-221197. **Web site:** http://www.hotelilgiardino.it/ **E-mail:** info@hotelilgiardino.it (10 rms., all w/toilet & shower.) 90€ single; 110€ double; 135€ triple; 160€ quad. Breakfast (8-10am) is included in the rates. Air-conditioned. Visa, MC. English spoken (Gianna), phones, cable TV w/CNN, wonderful charming hotel w/ nicely furnished bright pretty rms., most w/wonderful views of countryside, #6 (ground-flr. rm. w/2 twin beds or zip & lock queen-size bed, large bathroom & high ceiling), 11 (large rm. w/2 twin beds or zip & lock king-size bed, small bathroom & faces Siena's wall w/ view of tower & countryside) & 10 (queen-size bed, small bathroom & faces Siena's wall) are for a double; #7 (large ground-flr. rm. w/2 twin beds or zip & lock king-size bed, convertible sofa that turns into bunk beds, high ceiling, standard-size bathroom & fabulous view of countryside) & 17 (2 twin beds or zip & lock king-size bed & convertible sofa that turns into bunk beds) are for a double, triple or family; wonderful peaceful location about a 20-min. walk to the Piazza Il Campo, garden, pool/solarium, bar, restaurant, no elevator, 1 fl., free parking. This is a breathtaking oasis where you can enjoy magnificent views of Siena. Owned/managed by Umberto & Gianna Preve. They are planning on adding 10 more rooms w/views by next year. Catch bus #17 from train station.

HOTEL
2km from center. It is convenient only if you have a car.
PALACE HOTEL DUE PONTI: Viale Europa/S.S. 73 Levante. **Tel/Fax:** 0577-46055. **Mobile:** 347-3469575.
Web site: http://www.palacehoteldueponti.com/
E-mail: info@palacehoteldueponti.com (44 rms., all w/toilet & bath or shower.) 69€ single; 131€ double; 169€ triple. Owned/managed ᵇ⁻ ⁺ rianna & Federica Sandrucci (sisters) who also own Hotel Lea.
rm. *discount when you show them this book*. This hotel was built when I arrived. It will be completed before this book's ᵗation. Arianna gave me a tour of the unfinished rooms while ᵉscribed the furnishings. Buffet breakfast (7:30-9:30am, includes ᵇverages, assorted breads, pastries, ham, cheese, cereals, hard-ᵈ eggs, yogurt, juices & jams) is included in the rates & can be ᵈ in the room (6€ extra pp). Air-conditioned. Visa, MC, AX, ᴱnglish spoken, phones, cable TV w/CNN, all rooms are mod-ᵉidentically furnished & will have 2 twin beds or zip & lock ᶦze beds; Arianna's favorite rm. is #215 (large rm., bathroom w/bathtub & faces the garden) for a double or triple; minibars, 2 ground-flr. rms. have handicapped-access bathrooms, rooms will either face the noisy highway or the quiet gardens, rooftop garden w/ solarium & no view, children's play room, swimming pool, bar, restaurant, gardens, quiet isolated location, elevator, 2 flrs., free park-

ing. They offer half- and full-board rates. This hotel is fabulous if you have a car, otherwise e-mail the hotel for specific bus information to & from Siena (15-min. ride).

LAUNDROMATS (Lavanderia)
Ondablu: Via Casato Sotto 17. Daily: 8am-10pm. Behind the Piazza Il Campo; Wash & Dry Lavanderia: Via Pantaneto 38. Daily: 8am-10pm.

TAXI
Tel: 0577-49222 or 289350 or 44504.

INTERNET CAFES
The Netgate: Via G. Duprè 12. Tel 0577-226185; The Netgate: Via Porrione 88/90. Tel 0577-236412. Web site: http://www.thenetgate.it/ Sien@web: Via Citta 121 & Via Pantaneto 54; MegoWeb: Via Pantaneto 132. Hrs.: Daily 10am-11pm. Visa, MC, AX.

RESTAURANTS
NONNA GINA: Piazza Mantellini 2. Tel: 0577-280894. E-mail: osterianonnagina@yahoo.it Hrs.: Tues.-Sun. 12:30pm-2:30pm & 7:30pm-10:30pm. Closed Mon. Visa, MC. Specialty: Meat. Small outdoor street terrace. Wonderful quaint restaurant that serves delicious homemade food. Owned by a nice family, Dodo, (husband), Lella (wife/chef) & Elisa (daughter/waitress). Highly recommended by Hotel Bernini & Alex.

PAPEI: Piazza Mercato 6. Tel: 0577-287247. Hrs.: Tues.-Sun. 12noon-3pm & 7pm-10:30pm. Open for Mon. lunch. Closed Mon. evenings. Visa, MC, AX. Reservations recommended. Specialty: Meat. If you want fish, you have to order a day in advance. This is my favorite restaurant in Siena. Great ambience with an outdoor street terrace. They don't have liters of wine. They put a bottle on your table and you pay for what you drink. A full bottle is 8€ . Ask for Daniele or Giuseppe, the charming waiters who are also brothers. Owned/managed by Roberto Papei. Jiuliana (Roberto's mother), brother & cousin do the cooking. *Show owner Roberto Papei this book and they will give you a complimentary Vin Santo or Grappa.* Located behind the Piazza Il Campo.

SIRMIONE
Lake Garda, zip code 25019
Country code 39, city code 030

Sirmione's Tourist Information Center
Viale Marconi 8. **Tel:** 030-916114/916245. **Fax:** 030-916222. Hrs.: Nov.-March Mon.-Fri. 9am-12:30pm & 3pm-6pm; Sat. 9am-12:30pm. Longer hours & Sundays in summer. Located outside the old city. **Web site:** http://www.bresciaholiday.com/ **E-mail:** aptbs@ferriani.com

TRANSPORTATION TIPS
To get to Sirmione by rail, catch a train to the Desanzano del Garda train station. Don't look for a bus station at the Desanzano train station-there isn't any. Purchase your bus ticket (3€) to Sirmione at the bar inside the train station. Walk across the street to Bar Olympia, where there should be some bus drivers hanging out. Ask them for the departure times to Sirmione. It is a 1/2-hr. bus ride from the Desanzano train station to Sirmione. The bus will drop you off in front of the post office, with your back towards the post office, walk to your left, turn left onto Viale Marconi, continue straight through the arched wooden portal to the old city. Note: You can also catch a train to Peschiera train station. It is a 1-hr. bus ride from the Peschiera del Garda train station to Sirmione. The problem I had was finding a place to purchase my bus ticket to Sirmione. It was an exhausting challenge.

Or you can walk (15 min.) or taxi to Desanzano's port to catch (April-Oct.) a 30-min. boat ride to Sirmione. If you arrive by boat, the port is right in the middle of the center. Don't assume the boats run every day in high season. The condition of the weather dictates their schedule. Always check the day before departure. Navigazione Lago di Garda Tel: 800-551801.

Sirmione hotels listed alphabetically
CORTE REGINA	LUNA
DEGLI OLEANDRI	PACE
GIARDINO	SPERANZA
GRIFONE	

HOTELS

CORTE REGINA: Via Antica Mura 11. **Tel/Fax**: 030-916147. **Tel/Fax**: 030-9196470. **Web site**: http://www.corteregina.it/ **E-mail:** lorenzoronchi@libero.it (14 rms., all w/toilet & shower.) 60€ single; 85€ (small rm.) double; 97€ (standard rm.) double; 128€ (superior rm.) double; 111€ triple; 182€ quad; 199€ quint. Breakfast (8-10:30am) at 8€ pp can be served in the room. Air-conditioned. Visa, MC, AX, DC. English spoken (Lorenzo), phones, cable TV w/CNN, fabulous wonderful charming hotel w/beautifully & identically contemporary furnished modern nice-size pretty rms. that are named after flowers, marble tiled flrs., Tulipano (small rm. w/2 twin beds or zip & lock queen-size bed) & Geranio (narrow rectangular-shaped rm. w/2 twin beds positioned head-to-toe & faces the street) are for a single or discounted for a double; Azalea (standard rm. w/2 twin beds or zip & lock king-size bed & 2 small windows that face the back w/partial view of castle) is for a double; Mimosa, Ortensea & Camelia (all standard rms. w/2 twin beds or zip & lock king-size bed & balconies that face the street) are for a double; Narciso (standard rm. w/2 twin beds or zip & lock king-size bed & faces the street w/ rooftop & lake views) is for a double; Viola & Rosa (both standard rms. w/2 twin beds or zip & lock queen-size bed & face the street) are for a double; Bouganvillea (large 2nd flr. superior rm. w/2 twin beds or zip & lock king-size bed, huge handicapped-access bathroom & balcony that faces the back) is for a double but can fit an extra twin bed for a triple; Ciclamino (large superior rm. w/2 twin beds or zip & lock king-size bed, futon convertible chair/bed & faces the street) is for a double or triple; Iris & Ninfea (both w/2 rms. w/2 twin beds or zip & lock queen-size bed, convertible sofas, sloped wood-beamed ceilings & small views of the top of the castle) are for a double, triple or family; Bouganvillea (see above) & Tuliparo (see above) have connecting doors & make a great family room; modern standard-size bathrooms equipped w/hairdriers, phones & towel heaters, digital safety boxes (look behind the picture on the wall), minibars, beautiful tiled flrs., pretty terrace, wonderful quiet location, bar, restaurant w/Roman ruin under glass-covered floor (closed Thurs.), fabulous ambience, elevator, 2 flrs., free parking. Owned/managed by charming & accommodating Alba Sacchella & Lorenzo Ronchi (mother & son). *Free breakfast when you show them this book.* Lorenzo assures me that his convertible chair/beds & sofas are just as comfortable as his other beds. I have stayed at this hotel & loved it. Walk through the arched opening, continue straight on the main road, turn right onto Via Antica Mura. (Closed Nov. 5-March.)

DEGLI OLEANDRI: Via Dante 31. **Tel**: 030-9905780 or 916131. **E-mail:** hoteloleandri@libero.it (20 rms., all w/toilet & shower.) 47€ single; 65€ (no view) double; 70€ (view) double; 92€ (no view) triple; 98€ (view) triple; 116€ (rm. #1-no view) quad. Breakfast (7:30-10am) is included in the rates. Visa, MC, AX. English spoken (Barbara, Paolo & Carlotta), phones, TV, charming hotel w/nicely & identically furnished nice-size rms., #4 (1st flr. rm.), 5 (1st flr. rm.) & 28 (newly remodeled 2nd flr. rm. w/no view) all have twin beds & are for a single; #21, 23 & 24 (all large newly remodeled wonderful rms. w/2 twin beds or zip & lock queen-size bed, new bathrooms & large windows w/views of lake & rooftops) are for a double but can fit an extra twin bed for a triple; #26 (2nd flr. rm. that shares huge communal terrace w/views of lake & church) is for a double; #22 (view), 25 (view) & 20 (all newly remodeled rms. w/new bathrooms) are for a double; #6 (large 1st flr. rm. w/2 twin beds or zip & lock queen-size bed & no view) is for a double but can fit an extra twin bed for a triple; #1 (1st flr. rm. w/queen-size bed & twin bed) is perfect for a triple but too snug for a family; great terrace w/view of the lake, bar, private restaurant, wonderful quiet location, no elevator, 2 flrs. They offer half- and full-board rates. Owned/managed by Paolo & Carlotta Cichello (father & daughter). Walk through the arched opening, turn right and follow the wall, turn left to hotel. (Closed Nov.-Easter.)

GRIFONE: Via Bocchio 4. **Tel**: 030-916014. **Fax:** 030-916548. (16 rms., all w/toilet & bath or shower.) 37€ single; 64€ double; 85€ triple; 210€ quad. No breakfast is served. Cash only. English spoken (Cristina), wonderful charming hotel w/simply & identically furnished rms. w/lakeside views, shiny tiled flrs., #34 (2 twin beds or zip & lock queen-size bed, bathroom w/bathtub w/hand-held shower & large balcony w/fabulous view of the castle & lake) is for a double; #28 (corner rm. w/2 twin beds or zip & lock queen-size bed & large balcony w/fabulous view of the castle & lake) is for a double; #26 (corner rm. w/3 twin beds or 1 zip & lock queen-size bed & twin bed, bathroom w/bathtub w/hand-held shower & large balcony w/fabulous view of the lake) is for a double or triple; #36, 38, 40 & 42 (all 3rd flr. rms. w/2 twin beds or zip & lock queen-size bed, sloped ceilings, bathrooms w/showers & balconies w/fabulous views of the lake) are for a double; #24, 22 & 20 (all 2nd flr. rms. w/2 twin beds or zip & lock queen-size bed, bathrooms w/showers & fabulous views of the lake) are for a double; #16 (large 1st flr. rm. w/2 twin beds or zip & lock queen-size bed & wonderful view of lake) is for a double but can fit an extra twin bed for a triple; #14 (1st flr. rm. w/2 twin beds or zip & lock queen-size bed & small view) is for a double; #10 & 12 (both 1st flr. rms. w/2 twin beds or zip & lock queen-size bed & no views) have connecting doors but can be rented separately as a double or together as one family rm.; #20 & 22 (both 2nd flr. rms. w/ 2 twin beds or zip & lock queen-size bed) have connecting doors but can be rented separately as a double or together as one family rm.; #32 & 34 (both 3rd flr. rms. w/2 twin beds or zip & lock queen-size bed) have connecting doors but can be rented separately as a double or together as one family rm.; garden, wonderful quiet location, elevator only goes to 3rd flr., 4 flrs., free parking. Owned/managed by Nicola & Cristina Marcolini (brother & sister). I have stayed at this hotel & loved it. I just wished they took credit cards. Walk through the arched opening, turn right and follow the wall, turn right to hotel. (Closed Nov.-mid-March.)

PACE: Via Carpentini 17. **Tel**: 030-9905877. **Fax**: 030-9196097. **Web site:** http://www.pacesirmione.it/ **E-mail:** hotelpace@tin.it (22 rms., all w/toilet & shower.) 103€ double. Buffet breakfast (7:30-10:30am, includes cereals, cheese, ham & yogurt) at 6€ pp can be served in the room (5€ extra pp) or on the veranda in warm weather. Visa, MC, AX, DC. English spoken (Eleanor), phones, cable TV w/CNN, fabulous wonderful charming hotel w/nicely & identically furnished nice-size rms., #50 , 52, 58 & 60 (all w/2 twin beds or zip & lock queen-size bed & huge balconies that face the street w/wonderful views of the lake) are for a double; #88 & 74 (both corner rms. w/2 twin beds & 2 windows w/views of the lake) are for a double; #72 (small corner rm. w/2 twin beds & 2 windows w/views of the lake) is for a double; some rms. w/ceiling fans, warm ambience, Internet access available at 6€ per 1/2 hr., beautiful garden, private pier w/ sunbathing, veranda w/magnificent panoramic view, bar, 2 restaurants, wonderful quiet location, elevator stops in between flrs., 3 flrs.

Owned/managed by Gianna, Eleanor (charming) & Julia Barelli (mother & daughters). They offer half- and full-board rates. Walk through the arched opening, continue straight on the main road, turn left onto Via Carpentini. Cross street: Piazza Porto Valentino 5. (Closed Nov. 5-Dec. 5 & Jan. 10-Feb. 15.)

SPERANZA: Via Casello 6. **Tel**: 030-916116. **Fax:** 030-916403. (13 rms., all w/toilet & shower.) 47€ (rm. #23) single; 77€ double; 105€ triple. Breakfast (8-10am, includes pâté, cheese, assorted fresh breads, jams, cereals & juices) is included in the rates & can be served in the room. Air-conditioned. Visa, MC, AX, DC. English spoken (Franco & Aliza), phones, TV, wonderful charming hotel w/nicely & identically furnished nice-size rms. w/no views, #23 (2 twin beds that are positioned toe-to-toe) is perfect for a single but too snug for a double; #27 (large rm. w/2 twin beds or zip & lock queen-size bed, futon convertible chair/bed & large bathroom) & 26 (large rm. w/2 twin beds or zip & lock queen-size bed, futon convertible chair/bed & small bathroom) are for a double or triple; #16 & 18 (both w/2 twin beds or zip & lock queen-size bed, futon convertible chair/bed, small bathrooms & faces street) are for a double or triple; #24 (2 twin beds or zip & lock queen-size bed & small window that faces the main street) & 25 (2 twin beds or zip & lock queen-size bed, historical arch & small window that faces the main street) are for a double; #15 & 21 (both w/3 twin beds or 1 zip & lock queen-size bed & twin bed & face street) are for a triple; #11 (large rm. w/2 twin beds or zip & lock queen-size bed, 2 futon convertible chair/beds, small bathroom & faces the side street) is perfect for a double or triple but too snug for a family; modern bathrooms w/towel heaters, wonderful noisy location, marble staircase, elevator, 2 flrs. Owned/managed by Franco & Aliza Sacchella (husband & wife). Walk through the arched opening, continue straight on the main road, turn left onto Via Casello. (Closed Nov. 11-Feb.)

LAST OPTIONS
GIARDINO: Via Vittorio Emanuele 67. **Tel/Fax**: 030-916135. **Web site:** http://www.sirmione.it/ **E-mail:** giardino@sirmione.it (40 rms., all w/toilet & bath or shower.) 55€ single; 82€ double; 118€ triple. Breakfast (7:30-9:30am) at 8€ pp can be served in the room (1€ extra pp). Visa, MC. English spoken (Angela & Giuseppe), phones,

cable TV w/CNN, simple hotel w/plainly & identically furnished nice-size rms. w/balconies but no views, wooden flrs., rooms #27 & 28 (both small rms. w/twin bed & no balconies) are for a single; #1 (large rm. w/3 twin beds or 1 zip & lock king-size bed & twin bed, large bathroom w/bathtub w/hand-held shower & small balcony that faces the parking lot) is the only large room for a triple, no ambience, wonderful quiet location, no elevator. Owned/managed by charming Angela & Giuseppe Bertoldi (sister & brother) & their family since 1934. Angela was born in the hotel. (Closed Oct. 27-March.)

LUNA: Via Vittorio Emanuele 92. **Tel:** 030-9905836. **Fax:** 030-916381. (31 rms., all w/toilet & shower.) 69€ single; 85€ double. Call for triple rates. Breakfast (7:30-9:45am) at 6€ pp. Air-conditioned. Visa, MC, AX. English spoken (Mario), phones, TV, simple hotel w/plainly & identically furnished nice-size rms. w/balconies but no views, 4 rooms are for a single; no ambience, wonderful quiet location, elevator, 2 flrs. Owned/managed by Mario Lizzeri. Walk through the arched opening, continue straight on the main road, hotel is located opposite the park. (Closed Nov.-March.)

TAXI
030-916082.

RESTAURANTS
AL PESCATORE: Via G. Piana 20/22. **Tel:** 030-916216. **Fax:** 030-9199004. Hrs.: Thurs.-Tues. 11:30am-2:30pm & 4:30pm-10:30pm. Closed Wed. & Nov. 10-Dec. 20. Visa, MC, AX. Reservations recommended. Specialty: Fresh seafood & fish. Delicious food. It is one of the few restaurants I know of that doesn't have a 2-people minimum on ordering *risotto*. I usually travel alone and am not always able to order it. This is my favorite restaurant in Sirmione. Highly recommended by Lorenzo, Hotel Corte Regina.

BOTTE (LA): Via Antiche Mura 25. **Tel:** 030-9196257. **Fax:** 030-916273. Hrs.: Wed.-Mon. 11:45am-2:45pm & 7pm-10:45pm. Closed Tues. Visa, MC, AX. Reservations required. Specialty: Meat. Delicious food. *Show owner/chef Anna Maria or owner/manager Roberto Vanni (mother & son) this book and get a complimentary after-dinner drink.* Highly recommended by Lorenzo, Hotel Corte Regina.

SORRENTO
Amalfi Coast, zip code 80067
Country code 39, city code 081

Sorrento's Tourist Information Center
Via Luigi Maio 35. **Tel:** 081-8074033. **Fax:** 081-8773397. Hrs.: Mon.-Sat. 9am-6:30pm. Closed Sun. Longer hours in summer. From the station, turn left onto Corso Italia, walk to Piazza Tasso, turn right at end of square down onto Via Luigi Maio, walk through Piazza Sant'Antonio, continue right towards the port. The tourist office is located on the left as you enter the building.
Web site: http://www.sorrentotourism.com/
E-mail: aastsorrento@libero.it

TRANSPORTATION TIPS
Naples to Sorrento by train
Naples Centrale Stazione is the main train station facing Piazza Garibaldi. On the lower level of this station is where you can catch the independent local *Ferrovia Circumvesuviana* commuter trains to Sorrento. Tel: 081-7722444. When you arrive at the Naples Centrale station, look for the large blue signs *"Circumvesuviana."* Follow the signs, walk downstairs, buy your ticket at the *Circumvesuviana* window. Walk to the far left of the turnstiles, insert your ticket into the machine and walk downstairs to the tracks. Naples to Sorrento: 70-min. train ride. 3€ one way. No rail passes accepted. (There are no toilets on these local trains.)

To Sorrento by boat
CA.RE.MAR: Tel: 081-8073077. Fax: 081-8072479. Capri - Sorrento: Fast ferry 7€ one way. 20-min.; **LINEE MARITTIME:** Tel: 081-8071812. Fax: 081-5329071. Capri -Sorrento: Slow ferry 8€ one way. 40 min.; Capri -Sorrento: Hydrofoil 9€ one way. 20 min.; Naples to Sorrento: Hydrofoil 8€ one way. 35 min.; Ischia to Sorrento: Hydrofoil 13€ one way. 50 min. Cash only. Don't assume the boats run every day in high season. The condition of the weather dictates their schedule. Always check the day before departure.

SORRENTO

Sorrento hotels listed alphabetically
ASTORIA
CITY
CORSO (DEL)
DÉSIRÉE
ELIOS
IL NIDO
LORELEY & LONDRES
MIGNON
MINERVETTA (LA)
NICE
TONNARELLA (LA)
VILLA DI SORRENTO

HOTELS
CORSO (DEL): Corso Italia 134. **Tel:** 081-8071016. **Fax:** 081-8073157. **Web site:** http://www.hoteldelcorso.com/ **E-mail:** info@hoteldelcorso.com (20 rms., all w/toilet & shower.)
95€ single; 116€ double; 157€ triple; 189€ quad. Continental buffet breakfast (7:30-9:30am includes cheese, fruit, cereals, breads & juices) is included in the rates & served on the terrace in warm weather. Air-conditioned. Visa, MC, AX, DC. English spoken (Luca), phones, cable TV w/CNN, wonderful charming hotel w/simply furnished nice-size airy rms., #64 (patio w/view of rooftops & Vesuvius), 62, 63, 65 & 66 (all 2nd flr. nice-size rms. w/2 twin beds or zip & lock queen-size bed) are for a double; #60 (arched doorway & bathroom w/bathtub), 59 & 61 (all large rms. w/3 twin beds or 1 zip & lock queen-size bed & twin bed & face the street) are for a triple; #51, 52, 53, 54 & 55 (all huge rms. w/3 twin beds or 1 zip & lock queen-size bed & twin bed, large bathrooms w/showers & face back) are for a triple but can fit extra twin bed for a family; #70 (3rd flr. rm. that faces the street) is for a triple; 7 rms. w/balconies, newly renovated bathrooms w/hairdriers, solarium rooftop terrace, Internet access available at 6€ per 1/2 hr., wonderful noisy location because of the pedestrian traffic, rms. that face the back are quieter, bar, marble circular staircase, elevator only goes to 1st flr., 2 flrs. Owned/managed by Luca Marciano & his family for over 26 years. *5% rm. discount when you show them this book.* Luca is wonderful & accommodating. They are

constantly renovating the hotel to improve their services. From station, walk down the stairs to Corso Italia, turn left onto Corso Italia, walk for 2 1/2 blocks. (Closed Nov.-Feb.)

LORELEY & LONDRES: Via Califano 2. **Tel:** 081-8073187. **Fax:** 081-5329001. (27 rms., all w/toilet & bath or shower.) 101€ double; 127€ triple; 153€ quad; 180€ quint. The 7 rooms facing the noisy street are cheaper. Breakfast (7-10am) is included in the rates & served on the garden terrace. Air-conditioned (7 rms. that face noisy street). Visa, MC, AX, DC. English spoken (Anna Marie), no phones, no TV, wonderful charming ancient villa hotel w/old-fashioned simply furnished nice-size to large bright rms., shiny tiled flrs., #14 (fabulous corner rm. w/2 twin beds or zip & lock queen-size bed, bathroom w/ bathtub & 2 balconies w/wonderful views of coastline) & 25 (fabulous large corner rm. w/2 twin beds or zip & lock queen-size bed, large bathroom w/bathtub & floor-to-ceiling windows w/wonderful views of coastline) are for a double but can fit an extra twin bed for a triple; #15 (balcony) & 26 (both wonderful rms. w/2 twin beds or zip & lock queen-size bed, small bathrooms w/showers & wonderful views of sea & coastline) are for a double; #13 (terrace) & 24 (both w/wonderful sea views) are for a double; #22 (2 twin beds or zip & lock queen-size bed & window w/sea view) is for a double; #11 (sea view) is for a double; #12 (small balcony) & 23 (both wonderful large corner rms. w/2 twin beds or zip & lock queen-size bed, small bathrooms w/showers & wonderful views of sea, Naples, Ischia & Vesuvius) are for a double but can fit an extra twin bed for a triple; #5, 6, 7, 8, 9 & 10 (all nice-size air-conditioned rms. w/2 twin beds or zip & lock queen-size bed, small bathrooms w/showers & face the street w/no views) are for a double; #20 (large air-conditioned rm. w/3 twin beds or 1 zip & lock queen-size bed & twin bed, small bathroom w/shower & faces the street w/no view) is for a triple but can fit an extra twin bed for a family; #29 (huge ground flr. rm. w/4 twin beds or 1 zip & lock queen-size bed & 2 twin beds, small bathroom w/shower, high ceiling & wonderful views of sea, Naples, Ischia & Vesuvius) is for a family but can fit an extra twin bed for a quint; 15 rms. w/sea views, 8 of those rms. have balconies, most rms. have small bathrooms, garden/terrace restaurant w/fabulous view, elevator to private beach, bar, lots of warm ambience, wonderful location, marble staircase, no elevator, 2 flrs., free parking. They offer half-board rates. Owned by Giuseppina Ereolan (mother) & managed by Anna Marie (daughter). Same family owns Hotel Mignon. Wonderful, charming & accommodating Anna Marie has been in this hotel all her life. She tries hard to give you a room with a view. If you don't get a room w/a view on the first night, she keeps trying each night until you do. The hotel is located high on the cliffs on the eastern edge of town. From station, walk down the stairs to Corso Italia, turn right on Corso Italia, an immediate left at the gas station onto Via Capasso, which becomes Via Califano. Taxi 12€ . (Closed Nov.-until Easter.)

MIGNON: Via Antonino Sersale 9. **Tel/Fax:** 081-8073824. (11 rms., all w/toilet & bath or shower.) 63€ single; 85€ double; 106€ triple. Breakfast (8-9:30am) is included in the rates & is served in the room. Air-conditioned. Visa, MC, AX, DC. English spoken (Giovanna), no phones, TV, charming modern hotel w/nicely furnished nice-size rms., shiny tiled flrs., #21 (twin bed) is the only single rm.; #7 (corner rm.), 4, 5 & 6 (all nice-size rms. w/2 twin beds or zip & lock queen-size bed & balconies that face street) are for a double; #2 (large rm. w/2 twin beds or zip & lock queen-size bed & 2 large balconies that face street & back) is for a double but can fit an extra twin bed for a triple; #15 (nice-size rm. w/2 twin beds or zip & lock queen-size bed & balcony w/no view) is for a double; #10 (large rm. w/3 twin beds or 1 zip & lock queen-size bed & twin bed, small bathroom & huge terrace w/mountain view) & 9 (shares terrace w/rm. #10) are for a triple; #13 (large rm. w/3 twin beds or 1 zip & lock queen-size bed & twin bed & small balcony w/mountain view), 14 & 22 are for a triple but can fit an extra twin bed for a family; newly renovated bathrooms w/towel heaters & hairdriers, quiet location, marble staircase, no elevator, 2 flrs., free parking. Owned Giuseppina Ereolan (mother) & managed by Anna Marie (daughter). Same family owns Hotel Loreley. From station, walk down the stairs to Corso Italia, turn left onto Corso Italia, continue straight through Piazza Tasso, turn left at the Fortuna toy store onto Via Antonino Sersale.

NICE: Corso Italia 257. **Tel:** 081-8781650. **Fax:** 081-8071154. **E-mail:** hotelnice@hotmail.com (23 rms., all w/toilet & shower.) 64€ single; 77€ double; 109€ triple; 137€ quad. Breakfast (7:30-10am) is included in the rates. Air-conditioned (cost extra). Visa, MC, AX, DC. English spoken (Alfonso), phones, cable TV w/CNN, pleasant renovated hotel w/simply & identically furnished nice-size rms., shiny tiled flrs., #49 (nice-size 3rd flr. rm. w/twin bed, compact bathroom & faces back) & 37 are for a single; #50 (3rd flr. rms. w/2 twin beds or zip & lock queen-size bed, compact bathroom & faces street) is for a double; #32 (2 twin beds & small window that faces interior) is for a double; #33 & 35 (both rms. w/balconies facing the train station) are for a double; #47 (huge 3rd flr. rm. w/3 twin beds or 1 zip & lock queen-size bed & twin bed & faces interior) is for a triple but can fit an extra twin bed for a family; #52 & 45 (both huge 3rd flr. rms. w/4 twin beds or 1 zip & lock queen-size bed & 2 twin beds, small bathrooms & face back) are for a family, 7 rms. w/balconies (5 that face the street), rooftop terrace w/town view, wonderful noisy location, rms. that face the back are quieter, no elevator, 3 flrs. Owned/managed by charming & accommodating Alfonso. From station, walk (5 min.) down the stairs to Corso Italia, turn left onto Corso Italia to the hotel.

VILLA DI SORRENTO: Piazza Tasso/Via Fuorimura 6. **Tel:** 081-8781068. **Fax:** 081-8072679. **Web site:** http://www.belmare-travel.com/ **E-mail:** info@belmare-travel.com (21 rms., all w/toilet & bathtub w/hand-held shower.) 80€ single; 144€ double. Call for triple rates. Continental buffet breakfast (7-10am includes fruit, cereals, ham, jam, bread & juices) is included in the rates & can be served in the room (3€ extra pp). Air-conditioned. Visa, MC, AX. English spoken (Anna Maria & Simonetta), phones, cable TV w/ CNN, wonderful charming quaint hotel w/nicely & identically furnished nice-size bright rms., #15, 25, 35 & 44 are for a single; #41 & 42 (both top-flr. rms. w/2 twin beds or zip & lock queen-size bed & huge terraces w/wonderful views of sea, mountain & rooftops) are for a double; #21 (2 twin beds or zip & lock queen-size bed & faces side street) is for a double; #34 (queen-size bed) & 35 (2 twin beds) have connecting doors but can be rented separately as a double or together as one family rm.; #9 (queen-size bed & arched entrance) & 10 have connecting doors but can be rented separately as a double or together as one family rm.; rooms that face the garden are smaller, quieter & not as bright as the rooms that face the street, hairdriers, safes, wonderful ambience, fabulous noisy location, garden, eleva-

tor, 4 flrs. This hotel is not family-owned. From station, walk down
the stairs to Corso Italia, turn left onto Corso Italia, continue straight
to Piazza Tasso, turn left onto Via Fuorimura.

HOTELS
Punta Capo/Via Capo
You will not regret staying at any of these hotels. They are perched
on a cliff in splendid panoramic position with views of the Gulf of
Naples & Vesuvius. Just make sure you request a room with a view.
I suggest you taxi or bus to these hotels. Catch Sita bus #A from the
train station to Via Capo.

DÉSIRÉE: Via Capo 31B. **Tel/Fax:** 081-8781563. (22 rms., all w/
toilet & bath or shower.) 81€ (small rms. #17, 18, 20 & 22) double;
97€ (rms. #4, 13 & 14) double; 118€ (rms. #3, 8, 10 & 15) triple;
140€ quad. Breakfast (7:30-9:30am) is included in the rates. Cash
only. English spoken (Corinna), phones, no TV, wonderful charming
simple hotel w/simply furnished airy nice-size rms., shiny tiled flrs.,
#14 (fabulous lower lower-level rm. w/2 twin beds or zip & lock
king-size bed, bathroom w/bathtub & huge terrace w/magnificent
sea view) & 1 (magnificent sea view) are for a double; #13 (lower
lower-level large rm. w/2 twin beds or zip & lock queen-size bed,
bathroom w/bathtub, terrace w/view of hillside & window w/sea view)
& 6 (lower-level corner rm. w/2 twin beds or zip & lock queen-size
bed, bathroom w/bathtub, balcony w/view of hillside & window w/
sea view) are for a double; #2 (2 twin beds or zip & lock queen-size
bed, bathroom w/bathtub & window w/wonderful sea view) & 7
(lower-level rm. w/2 twin beds or zip & lock queen-size bed & window w/sea view) are for a double; #10 (balcony w/sea view) & 8 (sea
view) are for a double; #16 (2 twin beds or zip & lock queen-size
bed, large bathroom w/bathtub & balcony w/no view) is for a double
but can fit an extra twin bed for a triple; #17 (small rm. w/2 twin beds
or zip & lock queen-size bed, small bathroom w/shower & balcony
w/view of hillside) & 22 (small plain dark rm., small bathroom & no
view) are for a double; #15 (no view) is for a triple; #3 (large rm. w/
4 twin beds, bathroom w/bathtub, small terrace w/views of hillside
& sea) is for a family; walk down the stairs to the rms., 2 frigobars
(one on each flr.), roof-top terrace, lots of cats hanging out in the

reception, private elevator to private beach, fabulous peaceful location, no elevator, 2 flrs., free parking. Owned/managed by the very warm & accommodating Corinna Gargiulo. Same driveway & private beach as Hotel Tonnarella. (Closed Jan. 7-Feb.)

ELIOS: Via Capo 33. **Tel/Fax:** 081-8781812. (14 rms., all w/toilet & shower.) 59€ single; 90€ double. No breakfast served. Cash only. English spoken (Gianna), no phones, no TV, wonderful charming plain hotel w/simply furnished bright airy rms., shiny tiled flrs., #12 & 13 (lower-level rms. w/2 twin beds or zip & lock queen-size bed, newly tiled bathrooms & huge balconies w/wonderful sea views) are for a double; #1 (large rm. w/2 twin beds or zip & lock queen-size bed & huge balcony w/sea view) is for a double; #8 (nice-size rm. w/ 2 twin beds or zip & lock queen-size bed, small bathroom & large balcony w/sea view) is for a double; #2 & 3 (2 twin beds or zip & lock queen-size bed & small balconies w/sea views) are for a double; #14 (lower-level large rm. w/queen-size bed, newly tiled large bathroom w/bathtub & small balcony w/hillside view & partial corner sea view) is for a double; #7 (2 twin beds or zip & lock queen-size bed & balcony w/hillside view & tiny view of water) is for a double; #5 (small rm. w/2 twin beds or zip & lock queen-size bed & tiny balcony w/hillside view & tiny view of water) is for a double; #6 (nice-size rm. w/2 twin beds or zip & lock queen-size bed, private bathroom outside the room & small balcony w/hillside view & tiny view of water) is for a double; #11 & 10 (both w/2 twin beds, large bathrooms & no views) are for a double; #9 (3 twin beds or 1 zip & lock queen-size bed & twin bed, small bathroom & large balcony w/ sea view) is for a triple; #4 (large rm. w/balcony & no view) is for a triple or a family; most have small bathrooms, beautiful rooftop solarium/terrace & breakfast terrace w/magnificent panoramic sea views, warm family atmosphere, fabulous peaceful location, no elevator, 3 flrs., free parking. If this hotel took credit cards, I would be in heaven. Owned/managed by the wondeful & accommodating Luigi, Maria & Gianna Aiello (father, mother & daughter). Ask bus driver for Hotel Elios. (Closed Nov.-Feb.)

MINERVETTA (LA): Via Capo 25. **Tel:** 081-8773033. **Fax:** 081-8073069. **Web site:** http://www.tornasurriento.com/minervetta.htm/ Reservations accepted only by fax. (12 rms., all w/toilet & bath or shower.) 96€ single; 110€ double; 139€ triple; 168€ quad. Breakfast (7:30-9:30am) is included in the rates & served on the beautiful veranda in warm weather. Air-conditioned (3 rms. @16€ extra per day). Visa, MC, AX, DC. English spoken (Salvatore), phones, TV, wonderful charming warm hotel w/nicely furnished rms., all rooms have magnificent views of coastline & sea; shiny tiled flrs., #101, 102 & 103 (all lower-level rms. w/2 twin beds or zip & lock queen-size bed, bathrooms w/showers & tiny balconies) are for a double; #104 (huge lower-level rm. w/3 twin beds or 1 zip & lock queen-size bed & twin bed, large bathroom w/bathtub & floor-to-ceiling window) is for a double; #206 & 207 (both small air-conditioned rms. located 1/2 flight down w/2 twin beds or zip & lock queen-size bed, small bathrooms w/showers & large windows) are for a double; #201 (lower lower-level rm. w/3 twin beds or 1 zip & lock queen-size bed & twin bed, large bathroom w/bathtub & 2 floor-to-ceiling windows) is for a triple; #202 & 203 (both lower lower-level rms. w/3 twin beds or 1 zip & lock queen-size bed & twin bed, large bathrooms w/bathtubs & floor-to-ceiling windows) are for a triple; #105 (huge lower-level rm. w/2 twin beds or zip & lock queen-size bed, bunk beds, large bathroom w/bathtub & tiny balcony) & 204 (lower lower-level corner rm. w/2 twin beds or zip & lock queen-size bed, bunk beds, large bathroom w/bathtub & balcony) are for a family; #205 (large corner air-conditioned rm. w/2 twin beds or zip & lock queen-size bed, bunk beds & bathroom w/shower) is for a family; ceiling fans, private steps to the beach, bar, wonderful restaurant owned by same family for more 65 years (see below), terrace w/magnificent panoramic sea view, no elevator, 4 flrs., free parking. Owned/managed by wonderful & attentive Salvatore Morvillo. *5% rm. discount when you show him this book.* They offer half- and full-board rates.

TONNARELLA (LA): Via Capo 31. **Tel:** 081-8781153. **Fax:** 081-8782169. **Web site:** http://www.latonnarella.com/ **E-mail:** latonnarella@libero.it (21 rms., all w/toilet & bath or shower.) 121€ single; 142€ (no view) double; 148€ (view) double; 180€ triple; 209€ quad. Breakfast (7:30-9:30am) is included in the rates & can be served in the room or on the beautiful veranda in warm weather. Air-conditioned. Visa, MC, AX. English spoken (Pippo, Giuseppe, Smeralda & Rucco), phones, cable TV w/CNN, wonderful charming beautiful villa w/beautifully furnished rms., shiny tiled flrs., #4 (wonderful corner rm. w/2 twin beds or zip & lock king-size bed, small bathroom & 2 small terraces w/floor-to-ceiling windows w/magnificent sea views) & 3 (huge terrace w/magnificent sea view) are for a double; #21 (large rm. w/2 twin beds or zip & lock queen-size bed, private entrance & balcony w/fabulous sea view), 5 (wonderful corner rm. & small balcony w/sea view) & 9 (huge terrace w/magnificent sea view) are for a double; #12 (huge rm. w/2 twin beds or zip & lock queen-size bed, huge bathroom w/Jacuzzi shower & window w/ sea view) is for a double; #13 (romantic large attic rm. w/queen-size bed, sloped wood-beamed ceiling, Jacuzzi bathtub w/sea view & window w/sea view) & 14 (large attic rm. w/queen-size bed, sloped ceiling, small Jacuzzi bathtub & window w/sea view) are for a double; #6 (balcony w/sea view) is for a double or triple; #10 & 11 (both small rms. w/2 twin beds or zip & lock queen-size bed & windows w/small sea views) are for a double; #15 (nice-size attic rm. w/2 twin beds or zip & lock queen-size bed, huge bathroom w/corner Jacuzzi bathtub, sloped ceiling & small window w/no view) is for a double; #1 (large rm. w/3 twin beds or 1 zip & lock king-size bed & twin bed), 22 (large rm. w/private entrance) & 2 (all w/huge terraces w/ magnificent sea views) are for a triple; #20 (special fabulous large 2 rms. w/4 twin beds or 1 zip & lock queen-size bed & 2 twin beds, small balcony, hideaway terrace, large bathroom w/shower, step down to another large landscaped bathroom w/shower & hot tub, 2 TVs, minibar & small terrace w/magnificent sea view) is a honeymoon suite for a double or a room for a family; hairdriers, newly renovated bathrooms, elevator to private beach, bar, restaurant & terrace w/ panoramic sea view, fabulous peaceful location, elevator, 2 flrs., free parking. *5% rm. discount when you show owners/managers Cristina & Giuseppe Gargiulo this book.* They offer half- and full-board rates. Same driveway & private beach as Hotel Désirée.

HOTEL
5 km (3 miles) out of town.
I included this hotel even though it is located slightly out of town
because I had received many fabulous reports regarding it. Out of
curiosity I decided to put the hotel to the test to see how convenient it
was to get back and forth using both the hotel & town buses. It was
wonderful. I loved the tranquil location with its panoramic view and
fabulous owners. I never felt constricted or pressured by the hotel's
location outside of town. I was able to go back and forth to my hotel
using both the hotel's free minibus and the local buses. In the evenings, I went back into town to have dinner and stroll around and was
able catch the 11:30pm hotel bus back to the hotel with no problem.

IL NIDO: Via Nastro Verde 62. **Tel/Fax:** 081-8782766. **Tel/Fax:**
081-8073304. **Web site:** http://www.ilnido.it/ **E-mail:** info@ilnido.it
(26 rms., all w/toilet & bath or shower.) 80€ (no view) double; 90€
(partial view) double; 100€ (view) double; 115€ (view) triple; 131€
(view) quad. Call for quint rates. Breakfast (7:30-9:30am) is included
in the rates & can be served on the terrace in warm weather. Visa,
MC, AX, DC. English spoken (Gianni & Dino), phones, cable TV w/
CNN & BBC, fabulous warm charming newly renovated modern
hotel w/nicely identically furnished rms., shiny tiled flrs., #104 (bathroom w/bathtub), 105, 106 107, 108 & 109 (all large rms. w/3 twin
beds or 1 zip & lock king-size bed & twin bed & large balconies w/
wonderful views of sea, Sorrento coastline, Naples & Vesuvius) are
for a double or triple; #118 (balcony w/wonderful sea view) is for a
double; #112 (huge rm. w/2 twin beds or zip & lock king-size bed,
bathroom w/large shower & window w/wonderful sea view) is for a
double; #110 & 111 (both w/2 twin beds or zip & lock king-size bed
& large terraces w/sea views) are for a double; #103 (partial sea view)
& 114 (huge balcony w/partial sea view), 113 (faces back w/partial
sea view) & 103 (partial sea view) are for a double; #101, 102 & 123
(all w/3 twin beds or 1 zip & lock king-size bed & twin bed & face
the back w/no views) are for a double or triple; #115 (sea view) is
for a family or quint; all the 2 twin beds can also be made into a zip
& lock king-size bed, hairdriers, safes, minibars, bar, restaurant (food
is cooked & served by Gianni & Dino's parents from 7pm-8pm),
terrace w/magnificent breathtaking view of sea, Sorrento coastline,
Naples & Vesuvius, solarium, rooftop terrace, Internet access avail-

able at 5€ per hr., elevator, wonderful peaceful location perched on a cliff looking down on Sorrento, free parking. They offer half-board rates. Owned/managed by fabulous, warm, accommodating & generous Gianni & Dino Persico (brothers) who receive flags from their guests that come from different states within the U.S. When you arrive in Sorrento, call the hotel from the train station or the port and they pick you up (free of charge) from 3pm (check-in time) until 10pm in the hotel's minibus. The hotel's minibus shuttles guests to town and/or the port at least 3 times in the morning and 3 times in the afternoon. There is a prearrange pick-up from town and/or port about 6 times in the evening until 11:30pm. In between those times there is a town bus that goes to and from the hotel and town every other hour. In my case, I had arrived early in the morning so I caught the town bus to the hotel to drop off my bags. To purchase a bus ticket, walk down the stairs from the train station to the bar. Ask for a bus ticket to Il Nido. Cost 1€ one way. Bus stop: Il Nido hotel. 10-min. ride to hotel. Check the hotel's Web site or e-mail Gianni for specific details on transportation to & from the hotel.

LAST 2 HOTEL OPTIONS IN THE CENTER
ASTORIA: Via S. Maria Grazie 24. **Tel:** 081-8074030. **Fax:** 081-8771124. **E-mail:** info@abctravel.it (34 rms., all w/toilet & bath or shower.) 58€ single; 100€ double. Call for triple rates. Breakfast (7-9am) is included in the rates. Visa, MC. English spoken, phones, no TV, 17th-century plain no-atmosphere hotel w/simply furnished nice-size rms. w/no views, #16 (twin bed & compact bathroom) & 40 (balcony) are for a single; #30, 20 (opens up onto the communal terrace), 37, 38, 41 & 46 (all have balconies w/no views) are for a double; #23 (3 twin beds or 1 zip & lock queen-size bed & twin bed & faces back) & 45 (balcony w/no view) are for a triple; all the rooms for 2 people have 2 twin beds or zip & lock queen-size bed, small bathrooms, 7 rms. w/balconies w/no views, terrace/garden, bar, quiet location, no elevator, 3 flrs. on one side & 1 fl. on the other side. This hotel is not family-owned. They offer half-board rates. From station, walk down the stairs to Corso Italia, turn left onto Corso Italia, continue straight through Piazza Tasso, turn right onto Via Archi, turn left (after the wall) onto Via S. Maria Grazie. (Closed Jan.Feb.)

CITY: Corso Italia 221. **Tel/Fax:** 081-8772210.
E-mail: hotelcity@libero.it (13 rms., all w/toilet & shower.) 48€ single; 81€ double; 113€ triple; 136€ quad; 164€ quint. Breakfast (8-10am) is included in the rates. Visa, MC, AX. English spoken (Angela & Gianni), no phones, TV, plain hotel w/simple plainly furnished nice-size airy bright rms., #3 (2 twin beds or zip & lock queen-size bed, compact bathroom & small balcony that faces the street) is for a double; #7 (2 twin beds & faces back) is for a double; #9 (large rm. w/3 twin beds or 1 zip & lock queen-size bed & twin bed, small bathroom & faces back), 8 (large rm. that faces back) & 6 (faces back) are for a triple; #4 & 14 (both w/2 twin beds or zip & lock queen-size bed & bunk beds) are for a family; #5 (queen-size bed, twin bed, bunk beds & faces back) is for a quint; only 6 (all for 2 people) out of 13 rooms face the noisy street, no atmosphere, wonderful noisy location, no elevator, 2 flrs. Owned/managed by charming Gianni Magliulo. From station, walk down the stairs to Corso Italia, turn left onto Corso Italia and walk for 1 1/2 blocks.

LAUNDROMAT (Lavanderia)
Terlizzi: Corso Italia 30. Tel: 081-8781185. Daily: 8am-9pm. Self-service. Located around the corner from the dry cleaner. Owned/ managed by the dry cleaner who sells the coins for the machines. Hours for the dry cleaner are Mon.-Fri. 8am-1:30pm & 4pm-8pm. Because the dry cleaner is closed Sat. & Sun., you have to get your coins from the leather shop.

TAXI
Francesco Scialone taxi: Mobile Tel: 330703782. Recommended by Hotel Il Nido; Sorrento taxi: Tel: 081-8782204.

SUPERMARKETS
Standa: Corso Italia 223. Hrs.: Mon.-Sat. 8:30am-1:20pm & 5pm-8:55pm. Closed Sun; Via degli Aranci 27. Hrs.: Mon.-Sat. 8:30am-1:30pm & 4:30pm-8:30pm. Closed Thurs. afternoon & Sun; Super Sigma: Via Capo 10. Hrs.: Mon.-Sat. 8am-9pm & Sun. 8am-1pm. Visa, MC.

RESTAURANTS
FENICE (LA): Via degli Aranci 11. Tel: 081-8781652. Fax: 081-5324153. Tues.-Sun. Hrs.: 12noon-3pm & 7pm-12midnight. Closed Mon. Visa, MC, AX, DC. Reservations required. Delicious fresh food served in a wonderful garden environment. You can select your fresh fish & seafood from the fish tank in front of the restaurant. Cover charge: 1€ pp. *Show owners Fabrizio & Giuseppe or Luigi (charming waiter) this book and they will give you a complimentary Limoncello.* Highly recommended by Gianni, Hotel Il Nido.

MINERVETTA (LA): Via Capo 25. Tel: 081-8773033. Fax: 081-8073069. Web site: http://www.tornasurriento.com/minervetta.htm/ Hrs.: Daily 12noon-2pm & 7pm-12midnight. Closed Nov.-March. Visa, MC, AX, DC. Specialty: Fish and seafood. Reservations recommended, especially for dinner. This fabulous restaurant has been in the family for more than 65 years. They serve a huge selection of unbelievable delicious fresh fish and seafood, assorted meats, homemade local pastas along with a magnificent view of the sea and coastline (the best view in town). Wonderful ambience. Eat here and you won't want to eat anywhere else in Sorrento. Eight assorted fixed tourist menus available depending on your budget. No cover or service charges.

RED LION: Via Marziale 25. Tel/Fax: 081-8073089. Web site: http://www.theredlion.it/ E-mail: info@theredlion.it Hrs.: Daily 12noon-4pm & 7pm-2am. Closed Jan. 8-31. Visa, MC, DC. This simple family-owned restaurant with an English name has an extensive menu of homemade Italian food. It is a fun place to enjoy an affordable, delicious meal. Choose from 15 homemade pasta dishes, assorted meats and scrumptious pizzas. They even have banana splits & real milk shakes. No cover or service charges. *Show owner/manager Tonino Maresca this book and he will give you a complimentary after-dinner drink.* Highly recommended by Alfonso, Hotel Nice. From station, walk down the stairs to Corso Italia, turn left onto Corso Italia, turn left to restaurant.

VARENNA
Lake Como, zip code 23829
Country code 39, city code 031

Varenna's Tourist Information Center
Piazza Venini 1. **Tel/Fax:** 0341-830367. Hrs.: Mon.-Sat. 10am-12:30pm & 3:30pm-5:30pm; Sun. 10am-12:30pm. Longer hours in summer. Located next to the bell tower.
Web site: http://www.varennaitaly.com/
E-mail: prolocovarenna@tin.it

TRANSPORTATION TIPS
Before purchasing individual boat tickets to see the different towns, look into the all-day ticket (7€ pp). They are great, you can hop on & off the boats to the different towns. Visa, MC. **Web site:** http://www.navigazionelaghi.it/ **E-mail:** navicomo@navigazionelaghi.it If you are leaving Varenna by train, purchase your train ticket at the bar inside Hotel Beretta or the travel agency next to the hotel because the ticket window at the train station may not be open. If there are no train personnel available at the train station to designate the track number for your departure, look for the box under the clock that lights up the correct track number for your destination.

HOTELS
BERETTA: Via Per Esino 1. **Tel/Fax:** 0341-830132.
Web site: http://www.varennaitaly.com/beretta.index.htm
E-mail: hotelberetta@iol.it (10 rms., 8 w/toilet & shower.) 78€ double; 91€ (rms. #4, 5 & 9) double; 111€ triple; 126€ quad. The rooms without bathrooms are cheaper. Breakfast (8:30-10am) at 6€ pp can be served in the room (3€ extra pp) or served on the outdoor patio in warm weather. Visa, MC, AX, DC. Limited English spoken (Giulia), phones, TV, wonderful charming hotel w/nicely & identically pinewood furnished nice-size rms., #1, 2 & 3 (all wonderful newly renovated 1st flr. rms. w/queen-size beds, bathrooms & face the street) are for a double; #6 & 7 (large 2nd flr. rms. w/2 twin beds or zip & lock king-size bed & bathrooms) are for a double; #9 (wonderful corner rm. w/2 twin beds or zip & lock queen-size bed, no bathroom & balcony w/mountain view) & 8 (3 twin beds or 1 zip &

lock queen-size bed & twin bed, no bathroom & small window that faces the street) are for a double or triple and share a bathroom w/rm. #5 & 10 but will have private bathrooms sometime this year; #4 (wonderful 1st flr. rm. w/queen-size bed, twin bed, convertible sofa, huge bathroom & balcony that faces street) is for a double, triple or family; #5 (2nd flr. w/2 twin beds or zip & lock queen-size bed, no bathroom & large terrace w/wonderful mountain view) currently shares a bathroom w/rms. #10 (double bed & no bathroom), 9 (see above) & 8 (see above) but that will change sometime this year; quiet location but the rooms are above the hotel's bar, restaurant, no elevator, 2 flrs. Owned/managed by Tosca Proto. Tosca's brother owns Hotel Monte Codeno. To walk to the hotel from the train station, walk down the curvy road; as you go around the curve, look for the steps (shortcut) on your right, walk down the steps to Via Per Esino, turn right onto Via Per Esino.

MILANO: Via XX Settembre 29. **Tel/Fax:** 0341-830298. **Web site:** http://www.varenna.net/ **E-mail:** hotelmilano@varenna.net (8 rms., 7 w/toilet & shower.) 106€ double. Call for triple rates. The room without a bathroom is cheaper. Breakfast (8-10am) is included in the rates & is served on the terrace in warm weather. Visa, MC, AX, DC. English spoken (Bettina & Egidio), phones, no TV, wonderful charming hotel w/simply & identically pinewood furnished nice-size rms., original wooden flrs., #1 (1st flr. rm. w/2 twin beds or zip & lock king-size bed, small bathroom w/shower & super huge terrace w/ wonderful view of water) & 2 (1st flr. rm. w/2 twin beds or zip & lock king-size bed, bathroom w/bathtub & super huge terrace w/ wonderful view of water) are for a double; #5 & 6 (both large 2nd flr. rms. w/2 twin beds or zip & lock queen-size bed, small bathrooms w/showers & small balconies w/wonderful views of water) are perfect for a double but too snug for a triple; #8 (2nd flr. corner rm. w/2 twin beds or zip & lock queen-size bed, standard-size bathroom w/ shower & small balcony & patio door w/partial side views of water), 4 (1st flr. rm. w/2 twin beds or zip & lock king-size bed, standard-size bathroom w/shower & small balcony w/partial side view of water) & 7 (2nd flr. rm. w/2 twin beds or zip & lock queen-size bed, standard-size bathroom w/shower & small balcony w/partial side view of water) are for a double; #3 (1st flr. rm. w/2 twin beds or zip & lock king-size bed, private bathroom outside the room & small balcony w/partial side view of water) is for a double; terrace w/magnificent panoramic view, bar, wonderful quiet location, no elevator, 2 flrs. Newly (2002) owned/managed by Bettina & Egidio Mallone Schmidt (husband & wife). Taxi to hotel. (Closed Dec.-Feb.)

MONTE CODENO: Via Croce 2. **Tel:** 0341-830123. **Fax:** 0341-815227. **Web site:** http://www.varennaitaly.com/ **E-mail:** ferrcas@tin.it (11 rms., all w/toilet & shower.) 74€ single; 100€ double. Call for triple rates. Breakfast (7:30-10am) is included in the rates & can be served in the room (11€ extra pp). Visa, MC, AX, DC. English spoken (Marina & Rodolfo), phones, cable TV w/ CNN, charming simple hotel w/nicely & identically pinewood furnished rms. w/no views, shiny tiled flrs., #5 (small rm. w/twin bed & compact bathroom) & 9 (small 1st flr. rm. w/twin bed & small bathroom) are for a single but can fit an extra twin bed for a double at a discounted rate; #2 (large ground-flr. rm. w/2 twin beds or zip & lock queen-size bed) is for a double but can fit an extra twin bed for a triple; #6 (1st flr. rm. w/2 twin beds or zip & lock king-size bed, large bathroom & small view of mountain), 8 (1st flr. rm. w/2 twin beds or zip & lock king-size bed & small view of mountain) & 10 (quaint rm. w/2 twin beds or zip & lock queen-size bed, small bathroom & balcony w/tiny view of mountain) are for a double; #1 (ground-flr. rm. w/2 twin beds or zip & lock queen-size bed & handicapped-access bathroom) & 4 (ground-flr. rm. w/2 twin beds or zip & lock queen-size bed, handicapped-access bathroom & faces the back) are for a double; #7 (nice-size rm. 1st flr. rm. w/2 twin beds or zip & lock king-size bed & faces the back), 3 (ground-flr. rm. w/2 twin beds or zip & lock king-size bed) & 11 (small rm. w/2 twin beds or zip & lock queen-size bed & faces the back) are for a double; standard-size modern bathrooms, garden, bar, great restaurant, 5 steps up to the front door, no elevator, 2 flrs. Owned/managed by Rodolfo & Ferruccio Castelli (husband & wife). Rodolfo's brother owns Hotel Berretta. Taxi to hotel. To walk to the hotel from the train station, walk down the curvy road; as you go around the curve, look for the steps (shortcut) on your right, walk down the steps to Via Per Esino, turn right onto Via Per Esino, follow the road, turn left onto Via Croce. (Closed Nov.-Feb.)

OLIVEDO: Piazza Martiri 4. **Tel/Fax:** 0341-830115. (15 rms., 6 w/ toilet & bath.) **Web site:** http://www.olivedo.it/ **E-mail:** olivedo@tin.it 65€ single; 100€ double. Call for triple & quad rates. The rooms without bathrooms are cheaper. Breakfast (8-10am) is included in the rates & served on the garden terrace in warm weather. Cash only. English spoken (Laura), no phones, no TV, wonderful charming Victorian hotel w/beautifully old-fashioned & individually furnished bright airy nice-size to large rms., original wooden flrs., #3 (huge wonderful 1st flr corner rm. w/queen-size bed, bathroom w/bathtub w/hand-held shower & balcony w/wonderful view of water) & 18 (large wonderful corner rm. w/queen-size bed, bathroom w/bathtub w/hand-held shower & balcony w/wonderful view of water) are for a double; #21 & 11 (both w/bathrooms & great views) are for a double; #26 (huge wonderful corner rm. w/queen-size bed, twin bed, bathroom w/bathtub w/hand-held shower, balcony on the side & window w/wonderful view of water) is for a double or triple; #34 (quaint attic rm. w/queen-size bed, large bathroom w/ bathtub w/hand-held shower & small window in sloped ceiling w/no view) is for a double; #15 (French double bed, no bathroom & balcony w/wonderful view of water) is for a single; #2 (queen-size bed, shower outside the rm., toilet one flight up & balcony w/wonderful view of water), 25 (queen-size bed, no bathroom & balcony w/wonderful view of water) & 24 (2 twin beds, no bathroom & window w/ wonderful view of water) are for a double; all the rooms (except rms. #31, 33, 34 & 35) have views; the beds look like you can cuddle up & sleep in them all day, warm ambience, wonderful quiet location near the ferry dock, bar, great restaurant (see below), no elevator, 4 flrs., free parking. Owned by wonderful & charming Antonietta Illia & managed by Laura Columbo. *5% rm. discount when you show them this book.* They offer half-board rates which may be required in summer. Taxi to hotel. To walk to the hotel from the train station, walk down the curvy road, as you go around the curve, look for the steps (shortcut) on your right, walk down the steps to Via Per Esino, turn right onto Via Per Esino, follow the road, turn left onto Via Croce, turn right down to the waterfront. (Closed Nov.-Dec. 3.)

VILLA CIPRESSI: Via IV Novembre 18. **Tel:** 0341-830113. **Fax:** 0341-830401. **E-mail:** villacipressi@libero.it (21 rms., all w/toilet & shower.) 78€ single; 102€ (no view) double; 114€ (view) double; 126€ (suite) double; 155€ triple; 183€ quad. Breakfast (8-10am) is included in the rates & served on the garden terrace in warm weather. Visa, MC, AX, DC. English spoken (Elena, Cristian & Federico), phones, cable TV w/CNN, charming hotel w/plainly & identically pinewood furnished nice-size modern rms., carpeted flrs., #204 & 219 (both w/twin beds) are for a single; #213 (huge rm. w/2 twin beds or zip & lock queen-size bed & view of water) & 216 (2 twin beds or zip & lock queen-size bed & small view of water) are for a double; #217 (large rm. w/3 twin beds or 1 zip & lock queen-size bed & twin bed, large bathroom & small window view of water) is for a triple; #215 (loft suite w/4 beds & small view of water) & 214 (loft suite w/4 beds) are for a family; #217 (small view), 202 & 212 (all w/handicapped-access bathrooms) are for a double; standard-size bathrooms w/hairdriers & towel heaters, sterile ambience, bar, restaurant, wonderful quiet location, beautiful grounds w/gardens, elevator, 2 flrs. I am not as impressed with the rooms as I am with the hotel's surroundings. The rooms without views are not-so-bright but I don't think it is worth paying the extra money for the view. This hotel is not family-owned but managed by Federico Sangiani. *10% rm. discount when you show them this book.* They offer half-board rates. Taxi to hotel. (Closed Dec. 11-Feb.)

TAXI
Tel: 0341-830580. Tel: 0341-815061.

LAUNDROMAT (Lavanderia)
Via Croce 21. Hrs.: 9am-12:30pm & 3pm-7:30pm. Dry cleaning, drop-off & pick-up service only.

SUPERMARKET
Hrs.: Daily 7am-7:30pm. Located opposite the tourist office.

RESTAURANTS
IL CAVATAPPI: Via XX Settembre. **Tel:** 0341-815349. **Fax:** 0341-814772. Hrs.: Thurs.-Tues. 12noon-3pm & 7:30pm-12midnight. Closed Wed. Visa, MC, AX. Reservations required. This is a new

restaurant that recently opened in Varenna. I did not have the opportunity to eat here but Brad McEwen, tour guide for Rick Steves, assured me that the food is unbelievably delicious. I was trying to make reservations for the next day, only to find out that they would not be open. Brad introduced himself to me and starting raving about the restaurant. I am going by his high recommendation. Brad's e-mail: brdclsk@cs.com/ Owned/managed by Mario Nasazzi.

OLIVEDO: Piazza Martiri 4. **Tel/Fax:** 0341-830115. **Web site:** http://www.olivedo.it/ **E-mail:** olivedo@tin.it 12:30pm-2pm & 7:30pm-9:30pm. Cash only. Reservations recommended. The atmosphere is sterile but the food is unbelievably delicious & affordable. It is one of the few restaurants I know of that doesn't have a 2-people minimum on ordering *risotto*. I usually travel alone and am not always able to order it. You can even order homemade apple pie & ice cream for dessert. Owned by Antonietta Illia & chef Giuseppe (Antonietta's brother) who has been cooking at the hotel for more than 20 years.

VENICE (Venezia)
Veneto, zip code 30121
Country code 39, city code 041

Venice Tourist Information Centers
1.) Santa Lucia Train Station. **Tel:** 041-5298727. **Fax:** 041-719078. Hrs.: 8am-8pm, located on the left side of the train station. **2.)** Palazzina del Santi 2, San Marco. **Tel:** 041-5225150. **Fax:** 041-5298730. Hrs.: June-Sept. Mon.-Sat. 9:30am-6:30pm, Oct. to May, Mon.-Sat. 9:30am-12:30pm. **3.)** Castello 4421. Accepts phone calls only, no walk-ins. **Tel:** 041-5298711. **Fax:** 041-5230399. **4.)** Calle dell'Ascensione 71F, San Marco. **Tel/Fax:** 041-5208964. **Web site:** http://www.turismovenezia.it/ **E-mail:** apt-06@mail.regione.veneto.it

Floods: On one of my trips to Venice while researching hotels, it rained for five days in a row. Each of those days, the water in the canals overflowed into the streets and lobbies of hotels. In order to be able to continue my work, I was forced to buy fisherman's boots that came up to my knees because most of the hotels that were located near the canals had at least one foot of water in their reception areas.

TRANSPORTATION TIPS
Depending on the length of your stay in Venice, you may want to inquire about the different types of tickets that are available before buying the individual ticket that takes you to your hotel. There are 24-hr., 72-hr. or 7-day (34€ pp) tickets that give you unlimited usage during the ticket's time period. The 24-hr. period starts from the time you validate your ticket. They are great, you can hop on & off the boats without ever waiting on line to purchase an individual ticket or validate it only to miss the boat. I had a multiusage ticket to travel to and from restaurants from my hotel. The 7-day. ticket allows you to bring one luggage on board without charge. I had two bags (1 roll-on & 1 backpack) but they only count what you roll on board, not what is on your back, so I didn't have to pay for any bag coming or going to my hotel because I had the 7-day ticket (for which I got more than my money's worth.)

Venice hotels listed alphabetically

ADUA	GALLINI
AGLI ALBORETTI	LA RESIDENZA
AI DO MORI	LOCANDA CA' FÓSCARI
AL GAMBERO	LOCANDA CANAL
AL GAZZETTINO	LOCANDA FIORITA
AL GOBBO	LOCANDA LEONE BIANCO
ALLA SCALA	LOCANDA NOVO
ANTICO CAPON	LOCANDA SAN TROVASO
BERNARDI SEMENZATO	LOCANDA SILVA
BUCINTORO	MARTE & BIASIN
CANADA	MESSNER
CANEVA	PALAZZETTO DA SCHIO
CASA GEROTTO	RIVA
CALDERAN	ROSSI
CÀ SAN MARCUOLA	SAN GEREMIA
CASA PERON	SAN GIORGIO
CASA VERARDO	SAN SAMUELE
DONI	SANTA LUCIA
FALIER	SERENISSIMA
FONTANA	TIVOLI
GALLERIA	VILLA ROSA

VAPORETTO (water bus) STOPS FOR VENICE HOTELS

I have included vaporetto stops with all the hotel listings. You will notice that some hotels have two vaporetto stops. That is because the hotel is easily accessed from both stops. Please refer to the master vaporetto list below. This list will make it convenient for you when you arrive in Venice without reservations. You might end up walking around the city and will need to know what hotels are listed near your vaporetto stop. As you exit the train station facing the water, line #1 is to the right & lines #82 & N are to the left. Purchase your boat ticket (6€ pp) before you board or you'll pay a little extra to the conductor if you board without a ticket. There is a charge of 3€ for luggage. **Web site:** Venice transport system: http://www.actv.it/

VAPORETTI/WATER BUS
Accademia: Lines #82Red, 1, 3, 4 & N
Hotels: Agli Alboreti, Galleria, Locanda Fiorita

Arsenal: Lines #1 & 52Red
Hotel: Bucintoro

Ca' d'Oro: Lines #1 & N
Hotels: Bernardi Semenzato, Locanda Leone Bianco, Locanda Novo

Ca' Rezzonico: Line #1
Hotel: Antico Capon

Ferrovia: Lines #82Red, 1, 3, 4 & N
Hotels: Adua, Al Gobbo, Casa Gerrotto, Marte & Biasin, Rossi, San Geremia, Santa Lucia, Villa Rosa

Ospedale: Lines #41 & 52
Hotel: Locanda S.S. Giovannie E Paolo (See Hotel Galleria.)

Rialto: Lines #82Red, 1, 4 & N
Hotels: Al Gambero, Al Gazzettino, Alla Scala, Canada, Caneva, Gallini, Serenissima

Salute: Line #1
Hotels: Messner, Palazzetto Da Schio

San Angelo: Line #1
Hotels: Gallini, Locanda Fiorita, San Giorgio, San Samuele

San Marco: Lines #82Red, 1, 3, 4 & N
Hotels: Ai do Mori, Locanda Canal, Locanda Silva, Riva

San Marcuola: Lines #82Red & 1
Hotel: Cà San Marcuola

San Samuele: Lines #82Red, 1, 3 & 4
Hotel: San Samuele

San Tomà: Lines #82Red, 1 & N
Hotels: Casa Peron, Falier, Locanda Ca' Fóscari, Tivoli

San Zaccaria: Lines #82Red, 1 & N
Hotels: Casa Verardo, Doni, Fontana, La Residenza, Locanda Canal, Locanda Silva

Záttere: Lines #82Red, 82Green, 1 & N
Hotel: Locanda San Trovaso

HOTELS (San Marco/St. Mark's Square)
AI DO MORI: Calle Larga San Marco 658. **Tel:** 041-5204817 or 5289293. **Fax:** 041-5205328.
Web site: http://www.hotelaidomori.com/
E-mail: reception@hotelaidomori.com (11 rms., 9 w/toilet & shower.) 130€ (small rms. like #8) double; 141€ (large rms. like #2, 3, 6, 9 & 11) double; 184€ triple; 205€ quad; 245€ (rm. 4/5) quad; 264€ (rm. 4/5) quint. The rooms without bathrooms are cheaper. No breakfast served. Air-conditioned. Visa, MC. English spoken (Antonella), phones, cable TV w/BBC, charming hotel w/nicely & identically furnished bright small pretty rms., #8 (small quaint rm. w/standard-size bathroom, sloped wood-beamed ceiling & 2 windows) is for a double; #11 (wonderful compact quaint attic rm. w/queen-size bed, wood-beamed ceiling, small bathroom & wonderful rooftop terrace w/views of Basilica & clock tower) & 9 (large corner rm. w/small bathroom & 2 small windows w/rooftops view) are for a double; they have plans to renovate rm. #6 (wonderful large corner rm., wood-beamed ceiling, no bathroom & 2 windows w/views of Basilica & rooftops) to have a private compact bathroom & accommodate a double; #2 (bathroom w/bathtub) & 3 (bathroom w/shower) both w/ 2 twin beds or zip & lock queen-size bed, wood-beamed ceilings & face the clock tower are for a double; #5 (nice-size rm. w/2 twin beds or zip & lock king-size bed, futon convertible chair/bed, no bathroom & 2 windows that face the side street) & 4 (small rm. w/2 twin beds or zip & lock queen-size bed & no bathroom) share a bathroom w/bathtub & shower and because they have connecting doors are rented together as a family or quint rm.; modern bathrooms w/ hairdriers & towel heaters, they do not reserve specific rooms, bar,

reception is two flights up, wonderful location, lots of stairs, no elevator, 4 flrs. Owned/managed by Antonella Bernardi. **Vaporetto:** San Marco. Located just off St. Mark's square. From St. Mark's square, walk under the Torre l'Orologio clock tower, turn a quick right to the hotel.

AL GAMBERO: Calle Fabbri 4687. **Tel:** 041-5224384 or 5201420. **Fax:** 041-5200431. **Web site:** http://www.locandaalgambero.com/ **E-mail:** hotelgambero@tin.it or hotgamb@tin.it (27 rms., all w/toilet & bath or shower.) 121€ single; 165€ (no view) double; 183€ (view of canal) double; 225€ (no view) triple. Call for quad rates. Breakfast (7:30-9:30am) is included in the rates. Air-conditioned. Visa, MC. English spoken (Christian, Gianni & Luciana), phones, cable TV w/ CNN, charming hotel w/nicely to beautifully antique Venetian style furnished nonsmoking rms. that vary in decor; #206 (wonderful beautifully furnished rm. w/twin bed & faces the interior) & 401 (small rm. w/twin bed & terrace) are for a single; #203 (wonderful beautifully furnished rm. w/2 twin beds or zip & lock king-size bed, bathroom w/bathtub & tiny balcony w/2 floor-to-ceiling windows that face the canal) & 204 (wonderful beautifully furnished corner rm. w/ 2 twin beds or zip & lock king-size bed, bathroom w/bathtub & windows that face the canal) are for a double; #202 (view of canal) & 201 (faces the street) are for a double; #205 (wonderful beautifully furnished rm.), 312 (corner rm. that faces the street) & 404 are perfect for a triple but too snug for a family; modern bathroom w/hairdriers, minibars, if you get a room facing the street be aware that it is over a restaurant and you may smell fish, bar, restaurant, wonderful location, lots of stairs, no elevator, 4 flrs. Owned/managed by Sandro & Christian Rossi (father & son). **Vaporetto:** Rialto. Walk right along the canal, cross over the small footbridge, turn left turn onto Calle Fabbri. Hotel is on the right about 5 blocks up.

AL GAZZETTINO: Calle Mezzo 4971. **Tel:** 041-5286523. **Fax:** 041-5223314. **Web site:** http://www.algazzettino.com/ **E-mail:** algazzettino@virgilio.it (12 rms., all w/toilet & shower.) 65€ single; 135€ double; 157€ triple; 178€ quad. Call for quint rates. Breakfast (8-10am) is included in the rates. Air-conditioned. Visa, MC, AX. Limited English spoken (Luca, Mario & Jean), phones, no TV, charming simple hotel w/simply furnished rms., #16 (wonderful large rm. w/3 twin beds or 1 zip & lock king-size bed & twin bed, huge bathroom & terrace that overlooks the canal) is for a double or triple; #2 (view of canal) is for a double; #22 & 23 (both w/views of the canal) are for a double or triple; #12 (wonderful large rm. w/3 twin beds or 1 zip & lock queen-size bed & twin bed, compact bathroom & 2 windows w/ small balcony that overlook the canal) is for a double or triple; #31 (top-flr. rm. w/panoramic view but no canal view) is for a double or triple; #5, 15, 25 & 32 (all w/no views) are for a double; #3 (huge rm. w/4 twin beds or 1 zip & lock king-size bed & 2 twin beds & 2 large windows that face the canal) is the only room for a family or quint; bar, restaurant, lots of stairs, no elevator, 4 flrs. Owned/managed by Mario & Luca Lazzari (father & son). **Vaporetto:** Rialto. Walk straight ahead on Calle Larga Mazzini which becomes Calle San Salvatore Merceria, take it to the end, turn right onto Calle Ballotte, turn left onto Calle Mezzo. Ask hotel to fax you a map. (Closed Dec.15-Feb. 15.)

ALLA SCALA: Campo Manin (Corte Contarini Bovolo) 4306. **Tel:** 041-5210629. **Fax:** 041-5226451. (5 rms., 4 w/toilet & shower.) 90€ double; 126€ triple; 157€ quad. The room without a bathroom is cheaper. Breakfast (8:30-10:30am) at 7€ pp can be served in the room (1€ extra pp). Visa, MC. English spoken (Andrea & Alessandro, mother & son), no phones, no TV, quaint charming plain hotel w/ simply furnished nonsmoking pretty rms., #2 (large rm. w/2 twin beds or zip & lock king-size bed, roll-out twin bed, high ceiling w/ chandelier, small bathroom & faces the street) is for a double or triple but can fit an extra twin bed for a family; #1 (2 twin beds or zip & lock queen-size bed, cubicle bathroom where the sink slides, while you straddle the toilet so you can take a shower & faces the interior) & 4 (2 twin beds or zip & lock queen-size bed, cubicle bathroom where the sink slides, while you straddle the toilet so you can take a shower & faces the interior) are for a double; #5 (small rm. w/2 twin beds or zip & lock queen-size bed, high ceiling, private bathroom outside the room & faces the street) is for a double; #3 (huge rm. w/ 3 twin beds or 1 zip & lock king-size bed & twin bed, small bath-room w/shower & faces the interior) is for a triple but can fit an extra twin bed for a family; hairdriers, famous spiral stairway, warm ambi-ence, wonderful quiet location near the Scala Contarini Del Bovolo, no elevator, 1 fl. Owned/managed by the charming warm Andrea Della Fiorentina. **Vaporetto:** Rialto. Walk to your right along the waterfront, turn left onto Calle Carbon to Campo San Luca, turn right onto Salizzada San Luca, follow it to your left to Campo Manin, take Calle Vida from the square to Calle Locande, turn left, then a quick right onto Corte Contarini Bovolo. (Closed Aug.)

GALLINI: Calle Verona 3673. **Tel:** 041-5204515. **Fax:** 041-5209103. **E-mail:** hgallini@tin.it (40 rms., all w/toilet & bath or shower.) 110€ single; 166€ double; 182€ (suite) double; 227€ triple; 145€ (suite) triple. Breakfast (7:30-10am) is included in the rates & can be served in the room (2€ extra pp). Air-conditioned (10 rms. at 6€ extra per day). Visa, MC, AX, DC. English spoken (Adriano, Gabriella, Francesco & Franco), phones, TV (10 rms.), charming pleasant renovated hotel w/nicely & identically pinewood furnished nice-size rms., mixture of wooden & shiny tiled flrs. that were put down by Adriano, #353 (view of canal) & 310 (both 3rd flr. rms. w/ twin beds) are for a single; #352 (Adriano was born in this wonderful air-conditioned rm. w/2 twin beds or zip & lock king-size bed, convertible sofa, wood-beamed ceiling, minibar & 2 small windows w/ views of the canal) is for a double or triple; #354 (3rd flr. suite. w/2 twin beds or zip & lock king-size bed, roll-out bed, small window w/ view of the canal, bathroom w/shower & sitting room w/window that overlooks the canal) is for a double or triple; #308 (large 3rd flr. corner rm. w/2 twin beds or zip & lock queen-size bed, bathroom w/ large shower stall & 3 windows) is for a double; #311 (large 3rd flr. bright airy corner rm. w/2 twin beds or zip & lock queen-size bed, bathroom w/shower & 3 windows) is for a double; #304 & 305 (both 3rd flr. rms. w/2 twin beds or zip & lock queen-size bed, bathrooms w/showers & face the courtyard) are for a double; #125 (1st flr. rm w/2 twin beds or zip & lock queen-size bed, bathroom w/bathtub w/ hand-held shower & faces the interior) is for a double; #122, 202 & 205 (all w/2 twin beds or zip & lock queen-size bed & roll-out bed) are for a double or triple; #300 (air-conditioned rm. w/TV & minibar); #105 (TV & minibar); modern bathrooms on the 2nd flr., huge breakfast room, minibars (10 rms.), bar, lots of stairs, no elevator, 3 flrs. Owned/managed by Adriano & Gabriella Ceciliati (father & daughter) & their family for more than 50 years. *10% rm. discount when* *you show them this book.* They cannot reserve specific rooms. **Vaporetto:** Rialto or San Angelo. Walk the wavy road passing through Campo San Angelo onto Calle Mandola, turn right onto Calle Assasini, which becomes Calle Verona. (Closed Dec.-Jan.)

LOCANDA FIORITA: Campiello Nuovo, Santo Stefano 3457/A. **Tel:** 041-5234754. **Tel/Fax:** 041-5228043. **Web site:** http:// www.locandafiorita.com/ **E-mail:** info@locandafiorita.com (21 rms., 17 w/toilet & shower.) Fiorita (main bldg.): 86€ (rm. #3) single; 135€ double; 140€ double; 177€ triple; 230€ quad. Allogi Fiorita annex (2nd bldg.): 140€ double; 193€ triple; 251€ quad. Ca' Morosini (3rd bldg.): 214€ double. Call for single rates in the Allogi Fiorita & Ca' Morosini. The rooms without bathrooms are cheaper. Breakfast (8:30-10:30am) is included in the rates & served on the terrace (Fiorita main bldg.) in warm weather. Air-conditioned. Visa, MC, AX, DC. English spoken (Renato, Alessandra, Daniela & Carl), phones, cable TV w/CNN (only in Allogi Fiorita annex & Ca' Morosini), wonderful charming 3-in-1 hotel w/beautifully & individually Venetian style furnished rms., Fiorita (15th-century main bldg. w/10 rms.): #3 (small rm. w/twin bed, private bathroom outside the rm. & faces the street) is for a single; #1 (2 twin beds or zip & lock queen-size bed, wood-beamed ceiling, small bathroom & faces the square) & 8 (1 flight up to rm. near reception w/2 twin beds or zip & lock queen-size bed, compact bathroom & faces the side street) are for a double; #9 (1 flight up to rm. near reception w/2 twin beds or zip & lock queen-size bed, convertible chair/bed, small bathroom & faces the side street) is for a double or triple; #10 (private entrance located off the front porch w/queen-size bed, small bathroom & faces the square) is for a double; #6 (private bathroom outside the rm.) is for a double; Allogi Fiorita annex (17th-century w/8 rms.): #5 (2 flights up to small rm. w/French double bed, no bathroom & faces the street) is for a single; #2 (1 flight up to large rm. near breakfast room w/2 twin beds or zip & lock queen-size bed & 2 windows that overlook the canal) & 3 (1 flight up to small rm. w/double bed, small bathroom & 2 small windows that overlook the canal) are for a double; #1 (1 flight up to large rm. near breakfast room w/2 twin beds or zip & lock king-size bed, small bathroom & faces the street), 4 (1 flight up to large rm. w/2 twin beds or zip & lock king-size bed, small bathroom & 2 windows that face the street) & 6 (2 flights up to small rm. w/queen-size bed, standard-size bathroom, arched wood-beamed ceiling & faces the street) are for a double; #7 (2 flights up to rm. w/ queen-size bed, no bathroom & faces the canal) is for a double; #8 (5 steps up to large ground-flr. rm. w/2 twin beds or zip & lock king-size bed, sofa/twin bed, small bathroom & 2 windows that overlook the canal) is for a double or triple; Ca' Morosini (3rd bldg. w/3 rms.): #22 (small rm. w/French double bed & bathroom) is for a single; #21 (corner rm. w/high decorative antique ceiling, small bathroom & 3 windows that face the square) & 20 (large rm. & bathroom) are for a double; they are working on 9 more rooms for 2004, hairdriers, minibars (Ca' Morosini), warm ambience, wonderful quiet location in a square, no elevator, 1 fl. Owned/managed by a wonderful group of friends: Renato, Alessandra & Paolo. **Vaporetto:** Accademia or San Angelo. From Accademia, cross the Accademia Bridge, continue to the large Campo Santo Stefano, cross the Campo, at the far end after the church, turn left at the flower stand., walk up seven steps to the hotel.

SAN GIORGIO: Rio Terà Mandola 3781. **Tel:** 041-5235835. **Fax:** 041-5228072. **E-mail:** hotelsangiorgio@tin.it (16 rms., all w/toilet & shower.) 115€ single; 150€ double; 195€ triple. Call for quad & quint rates. Continental buffet breakfast (7:30-9:30am) is included in the rates & can be served in the room (1€ extra pp). Air-conditioned (10€ extra per day). Visa, MC. English spoken (Manuela & Gabriella), phones, TV, wonderful charming hotel w/beautifully & identically Venetian style furnished pretty rms., shiny tiled flrs., #28 & 25 (both w/twin bed & face interior) are for a single; #22 (small rm. w/French double bed) is perfect for a single but too snug for a double; 27 (nice-size rm. w/2 twin beds or zip & lock queen-size bed) is for a double; #23, 24 & 26 (all w/2 twin beds & face the back) are for a double; #11 (3 twin beds or 1 zip & lock king-size bed & twin bed & faces the back) is the only room for a triple but has connecting doors w/rm. #12 (double) & can be rented together for a family or quint; #16 is the smallest but still very pretty, chandeliers, modern bathrooms w/hairdriers, minibars, safety boxes, warm ambience, wonderful quiet location, no elevator, 3 flrs. Owned by Renzo Cristofoli & managed by the wonderful Gabriella Gazzola for more than 30 years. **Vaporetto:** San Angelo. Walk to your left along the waterfront, turn right onto Calle Traghetto through Campo San Benedetto, turn right onto Calle Magazen, turn left onto Rio Terà Mandola, turn left onto Calle Mandola. (Closed Jan.)

SAN SAMUELE: Salizzada San Samuele 3358, 1st fl. **Tel/Fax:** 041-5205165 or 5228045. (10 rms., 7 w/toilet & shower.) 110€ double. Call for triple rates. The rooms without bathrooms are cheaper. Breakfast (8-10am) at 5€ pp. Cash only. English spoken (Domenico & Roberto), phones, no TV, charming plain hotel w/simply & identically furnished large bright airy rms., original flrs., #5 (small rm. w/ twin bed & no bathroom) & 7 (no bathroom) are for a single; #4 (2 twin beds or zip & lock queen-size bed, small bathroom & 2 windows that face the street) & 2 (1st flr. rm. w/2 twin beds or zip & lock queen-size bed, small bathroom & faces the street) are for a double; #3 (huge rm. w/2 twin beds or zip & lock queen-size bed, futon convertible chair/bed, small bathroom & 2 windows that face the street) is for a double or triple; #10 (queen-size bed, small bathroom & faces the garden) is for a double; #8 (not-so-bright nice-size rm. w/2 twin beds or zip & lock queen-size bed, small bathroom & faces the side street) & 9 (5 steps down into not-so-bright nice-size rm. w/2 twin beds or zip & lock queen-size bed, small bathroom & faces the interior) are for a double; #1 (1st flr. rm. w/3 twin beds or 1 zip & lock queen-size bed & twin bed, small bathroom & faces the street) is for a triple; #6 (corner rm. w/no bathroom & 2 windows that face the street) is for a double; the 3 rooms w/o bathrooms share 2 communal bathrooms; wonderful quiet location, reception is one flight up, no elevator, 2 flrs. This hotel is not family-owned. Charming Roberto is responsible for keeping the flowers fresh at the hotel. **Vaporetto:** San Angelo or San Samuele. From San Samuele boat stop, take Calle Carrozze from Campo San Stefano straight to Salizzada San Samuele.

SERENISSIMA: Calle Carlo Goldoni 4486. **Tel:** 041-5200011. **Fax:** 041-5223292. **Web site:** http://www.hotelserenissima.it/ **E-mail:** info@hotelserenissima.it (37 rms., all w/toilet & bath or shower.) 103€ single; 180€ double; 230€ triple; 269€ quad. Breakfast (7-10am) is included in the rates & can be served in the room (5€ extra pp). Air-conditioned (June-Sept.). Visa, MC, AX. I always stay at this hotel when I am in Venice. I love it. English spoken (Salvaltore & Roberto), phones, cable TV w/CNN, fabulous wonderful charming hotel w/beautifully & identically contemporary Venetian style furnished modern nice-size rms., original wooden flrs., #157 (small 1st flr. rm. w/twin bed & bathroom w/small bathtub & faces the back) is for a single; #256 (2nd flr. rm. w/French double bed, nice-size bathroom w/shower & faces the back) is for a single; there are 7 other rooms for singles, most are on the 4th flr. w/twin beds; #251 (bright airy 2nd flr. rm. w/2 twin beds or zip & lock king-size bed, compact bathroom w/shower & 2 tiny balconies w/2 large windows that face the street) is for a double; #261 (double bed, bathroom w/ bathtub, please notice the frescoed door that Roberto had specially painted & 2 windows that face the street) is for a double; #153 (1st flr. rm. w/2 twin beds or zip & lock queen-size bed, small bathroom & faces the street) & 154 (1st flr. rm. w/2 twin beds or zip & lock king-size bed, small bathroom & faces the back) are for a double; #252 & 253 (both bright airy 2nd flr. rms. w/2 twin beds or zip & lock king-size bed, compact bathrooms w/showers & 2 windows that face the street) are for a double; #156 (1st flr. rm. w/3 twin beds or 1 zip & lock king-size bed & twin bed, bathroom w/bathtub & faces the back), 160 (1st flr. rm. w/3 twin beds or 1 zip & lock king-size bed & twin bed & small bathroom w/shower) & 260 (2nd flr. rm. w/ 3 twin beds or 1 zip & lock king-size bed & twin bed & small bathroom w/shower) are for a double or triple; hairdriers, bar, fabulous quiet location about a 5-min. walk to St. Mark's square and the Rialto bridge, no elevator, 4 flrs. Owned/managed by wonderful, charming & attentive Roberto DalBorgo. Salvaltore is also quite charming. *10% rm. discount when you show them this book.* The hotel is regularly visited by famous artists. The young blond woman in the fabulous paintings on the wall is Roberto's mother. You may recognize her as the hard-working elderly woman who serves you your breakfast. If you are an artist, ask to see Roberto's treasured book of artwork sketched by various artists from all over the world. **Vaporetto:** Rialto. (I prefer the #1 line which puts you closer to where you have to walk.) Walk to your right along the waterfront, turn left onto Calle Carbon straight through Campo San Luca bearing left onto Calle Carlo Goldoni. (Closed Dec. & Jan.)

HOTELS (Castello)

BUCINTORO: Riva Schiavoni Biagio 2135. **Tel:** 041-5223240. **Fax:** 041-5235224. (28 rms., 23 w/toilet & bath or shower.) 98€ single; 176€ double; 233€ triple. Call for quad rates. The rooms without bathrooms are cheaper. Breakfast (7:30-9:30am) is included in the rates & can be served in the room (6€ extra pp). Cash only. English spoken (Donatello), phones, no TV, wonderful charming hotel w/ nicely pinewood furnished pretty rms. that have a view of either the Grand Canal or the Venetian lagoon, shiny tiled flrs., #12 (small rm. w/twin bed, compact bathroom w/shower & view of the Venetian lagoon) & 4 other rms. w/private bathrooms & views are for a single; #14 (nice-size rm. w/2 twin beds or zip & lock queen-size bed, bathroom w/bathtub & view of the Venetian lagoon), 30 (nice-size rm. w/ 2 twin beds or zip & lock queen-size bed, compact bathroom w/ shower & view of the Venetian lagoon) & 23 (small rm. w/2 twin beds, low ceiling, small bathroom w/bathtub & view of the Venetian lagoon) are for a double; #26 (large 1st flr. rm. w/3 twin beds, bathroom w/bathtub & window w/view of Grand Canal) & 5 (nice-size rm. w/3 twin beds, bathroom w/bathtub & window w/view of Grand Canal) are for a triple; #15 (2 twin beds, no bathroom & view of the Venetian lagoon) & 14 (see above) have connecting doors but can be rented separately as a double or together as one family rm., the 5 rooms w/o bathrooms share 3 communal showers & 2 communal toilets; hairdriers, lots of stairs, wonderful quiet location off the Grand Canal, no elevator, 4 flrs. Owned/managed by Augusta Bianchi. **Vaporetto:** Arsenal. Turn right, walk along the waterfront over the bridge to the hotel. (Closed Dec.-Jan. Call to confirm.)

CANADA: Campo San Lio 5659. **Tel:** 041-5229912. **Fax:** 041-5235852. (25 rms., all w/toilet & bath or shower.) 122€ single; 160€ double; 166€ (rm. 12B) double; 196€ triple; 255€ quad. Breakfast (7:30-10am) is included in the rates & can be served in the room. Air-conditioned (6 rms. at 15€ extra per day). Visa, MC. English spoken (Giuseppe), phones, no TV, charming hotel w/simply to nicely furnished nice-size rms., #17, 20 & 21 (all w/views of the canal) are for a double; #12B (wonderful airy bright honeymoon rm. & terrace w/rooftops view) & 18 (air-conditioned rm. w/2 twin beds or zip & lock king-size bed & terrace w/no view) are for a double; #8 (queen-size bed & balcony that faces the back w/no view) & 14 (queen-size bed & 1/2 size bathtub w/hand-held shower) are for a double; #6 (large rm. w/3 twin beds or 1 zip & lock queen-size bed & twin bed & small window w/view of canal) is for a triple; #9 (huge w/4 twin beds or 1 zip & lock queen-size bed & 2 twin beds, 1/2-size bathtub w/hand-held shower & view of canal) is for a family; the rooms on the 2nd flr. are nicely furnished & the rooms on the 3rd flr. are simply furnished, bar, reception is two flights up, lots of stairs, wonderful noisy location, no elevator, 2 flrs. Located on a small pleasant square. **Vaporetto:** Rialto. Walk straight ahead on Calle Larga Mazzini, turn left onto Calle San Salvatore Merceria through Campo San Bartolomeo, turn right after Calle Pirietta, turn left past Calle Zocca into Calle Calle Ponte Antonio which becomes Salizzada San Lio, look to your left for the hotel on Campo San Lio.

CANEVA: Ramo dietro La Fava 5515. **Tel:** 041-5228118. **Fax:** 041-5208676. (22 rms., 14 w/toilet & bath or shower.) 69€ single; 105€ double; 133€ triple; 170€ quad. The rooms without bathrooms are cheaper. Breakfast (8-10am) is included in the rates. Air-conditioned. Visa, MC, AX. English spoken (Valentina), phones, TV, charming simple hotel w/simply furnished nice-size bright rms., #26 (bathroom & view of the canal) is for a single; #34 (2 twin beds or zip & lock queen-size bed, small bathroom w/bathtub & small balcony w/ view of the canal) is for a double; #30, 31, 32, 33, 35 & 36 (all w/2 twin beds or zip & lock queen-size bed, compact bathrooms w/showers & small balconies w/views of the canal) are for a double; #38 & 39 (both w/bathrooms & windows w/views of the canal) are for a double; #20 (bathroom & no view) is for a family; #29 (small balcony) & 41 (both w/2 twin beds or zip & lock queen-size bed, no bathrooms & views of the canal) are for a double; bathrooms w/ hairdriers, wonderful quiet location, no elevator, 2 flrs. Owned/managed by Massimo & Valentina Cagnato (father & daughter). *10% rm. discount when you show them this book and pay in cash.* **Vaporetto:** Rialto. Walk straight ahead on Calle Larga Mazzini, turn left onto Calle San Salvatore Merceria to Campo San Bartolomeo, take Calle Stagneri from Campo San Bartolomeo, cross the bridge to Campo Fava, turn right, Calle Ramo dietro La Fava starts to the right after the church of the Fava. (Closed Dec. & Jan.)

CASA VERARDO: Ponte Storto 4765. **Tel:** 041-5286138 or 5286127. **Fax:** 041-5232765. **Web site:** http://www.casaverardo.it/ **E-mail:** casaverardo@tin.it (25 rms., all w/toilet & bath or shower.) 142€ (compact rms. #103 & 203) double; 155€ (medium 1st flr. rms. #104 & 105) double; 164€ (large 1st flr. rms. #101, 102 & 106) double; 168€ (small rms. w/o views on 2nd & 3rd flrs.) double; 196€ (medium rms. on 2nd & 3rd flrs.) double; 211€ (large rms. on 2nd & 3rd flrs.) double. Call for single, room w/terrace, triple & quad rates. Buffet breakfast (7:30-10:30am) is included in the rates & can be served in the room (4€ extra pp) or on the terrace in warm weather. Air-conditioned (2nd & 3rd flr. rms.) Visa, MC, AX (3 nights minimum.) English spoken (Daniela, Diana, Piero, Enrico & Jolanda), phones, cable TV w/CNN, wonderful quaint charming 14th-century grand style palazzo hotel w/beautifully furnished bright rms. that vary in size, shape & decor. They were in the middle of finishing the renovations on the 2nd & 3rd flrs. Most will have newly renovated nice-size to large bathrooms w/bathtubs, showers, hairdriers & towel heaters, safety boxes, many rms. w/floor-to-ceiling windows, minibars (2nd & 3rd flrs.), the 6 attic rooms on 3rd flr. have sloped wood-beamed ceilings, there is only one single room on the 3rd flr., they have plans to have 2 ground-flr. rooms that will have handicapped-access bathrooms, there is one room w/a private terrace. #103 (compact 1st flr. rm. w/French double bed, small bathroom w/shower & floor-to-ceiling window) & 203 (compact 2nd flr. rm. w/French double bed) are perfect for a single but too snug for a double; #104 (nice-size 1st flr. rm. w/2 twin beds or zip & lock king-size bed, small bathroom w/shower & 2 windows that face the street) is for a double; #105 (large 1st flr. rm. w/3 twin beds or 1 zip & lock king-size bed & twin bed, small bathroom w/shower & floor-to-ceiling window that faces the side street) is for a double or triple; #101 (huge 1st flr. rm. w/3 twin beds or 1 zip & lock king-size bed & twin bed, convertible sofa & cubicle bathroom w/shower) & 106 (magnificent huge 1st flr. rm. w/2 twin beds or zip & lock king-size bed, convertible chair/bed, small bathroom w/shower & floor-to-ceiling windows that face the courtyard) are for a double or triple; impressive sitting room, Internet access available at 6€ per 1/2 hr., rooftop terrace w/magnificent panoramic view, bar, wonderful quiet location near the canal, elevator, 2 flrs. Owned/managed by the wonderful charming Francesco &

Daniela Mestre (husband & wife). *5% rm. discount when you show them this book.* Sometimes they will meet you at the vaporetto dock. **Vaporetto:** San Zaccaria.Walk straight ahead on Calle Rasse, turn left onto Salizzada Provolo to Campo SS Filippo e Giacomo, turn right from the Campo onto Calle Rimpetola Sacrestia, cross the first small footbridge (Ponto Storto), the hotel is located on the right facing the bridge. Ask hotel to fax you a map.

DONI: Calle Vin 4656. **Tel/Fax:** 041-5224267. **E-mail:** albergodoni@libero.it (12 rms., 3 w/toilet & shower.) 116€ double; 152€ triple; 189€ quad. The rooms without bathrooms are cheaper. Breakfast (8-10am) is included in the rates. Visa, MC. English spoken (Nikos & Tessa Bortoluzzi), renovated plain 15th-century palace hotel w/plainly furnished airy nonsmoking not-so-bright rms., wooden flrs., none of the rooms that overlook the canal have a private bathroom, #22 (huge 3rd flr. corner rm. w/2 twin beds or zip & lock king-size bed, futon convertible chair/bed, standard-size bathroom & 2 windows that face the back) & 15 (large 2nd flr. rm. w/2 twin beds or zip & lock queen-size bed, futon convertible chair/bed, compact bathroom & 2 windows that face the back) are for a double or triple; #8 (fabulous huge rm. w/2 twin beds or zip & lock queen-size bed, futon convertible chair/bed, original frescoed ceiling, small bathroom & 2 windows that face the back) is for a double, triple or family; #21 (large 3rd flr. rm. w/2 twin beds, futon convertible chair/bed, no bathroom & 2 windows that overlook the canal) is for a double or triple; #3 (wonderful rm. w/double bed, no bathroom & view of canal) & 12 (double bed, no bathroom & view of the canal) are for a double; the 9 rooms w/o bathrooms share 2 1/2 communal bathrooms; ceiling fans, wonderful quiet location near canal, lots of stairs, no elevator, 4 flrs. Owned by Annabella Doni & managed by Nikos & Tessa Bortoluzzi (brother & sister) & their family for more than 60 years. **Vaporetto:** San Zaccaria. For directions, see Hotel Campiello. (Closed Jan.)

FONTANA: Campo San Provolo 4701. **Tel:** 041-5220579 or 5210533. **Fax:** 041-5231040. **Web site:** http://www.hotelfontana.it/ **E-mail:** htlcasa@gpnet.it (14 rms., all w/toilet & shower.) 115€ single; 180€ double; 215€ triple; 250€ quad. Buffet breakfast (7:30-9:30am, includes yogurt, cheese, cereals, assorted breads & juices.)

is included in the rates. Visa, MC, AX, DC. English spoken (Gabriele & Diego, cousins), phones, cable TV w/CNN, wonderful charming renovated convent hotel w/nicely furnished bright airy nice-size to large rms., #15 (small 4th flr. rm. w/twin bed & small window w/no view) is for a single; #12 (2 small rms. w/2 twin beds, small bathroom & terrace w/view of church), 8 (nice-size 2nd flr. rm. w/2 twin beds or zip & lock queen-size bed, small bathroom & faces the garden), 6 (large 2nd flr. rm. w/2 twin beds or zip & lock queen-size bed, small bathroom & 2 windows that face the square), 10 (nice-size 3rd flr. rm. w/2 twin beds or zip & lock queen-size bed, small bathroom & faces the square) & 16 (small 4th flr. rm. w/2 twin beds) are for a double; #11 (nice-size 3rd flr. rm. w/2 twin beds or zip & lock queen-size bed, roll-out bed, standard-size bathroom & terrace w/view of church) is for a double or triple; #5 (large 2nd flr. rm. w/2 twin beds or zip & lock queen-size bed, 2 roll-out twin beds, standard-size bathroom & faces the square) & 9 (nice-size 3rd flr. rm. w/2 twin beds or zip & lock queen-size bed, 2 roll-out twin beds, standard-size bathroom & faces the square) are for a double, triple or family; #7 (huge 2nd flr. rm. w/4 twin beds or 1 zip & lock queen-size bed & 2 twin beds, standard-size bathroom & faces the garden) is for a family; #14 (wonderful unusually shaped 4th flr. 2 rms.: 1 rm. w/2 twin beds & rooftops view, 2nd rm. w/2 twin beds or zip & lock queen-size bed & wonderful view of garden & church & large bathroom w/bathtub & shower that parallels both rooms) is for a family; ceiling fans, warm ambience, bar, wonderful location, lots of stairs, no elevator, 4 flrs. Owned by Bentivoglio & Lino Stainer (grandparents) & managed by charming Gabriele & Diego Stainer (grandsons) since 1969. *10% rm. discount when you show them this book and pay in cash.* They plan on building an elevator by 2004. **Vaporetto:** San Zaccaria. Turn right, walk straight up Riva Schiavoni (waterfront) over 2 bridges, turn 1st left after Calle Vin into Campo San Zaccaria, walk through the square, bearing to your left straight onto Campo San Provolo.

LA RESIDENZA: Campo Bandiera e Moro 3608. **Tel:** 041-5285315. **Fax:** 041-5238859. **Web site:** http://www.venicelaresidenza.com/ **E-mail:** info@venicelaresidenza.com (14 rms., all w/toilet & bath or shower.) 101€ single; 176€ double; 205€ triple; 245€ quad. Breakfast (7:45-9:30am) is included in the rates. Air-conditioned. Visa, MC. English spoken (Giovanni & Schenal), phones, TV, fabulous wonderful charming Venetian Palace hotel w/beautifully old-fashioned Venetian style furnished nice-size to huge pretty nonsmoking rms., #221 (huge rm. w/queen-size bed, high ceiling w/chandelier, nice-size bathroom w/large shower stall & faces the square) is for a double; #224 (nice-size rm. w/queen-size bed, high ceiling w/chandelier, large bathroom w/large shower stall & faces the street) is for a double; #223 (huge rm. w/2 twin beds or zip & lock king-size bed, nice-size bathroom w/large shower stall & faces the square) is for a double but can fit an extra twin bed for a triple; #222 (fabulous huge corner rm. w/3 twin beds or 1 zip & lock queen-size bed & twin bed, high ceiling w/chandelier, large bathroom w/large shower stall & 2 windows that face the square) is for a double or triple but can fit an extra twin bed for a family; modern bathrooms w/hairdriers & towel heaters, most /large shower stalls, minibars, wonderful quiet location, no elevator. Owned/managed by Giovanni Ballestra. *5% rm. discount when you show him this book.* **Vaporetto:** San Zaccaria. Turn right, walk straight up Riva Schiavoni (waterfront), turn left onto Calle Dose which leads you straight to the hotel.

LOCANDA CANAL: Fondamenta Rimedio 4422/C. **Tel:** 041-5234538. **Fax:** 041-2419138. (7 rms., 2 w/toilet & shower.) 121€ double. Call for triple & quad rates. The rooms without bathrooms are cheaper. Breakfast (8-9:30am) is included in the rates & can be served in the room (6€ extra pp). Cash only. English spoken (Pasquale, Silvia, Francesco & Renato) no phones, no TV, plain 13th-century hotel w/plainly furnished large bright rms., original flrs., #2 (nice-size rm. w/2 twin beds or zip & lock queen-size bed, high ceiling, small bathroom & faces the street) & 6 (large rm. w/2 twin beds or zip & lock queen-size bed, high ceiling w/mini chandelier, standard-size bathroom & faces the back) are for a double; #1 (large rm. w/3 twin beds or 1 zip & lock queen-size bed & twin bed, high ceiling w/ mini chandelier, freestanding prefabricated shower in the middle of the room, no toilet & 2 windows w/views of the canal) is for a double or triple; #3 (nice-size rm. w/2 twin beds or zip & lock king-size bed, high ceiling w/mini chandelier, freestanding prefabricated shower in the middle of the room, no toilet & faces the street) is for a double;

#4 (nice-size rm. w/2 twin beds or zip & lock queen-size bed, no bathroom & 2 windows that face the street) is for a double; #5 (nice-size rm. w/2 twin beds or zip & lock queen-size bed, futon convert-ible chair/bed, no bathroom & window that faces the street) is for a double or triple; #7 (freestanding prefabricated shower in the middle of the room & no toilet); they do not reserve specific rooms, wonder-ful quiet location off the canal, reception is two flights up, no eleva-tor, 1 flr. Owned by Pasquale Tortorella & managed by Silvia. Same family owns the more expensive & wonderful Hotel Campiello not reviewed in this book. **Vaporetto:** San Zaccaria or San Marco. From St. Mark's square, walk under the Torre l'Orologio clock tower, turn right onto Calle Larga San Marco, turn left onto Call dell'Anzelo, cross the bridge on the right and it becomes Calle Rimedio, turn left at the canal onto Fondamenta Rimedio. (Closed 10 days in Jan.)

LOCANDA SILVA: Fondamenta Rimedio 4423. **Tel:** 041-5227643 or 5237892. **Fax:** 041-5286817. **E-mail:** albergosilva@libero.it (24 rms., 15 w/toilet & shower.) 115€ double; 155€ triple; 185€ quad. The rooms without bathrooms are cheaper. Breakfast (8-10am) is included in the rates. Cash only. English spoken (Sandra Perut), phones, no TV, charming plain hotel w/plainly furnished nice-size rms., #14 (twin bed, no bathroom & 2 windows w/views of canal) is for a single; #18 & 19 (both rms. w/twin beds, no bathrooms & views of canal) are for a single; #1 & 2 (both w/2 twin beds or zip & lock double bed, compact bathrooms & views of canal) are for a double; #16 & 17 (both w/bathrooms & views of canal) are for a double; #3 (2 twin beds, futon convertible chair/bed, compact bathroom & 2 windows that face the canal) is for a double or triple; #8 (3 twin beds, compact bathroom & faces the street) is for a double or triple; #10 (4 twin beds small bathroom & faces the side street) is for a family; wonderful quiet location off the canal, lots of stairs, no elevator, 4 flrs. Owned/managed by Ettore Perut, a very unusual & wonderful elderly man who speaks no English. **Vaporetto:** San Zaccaria or San Marco. For directions, see Hotel Locanda Canal. This hotel is right next to the Hotel Locanda Canal. Between these two simple hotels, I prefer this hotel. (Closed Dec.-Jan.)

RIVA: Ponte dell'Anzelo/Angelo 5310. **Tel:** 041-5227034. **Fax:** 041-5285551. (29 rms., 22 w/toilet & shower.) 105€ single; 126€ (small rms.) double; 141€ (large rms.) double; 172€ triple; 210€ quad. The rooms without bathrooms are cheaper. Breakfast (8-9:30am) is included in the rates. Cash only. English spoken (Sandro & Iris), no phones, no TV, charming old-fashioned simple renovated palace hotel w/simply furnished bright rms., marble flrs., #24 & 26 (both wonderful large rms. w/2 twin beds or zip & lock queen-size bed, high ceilings, compact bathrooms & 2 large windows w/views of the canal) are for a double; #1, 2, 3 & 4 (all small rms., w/compact bathrooms & small windows w/views of the canal) are for a double; #7 (queen-size bed, compact bathroom & 2 small windows w/views of the canal) is for a double; #19 (queen-size bed, compact bathroom & faces the side street) is for a double; #27 (wonderful huge rm. w/3 twin beds or 1 zip & lock queen-size bed & twin bed, high wood-beamed ceiling, standard-size bathroom & 2 large windows w/views of the canal), 8 (3rd flr. wonderful corner rm. w/3 twin beds or 1 zip & lock queen-size bed & twin bed, wood-beamed ceiling, compact bathroom & 3 windows w/views of the canal) & 12 (small rm. w/ queen-size bed, twin bed, compact bathroom & rooftop terrace w/ panoramic view of Basilica & canal that you share with the hotel's laundry) are for a double or triple; #18 (large rm. w/3 twin beds, wood-beamed ceiling, compact bathroom & faces the side street) is for a double or triple; #10 (4th flr. rm. w/queen-size bed, wood-beamed ceiling, no bathroom & view of canal) & 11 (4th flr. rm.) share 1 bathroom; most w/compact bathrooms, charming breakfast & reception rooms furnished w/18th-century furniture, marble staircase, wonderful quiet location on delightful side of a canal at the junction of 3 canals where you can watch the gondolas go by, lots of stairs, no elevator, 4 flrs. Owned by charming Sandro Nart, doctor of medicine & managed by wonderful & attentive Iris. **Vaporetto:** San Marco. Exit St. Mark's square by walking under the clock tower, turn right onto Calle Larga San Marco, turn left onto Calle l'Anzelo, follow the street straight over 2 small bridges to the hotel. (Closed mid-Nov.-until Carnivale.)

HOTELS (Dorsoduro)

AGLI ALBORETTI: Rio Terà Antonio Foscarini 884. **Tel:** 041-5230058. **Fax:** 041-5210158. **Web site:** http://www.aglialboretti.com/ **E-mail:** alborett@gpnet.it (24 rms., all w/toilet & bath or shower.) 98€ single; 155€ double; 189€ triple; 222€ quad. Breakfast (7:30-9:30am) is included in the rates & can be served in the room (4€ extra pp) or in the garden in warm weather. Air-conditioned. Visa, MC, AX. English spoken (Anna, Isabella & Cinzia), phones, cable TV w/CNN, wonderful charming hotel w/beautifully & identically Venetian style furnished modern rms., bright red carpeted flrs., #102 (nice-size 1st flr. rm. w/twin bed, bathroom w/large shower stall & faces the back) is for a single; #116 (faces garden) & 118 (both nice-size rms. w/2 twin beds or zip & lock queen-size bed & bathroom w/ showers) are for a double; #104 (1st flr. rm. w/2 twin beds that are positioned head-to-head, small bathroom w/bathtub & terrace that faces the back) & 108 (2 steps down into a rm. w/queen-size bed, compact bathroom w/shower & 2 windows that face the street) are for a double; #101 (wonderful large 1st flr. rm. w/2 twin beds or zip & lock queen-size bed, futon convertible chair/bed, compact bathroom w/shower & small window that faces the street) & 109 (large rm. w/2 twin beds or zip & lock queen-size bed, futon convertible chair/bed, cubicle bathroom w/shower & 2 windows that face the street) are for a double or triple; the entrance to the 5 wonderful rooms on the 4th flr. is outside the main bldg. with lots of stairs but a wonderful rooftop terrace: #45 (small 4th flr. rm. w/2 twin beds, small bathroom & partial view of water) is for a single or double; #43 (corner 4th flr. rm. w/2 twin beds or zip & lock king-size bed, small bathroom w/bathtub & rooftops view) is for a double; #42 (huge 4th flr. rm. w/2 twin beds or zip & lock king-size bed, small bathroom w/ bathtub, convertible sofa, futon convertible chair/bed & 2 windows that face the garden) is for a double, triple or family; #41 (huge 4th flr. rm. w/2 twin beds or zip & lock king-size bed, small bathroom w/ bathtub, convertible sofa, futon convertible chair/bed & small window that faces the back) is for a double, triple or family; #44 (4th flr. combination of 2 rms. w/4 twin beds or 1 zip & lock king-size bed & 2 twin beds, bathroom w/shower that parallels both rooms & lots of windows w/rooftops view) is for a family; hairdriers, Venetian garden, bar, well-known restaurant (closed 3 wks. in Aug.), wonderful quiet location, lots of stairs, no elevator, 4 flrs. Owned/managed by Anna Linguerri. They offer half- and full-board rates. **Vaporetto:** Accademia. Located at the foot of the Ponte dell'Accademia (bridge), to the left of the Campo Carita. (Closed Jan.)

ANTICO CAPON: Campo Santa Margherita 3004/B. **Tel/Fax:** 041-5285292. **Web site:** http://www.hotelanticocapon.com/ **E-mail:** hotelanticocapon@hotmail.com (7 rms., all w/toilet & shower.) 99€ single or double. Call for triple or quad rates. Breakfast (8-11am) is included in the rates & served outside at a restaurant. Visa, MC. English spoken (Elias, George & Stafania), phones, TV, charming simple hotel w/plainly furnished old small rms., #7 (small rm. w/French double bed, compact bathroom & faces the back w/no view) is for a single or 2 slim people in love; #3 (2nd flr. rm. w/2 twin beds or zip & lock queen-size bed, compact bathroom w/shower directly over the toilet, sink in the room separate from the bathroom & 2 windows that face the square), 4 (bright rm. w/2 twin beds or zip & lock queen-size bed, compact bathroom w/shower directly over the toilet, sink in the room separate from the bathroom & 2 windows that face the square) & 5 (queen-size bed, compact bathroom & 1 tiny window that faces the square) are for a double; #6 (nice-size rm. w/2 twin beds or zip & lock queen-size bed, compact bathroom w/shower directly over the toilet, sink in the room separate from the bathroom & 2 windows that face the back), 1 (2 twin beds, compact bathroom w/ shower directly over the toilet, sink in the room separate from the bathroom & faces the back) & 2 (queen-size bed, compact bathroom & faces the back) are for a double; they add roll-out bunk beds to rms. #5 & 6 for a triple or family but it makes the small rms. even smaller; ceiling fans, original 12th-century wooden wall near stairs, wonderful noisy location that is used during Carnivale, no elevator, 2 flrs. The hotel has an arrangement with 2 restaurants in the square to serve breakfast to the guests. Owned/managed by the wonderful & accommodating Elias Mennanna. He has galoshes on hand to loan to his guests when the canals flood. Most mornings there is a fruit and vegetable market in the square which becomes a playground for children in the late afternoons. **Vaporetto:** Ca' Rezzonico. Walk towards Campo Santa Margherita.

CASA PERON: Salizzada San Pantalon/Calle Vinanti 84/85. **Tel:** 041-710021. **Tel/Fax:** 041-711038. (11 rms., 7 w/toilet & shower.) 95€ double. Call for triple & quad rates. The rooms without bathrooms are cheaper. Breakfast (8-10am) is included in the rates. Air-conditioned (6 rms. at 11€ extra per day). Visa, MC, AX. English spoken (Gianrico), simple hotel w/plainly & identically furnished small rms., shiny tiled flrs., #7 (small rm. w/double bed, sloped ceiling, freestanding prefabricated shower in the middle of the room & toilet) & 5 (3rd flr. rm. w/queen-size bed, small bathroom & terrace w/rooftops view) are for a double; #6 (large 3rd flr. air-conditioned rm. w/double bed, roll-out bunk beds, small bathroom & 2 windows) is for a double, triple or family; #1 (twin bed, freestanding prefabricated shower in the middle of the room, no toilet & balcony that faces the back) is for a single; #8 (large air-conditioned rm. w/king-size bed, freestanding prefabricated shower in the middle of the room shower, no toilet & balcony that faces the street) is for a double; #9, 10 & 11 (all of which I did not see) are air-conditioned rms. w/compact bathrooms for a double; #5 is 3rd flr. rm. w/bathroom & balcony; #4 has a bathroom; ceiling fans, warm ambience, wonderful location, lots of stairs, no elevator, 3 flrs. Pietro (Peter) is a nonstop Italian-talking parrot. Owned/managed by Gianrico & Luana Scarpa (husband & wife). **Vaporetto:** San Tomà. (Closed Jan.)

FALIER: Salizzada San Pantalon 130. **Tel:** 041-710882 or 711005. **Fax:** 041-5206554. **Web site:** http://www.hotelfalier.com/ **E-mail:** falier@tin.it (19 rms., all w/toilet & shower.) 168€ double. Breakfast (8-10am) is included in the rates & can be served in the room (2€ extra pp) or in the garden/patio in warm weather. Air-conditioned. Visa, MC, AX. English spoken (Sutera), phones, cable TV w/ CNN, wonderful charming renovated hotel w/simply & identically furnished modern rms., #41 (lovely quaint 4th flr. attic room w/2 twin beds or zip & lock queen-size bed, arched wood-beam ceiling, small bathroom, small window in room that faces the back & private terrace outside the room) is for a double; most of the rooms are similar to #23 w/2 twin beds or zip & lock queen-size bed, small bathroom & faces the street, but some of the rooms have French double beds which are beds for 2 slim people in love; there are 6 rooms on each floor including the ground flr., all the ground-flr. rooms face the noisy street, hairdriers, bar, interior garden/patio, wonderful noisy location, lots of stairs, no elevator, 4 flrs. Owned/managed by Salvatore Sutera Sardo. *10% rm. discount when you show him this book.* **Vaporetto:** San Tomà.

GALLERIA (LA): Rio Terà Antonio Foscarini 878/A. **Tel:** 041-5232489. **Tel/Fax:** 041-5204172. **Web site:** http://www.hotelgalleria.it/ **E-mail:** galleria@tin.it (10 rms., 6 w/toilet & shower.) 141€ (Grand Canal view) double; 187€ triple; 231€ quad. The rooms without views (#1 & 2) & no bathrooms are cheaper. Breakfast (8-9:30am) is included in the rates & served in the room. Visa, MC, AX, DC. English spoken (Luciano & Stefano), phones, no TV, wonderful charming 17th-century palace hotel w/beautifully & individually antiquish Venetian style furnished rms. that vary in size, original wooden flrs., #9 & 7 (small rms. w/ queen-size beds, chandeliers, compact bathrooms & overlook the Grand Canal) are for a single or double; #8 (Stefano's favorite magnificent rm. w/2 twin beds or zip & lock queen-size bed, small bathroom & arched window w/2 large wicker chairs in sitting area that overlooks the Grand Canal) is for a double; #2 (2 twin beds or zip & lock queen-size bed, decorative ceiling, compact bathroom & faces the Accademia bridge) is for a double; #10 (huge rm. w/4 twin beds or 1 zip & lock queen-size bed & 2 twin beds, high 16th-century frescoed ceiling, small bathroom & 2 windows overlooking the Grand Canal & Accademia bridge) is for a family; #5 (wonderful corner rm. w/2 twin beds or zip & lock queen-size bed, chandelier, 18th-century armoire, decorative nonworking marble fireplace, no bathroom & 2 huge windows that overlook the Grand Canal) is for a double; #6 (no bathroom & view of Grand Canal), 3 (king-size bed, no bathroom & faces the Accademia bridge) & 4 (2 twin beds or zip & lock queen-size bed, no bathroom & faces the Accademia bridge) are for a double; hairdriers, ceiling fans, beautiful doors, some w/ frescoed or carved ceilings, great ambience, wonderful quiet location, narrow spiral staircase, no elevator, 1 fl. Owned/managed by Luciano Benedetti & charming Stefano Franceschini. **Vaporetto:** Accademia. Located at the foot of the Ponte dell'Accademia (bridge), to the left of the Campo Carita. (Closed Dec. 23-27.) The same family has opened up a new hotel. **Locanda S.S. Giovannie E Paolo:** Calle Ospedale 4529, Cannarggio. 8 air-conditioned rms., all w/toilet & bath or shower, phones, no TV, 3 rooms for a double & 5 rooms for a triple or family. No elevator, 3 flrs. Credit cards. Same prices as Hotel Galleria. Vaporetto: Ospedale. It will be completed before this book's publication.

LOCANDA CA' FÓSCARI: Calle Frescada 3887B. **Tel:** 041-710401. **Fax:** 041-710817. **E-mail:** valtersc@tin.it (11 rms., 5 w/ toilet & shower.) 71€ single; 116€ double. Call for triple & quad rates. The rooms without bathrooms are cheaper. Breakfast (8-9:30am) is included in the rates. Visa, MC. English spoken (Valter & Giuliana), no phones, no TV, wonderful charming simple hotel w/simply & individually old-fashioned furnished nice-size to large bright airy rms, original flrs., #10 (twin bed, compact bathroom & 2 windows that face the back) is the only rm. for a single; #9 (corner rm. w/2 twin beds or zip & lock king-size bed, compact bathroom & 2 windows) & 1 (2 twin beds or zip & lock king-size bed, convertible chair/bed, compact bathroom & faces the street) are for a double; #6 (large rm. w/2 twin beds or zip & lock king-size bed, convertible chair/bed, compact bathroom & faces the back) & 5 (2 twin beds or zip & lock king-size bed, compact bathroom & faces the interior) are for a double; the 6 rooms w/o bathrooms: #2 (corner rm. w/2 twin beds or zip & lock king-size bed, no bathroom & 2 windows that face the street), 11 (corner rm. w/2 twin beds or zip & lock king-size bed, no bathroom & 2 windows that face the street), 7 (corner rm. w/2 twin beds or zip & lock king-size bed, fold-up bed, no bathroom & 2 windows that face the garden), 3 (wonderful corner rm. w/3 twin beds or 1 zip & lock king-size bed & twin bed, no bathroom & 3 windows that face the garden), 8 (4 twin beds or 1 zip & lock king-size bed & 2 twin beds, no bathroom & 3 windows) & 4 share 2 communal bathrooms; wonderful ambience, 1am curfew, wonderful location, lots of stairs, no elevator, 3 flrs. Owned/managed by Valter & Giuliana Scarpa (husband & wife). **Vaporetto:** San Tomà. Turn left, walk across the 1st canal, turn right, turn left onto Calle Frescada. (Closed last wk. in July, 1st wk. in Aug. & mid-Nov.-Jan. 15.)

LOCANDA SAN TROVASO: Fondamenta Borgo Eremite 1351. **Tel:** 041-2771146. **Fax:** 041-2777190.
Web site: http://www.locandasantrovaso.com/
E-mail: info@locandasantrovaso.com or s.trovaso@tin.it or (7 rms.,

all w/toilet & shower.) 95€ single; 125€ (no view) double; 135€ (view) double; 160€ triple; 190€ quad. Breakfast (anytime-11:30am) is included in the rates & served in the room on the terrace in warm weather. Visa, MC, AX. English spoken (Mark, Cristina & Alessandro), no phones, no TV, fabulous wonderful charming new (2001) hotel w/beautifully old-fashioned Venetian style furnished pretty rms., #5 (2nd flr.) & 3 (small rms. w/2 twin beds or zip & lock king-size bed & face the garden) are for a single or double; #4 (2nd flr. rm.) & 2 (both are large bright airy rms. w/2 twin beds or zip & lock king-size bed, fold-out beds & 2 windows that face the canal) are for a double or triple; * (star) & 6 (both are nice-size rms. w/2 twin beds or zip & lock king-size bed & face the garden) are for a double; #1 (huge ground flr. rm. w/3 twin beds or 1 zip & lock king-size bed & twin bed, fold-out bed, large bathroom & faces the canal) is for a triple or family; modern bathrooms, ceiling fans, rooftop terrace w/view of canal, wonderful quiet location overlooking the canal, no elevator, 2 flrs. Owned/managed by Mark, Cristina & Alessandro Storelli (father, mother & son). Alessandro is wonderful & accommodating. Alessandro's cousin owns the delightful Osteria Alberto restaurant (see below). **Vaporetto:** Záttere. Walk to your left on Fondamente Zattere Ponte Lungo, turn right onto Calle Trevisan over the bridge, walk down the road that parallels the canal.

MESSNER: Rio Terà Catacumeni/Fondamenta Ca' Bala 216/217. **Tel:** 041-5227443. **Fax:** 041-5227266. **E-mail:** messner@italy.com (34 rms., 30 w/toilet & shower.) 92€ (annex) single; 103€ (main bldg.) single; 130€ (annex) double; 151€ (main bldg.) double; 157€ (annex) triple; 180€ (main bldg.) triple; 180€ (annex) quad; 206€ (main bldg.) quad; Breakfast (8-10am) is included in the rates & can be served in the room (3€ extra pp) or in the garden in warm weather. Air-conditioned (main bldg.). MC, Visa, AX, DC. English spoken (Alex, Antonio & Giorgio), phones, no TV, charming 3-in-1 hotel w/ simply & identically pinewood modern furnished rms., Main bldg. (11 rms. w/carpeted flrs. but only 3 face the canal): #7 & 9 (both wonderful corner rms. w/2 twin beds or zip & lock queen-size bed, small bathrooms & 2 windows w/wonderful views of canal) are for a double; #8 (wonderful rm. w/2 twin beds or zip & lock queen-size bed, roll-out bunk beds, private bathroom outside the room & floor-to-ceiling window w/wonderful view of canal) is for a double, triple or family; #1 (corner rm. w/2 twin beds or zip & lock queen-size bed, roll-out bed & faces the garden) is for a double or triple; #3 & 4 (both w/2 twin beds or zip & lock queen-size bed, roll-out bunk beds & face the garden) are for a double, triple or family; #10 & 11 (both w/2 twin beds or zip & lock queen-size bed, roll-out bunk beds & no views) are for a double, triple or family; annex bldg. #1 (has 2 fabulous rms.): #37 (wonderful large ground-flr. rm. w/3 twin beds or 1 zip & lock queen-size bed & twin bed, wood-beamed ceiling, small bathroom & faces the side street) is for a triple; #36 (wonderful large ground-flr. rm. w/2 twin beds or zip & lock queen-size bed, roll-out bunk beds, kitchenette, wood-beamed ceiling, large bathroom & 2 windows that face the canal) is for a family; annex bldg. #2 (21 rms. w/shiny tiled flrs. & no views): #24 & 23 (both small rms. w/2 twin beds or zip & lock queen-size bed, compact bathrooms & small windows near the ceiling w/no views) are perfect for a single but too snug for a double; #19 (small charming corner rm. w/2 twin beds, arched wood-beamed ceiling, small bathroom & window w/partial view of canal) is for a double; #22, 21 & 20 (all small rms. w/2 twin beds or zip & lock queen-size bed, roll-out bunk beds, small bathrooms & no views) are perfect for a double but too snug for a triple; #31 (2 twin beds or zip & lock queen-size bed, wood-beamed ceiling, small bathroom & no view), 16 (not-so-bright small ground-flr. rm. w/2 twin beds or zip & lock queen-size bed, small bathroom & small window near the ceiling w/no view) & 35 (small rm. w/2 twin beds or zip & lock queen-size bed, small bathroom & no view) are for a double; #28 & 25 (both bright rms. w/2 twin beds or zip & lock queen-size bed, roll-out beds, compact bathrooms & face the garden) are for a double or triple; #17 (2 windows) & 18 (both not-so-bright ground-flr. rms. w/2 twin beds or zip & lock queen-size bed, roll-out bunk beds, small bathrooms & no views) are for a double or triple; #33 & 32 (both w/3 twin beds or 1 zip & lock queen-size bed & twin bed & no views) is for a triple; #26 & 27 (both bright rms. w/ 3 twin beds or 1 zip & lock queen-size bed & twin bed, private bathrooms outside the rooms & face the garden) are for a triple; #34 (nice-size rm. w/2 twin beds or zip & lock queen-size bed, roll-out bunk beds, small bathroom & no view) is for a family; if you stay in the annex, you have to walk outside to the main bldg. to have breakfast; modern bathrooms, hairdriers, garden/patio near the canal, bar, restaurant, wonderful quiet location, lots of stairs, no elevator, 3 flrs. Owned by Bruno Nardi (father) & managed by Alessandro Nardi (son). *10% rm. discount when you show them this book.* Antonio is wonderful, attentive & informative. They offer half- and full-board rates. The hotel has 2 entrances in the main bldg. in case the canals overflow into the main entrance. **Vaporetto:** Salute. As you exit the boat facing the La Salute Church, turn right paralleling the canal, walk straight ahead to the first small bridge through the tunnel, continue straight through Campo San Gregorio, continue straight on Calle Gregorio, just before you get to the next canal turn left onto Fondamenta Ca' Balà. (Closed Dec.)

PALAZZETTO DA SCHIO: Fondamenta Soranzo Fornace 316B. **Tel/Fax:** 041-5237937. **Web site:** http://www.web.tin.it/sangregorio/ **E-mail:** avenezia@tin.it (4 apts., all w/toilet & bath or shower.) 195€ double. Call for triple & quad rates. 2-night minimum. Cash only. Air-conditioned (apts. #2 & 3). English spoken (Contessa), fabulous wonderful charming 16th-century bldg. w/4 beautifully & individually antique Venetian style furnished apts.: large 2-bedroom apt. #4 (huge master bedroom w/king-size bed, high ceiling, bathroom w/shower & 2 windows w/views of canal, huge 2nd bedroom w/2 twin beds & 2 windows w/views of canal, huge bathroom w/bathtub, living room w/ 2 windows that have views of canal, portable air-conditioned unit & kitchen); large 2-bedroom apt. #3 (4 flights up to air-conditioned master bedroom w/queen-size bed, low wood-beamed ceiling & 2 windows w/views of canal, large bathroom w/bathtub w/hand-held shower, 2nd bedroom w/2 twin beds, small bathroom w/shower, wood-beamed ceiling & 2 windows w/views of canal, living room w/convertible sofa, wood-beamed ceiling & 2 windows that have views of canal & rooftops & small kitchen); small 1-bedroom apt. #5 (1st flr. bedroom w/ king-size bed & 2 windows, high ceiling, 2nd room w/short ladder to get to the 2 twin beds, dining/living room w/huge antique dining table, large bathroom w/old-fashioned bathtub w/shower, breakfast table, portable air-conditioned unit, kitchen & faces the garden); small 1-bedroom apt. #2 (4 flights up to air-conditioned bedroom w/queen-size bed & low wood-beamed ceiling, bathroom w/shower, small living room w/convertible sofa twin bed, fabulous huge kitchen w/dining area & 16th-century sink & faces the garden); each of the apts.

have phones, TV, fully equipped kitchens w/dishwashers, washing/ drying machines, shopping carts, carpeted &/or wooden flrs., wonderful quiet location, off the canal, no elevator. Sometimes the Contessa rents out her beautiful huge 2nd flr. apt. #1 where she resides during the months of July & Aug. when she goes on holiday. Contessa will e-mail you a detailed floor plan, the requirements for renting the apts. and a very detailed description including pictures of each of the 4 apts. **Vaporetto:** Salute. For directions, see Hotel Messner. Fondamenta Soranzo Fornace parallels Fondamenta Ca' Bala.

TIVOLI: Calle Foscari 3838. **Tel:** 041-5242460. **Fax:** 041-5222656. (22 rms., 19 w/toilet & shower.) **Web site:** http://www.hoteltivoli.it/ **E-mail:** hoteltivoli@tin.it 91€ single; 150€ double; 185€ triple; 220€ quad. The rooms without bathrooms are cheaper. Breakfast (8-10am) is included in the rates & can be served in the room (5€ extra pp) or on the patio in warm weather. Visa, MC. English spoken (Gina & Andrea), phones, cable TV w/CNN, wonderful charming hotel w/ nicely & identically old-fashioned furnished rms., wooden flrs., #26 (nice-size rm. w/2 twin beds or zip & lock queen-size bed, standard-size bathroom & faces the street) is for a double; #34 (wonderful large 3rd flr. attic rm. w/king-size bed, twin bed, wood-beamed wall, sloped ceiling, small bathroom & terrace that faces the back w/no view) & 30 (wonderful large rm. w/3 twin beds or 1 zip & lock king-size bed & twin bed, chandelier, small bathroom & 2 windows) are for a triple; there are 2 ground-flr. rms. that face the communal patio, modern bathrooms w/hairdriers, floor fans, patio, bar, lots of stairs, no elevator, 3 flrs. Owned/managed by wonderful charming Renato & Gina Gardin & Andrea (husband, wife & son-in-law) for more than 45 years. They are constantly renovating the hotel. **Vaporetto:** San Tomà. (Closed Dec. 15-Jan. 15.) From Hotel Locanda Ca' Fóscari, turn right onto Calle Crosera, walk straight to Hotel.

Note: I was not pleased with either the rooms or ambience at the Hotel Alla Salute Cici or the Locanda Antica Montin. Locanda Antica Montin is well-known for their restaurant and should continue to focus on it. If you like the locations of the Locanda Antica Montin or the Hotel Alla Salute Cici, then try the wonderful Locanda Trovaso which is opposite the Locanda Antica Montin or the Hotel Messner which is next door to the Hotel Alla Salute Cici.

HOTELS (Cannaregio)

ADUA: Lista Spagna 233A. **Tel:** 041-716184. **Fax:** 041-2440162. (13 rms., 9 w/toilet & bath or shower.) 129€ double; 157€ triple; 184€ quad. The rooms without bathrooms are cheaper. Breakfast (7:30-11am) at 6€ pp can be served in the room. Air-conditioned. Visa, MC, AX, DC. English spoken (Luciano & Lucia), phones, cable TV w/ CNN, wonderful charming newly renovated hotel w/nicely & identically modern furnished nice-size pretty rms., shiny tiled flrs., #2 (corner rm. w/queen-size bed, small bathroom w/shower & balcony that faces street) & 8 (2 twin beds or zip & lock king-size bed, bathroom w/shower & faces the street) are for a double; #6 (2 twin beds or zip & lock queen-size bed, small bathroom w/shower & faces the back) & 3 (2 twin beds or zip & lock king-size bed, small bathroom w/shower & faces the back) are for a double; #14 (large rm. w/3 twin beds or 1 zip & lock queen-size bed & twin bed & bathroom w/bathtub) & 9 (large rm. w/king-size bed, twin bed, small bathroom w/shower & 2 windows that face the street) are for a triple; #7 (small rm. near reception w/2 twin beds & shares outside bathroom in the hall w/staff) is for a double; #11, 12 (both w/terraces but no views) & 10 share 1 communal bathroom; modern bathrooms, 1am curfew, noisy pedestrian location, no elevator, 2 flrs. Owned/managed by Luciano & Lucia Stefani (brother & sister). *5% rm. discount when you show them this book.* **Vaporetto:** Ferrovia. Exit the train station, turn left, walk straight up Lista Spagna, hotel is about 2 blocks up on your right.

AL GOBBO: Campo San Geremia 312. **Tel:** 041-715001 or 714765. (9 rms., 6 w/toilet & shower.) 77€ single; 89€ (rm. #8) double; 99€ double; 128€ triple; 144€ quad. The rooms without bathrooms are cheaper. Breakfast (8-10am) is included in the rates. Visa, MC (call to confirm). English spoken (Emanuela, who is wonderful), no phones, cable TV w/CNN (2 rms.), charming hotel w/simply furnished rms., #8 (French double bed, cubicle bathroom & faces the square) is for a single or discounted for 2 slim people in love; #10 (corner rm. w/2 twin beds or zip & lock queen-size bed, compact bathroom & faces the square) is for a double; #1 (room near reception w/2 twin beds or zip & lock king-size bed, roll-out twin bed, small bathroom, cable TV w/CNN & faces the square) & 2 (room near reception w/cable TV w/CNN & faces the garden) are for a double; #6 (2 twin beds or zip & lock king-size bed, small bathroom & faces the garden) is for a double; the 3 rooms w/o bathrooms share 1 communal shower & toilet, 1:30am curfew, wonderful noisy location, no elevator, 3 flrs. Owned/managed by Maria Vinco. **Vaporetto:** Ferrovia. Exit the train station, turn left onto Lista Spagna, walk straight up Lista Spagna into Campo San Geremia. (Closed mid-Dec.to mid-Jan.)

BERNARDI SEMENZATO: Calle dell'Oca, SS. Apostoli 4363-66. **Tel:** 041-5227257. **Fax:** 041-5222424. **Web site:** http://www.hotelbernardi.com/ **E-mail:** mtpepoli@tin.it (20 rms., 15 w/ toilet & shower.) 85€ single; 112€ double; 133€ triple; 155€ quad. Call for quint rates. The rooms without bathrooms are cheaper. Breakfast (8-10am) is included in the rates & can be served in the room (2€ extra pp). Air-conditioned (5€ extra per day). Visa, MC, AX, DC. English spoken (Leonardo), phones, cable TV w/CNN & BBC, wonderful charming 2-in-1 hotel w/nicely to beautifully & identically handmade Venetian style furnished rms., Main bldg. (12 nicely furnished rms. w/shiny tiled flrs.): #26 (Maria Teresa's favorite attic rm. w/queen-size bed, arched wood-beamed ceiling, carpeted flr., standard-size bathroom & 2 windows that face the back) is for a double; #25 (attic rm. w/ queen-size bed, arched wood-beamed ceiling, carpeted flr., standard-size bathroom & faces the side street) & 10 (queen-size bed, high wood-beamed ceiling, standard-size bathroom & faces the back) are for a double; #6 & 5 (both large rms. w/ queen-size bed & twin bed) are for triple; #9 (queen-size bed, arched wood-beamed ceiling, no bathroom & faces the back) is for a double; the 4 rooms w/o bathrooms share 2 communal bathrooms; annex (8 beautifully furnished rms. w/original wooden flrs. & bathrooms w/ hairdriers & towel heaters): #2 (fabulous huge rm. w/queen-size bed, twin bed, large bathroom & faces the garden) is for a triple but can fit extra twin beds for a family or quint; #5 (fabulous huge corner rm. w/canopy queen-size bed, twin bed, high decorative wood-beamed ceiling w/antique wrought-iron chandelier, decorative marble non-working fireplace, antique huge wall mirror, standard-size bathroom & 3 windows that face the back) is for a triple but can fit an extra twin bed for a family; #1 (wonderful queen-size bed, twin bed, high ceiling, decorative marble nonworking fireplace, marble flr., large bathroom & faces the side street) is for a triple; #8 (fabulous huge corner rm. w/canopy queen-size bed, convertible sofa, high ceiling

& 3 windows that overlook the canal) & 7 (queen-size bed, twin bed, private bathroom outside the room & no view) can be rented separately or together as a huge suite; modern hand-painted Venetian tiled bathrooms selected by Maria Teresa, summer rooftop terrace (ask permission to visit), 1am curfew (main bldg.), wonderful location, no elevator, 3 flrs. Owned/managed by wonderful, attentive & accommodating Leonardo & Maria Teresa Biasin. *5% rm. discount when you show them this book.* **Vaporetto:** Ca' d'Oro. From the water stop, walk up Calle Ca' d'Oro, turn right onto Strada Nova, continue straight to Campo SS. Apostoli, turn left at the church of Santi Apostoli onto Campiello Salizzada Pistor, turn left onto Calle dell'Oca. Located in a small alleyway. (Closed 1st 2 wks. in Dec. & mid-Jan. to 2 wks. before Carnivale.)

CASA GEROTTO CALDERAN: Campo San Geremia 283.
Tel/Fax: 041-715562. **Tel/Fax:** 041-715361.
Web site: http://www.casagerotto.com/
E-mail: info@casagerotto.com **Reservation E-mail:** agev@iol.it (34 rms., 12 w/toilet & bath or shower.) 85€ single; 118€ double; 148€ triple; 180€ quad. The rooms without bathrooms are cheaper. Cash only. English spoken, no phones, TV (request only), charming simple hotel w/simply furnished airy bright large rms., 12:30am curfew, rooms that face the square are brighter but noisier, small bathrooms, wonderful noisy location, lots of stairs, no elevator, 4 flrs. Owned/ managed by Olindo & Mara Milani (husband & wife) who also own the fabulous Hotel Cà San Marcuola. **Vaporetto:** Ferrovia. Exit the train station, turn left onto Lista Spagna, walk straight up Lista Spagna into Campo San Geremia.

CÀ SAN MARCUOLA: Campo San Marcuola 1763.
Tel: 041-2759217. **Tel/Fax:** 041-716048.
Web site: http://www.casanmarcuola.com/
E-mail: info@casamarcuola.com (17 rms., all w/toilet & bath or shower.) 98€ single; 130€ double; 170€ (rm. #202) double; 170€ triple; 205€ (rm. #202) triple; 201€ quad. Breakfast (8-11am) at 6-12€ pp can be served in the room (12€ extra pp). Visa, MC, AX, DC. Air-conditioned. English spoken (Michela & Loretta), phones, cable TV w/CNN, fabulous wonderful charming new (2001) hotel w/beau-

tifully furnished large pretty rms., #302 (huge rm. w/king-size bed, small bathroom & faces the canal) & 307 (nice-size rm. w/king-size bed, wood-beamed ceiling, large bathroom & faces the square) are for a double; another room has a small balcony w/floor-to-ceiling window that faces the square; #306 (huge rm. w/king-size bed, twin bed, small bathroom & terrace that faces the square) & 203 (standard rm. w/king-size bed, twin bed & high ceiling) are for a double or triple; #202 (huge honeymoon rm. w/king-size bed, twin bed, convertible sofa, high wood-beamed ceiling w/glass chandelier & balcony that faces the canal) is for a double, triple or family; #303 (corner rm. w/ king-size bed, 2 twin beds, huge bathroom w/bathtub w/hand-held shower & 2 windows w/views of the canal) & 201 (king-size bed, 2 twin beds, high ceiling & overlooks the canal) are for a family; high ceilings, modern bathrooms w/hairdriers, minibars, nonsmoking rms. available, wonderful location close to the waterbus stop, elevator, 2 flrs. Owned/managed by Orlindo Milani & Stefano Zoccoletti who also own Casa Gerotto. *Free breakfast when you show them this book.* **Vaporetto:** San Marcuola. Exit the boat, walk straight ahead, look to your right for the two huge stone lions in front of the hotel.

LOCANDA LEONE BIANCO (White Lion): Corte Leon Bianco 5629, 2nd fl **Tel:** 041-5233572. **Fax:** 041-2416392. **Web site:** http://www.leonbianco.it/ **E-mail:** info@leonbianco.it (7 rms., all w/toilet & shower.) 142€ (rms. #5, 6 & 7, all w/views of small canal) double; 165€ (rms. #2, 3 & 4, all w/views of Grand Canal) double; 165€ (jr. suite #9) double. Call for triple, quad & quint rates. Breakfast (8-10am) is included in the rates & served in the room. Visa, MC, AX, DC. English spoken, fabulous wonderful charming 13th-century renovated mansion hotel w/beautifully & individually old-fashioned 18th-century Venetian style furnished large to huge magnificent rms., #2 (huge rm. w/double bed, standard-size bathroom & overlooks the Grand Canal) is for a double but can fit an extra twin bed for a triple; #3 (huge rm. w/double bed, small bathroom & overlooks the Grand Canal w/view of the Rialto bridge) is for a double but can fit an extra twin bed for a triple; #4 (overlooks the Grand Canal) is for a double; triple or family; #6 (large rm. w/2 twin beds or zip & lock queen-size bed, 2 steps up to large bathroom & overlooks the small canal) is for a double; #5 (huge rm. w/2 twin beds or zip &

lock queen-size bed, chandelier, standard-size bathroom & overlooks the small canal w/side view of Grand Canal) is for a double; triple or family; #9 (huge rm. w/2 twin beds or zip & lock king-size bed, sofa, mural wall, chandelier, sitting area, huge bathroom w/bathtub & faces interior) is for a double, triple, family or quint; #7 (overlooks the small canal); 17th-century original doors, hairdriers, wonderful quiet location, no elevator, 1 flr. Owned/managed by Ferruccio, Franco & Andrea Spellanzon (husband, wife & son). **Vaporetto:** Ca' d'Oro. Exit the boat, walk over the bridge, turn right, walk straight through the alley, open black iron gate, look to the right.

LOCANDA NOVO: Campo S.S. Apostoli 4529, Cannargio. **Tel:** 041-2411496. **Fax:** 041-2415989. **Web site:** http://www.locandanovo.com/ **E-mail:** info@locandanovo.com (10 rms., 9 w/toilet & shower.) 142€ double; 175€ triple. Call for quad, quint & sextet rates. Buffet breakfast (8-10am) is included in the rates. Visa, MC (3% surcharge). English spoken (Alberto), no phones, no TV, fabulous wonderful charming hotel w/beautifully old-fashioned Venetian style furnished large pretty rms. that bear the names of well-known historical characters, #9/Casanova (large rm. w/2 twin beds or zip & lock king-size bed, high ceiling, standard-size bathroom & small terrace that faces the street) is for a double; #5/Otello the Doges (nice-size rm. w/2 twin beds or zip & lock king-size bed & standard-size bathroom) & 6/ Vivaldi (2 twin beds or zip & lock king-size bed, standard-size bathroom & 2 small windows) are for a double; #11 (newly renovated 2nd flr. attic rm. w/2 twin beds or zip & lock king-size bed & bathroom) is for a double; #3 (double bed w/decorative high ceiling w/ chandelier & private bathroom outside the room) is for a double; #8/ Caterina Cornaro (huge rm. w/3 twin beds or 1 zip & lock king-size bed & twin bed, high ceiling w/chandelier, large bathroom & 4 windows) is for a triple but can fit an extra twin bed for a family; #7/ Marco Polo (huge rm. w/3 twin beds or 1 zip & lock king-size bed & twin bed & standard-size bathroom) is for a triple but can fit an extra twin bed for a family; #10 (newly renovated 2nd flr. attic 2-rms. w/ double bed, 2 twin beds, sloped wood-beamed ceiling & bathroom) is for a family; #4 (huge rm. w/4 twin beds or 1 zip & lock king-size bed & 2 twin beds, sitting area, high ceiling w/chandelier, large bathroom w/large shower stall) is for a family but can fit an extra twin bed for a quint; #5 & 4 have connecting doors which can be rented separately or together for a sextet or septet; #2 is considered to be the worst room because it is small & near the reception, new modern bathrooms, floor fans, wonderful quiet location, no elevator, 2 flrs. Owned/managed by Claudio Novo & wonderful, accommodating Ivan Ballarin. **Vaporetto:** Ca' d'Oro. From the water stop, walk up Calle Ca' d'Oro, turn right onto Strada Nova, continue straight onto Campo SS. Apostoli.

MARTE & BIASIN: Via Ponte Guglie 338. **Tel:** 041-716351. **Fax:** 041-720642. **Web site:** http://www.hotelmartebiasin.com/ **E-mail:** info@hotelmartebiasin.com (40 rms., 21 w/toilet & bath or shower.) 72€ single; 115€ double; 130€ triple; 150€ quad. The rooms without bathrooms are cheaper. Breakfast (8-10am) at 6€ pp can be served in the room. Visa, MC, AX. English spoken (Antonella & Silvana), phones, TV, pleasant charming 2-in-1 hotel w/simply furnished rms., shiny tiled flrs., Hotel Marte has 14 rms. (13 w/bathrooms): #102 (nice-size rm. w/double bed, small bathroom & window w/wonderful view of canal), 101 (double bed, small bathroom & window w/ wonderful view of canal) & 104 (double bed, small bathroom & faces the street) are for a double; #103 (wonderful rm. w/double bed, futon convertible chair/bed, small bathroom & tiny balcony w/view of the bridge & canal), 110 (double bed, twin bed, small bathroom & faces the street) & 114 (nice-size rm. w/double bed, twin bed, small bathroom & faces the garden) are for a double or triple; #112 (double bed, 2 twin beds & no view) is for a family; #111 (double bed, no private bathroom & faces the back) is for a double; directly across the canal from Hotel Marte is Hotel Biasin (I like this one better) which has 26 rms. (8 w/bathrooms but only 4 rms. face the canal): #2 (wonderful 1st flr. rm. w/double bed, sofa, wood-beamed ceiling, compact bathroom & 2 windows that have fabulous views of the canal) is for a double; #1 (wonderful small 1st flr. corner rm. w/ double bed, twin bed, wood-beamed ceiling, small bathroom & 3 windows that have fabulous views of the canal) & 10 (corner rm. w/ double bed, twin bed, small bathroom & 3 windows that have fabulous views of the canal) are for a double or triple; #17 (small rm. w/ queen-size bed, twin bed, standard-size bathroom & faces the back), 19 (small rm. w/double bed, twin bed, compact bathroom & faces the interior) & 20 (small rm. w/queen-size bed, twin bed, small bath-room & faces the back) are for a double or triple; #11 (small rm. w/ double bed, 3 twin beds, wood-beamed ceiling, small bathroom & faces the canal) is perfect for a family but too snug for a quint; frigobars (Hotel Marte), hairdriers, Internet access available at 3€ per 1/2 hr., wonderful location, walk up 2 flights of stairs to recep-tion, no elevator, 2 flrs. *Discount when you show owner Metilde Grinzato or managers Antonella Zanetti & Silvana Vianello this book.* **Vaporetto:** Ferrovia. Exit the train station, turn left onto Lista Spagna, walk straight up Lista Spagna through Campo San Geremia, from the square take Salazzada Geremia to Ponte Guglie (bridge), turn left at the bridge onto Fondamenta Savorgnan and to the hotel.

ROSSI: Calle Procuratie 262. **Tel:** 041-715164. **Tel/Fax:** 041-717784. (14 rms., 10 w/toilet & shower.) 99€ double; 123€ triple; 146€ quad. The rooms without bathrooms are cheaper. Breakfast (7:30-9:45am) is included in the rates & can be served in the room (3€ extra pp). Air-conditioned. Visa, MC. English spoken (Giuseppe, Giovanni & Francesco), phones, pleasant hotel w/simply & identically furnished rms. w/no views, original flrs., #206 (bright airy rm. w/2 twin beds or zip & lock king-size bed & 2 windows) is for a double; #210 (large rm. w/queen-size bed, roll-out twin bed, bathroom w/shower & faces the interior) is for a double or triple; 2 rms. w/balconies have no bathrooms; small bathrooms, some showers w/o curtains, ceiling fans, quiet location, no elevator, 3 flrs. Owned/managed by Francesco Cozzarini. **Vaporetto:** Ferrovia. Exit the train station, turn left onto Lista Spagna, walk straight up Lista Spagna, after you pass the Hotel Adua, turn 1st left under the arch onto Calle Procuratie. (Closed Jan.-Feb. 15.)

SAN GEREMIA: Campo San Geremia 290/A. **Tel:** 041-716245 or 716260. **Fax:** 041-5242342. **E-mail:** sangeremia@yahoo.it (21 rms., 17 w/toilet & bath or shower.) 105€ single; 145€ double; 175€ triple; 200€ quad. The rooms without bathrooms are cheaper. Continental buffet breakfast (8-10am, includes ham, cheese, yogurt, cereals, as-sorted pastries & juices) is included in the rates & can be served in the room (2€ extra pp) or on the terrace in warm weather. Visa, MC, AX, DC. English spoken (Claudio), phones, cable TV w/CNN & BBC, wonderful charming quaint hotel w/nicely furnished small rms.,

#201 (queen-size bed, small bathroom & overlooks the square), 302 (nice-size rm. w/2 twin beds or zip & lock queen-size bed, cubicle bathroom & faces the square) & 418 (3rd flr. rm. w/terrace that faces the garden) are for a double; #420 (large 3rd flr. rm. w/2 twin beds or zip & lock king-size bed, futon convertible chair/bed & terrace that faces the square) is for a double or triple; #102 (king-size bed, futon convertible chair/bed, cubicle bathroom w/shower & faces the square) is for a double or triple; #419 (large 3rd flr. rm. w/2 twin beds, queen-size bed & terrace that faces the square) is for a family; #101, 202, 202 & 301 all face the square; #206 is the smallest room for a double; small to cubicle bathrooms, hairdriers, charming quaint breakfast room w/nonworking fireplace & wood-beamed ceiling, bar, street terrace, wonderful noisy location, lots of stairs, no elevator, 3 flrs. Owned/managed by Claudio Casagrande & Francesco Sconocchia. *5% rm. discount when you show them this book.* **Vaporetto:** Ferrovia. Exit the train station, turn left onto Lista Spagna, walk straight up Lista Spagna into Campo San Geremia. (Closed Dec.-Jan.)

SANTA LUCIA: Calle Misercordia 358. **Tel:** 041-715180. **Tel/Fax:** 041-710610. (15 rms., 10 w/toilet & shower.) 116€ double; 146€ triple; 178€ quad. The rooms without bathrooms are cheaper. Breakfast (8-10am) is included in the rates & can be served in the room or on the patio in warm weather. Visa, MC, AX, DC. English spoken (Gianni & Alessandra), phones, TV, charming simple hotel w/simply furnished nice-size ground-flr. rms., #25 (2 twin beds, wooden flrs., high ceiling w/chandelier & opens out to the garden) & 14 (2 twin beds or zip & lock queen-size bed & faces walkway) are for a double; #26 (large corner rm. w/king-size bed, twin bed, roll-out twin bed, large bathroom & 2 large windows) is for a family; the 5 rooms (#10, 12, 22, 23 & 24) w/o bathrooms share 2 communal bathrooms; patio w/no view, quiet location, no elevator, 1 fl. Owned/managed by Gianni & Alessandra Parcianello (husband & wife). **Vaporetto:** Ferrovia. Exit the train station, turn left onto Lista Spagna, Calle Misercordia is the 2nd left turn. (Closed Dec.-Jan.)

VILLA ROSA: Calle Misercordia 389. **Tel:** 041-718976. **Tel/Fax:** 041-716569 **E-mail:** villarosa@ve.nettuno.it (33 rms., all w/toilet & shower.) 90€ (rm. #14) single; 113€ (rm. #20) single; 130€ double; 162€ triple; 188€ quad. Breakfast (8-10am) is included in the rates

& can be served in the room (5€ extra pp). Air-conditioned (extra cost per day.) Visa, MC, AX, DC. English spoken (Martina & Maria), phones, cable TV w/CNN & BBC, charming simple hotel w/simply & identically furnished not-so-bright nice-size rms., mixture of original & shiny tiled flrs., #14 (small noisy lower-level rm. w/twin bed & faces the noisy pedestrian walkway) is for a single; #26 (wonderful rm. w/2 twin beds or zip & lock queen-size bed & faces garden) & 25 (large rm. w/king-size bed step up to bathroom, high wood-beamed ceiling & faces the garden) are for a double; #39 (wonderful large 3rd-flr. attic rm. w/2 twin beds or zip & lock queen-size bed, high arched wood-beamed ceiling & faces patio) is for a double; #43, 44 & 45 (all are ground-flr. rms. w/2 twin beds or zip & lock queen-size bed, wood-beamed ceilings & face the patio) are for a double; #33 (2 twin beds or zip & lock double bed & terrace w/no view) & 18 (large lower-level rm. w/2 twin beds & faces the patio w/no privacy) are for a double; #29 (3 twin beds or 1 zip & lock queen-size bed & twin bed & terrace w/no view) is for a triple; #34 (large rm. w/2 twin beds or zip & lock queen-size bed, bunk beds, high wood-beamed ceiling & faces garden) is for a family; #40 (wonderful large 3rd-flr. attic rm. w/ 4 twin beds & small window in sloped ceiling) is for a family; #19 (terrace w/no view), 16 (lower-level rm. that faces interior) & 27 (all have queen-size beds & roll-out bunk beds) are for a family; #42 (walk outside through the patio to large rm. w/queen-size bed, twin bed, futon convertible chair/bed, wood-beamed ceiling & faces patio w/no privacy) is for a family; #10, 11, 15 & 24 face the noisy pedestrian walkway; small bathrooms, ceiling fans, hairdriers (5 rms.), the 7 rooms that face the pedestrian walkway are noisy, no elevator, 3 flrs. Owned/ managed by Ugo Marazzi. **Vaporetto:** Ferrovia. Exit the train station, turn left onto Lista Spagna, Calle Misercordia is the 2nd left turn. (Closed Nov.-March 1.)

LAUNDROMATS (Lavanderia)
Bea Vita: Rama Chiovereti 665A, San Polo. Tel: 041-5244131. Hrs.: Daily 8am-10pm. Self-service. Located across from the train station. Cross over the Ponte degli Scalzi bridge in front of the station, turn right, turn left, turn right onto Rama Chiovereti. Gabriella: Rio Terà Colonne 985, San Marco. Tel: 041-5221758. Mon.-Fri. 8am-7pm. Closed Sat. & Sun. Drop off & Pick-up only; Gettone SS. Apostoli: Salizzada Pistor 4553/A, Cannaregio. Tel: 041-5226650. Mon.-Fri.

8:30am-12noon & 3:30pm-7pm. Closed Sat. & Sun. Drop off & pick-up only; Lavaget: Fondamenta Pescaria 1269, Cannaregio. Tel: 041-715976. Mon.-Fri. 8:30am-12:30pm & 4pm-6:30pm. Closed Sat. & Sun. Drop off & Pick-up only.

BOOKSTORES
Libreria Demetra: Campo San Geremia 282, Cannaregio. Tel/Fax: 041-2750152. Hrs.: 9am-12midnight. Visa, MC; Libreria Emiliana: San Marco 4487. Tel/Fax: 041-5220793. Web site: http://elmoro.com/emiliana/ E-mail: libremil@tin.it

SHOPPING/HANDBAGS
Francis Model: Ruga Rialto 773/a, San Polo. Tel: 041-5212889. Hrs.: Daily 9:30am-7:30pm. This is the first retail store (other than book-stores) I have ever included in any of my books. On other trips to Italy, I usually pick up a purse for my friend Pam. This family has been making handbags at the store for more than 50 years. They are beautiful, handmade and affordable. Vaporetto: Rialto.

INTERNET CAFES
Planet Internet: Campo San Geremia 1519, Cannaregio. Tel: 041-5244188. Fax: 041-2757626. Vaporetto: Ferrovia; Net House: Campo San Stefano 2967-2958, Dorsoduro. Tel: 041-2771190. Vaporetto: Accademia. The Netgate: Dorsoduro 3812a. Tel 041-2440213. Netgate also plans on opening up a location at the train station. Web site: http://www.thenetgate.it/

SUPERMARKETS
Standa: Strada Nova 3660/Campo San Felice, Cannaregio. Hrs.: Mon.-Fri. 8:30am-7:20pm & Sat. 9am-7:20pm. Visa, MC; Calle L'Anconeta 1976, Cannaregio. Hrs.: Mon.-Sat. 9am-1pm & Mon., Tues. & Thurs.-Sat. 3:45pm-7:15pm. Closed Wed. afternoon & Sun; Rosa, Massimo & Federico: Calle Fabbri 4713, San Marco. Hrs.: Mon.-Sat. 8am-1pm & 4:30pm-7:30pm. Closed Sun.

DELICATESSEN
CASA GRAPPA: Ruga Rialto 779/a, San Polo. Tel: 041-5236578. Hrs.: Daily 9am-7pm. Visa, MC. Fabulous gourmet shop. My closest friends Jeff Fischgrund and Geovanni Brewer and I think this is the best gourmet delicatessen in all of Venice. They have the best Parma ham and cheese, grappa and lots of Venetian specialties you'll want to take home. Ask for Luciano, Luciana or Nicola Muschini (father, mother & son); they will be happy to help you with your selections. Located near the Rialto bridge. Vaporetto: Rialto.

RESTAURANTS
AI BARBACANI: Calle Paradiso 5746, Castello. Tel: 041-5210234. Fax: 041-5204691. E-mail: aibarbaconi@libero.it Hrs.: Tues.-Sun. 12noon-2pm & 7:30pm-10:30pm. Closed Mon. & Jan. Visa, MC, AX, DC. Reservations required, especially for the special table. This has become my favorite restaurant in Venice. I ate here 3 times on this last trip. They have soft music and a fabulous table for two that faces the canal. If you are lucky enough to get this table (and I was), you can eat while looking at the canal and every now and then a gondola goes by the window. There is a table that seats four that is behind the table with almost the same view. I had one of the best meals I ever had in Venice and am sorry my husband wasn't with me to enjoy this experience. Don't dismay if you don't get the most romantic table in the house. The food is so fresh and good you won't care. *You don't have to show owners/managers Antonio & Roberta (husband & wife) this book to get complimentary limoncello or grappa. Every customer gets one but they will give you a free coffee to compliment your drink if you show this book.* Antonio & Roberta really know how to make your night in Venice very special, which is why I ate here so many times. E-mail Roberta for specific directions to the restaurant. Highly recommended by my closest friends Jeff Fischgrund & Geovanni Brewer; Roberto, Hotel Serenissima and Francesco & Daniela, Hotel Casa Verado. Vaporetto: Rialto.

ALLA MADONNA: Calle Madonna 594, San Polo. Tel: 041-5223824. Fax: 041-5210167. Hrs.: Thurs.-Tues. 12noon-3pm & 7pm-10:30pm. Closed Wed., first 2 wks. in Aug. & Jan. Visa, MC, AX. Reservations required. Great large restaurant that serves fresh delicious food. Waiters are charming in a sterile atmosphere. Highly recommended by Stefano, Hotel Galleria. Vaporetto: Rialto.

OSTERIA DA ALBERTO: Calle Largo Giacinto Gallina 5401, Cannaregio. Tel/Fax: 041-5238153. Web site: http://www.meetingvenice.it/daalberto/ Hrs.: Mon.-Sat. 12noon-3pm & 7pm-10:30pm. Closed Sun., 1 wk. in Jan., & July 15-Aug 7. Visa, MC. Reservations advised for dinner. Great restaurant that serves fresh delicious food. Highly recommended by Ferruccio & Franco, Hotel Locanda Leon Bianco. Vaporetto: Fonda Nuove/Nove.

OSTERIA DA CARLA: Corte Contarina 1535. Tel: 041-5237855. Hrs.: 1pm-2:30pm & 6:30pm-9:30pm. Closed Sun. & holidays. Visa, MC. Small quaint simple restaurant that serves plain good food. No atmosphere. The only problem I have is you have to strain to hear an Italian accent. The place is filled with tourists. Highly recommended by Alessandro, Hotel Locanda Fiorita. Vaporetto: San Marco.

OSTERIA VINI DA GIGIO: Fondamenta Chiesa 3628a, Cannaregio. Tel: 041-5285140. Fax: 041-5228597. Closed Mon., last 2 wks. in Jan & last 2 wks. in Aug. Visa, MC, AX, DC. Quaint cozy rustic restaurant that serves delicious food. Nonsmoking rm. available. Owned by Paolo Lezzari. Highly recommended by Ferruccio & Franco, Hotel Locanda Leon Bianco. Vaporetto: San Marculo.

TRATTORIA DA REMIGIO: Calle Bosello/Salizzada Greci 3416, Castello. Tel: 041-5230089. Hrs.: Wed. -Sun. 12:30pm-2:30pm & 7:30pm-10:30pm. Open Mon. lunch. Closed Mon. dinner, Tues., 2 wks. July-Aug. & 4 wks. Dec.-Jan. Visa, MC, AX, DC. Reservations required. Small wonderful restaurant that offers fresh fish, assorted meats & homemade pasta. *Show Fabio Bianchi or Pino this book and get a complimentary after-dinner drink*. Highly recommended by Stefano, Hotel Galleria. Vaporetto: San Zaccaria.

GOOD CHEAP FOOD NEAR TRAIN STATION
AL CICHETO: Calle Misercordia 367, Cannaregio. Tel: 041-716037. Hrs.: Mon-Fri. 7:30am-6pm. Cash only. Small restaurant/bar. This place serves fabulous fresh sandwiches & good homemade

food. They cater to the workers and make just enough so that they run out of food every day. Located down the same alley as Hotel Villa Rosa. Owned/managed by Mateo, Marco & Simone. Vaporetto: Ferrovia.

TRATTORIA PIZZERIA LE COMPANE: Rio Terà San Leonardo 1402, Cannaregio. Tel: 041-718345. Hrs.: Daily 11am-3pm & 6pm-12midnight. Visa. MC. Serves the best pizza near the train station. Eat only the pizza, not the pasta. Highly recommended by Maria Teresa, Hotel Bernardi Semenzato. Vaporetto: San Marculo.

VERONA
Veneto, zip code 37121
Country code 39, city code 045

Verona's Tourist Information Centers
1.) Piazza Brå./Via Degli Alpini 9. **Tel:** 045-8068680. **Fax:** 045-8003638. Hrs.: Mon.-Sat. 9am-7pm. Sun. 9am-3pm. **2.)** Piazza XXV Aprile/Porta Nuova train station. **Tel:** 045-8000861. Hrs.: Mon.-Sat. 9am-6pm. Closed Sun. **Web site:** http://www.tourism.verona.it/ **E-mail:** info@tourism.verona.it

TRANSPORTATION TIPS
Purchase your bus ticket at the newsstand inside the train station. Look for the bus depot marked "A" directly in front of the train station. There is a display listing several bus numbers departing for Piazza Brå. You'll know you reached Piazza Brå when you enter the arched gate.

Verona hotels listed alphabetically
ANTICA PORTA LEONA
AURORA
CAVOUR
EUROPA
MAZZANTI
TORCOLO

HOTELS
ANTICA PORTA LEONA: Corticella Leoni 3. **Tel:** 045-595499. **Fax:** 045-595214. **E-mail:** htlanticaportaleona@tiscalinet.it (38 rms., all w/toilet & bath or shower.) 98€ (Feb. & March) single; 105€ (July & Aug.) single; 118€ (Feb. & March) double; 143€ (July & Aug.) double; 176€ triple; 203€ (rm. #002) quad. Rates are lower during the other months. Buffet breakfast (7:30-10:30am, includes ham, cheese, yogurt & cereals) is included in the rates & can be served in the room. Air-conditioned. Visa, MC, AX, DC. English spoken (Paolo & Carlo), phones, cable TV w/CNN, fabulous wonderful charming hotel w/newly renovated darkwood furnished not-so-bright nice-size rms., carpeted flrs., 14 rms. (all small rms. w/twin beds) are

for a single; if you are 2 people on a budget, they can squeeze a cot bed into a single room for a discounted price; the rooms for a double either have a queen-size bed or 2 twin beds; the rooms for a triple have 3 twin beds or 1 zip & lock queen-size bed & twin bed; only 4 rms. (1 single, 2 doubles & 1 triple) on the 2nd flr. have a high window near the ceilings that have no views; modern standard-size bathrooms w/hairdriers, ceiling fans, bar, restaurant, wonderful location, no elevator, 2 flrs. Owned/managed by Paolo & Carlo Casaro (brothers) & their family for more than 16 years. They offer half-board rates. Taxi to hotel. Cross street: Via Leoni. (Closed Dec. & Jan.)

AURORA: Piazza Erbe 4a/Via Pelliciai 2. **Tel:** 045-594717/597834. **Fax:** 045-8010860. (19 rms., 17 w/toilet & bath or shower.) 129€ double; 163€ triple. Call for quad rates. The 2 rooms (both singles) without bathrooms are cheaper. Buffet breakfast (7:30-10am, includes ham, cheese, yogurt & cereals) is included in the rates & can be served in the room (5€ extra pp). Air-conditioned. Visa, MC, AX, DC. English spoken (Elena), phones, cable TV w/CNN, wonderful charming renovated 15th-century hotel w/nicely furnished contemporary nice-size rms., 3 rms. (1 w/balcony) face the square, charming terrace w/view of the square, wonderful noisy pedestrian location, walk up 1 flight to the elevator, 4 flrs. Owned/managed by Olivieri Bepino. Taxi to hotel. Elena specifically requested that I do not give detailed information on any of the rooms.

CAVOUR: Vicolo Chiodo 4. **Tel:** 045-590166. **Tel/Fax:** 045-590508. (22 rms., all w/toilet & shower.) 83€ single; 126€ (standard rms.) double; 156€ (superior rms.) double; 171€ triple. Breakfast (8-10am) at 9€ pp can be served in the room (3€ extra pp). Air-conditioned. Cash only. English spoken (Patricia & Paolo), phones, TV, wonderful charming renovated 19th-century charming 2-in-1 hotel w/not-so-bright nice-size to large rms. w/no views, annex (large newly renovated superior nicely & identically furnished rms. w/large to huge bathrooms): #39 & 37 (both superior rms. w/2 twin beds or zip & lock queen-size bed, wood-beamed ceilings, large bathrooms & huge terraces w/no views) are for a double; #42 & 38 (both superior rms. w/2 twin beds or zip & lock queen-size bed & large bathrooms) are for a double; if you stay in the annex, you have to walk outside to the main bldg. to have breakfast; main bldg. (standard plainly & identically pinewood furnished rms.); there are only 2 rooms on the 3rd flr. and they are both standard single rooms w/twin beds; #24 (standard 2nd flr. rm. w/balcony), 21 (standard 2nd flr. rm. w/balcony) & 23 (standard 2nd flr. rm.) all w/2 twin beds or zip & lock queen-size bed & are for a double; #22 (standard 1st flr. rm.), 28 (standard 2nd flr. rm.) & 30 (standard 2nd flr. rm.) all w/3 twin beds or 1 zip & lock queen-size bed & twin bed & small bathrooms & are for a triple; wooden ceilings, wonderful quiet location, elevator (annex), 3 flrs., no elevator (main bldg.), 3 flrs., parking (16€ per day). Owned/managed by Carolina Giovannini & Patricia Puccetti and their family for more than 30 years. They prefer a mature clientele and do not accept children. Take the bus to the entrance (arched gate) near Piazza Brå. As you walk through the gate towards Piazza Brå, turn left onto Via Roma, turn right onto Via Cattaneo, turn left onto Vicolo Chiodo. (Closed Jan.-Feb.)

EUROPA: Via Roma 8. **Tel:** 045-594744. **Fax:** 045-8001852. **E-mail:** hoteleuropavr@tiscalinet.it (46 rms., 42 w/toilet & bath or shower.) 105€ single; 162€ double; 196€ triple. Call for quad rates. The single rooms without bathrooms are cheaper. Buffet breakfast (7:30-10am, includes ham, cheese, yogurt & cereals) is included in the rates & can be served in the room (3€ extra pp). Air-conditioned. Visa, MC, AX, DC. English spoken (Renato), phones, cable TV w/ CNN, wonderful charming modern hotel w/nicely & identically furnished nice-size pretty airy rms. w/no views, mixture of shiny tiled or wooden flrs., #411 (nice-size nonsmoking rm. w/twin bed) is for a single; #211 (small smoking rm. w/twin bed & small bathroom w/ shower) is for a single; #207 (small balcony), 107, 307 & 407 (all w/ twin beds & private bathrooms down the hall) are for a single; #206 (corner nonsmoking rm. w/2 twin beds or zip & lock queen-size bed, bathroom w/bathtub w/hand-held shower & 2 balconies) is for a double; #406 (corner smoking rm. w/2 twin beds or zip & lock queen-size bed, bathroom w/bathtub w/hand-held shower & 2 balconies) is for a double; #205 (nice-size smoking rm. w/2 twin beds or zip & lock queen-size bed, small bathroom w/shower & balcony that faces the theater) is for a double; #106 & 306 (both corner smoking rms. w/2 twin beds or zip & lock king-size bed, bathrooms w/bathtubs w/

hand-held showers & 2 windows) are for a double; #114 (wonderful huge smoking rm. w/2 twin beds or zip & lock king-size bed, futon convertible chair/bed & bathroom w/bathtub w/hand-held shower) is for a double or triple; #108 (large nonsmoking rm. w/2 twin beds or zip & lock king-size bed) & 105 (nonsmoking rm. w/2 twin beds or zip & lock queen-size bed & small bathroom w/shower) are for a double; #408 (nonsmoking rm. w/3 twin beds) is for a triple; #208 & 308 (both smoking rms. w/3 twin beds & small bathrooms w/showers) are for a triple; #104 (nonsmoking rm. w/queen-size bed & small bathroom) & 103 (smoking rm. w/2 twin beds & small bathroom w/bathtub w/hand-held shower) have connecting doors but can be rented separately as a double or together as one family rm.; #204 & 203 (both smoking rms.) have connecting doors but can be rented separately as a double or together as one family rm.; new modern marble bathrooms w/hairdriers, 20 rms. w/printed nonsmoking signs on the door, minibars, digital safety boxes, elevator, 4 flrs., parking (11€ per day). Owned/managed by Luigi Chiecchi Dott. Take the bus to the entrance (arched gate) near Piazza Brå. As you walk through the gate towards Piazza Brå, turn left onto Via Roma.

MAZZANTI: Via Mazzanti 6. **Tel:** 045-591370/8006813. **Fax:** 045-8011262. (23 rms., 18 w/toilet & bath or shower.) 74€ single; 110€ double; 136€ triple. Call for quad rates. The rooms without bathrooms are cheaper. Breakfast (7:30-10am) is included in the rates & can be served in the room (3€ extra pp). Air-conditioned (14 rms.). Visa, MC, AX. English spoken (Benedetto), phones, TV (18 rms.), charming plain hotel w/simply & identically pinewood furnished nice-size rms., #24 (large air-conditioned rm. w/queen-size bed & 2 windows), 10 (air-conditioned rm. w/queen-size bed) & 4 (air-conditioned rm. w/queen-size bed) are for a double; #20 (large air-conditioned rm. w/3 twin beds or 1 zip & lock queen-size bed & twin bed) is for a triple; the singles w/o private bathrooms are not air-conditioned; wonderful location near Piazza Signori, no elevator, 3 flrs. Owned by Flavia Raspino & managed by Benedetto. Taxi to hotel. (Closed 15 days including Christmas in Dec.)

TORCOLO: Vicolo Listone 3. **Tel:** 045-8007512. **Fax:** 045-8004058. **Web site:** http://www.hoteltorcolo.it/ **E-mail:** hoteltorcolo@virgilio.it (19 rms., all w/toilet & shower.) 59€ (Jan.-March & Nov.-Dec.) single; 72€ (April-June, Sept.-Oct., Christmas, New Years & holidays) single; 77€ (July & Aug.) single; 83€ (Jan.-March & Nov.-Dec.) double; 117€ (April-June, Sept.-Oct., Christmas, New Years & holidays) double; 131€ (July & Aug.) double. Call for triple rates. Rates are lower during the other months. Breakfast (7:30-10:30am) at 9€ pp can be served in the room or on the terrace in warm weather. Visa, MC, AX, DC. Air-conditioned. English spoken (Caterina who is wonderful), phones, cable TV w/CNN & BBC, fabulous charming hotel w/nicely & identically furnished modern rms., #33, 23, 21 & 14 (all w/small double beds & small bathrooms) are for a single; #34 (beautiful original old-fashioned furnished 3rd flr. attic rm. w/2 twin beds or zip & lock king-size bed, separate freestanding prefabricated shower, sloped ceiling, small bathroom w/toilet, the most requested room for a double & where Silvia's parents spent their honeymoon); #24 (large 2nd flr. corner rm. w/2 twin beds or zip & lock queen-size bed, separate free standing prefabricated shower & small bathroom w/toilet), 31 (nice-size quaint corner 3rd flr. attic rm. w/2 twin beds or zip & lock queen-size bed, low wood-beamed arched ceiling & 2 windows that face the street) & 36 (3rd flr. attic rm. w/2 twin beds or zip & lock king-size bed, sloped ceiling, huge bathroom w/bathtub w/hand-held shower & small window) are for a double; #25 (nice-size rm. w/3 twin beds or 1 zip & lock king-size bed & twin bed, separate freestanding prefabricated shower, small bathroom w/toilet & 2 windows that face the street) & 16 are for a triple; hairdriers, minibars, terrace, warm ambience, wonderful quiet location, elevator, 4 flrs. Owned/managed by wonderful, informative & attentive Silvia Pomari & Diana Castellani. I have stayed at this hotel a couple of times and loved it each time. Take the bus to the entrance (arched gate) near Piazza Brå. Walk through the gate towards Piazza Brå, continue walking straight on the left side of the arena, turn left after the restaurant Tre Corone to hotel. (Closed Jan. 10-Feb. 7.)

LAUNDROMAT (Lavanderia)
Onda Blu: Via XX Settembre 62a. Hrs.: Daily 8am-10pm. Not centrally located. Walk across Ponte Navi (bridge) to get to Via XX Settembre. Cross street: Via Colombine.

TAXI
Tel: 045-532666.

BOOKSTORE
Touring Club Italiano: Via Valverde 75. Tel: 045-595697. Great for maps. Web site: http://www.touringclub.it/

RESTAURANT
COLONNA: Largo Pescheria Vecchia 4. Tel: 045-596718. Fax: 045-8100563. Hrs.: Mon.-Sat. 12noon-3pm & 7pm-9:30pm. Closed on Sun. Visa, MC, AX. Reservations required. Great food, wonderful atmosphere and affordable prices. Highly recommended by Elena, Hotel Aurora.

APPENDIX I

PACKING THE UNUSUAL

Alarm clock radio: Helps you to catch those early-morning trains.

Apple slicer/peeler: Fruit makes a great snack. Assume the fruit has not been washed and you have no place to wash it. The slicer and peeler are handy when you are traveling on the train where the warning signs over the sink say "Do Not Drink the Water." **Note:** This item should be packed only in your check-on luggage, not your carry-on luggage.

ATM: Please refer to the section "Before You Leave Home" in the front of this book for detailed information on this subject.

Batteries: For alarm clock, radio, flashlight, camera and tape recorder. Don't forget lots of film, which usually costs more in Europe.

Cable lock: A lightweight adjustable-length cable lock. Great for locking your bags on trains and ships. I travel alone by train to do my research so I lock my bags to the overhead rack.

Calculator: Perfect for figuring out exchange rates.

Clothesline, clothes-pegs, sink stopper and soap: Take advantage of those sinks and don't forget the soap suds!

Earplugs: A lifesaver when your roommate's snoring becomes unbearable. They also come in handy for those rooms that sound like they're in the middle of a highway. Include an eye mask to help you sleep in hotels, on planes or trains.

Eyeglasses: Bring a backup pair of sunglasses/eyeglasses, photocopy of the prescription and a retainer cord. I have had to replace lost eyeglasses more than once.

Facecloths: European hotels do not supply them.

PACKING THE UNUSUAL

Flashlight (purse-size): You never know when you will need one.

Guidebooks: Travel guide (your favorite), language book and, of course, do not forget this one! Please refer to the section "Before You Leave Home" in the front of this book for detailed information about why it is important to purchase certain books prior to leaving home.

Hand sanitizers or towelettes: You can never pack enough of these.

Highlighter: Handy to use for highlighting maps and sections in your travel guide.

Inflatable neck cushion: Handy for planes, trains, buses and resting your head while on the beach.

Magnifying glass: Great for reading maps. Even better if it comes with a light.

Maps: Please refer to the section "Before You Leave Home" in the front of this book for a detailed explanation about why it is important to purchase your maps prior to leaving home.

Mosquito spray & citronella candles: Window screens are rare. A definite must for the summer.

Night light (international voltage): Comes in very handy when you are trying to find your toilet in the middle of the night, especially if you change hotel rooms as often as we do.

Notebook (small, spiral): Perfect for recording your memories. The notebook also comes in handy when negotiating room prices and taking down train information. I also pack a microcassette recorder to record my trip.

Novels (paperbacks): They help pass the time when you encounter the inevitable long train lines. When you finish reading them, give them away to other English-speaking tourists. It's a great way to introduce yourself. They are three times the cost in Italy.

PACKING THE UNUSUAL

Photocopies: Make copies of your passport, credit card numbers (including their domestic and international numbers in case they are stolen or lost), a record of traveler's checks and airline tickets. Also, make copies of medication and eyeglass prescriptions. Leave two copies at home with friends/family and take two with you. Remember to pack the copies separate from the originals.

Photo ID: You can use these photos if you have to replace your passport.

Plastic bags: Small, medium and large resealable plastic bags to be used for carrying food, stuff, wet or dirty clothes and brochures you pick up along the way. Also use them as hot or cold compresses, as well as for the plastic bottles filled with liquid in your suitcase.

Pre-printed address labels: Makes your life so much easier when you can just stick a pre-printed or handwritten address label on a postcard to friends back home. This is great if you are traveling with children. You can have their friends' names on pre-printed address labels.

Prunes, figs or something similar: Fiber is not big on Italian menus, and all that rice and pasta does not exactly help your digestive system. Sometimes it needs a little assistance. Whatever works.

Reading light: Perfect for reading books on planes, trains or in hotels. Also, not all hotels have overhead reading lights or they are not bright enough. I recommend the *Light Voyager Booklight* because it is convenient to pack and gives off a lot of light.

Security undercover wallets: Invest in a deluxe undercover wallet that is worn underneath your clothes. They come in different shapes and styles to be worn around your waist, shoulders, legs or neck. Buy whatever is comfortable for you but get one. Also get a small pouch with a loop in the back that slips onto your belt. I use the Eagle Creek's *Departure Pouch*. Use this pouch to carry your day's money, train tickets and the one credit card to avoid having to go into your secured undercover wallet. Look in the section under "Before You Leave Home" to get more information on pickpockets.

PACKING THE UNUSUAL

Sea bands: (For motion sickness.) Wear them on your wrists and use them for traveling by buses or cars while they are navigating scary narrow roads. Even short boat rides can be bumpy going across the water.

Self-adhesive labels: Stick small labels (1/2" x 3/4") on used rolls of film to identify the city you are currently shooting. This will assist you when you develop all those rolls of film and cannot remember which city you were in when you shot the pictures.

Survival kit: Combination of rubber bands, safety pins, shoelaces, sewing kit, bobby pins, transparent tape, pens, Bandaids™ and Visine™ eye drops (for those late nights).

Toilet paper (1/2 roll): Toilet paper may not always be available when you use the public toilets and sometimes a pack of tissues is just not enough. Most public toilets at train, bus stations and on trains don't have toilet paper.

Toilet seat covers: When you finally find a public toilet bowl that has a seat on it, you may not always have the strength to bend your knees and hold yourself up. After hiking for 5 hours, a friend of mine said she did not care what type of disease she might contract from sitting on the toilet. Perfect for toilets on trains, public restrooms in bus stations & restaurants.

Umbrella (collapsible): Just when you think you don't need one, it rains.

Utility web straps (3/4" x 24"): Great for tying your jacket to your purse straps.

Vaseline™: Use it to rub on the bottom of your feet to cut down on friction and to avoid getting blisters from all that walking on cobble streets. Add baby powder, blister/corn pads, inner cushion soles, moleskin and Second Skin™ to your list.

Walkie Talkies: I can't say enough good things about them. Perfect for when you want to split up for a couple of hours.

PACKING THE UNUSUAL

Water bottle carrier: So you can always have fresh water handy.

Wine bottle opener/corkscrew/wine cap: We eat a lot of our dinners on late-night trains and a bottle of wine complements the meal. We also like to bring a bottle back to our room at night. Include a set of camping utensils. **Note:** These items should be packed only in your check-on luggage, not your carry-on luggage.

Most of these items are carried by your local favorite travel bookstore or drugstore. If you have difficulty locating these items, you can contact Magellan's at (800) 962-4943 or Web site http://www.magellans.com/ They extend a one-time 15% discount on your first order to readers of this book. Code TO1.

APPENDIX II

ITALIAN TOURIST BOARD OFFICES IN NORTH AMERICA
http://www.italiantourism.com/ or http://www.enit.it.com/

New York, NY: 630 Fifth Avenue, Suite 1565, New York, NY 10011. Tel: (212) 245-4882 brochures only. Tel: (212) 245-5618. Fax: (212) 586-9249. E-mail: enitny@italiantourism.com

Los Angeles, CA: 12400 Wilshire Blvd., Suite 550, Los Angeles, CA 90025. Tel: (310) 820-0098 brochures only. Tel: (310) 820-1898. Fax: (310) 820-6357. E-mail: enitla@earthilink.net

Chicago, IL: 500 N. Michigan Ave., Suite 2240, Chicago, Il 60611. Tel: (312) 644-0990 brochures only. Tel: (312) 644-0996. Fax: (312) 644-3019. E-mail: enitch@italiantourism.com

Toronto, ON: 175 Bloor Street East, Suite 907, South Tower Toronto, ON M4W 3R8 Canada. Tel: (416) 925-4882. Fax: (416) 925-4799. E-mail: enit.canada@on.aibn.com

For each city in this book, I have included the phone, fax numbers and most Web sites of the city's local tourist office. Take advantage of this and write, fax or e-mail them prior to your leaving home. Request that they send you information on the city, a detailed list of local events for the month you plan to visit the city, a list of hotels and, most important, a map of the city.

APPENDIX III

TELEPHONES/FAXING

Calling from United States to Italy: For example, Hotel Perseo in Florence, Italy, from Los Angeles, California. Dial 011 (U.S. international access code), 39 (Italy's country code), Florence city code including the zero (055, each city's code is listed at the top of each chapter in this book), then dial the remaining local telephone number (Hotel Perseo: 212504) listed for each hotel in this book. For example: 011-39-055-212504.

Faxing & e-mailing hotels from United States to Italy: Everything that is stated above for calling also applies to faxing, except many of the hotels do not have a dedicated fax line. I used to fumble my way through a conversation requesting a fax tone so that I could fax that person's hotel. I was successful less than 50% of the time. I would hang up out of frustration and mail the hotel a letter requesting the information I was trying to get by fax. I have now discovered an easier way to fax Italy. I dial the fax number listed for the hotel in this book on the keypad of my fax machine without using the speaker phone. After I dial the number, I press "start." If it doesn't go through the first time, the machine automatically redials the fax number and the fax will go through the 2nd or 3rd time. I have a 95% success rate using this method of faxing. As far as e-mailing the hotels, I have verified all Web sites and e-mail addresses for the hotels listed in this book. However, every now and then I get an e-mail error message when I try to e-mail a hotel in Italy. I was told it had something to do with the phone lines in Italy. I have included a convenient hotel fax form at the end of this book and on my Web site at: www.HelloEurope.com/ See hotel reservations in "Tips on Hotels Accommodations" for more details on faxing hotels.

Italian calling cards: Most public (street phone box) phones are now operated by prepaid phone cards (*carte telefoniche*). There are 2 types of prepaid phone cards: One is inserted into a slot in the phone, then you dial your number slowly. The other is the international calling card that has a private access code with easy-to-follow instructions on the back of the card for making calls out of the country. Both cards are sold at post offices, train stations, newsstands and tobacco shops in Italy. When I don't use my cellular phone (see "Before You Leave Home"), I like to use the international calling card. I use this card to call back home to the U.S., to make local calls within Italy and to call other countries in Europe. They sell for 6€ (90 minutes) or 11€ (180 minutes). I also like them because there seem to be more public phones using the type of calling cards with access codes than the cards that have to be inserted into the phone slots. The other reason I like the card with the code is whenever I use the cards that have to be inserted, I always walk away and forget to take the card out of the phone. After using and comparing 5 different companies that sell these international calling cards in Italy, I prefer the brand name *Europa,* which may not always be available. I found this particular card to be the best value for my money.

Using the calling cards with access codes
This type of card is not inserted into public phones. There is a secret access code on the back of the calling card. Scratch the black ink off it and a numbered code will be revealed. Dial the toll-free number printed on the card. You will hear a pre-taped message that will give you a choice of languages to hear the directions for using the card. Press the number for the preferred language, enter the secret code and wait for confirmation. When dialing out of the country, dial 00, the country code and telephone (see below for detailed instructions in calling another country). I was able to use this type of calling card from most hotel rooms. (It depends on the type of phone system the hotel uses.) You have to be patient and may have to try it several times before it works. When you use the card on the phone in your hotel room, dial O, wait for the dial tone (beeping sounds), then follow the instructions listed below. When I am unable to use my international calling card on the phone in my hotel room to call my family and friends back home in the U.S., I make a quick call on my cellular phone to leave my contact information so they can call me back in the room. It is much more convenient & cheaper to do this versus trying to go outside the hotel to find a public telephone booth or using the hotel phone to make the expensive call. I was also able to use this card most of the time to make local calls within Italy. Every now and then the card did not work when trying to call certain

cities. For example: I was unable to call Cortina d'Ampezzo (Dolomites) from Rome. I had to use the Italian phone card that inserts into the phone slot.

Calling from Italy to United States: Florence to my office in Los Angeles, California. Dial 00 (international access code), then 1 (U.S.'s country code), then Los Angeles's area code (323) and my office phone number (939-0821). For example: 00-1-323-939-0821.

Calling from Italy to a hotel in another country in Europe: Florence, Italy, to Hotel Prince Albert Concordia in Paris, France. Dial 00 (international access code), then the country's access code (France is 33), then area code (Paris is 01, but always drop the zero when not in France) and the hotel's phone number 43473950. For example: 00-33-1-43473950.

Calling long distance within Italy: Rome, Italy to Hotel Perseo in Florence, Italy. Dial Florence's city code 055 (each city's code is listed at the top of each chapter in this book), then hotel's Perseo phone number 212504. For example: 055-212504.

Cellular phone: Please see "Before You Leave Home" on the advantages of renting a cellular phone for abroad.

U.S. phone companies' access codes.:
AT&T = 172-1011; Sprint = 172-1877; MCI = 172-1022.

Clock time: Europe uses the 24-hour clock.
9am is 0900hr., 12noon is 1200hr., 6pm is 1800hr., 12midnight is 2400hr.

World Clock Web site: http://www.stud.unit.no/USERBIN/steffent/verdensur.pl/

APPENDIX IV

ITALIAN PHRASES FOR CHECKING IN

Good morning!
Buon giorno!
boo-OHn jee-OHr-noh!

Good afternoon!
Buon pomeriggio
boo-OHn poamayREEDjeo

Good evening (night)!
Buona sera (notte)
boo-OH-nah sAY-rah (nOHt-teh)

Hello! (telephone)   Good-bye
pronto!   **Arrivederci**
prOHn-toh!   *ahr-ree-veh-dAYr-chee*

Sir   Madame   Miss
Signore   **Signora**   **Signorina**
see-ny-OH-reh   *see-ny-OH-rah*   *see-ny-oh-rEE-nah*

Please
Per piacere
pEHr pee-ah-chAY-reh

Thank you (very much)!
(Mille) grazie!
(mEEl-leh) grAH-tsee-eh!

You're welcome
prego (They say *prego*, *prego* for almost everything.)
PRAYgoa

My name is ...
Mi chiamo ...
mee kee-AH-moh ...

ITALIAN PHRASES FOR CHECKING IN

Do you speak English?
Parla inglese?
pAHr-lah een-glAY-seh?

Yes or no?
Si o no?
see oh noh?

I don't speak Italian.
Io non parlo italiano.
EE-oh nohn pAHr-loh ee-tah-lee-AH-noh.

I understand.
Capisco.
kah-pEE-skoh.

Do you understand?
Capisce?
kah-pEE-sheh?

I don't understand.
Non capisco.
nohn kah-pEE-skoh.

Do you have any vacancies?
Avete camere libere?
ahVAYtay KAAmayray LEEbayray?

I would like a single (double) room tonight.
Vorrei una camera singola (dopia) per stanotte.
vohr-rEH-ee oo-nah kAH-meh-rah sEEn-goh-lah
(dOHp-pee-ah) pehr stah-nOHt-teh.

---

for two people
per due persone
pehr DOO-ay pehr-SOH-nay

ITALIAN PHRASES FOR CHECKING IN

with (without)
con (senza)
kohn (sEHn-tsah)

---

with a toilet
con toilette
kohn too-ah-lEHt

---

with a shower/with a bathtub
con doccia/con vasco da bagno
kohn dOH-chee-ah/kohn VAH-skoh dah bAH-ny-oh

---

with a private bath
con bagno propio (privato)
kohn bAH-ny-oh prOH-pee-oh (pree-vAH-toh)

---

with (without) breakfast
con (senza) colazione
kohn (sEHn-tsah) koh-lahtsee-OH-neh

---

with twin beds
con due letti singoli
kon DOOay LEHTtee SEENG-goh-lee

---

with double bed
con letto matrimoniale
kon LEHTtoa mahtreemoaneeAAlay

---

with balcony
con balcone
kon bahl-KOH-nay

May I see the room?
Potrei vedere la camera?
poh-trEH-ee veh-dAY-reh lah kAH-meh-rah?

How much is the room?
Quanté la camera?
koo-ahn-tEH lah kAH-meh-rah?

ITALIAN PHRASES FOR CHECKING IN

Do you have something cheaper?
Ha qualche cosa meno costoso?
ah koo-AHl-keh kOH-sah mAY-noh koh-stOH-soh?

Is everything included?
E tutto compreso?
EH tOOt-toh kohm-prAY-soh?

Is it cheaper if I stay _____ nights?
E piu economico se mi_____ notti?
eh pew ay-koh-NOH-mee-koh seh me _____NOTti?

The room is very nice. I'll take it.
La camera é molto bella. La prendo.
lah kAH-meh-rah EH mOHl-toh bEHl-lah.
Lah prAYn-doh.

We'll be staying one (1) night.
Resteremo una notte.
rehs-teh-rAY-moh OO-nah nOHt-teh.

---

for tonight
per stanotte
pehr stah-NOT-tay

---

two (2) nights
due notti
dOO-eh nOHt-tee

3
tre
trEH

4
quattro
koo-AHt-troh

5
cinque
chEEn-kweh

6
sei
sEH-ee

7
sette
sEHt-teh

8
otto
OHt-toh

9
nove
nOH-veh

10
dieci
dee-EH-chee

11
undici
OOn-dee-chee

12
dodici
dOH-dee-chee

13
tredici
trEH-dee-chee

20
venti
vAYn-tee

30
trenta
trEHn-tah

40
quaranta
kwarAHn-tah

50
cinquanta
cheen-kwAHn-tah

60
sessanta
sehs-sAHn-tah

70
settanta
seht-tAHn-tah

80
ottanta
oht-tAHn-tah

90
novanta
noh-vAHn-tah

100
cento
chEHn-toh

101
centouno
chEHn-toh OO-nah

102
centodue
chEHn-toh dOO-eh

200
duecento
doo-eh-chEHn-toh

300
trecento
treh-chEHn-toh

400
quattrocento
kwatroh-chEHn-toh

500
cinquecento
cheenkweh-chEHn-toh

APPENDIX V

ANNUAL SCHEDULE OF HOLIDAYS, FESTIVALS AND EVENTS

Call, write or fax the Tourist Office of Italy (see Appendix II) for more information because some of the dates vary from year to year. Also, some of the events continue into the next month.

JANUARY

Jan. 1: "Primo dell A'Anno" (New Year's Day) national holiday.
Jan. 6: Epiphany Celebrations (national holiday). All the towns and villages in Italy stage Roman Catholic Epiphany observances.

FEBRUARY

Two wks. before Lent: **Venice** & **Sorrento** Carnevale (Carnival).

MARCH

Two wks. before Lent: **Venice** & **Sorrento** Carnevale (Carnival).
March 19: **Rome** & **Naples** celebrate "Festa di Giuseppe."

APRIL

April: **Rome** celebrates "Festa della Primavera." The Spanish steps are layered with azaleas.
Good Friday: **Rome**, Pope leads a candlelight procession at 9pm in the Colosseum.
Easter wk./Sunday: Easter national holiday. Something special happens all over Italy.
Easter Sunday: **Rome**, Pope gives a televised annual blessing from St. Peter's balcony at 12noon.
Florence celebrates "Scoppio del Carro" (Explosion of the Cart).
1st Sunday after Ascension day: **Venice** hosts "La Vogalonga." Anybody with an oar who can row can participate.
April 25: Liberation Day national holiday.
April 25: **Venice** honors St. Mark (patron saint).

ANNUAL SCHEDULE OF HOLIDAYS, FESTIVALS AND EVENTS

MAY
Florence celebrates "Maggio Musicale Fiorentino" (Musical May Florentine).
1st Sunday in May: **Naples** celebrates San Gennaro (patron saint).
May 1: "Festa del Lavoro" (Labor Day) national holiday.
May 6: **Rome**, swearing-in of the new guards at the Vatican in St. Peter's square.
May 14: **Capri** honors St. Costanzo (patron saint).
2nd Sunday in May: **Camogli** celebrates "Sagra del Pesce" (Fish Feast).
Last Sunday in May: **Orvieto** celebrates "Festa della Palombella."

JUNE
Milan hosts "Festa dei Navigli" a folklore celebration.
June: **Camogli** hosts Sailing Regattas.
June 2: Some cities celebrate Proclamation of Republic.
June 3: **Orvieto** celebrates "Festival of Palombella."
June 3: **Cortona** hosts "Archidado Games"(competitive crossbow games).
1st Sunday in June: **Pisa** celebrates "Gioco del Ponte" (Battle of the Bridge).
June 13: **Anacapri** honors St. Antonio di Padova (patron saint).
1st or 2nd wk.: **Orvieto** celebrates "Corpus Domini" (Corpus Christi), a 1264 miracle.
June 24: **Florence** honors St. John the Baptist (patron saint).
June 24 & 28: **Florence** celebrates "Gioco del Calcio" (soccer match).
June 29: **Genova** celebrates "Palio Marinaro dei Rioni" (rowing race).
June 29: **Rome** honors Sts. Peter and Paul (patron saints).
End of June: **Orvieto** & **Perugia** celebrate Rockin' Umbria (rock festival).

JULY
July: **Rome** hosts "Tevere Expo" arts & crafts booths, fireworks and folk music festivals.
July 2: **Siena** celebrates "Il Palio delle Contrade" (Palio horse race) and Aug. 16.
July 12: **Lucca** celebrates "Festa di San Paolino & Palio della balestra."

July 16: **Naples** celebrates "Feast of Madonna del Carmine."

Mid-July for 2 wks.: **Perugia** hosts the "Umbria Jazz Festival."

3rd Sunday in July: **Venice** commemorates "Il Redentore" (Feast of the Redeemer).

Last wk. of July: **Rome** turns its Trastevere neighborhood into "Festa de Noantri" (village fair).

Verona hosts the "Arena Outdoor Opera Season."

AUGUST

1st Sunday in August: **Camogli** celebrates "Stella Maris" (Our Lady of the Sea).

Aug. 15: "Ferragosto Assumption of the Virgin" national holiday.

Aug. 16: **Siena** celebrates "Il Palio delle Contrade" (Palio horse race).

Aug. 17-28: **Camogli** celebrates "King of Camogli."

Late Aug. to early Sept.: **Venice** hosts the "International Film Festival."

Late Aug. to early Sept.: **Perugia** hosts the "International Puppet Festival."

SEPTEMBER

1st Sunday in Sept.: **Venice** participates in "Regata Storica" (historical regatta) horse races preceded by a spectacular procession of period boats on the Grand Canal.

Mid-Sept.: **Perugia** hosts the "Sagra Musicale Umbria" (Umbrian Festival of Sacred Music).

Sept. 14-19: **Naples** hosts its Pizza Festival.

Sept. 19: **Naples** honors St. Gennaro (patron saint).

OCTOBER

Oct. 3-4: **Assisi** honors St. Francis (patron saint).

Oct. 4: **Bologna** honors St. Petronio (patron saint).

Oct. 10: **Genova** hosts a 10-day boat show.

Oct. 13-21: **Perugia** hosts the "Eurochocolate." Trade fair for chocolate lovers.

Last wk. of Oct.-1st wk. in Nov.: **Perugia** hosts the "Antique Trade Fair."

NOVEMBER
Nov. 1: "Ognissanti" (All Saints' Day) national holiday.
Nov. 4: Some cities celebrate national unity day.

DECEMBER
Dec. 7: **Milan** honors St. Ambrose (patron saint).
Dec. 8: "Festa del Madonna Immacolata" (Immaculate Conception of the Virgin Mary) national holiday.
Mid-Dec.: **Rome** hosts the "Epiphany Fair" in Piazza Navona.
Dec. 25: "Natale" (Christmas) national holiday. **Rome**, Pope gives a televised annual blessing from St. Peter's balcony at 12 noon.
Dec. 26: "Saint Stefano" national holiday.
Dec. 31: New Year's Eve.
Dec. 30-Jan. 3: **Orvieto** hosts the "Umbria Jazz Winter."
Note: If a public holiday falls on a Tuesday or Thursday, many businesses also close on the nearest Monday or Friday for a long weekend.

Pronto! I am a reader of the travel guide book
Hello Italy!
BEST BUDGET HOTELS in Italy

I am interested in information on the availability of rooms at your hotel. Please fill in the answers, sign the form and fax it back to me. I will fax the form back to you with my signature.

Date of Fax:_____ From (print):_____

Telephone #:_____ Fax #:_____

E-mail address:_____Country:_____

My address:_____

Name of Hotel :_____City:_____

Telephone #:_____Fax #:_____

Hotel's e-mail address:_____

Hotel's address:_____

Date of reservations: Arrival_____ Departure_____

(To avoid any confusion, write day/month/year in this order)

# of people:___ # of children:__ ages___ # of nights:__ # of rooms:__

Type of bed (s) I prefer: Twin____ Double_____ Queen/King_____

Type of bathroom inside room: Toilet___Shower___ Bathtub_____

Balcony/Terrace _____ View_____ Cheapest room_____

Back or front of hotel_____ Parking (cost per day)_____

Breakfast (yes/no)____ cost (Euro)_____

Cost of room per night with tax and breakfast (Euro)_____

Cost of room per night with tax without breakfast (Euro)_____

Method of paying: Cash (or Euro)___ Visa__ MC___AX___DC___

I will mail a check __or use my credit card __ for __night(s) deposit.

Credit card information:_____Exp. ____

Name on card (print) _____

Signature_____

Hotel manager's name (print)_____

Hotel manager's signature_____

The book mentions that _____ at your hotel will give a ____discount off the nightly cost of the room if I show the book to your staff when I arrive. Will you be able to give me the discount? (yes/no)_____.

(This form is available on: http://www.HelloEurope.com/)

INDEX

INDEX

Hello Italy!
$19.95
ISBN 0-9653944-8-4

Hello France!
$18.95
ISBN 0-9653944-0-9

Hello Britain & Ireland!
$18.95
ISBN 0-9653944-9-2

Hello Spain!
$18.95
ISBN 0-9653944-1-7

Margo's fascination and passion for travel are rooted in a background that reflects an incredible journey of triumph over tragedy. Abandoned at age four, Margo was raised in orphanages, where she remained until her late teens. She survived numerous episodes of abuse and through a resilient spirit managed to escape by reading about faraway places, educating herself in the process. She has traveled extensively throughout Europe, personally visiting each hotel listed in these guides. To call the "Hello" hotel guidebook series a "labor of love" is truly an understatement. Margo Classé's life philosophy is simple: "Difficulties are opportunities to prove your greatness by overcoming them." So go ahead, take a chance, take a trip and have a fabulous time with the adventure. Margo and her husband, Tyrell, live in Los Angeles, California.

The following recipe is compliments of Carlo Cuomo, owner of Hotel Bougainville, Positano, Italy.

LIMONCELLO A CARLOS POSITANO

INGREDIENTS

7 lemons - one of them should be green, not ripe.
(This will make it taste stronger.)

1 liter of pure 100% grain alcohol

1 liter of water

2 2/3 cups sugar

Skin the lemons, using only the top layer (yellow part) of skin. The white part of the lemon skin must not be used.

Put the skins into the liter of pure alcohol. Let stand for 6 days.

After the 6 days, bring a liter of water to a boil and add 2 2/3 cups of sugar while it is boiling. Allow the water to cool to room temperature.

When the water is room temperature, combine it with the alcohol and lemon skins and stir.